ANNUAL EDIT

United States History
Volume 1—Colonial Through Reconstruction
Twenty-First Edition

EDITOR

Robert James Maddox (Emeritus)
Pennsylvania State University
University Park

Robert James Maddox, distinguished historian and professor emeritus of American history at Pennsylvania State University, received a BS from Fairleigh Dickinson University in 1957, an MS from the University of Wisconsin in 1958, and a PhD from Rutgers in 1964. He has written, reviewed, and lectured extensively, and is widely respected for his interpretations of presidential character and policy.

ANNUAL EDITIONS: UNITED STATES HISTORY, VOLUME 1, TWENTY-FIRST EDITION

Published by McGraw-Hill, a business unit of The McGraw-Hill Companies, Inc., 1221 Avenue of the Americas, New York, NY 10020. Copyright © 2011 by The McGraw-Hill Companies, Inc. All rights reserved. Previous edition(s) 1987–2008. No part of this publication may be reproduced or distributed in any form or by any means, or stored in a database or retrieval system, without the prior written consent of The McGraw-Hill Companies, Inc., including, but not limited to, in any network or other electronic storage or transmission, or broadcast for distance learning.

Some ancillaries, including electronic and print components, may not be available to customers outside the United States.

Annual Editions® is a registered trademark of The McGraw-Hill Companies, Inc.

Annual Editions is published by the **Contemporary Learning Series** group within The McGraw-Hill Higher Education division.

1 2 3 4 5 6 7 8 9 0 WDQ/WDQ 1 0 9 8 7 6 5 4 3 2 1 0

ISBN 978–0–07–805054–1
MHID 0–07–805054–5
ISSN 0733–3560

Managing Editor: *Larry Loeppke*
Director Specialized Production: *Faye Schilling*
Developmental Editor: *Debra A. Henricks*
Editorial Coordinator: *Mary Foust*
Editorial Assistant: *Cindy Hedley*
Production Service Assistant: *Rita Hingtgen*
Permissions Coordinator: *Leonard Behnke*
Senior Marketing Manager: *Julie Keck*
Senior Marketing Communications Specialist: *Mary Klein*
Marketing Coordinator: *Alice Link*
Senior Project Manager: *Joyce Watters*
Design Specialist: *Margarite Reynolds*
Production Supervisor: *Sue Culbertson*
Cover Graphics: *Kristine Jubeck*

Compositor: Laserwords Private Limited
Cover Image: Royalty-Free/CORBIS (inset); Library of Congress Prints and Photographs Division [LC-USZC2-1956] (background)

Library in Congress Cataloging in Publication Data
Main entry under title: Annual Editions: United States History, Vol. 1: Colonial Through Reconstruction. 21e.
  1. United States—History—Periodicals. 2. United States—Historiography—Periodicals. 3. United States—Civilization—Periodicals. I. 1. Maddox, Robert James, *comp.* II Title: United States History, Vol. 1: Colonial Through Reconstruction.
658'.05

Editors/Academic Advisory Board

Members of the Academic Advisory Board are instrumental in the final selection of articles for each edition of ANNUAL EDITIONS. Their review of articles for content, level, and appropriateness provides critical direction to the editors and staff. We think that you will find their careful consideration well reflected in this volume.

ANNUAL EDITIONS: United States History, Volume 1
21st Edition

EDITOR

Robert James Maddox (Emeritus)
Pennsylvania State University
University Park

ACADEMIC ADVISORY BOARD MEMBERS

Preface

In publishing ANNUAL EDITIONS we recognize the enormous role played by the magazines, newspapers, and journals of the public press in providing current, first-rate educational information in a broad spectrum of interest areas. Many of these articles are appropriate for students, researchers, and professionals seeking accurate, current material to help bridge the gap between principles and theories and the real world. These articles, however, become more useful for study when those of lasting value are carefully collected, organized, indexed, and reproduced in a low-cost format, which provides easy and permanent access when the material is needed. That is the role played by ANNUAL EDITIONS.

The writing of history has changed dramatically since the first edition of this anthology. A look at the table of contents will show that individuals and groups previously ignored or downplayed are now being given much fuller attention. The westward expansion of this nation, for instance, usually was depicted as a triumphant migration that overcame great obstacles to "settle" the frontier. But what whites considered a process of civilization was to Native Americans a disastrous invasion of their lands. Some tribes were demoralized by the destruction of buffalo herds upon which their cultures and sustenance rested. Most Native Americans were finally herded onto reservations where they became little more than wards of the federal government. Attempts to tell the story from their standpoint, as in the article "How the West Was Lost," enrich our understanding of the past.

A similar process has taken place with regard to the treatment of women, blacks, and others who were marginalized in conventional histories. Earlier accounts, when they treated such groups at all, tended to focus attention on notable leaders rather than the rank-and-file members. This was understandable as source material about prominent figures was more readily available. The development of history "from the bottom up" has produced a great deal of writing about the lives of ordinary people as exemplified by several essays in this volume. "Steven Hahn Sings the Slaves Triumphant," for instance, reveals the important role played by common black people in bringing about emancipation. This tendency toward inclusion has to be applauded.

Another recent development in writing about the past has been an emphasis on viewing issues within broader contexts as opposed to those obtained in one or another colony or in the United States as a whole during its early national period. One essay included in this edition, for example, analyzes the U.S. Civil War and its aftermath as it played out on the world stage. Events that previously were treated in isolation are now presented within the framework of how they influenced or were influenced by other people and other nations. *Transnational history,* as it has been called, can provide insights previously lacking in conventional histories.

There has been a downside. A deplorable tendency in recent historical writing has been the practice of enlisting the past to promote specific agendas, however admirable those agendas might be. "Objective" history is impossible to attain, of course, because each of us carries intellectual baggage that pushes us toward one interpretation rather than another. But efforts to create a "usable past" often have resulted in gross distortions of the historical record.

It is tempting for both authors and readers to analyze and judge the past from the standpoint of present-day knowledge and assumptions. How easy it is to criticize people born in the 18th century, for instance, on the grounds that the ideas they held and the practices they followed have since become discredited. Who could believe in witchcraft? Who could defend slavery? Who could see "the natural order of things" in the relegation of women and other groups to second-class citizenship? The fact is that many intelligent and reasonable people in earlier times held such beliefs. Treating our predecessors with contempt because they did not hold the beliefs that many of us now take for granted can be comforting because it assures us of our own intellectual and moral superiority. One should keep in mind, however, many of today's "truths" will seem equally wrong-headed to people looking back at us hundreds of years from now, assuming we do not destroy the planet before then.

Annual Editions: United States History, Volume I is designed for non-specialized survey courses. We have attempted to present a fair sampling of articles that incorporate newer approaches to the study of history as well as more traditional ones. The sources from which these essays have been taken for the most part are intended for the general reader: They require no particular expertise to understand them, and they avoid the dreadful jargon that permeates so much of modern academic writing.

This volume contains a number of features designed to aid students, researchers, and professionals. These include a *topic guide* for locating articles on specific subjects; and the *table of contents,* which includes *abstracts* that summarize each essay and provide key concepts in bold italics. Articles are organized into four units, each preceded by an overview that provides a background for informed reading of the articles, emphasizes critical issues, and presents *challenge questions.*

Every revision of *Annual Editions: United States History, Volume I* replaces about fifty percent of the previous articles with new ones. We try to update and improve the quality of the sections, and we would like to consider alternatives that we may have missed. If you find an article that you think merits inclusion in the next edition, please send it to us (or at least send us the citation, so that the editor can track it down for consideration). We welcome your comments about the readings in this volume, and a postage-paid reader response card is included in the back of the book for your convenience. Your suggestions will be carefully considered and greatly appreciated.

Robert James Maddox

Robert James Maddox
Editor

Contents

UNIT 1
The New Land

The concepts in bold italics are developed in the article. For further expansion, please refer to the Topic Guide.

UNIT 2
Revolutionary America

The concepts in bold italics are developed in the article. For further expansion, please refer to the Topic Guide.

UNIT 3
National Consolidation and Expansion

The concepts in bold italics are developed in the article. For further expansion, please refer to the Topic Guide.

UNIT 4
The Civil War and Reconstruction

The concepts in bold italics are developed in the article. For further expansion, please refer to the Topic Guide.

The concepts in bold italics are developed in the article. For further expansion, please refer to the Topic Guide.

Correlation Guide

The *Annual Editions* series provides students with convenient, inexpensive access to current, carefully selected articles from the public press. **Annual Editions: United States History, Volume 1: Colonial through Reconstruction, 21/e** is an easy-to-use reader that presents articles on important topics in the study of United States History. For more information on *Annual Editions* and other *McGraw-Hill Contemporary Learning Series* titles, visit www.mhhe.com/cls.

This convenient guide matches the units in **Annual Editions: United States History, Volume 1, 21/e** with the corresponding chapters in three of our best-selling McGraw-Hill History textbooks by Brinkley and Davidson et al.

Annual Editions: United States History, Volume 1, 21/e	The Unfinished Nation: A Concise History of the American People, Volume 1, 6/e by Brinkley	American History: A Survey, Volume 1, 13/e by Brinkley	U.S.: A Narrative History, Volume 1, to 1877, 5/e, by Davidson et al.
Unit 1: The New Land	**Chapter 1:** The Meeting of Cultures **Chapter 2:** Transplantations and Borderlands **Chapter 3:** Society and Culture in Provincial America **Chapter 4:** The Empire in Transition	**Chapter 1:** The Meeting of Cultures **Chapter 2:** Transplantations and Borderlands **Chapter 3:** Society and Culture in Provincial America **Chapter 4:** The Empire in Transition	**Chapter 1:** The First Civilizations of North America **Chapter 2:** Old Worlds, New Worlds (1400–1600) **Chapter 3:** Colonization and Conflict in the South (1600–1750) **Chapter 4:** Colonization and Conflict in the North (1600–1700)
Unit 2: Revolutionary America	**Chapter 5:** The American Revolution **Chapter 6:** The Constitution and the New Republic **Chapter 7:** The Jeffersonian Era	**Chapter 5:** The American Revolution **Chapter 6:** The Constitution and the New Republic **Chapter 7:** The Jeffersonian Era	**Chapter 5:** The Mosaic of Eighteenth-Century America (1689–1771) **Chapter 6:** Toward the War for American Independence (1754–1776) **Chapter 7:** The American People and the American Revolution (1775–1783) **Chapter 8:** Crisis and Constitution (1776–1789) **Chapter 9:** The Early Republic (1789–1824)
Unit 3: National Consolidation and Expansion	**Chapter 8:** Varieties of American Nationalism **Chapter 9:** Jacksonian America **Chapter 10:** America's Economic Revolution **Chapter 11:** Cotton, Slavery, and the Old South **Chapter 12:** Antebellum Culture and Reform **Chapter 13:** The Impending Crisis	**Chapter 8:** Varieties of American Nationalism **Chapter 9:** Jacksonian America **Chapter 10:** America's Economic Revolution **Chapter 11:** Cotton, Slavery, and the Old South **Chapter 12:** Antebellum Culture and Reform **Chapter 13:** The Impending Crisis	**Chapter 10:** The Opening of America (1815–1850) **Chapter 11:** The Rise of Democracy (1824–1840) **Chapter 12:** The Fires of Perfection (1820–1850) **Chapter 13:** The Old South (1820–1860) **Chapter 14:** Western Expansion and the Rise of the Slavery Issue (1820–1850)
Unit 4: The Civil War and Reconstruction	**Chapter 14:** The Civil War **Chapter 15:** Reconstruction and the New South	**Chapter 14:** The Civil War **Chapter 15:** Reconstruction and the New South	**Chapter 15:** The Union Broken (1850–1861) **Chapter 16:** Total War and the Republic (1861–1865) **Chapter 17:** Reconstructing the Union (1865–1877)

Topic Guide

This topic guide suggests how the selections in this book relate to the subjects covered in your course. You may want to use the topics listed on these pages to search the Web more easily.

On the following pages a number of websites have been gathered specifically for this book. They are arranged to reflect the units of this Annual Editions reader. You can link to these sites by going to *http://www.mhhe.com/cls*.

All the articles that relate to each topic are listed below the bold-faced term.

Internet References

The following Internet sites have been selected to support the articles found in this reader. These sites were available at the time of publication. However, because websites often change their structure and content, the information listed may no longer be available. We invite you to visit http://www.mhhe.com/cls for easy access to these sites.

Annual Editions: United States History, Volume 1

General Sources

American Historical Association (AHA)
http://www.historians.org

This site is an excellent source for data on just about any topic in American history. All affiliated societies and publications are noted, and AHA and its links provide material related to myriad fields of history.

American Studies Web
http://www.georgetown.edu

Links to a wealth of Internet resources for research in American studies, from agriculture and rural development, to government, to race and ethnicity, are provided on this eclectic site.

Harvard's John F. Kennedy School of Government
http://www.ksg.harvard.edu

Starting from this home page, click on a huge variety of links to information about American history, politics, and government, including material related to debates of enduring issues.

History Net
http://www.thehistorynet.com

Supported by the National Historical Society, this site provides information on a wide range of topics. The articles are of excellent quality, and the site has book reviews and even special interviews. It is also frequently updated.

Library of Congress
http://www.loc.gov

Examine this website to learn about the extensive resource tools, library services/resources, exhibitions, and databases available through the Library of Congress in many different subfields of government studies.

Smithsonian Institution
http://www.si.edu

This site provides access to the enormous resources of the Smithsonian, which holds some 140 million artifacts and specimens for "the increase and diffusion of knowledge." Learn about American social, cultural, economic, and political history from a variety of viewpoints here.

UNIT 1: The New Land

Early America
http://earlyamerica.com/earlyamerica/index.html

Explore the "amazing world of early America" through early media data at this site. Topics include Pages of the Past, Lives of Early Americans, Notable Women of Early America, Milestone Events, and many more.

1492: An Ongoing Voyage/Library of Congress
http://lcweb.loc.gov/exhibits/1492

Displays examining the causes and effects of Columbus's voyages to the Americas can be accessed on this website. "An Ongoing Voyage" explores the rich mixture of societies coexisting in five areas of this hemisphere before European arrival. It then surveys the polyglot Mediterranean world at a dynamic turning point in its development.

The Mayflower Web Page
http://www.mayflowerhistory.com

The Mayflower Web Page represents thousands of hours of research, organization, and typing; it grows daily. Visitors include everyone from kindergarten students to history professors, from beginning genealogists to some of the most noted genealogists in the nation. The site is a merger of two fields: genealogy and history.

UNIT 2: Revolutionary America

The Early America Review
http://www.earlyamerica.com/review

Explore the website of The Early America Review, an electronic journal of fact and opinion on the people, issues, and events of eighteenth-century America. The quarterly is of excellent quality.

House of Representatives
http://www.house.gov

This home page of the House of Representatives will lead to information about current and past House members and agendas, the legislative process, and so on.

National Center for Policy Analysis
http://www.public-policy.org/web.public-policy.org/index.php

Through this site, click onto links to read discussions of an array of topics that are of major interest in the study of American history, from regulatory policy and privatization to economy and income.

Supreme Court/Legal Information Institute
http://supct.law.cornell.edu/supct/index.html

Open this site for current and historical information about the Supreme Court. The archive contains a collection of nearly 600 of the most historical decisions of the Court.

U.S. Senate
http://www.senate.gov

The U.S. Senate home page will lead to information about current and past Senate members and agendas, legislative activities, committees, and so on.

The White House
http://www.whitehouse.gov

Visit the home page of the White House for direct access to information about commonly requested federal services, the White House Briefing Room, and all of the presidents and vice presidents. The "Virtual Library" provides an opportunity to search White House documents, listen to speeches, and view photos.

The World of Benjamin Franklin
http://www.fi.edu/franklin

Presented by the Franklin Institute Science Museum, "Benjamin Franklin: Glimpses of the Man" is an excellent multimedia site that lends insight into Revolutionary America.

Internet References

UNIT 3: National Consolidation and Expansion

Consortium for Political and Social Research
http://www.icpsr.umich.edu

At this site, the Interuniversity Consortium for Political and Social Research offers materials in various categories of historical, social, economic, and demographic data. Presented is a statistical overview of the United States beginning in the late eighteenth century.

Department of State
http://www.state.gov

View this site for an understanding into the workings of what has become a major U.S. executive branch department. Links explain what the Department does, what services it provides, what it says about U.S. interests around the world, and much more information.

Mystic Seaport
http://amistad.mysticseaport.org

The complex Amistad case is explored in a clear and informative manner on this online educational site. It places the event in the context of the issues of the 1830s and 1840s.

Social Influence Website
http://www.workingpsychology.com/intro.html

The nature of persuasion, compliance, and propaganda is the focus of this website, with many practical examples and applications. Students of such topics as the roles of public opinion and media influence in policy making should find these discussions of interest.

University of Virginia Library
http://www.lib.virginia.edu/exhibits/lewis_clark

Created by the University of Virginia Library, this site examines the famous Lewis and Clark exploration of the trans-Mississippi west.

Women in America
http://xroads.virginia.edu/~HYPER/DETOC/FEM

Providing the views of women travelers from the British Isles, France, and Germany on the lives of American women, this valuable site covers the years between 1820 and 1842 and is informative, stimulating, and highly original.

Women of the West
http://www.wowmuseum.org

The home page of the Women of the West Museum offers several interesting links that include stories, poems, educational resources, and exhibits.

UNIT 4: The Civil War and Reconstruction

The American Civil War
http://sunsite.utk.edu/civil-war/warweb.html

This site provides a wide-ranging list of data on the Civil War. Some examples of the data that are available are army life, the British connection, diaries/letters/memos, maps, movies, museums, music, people, photographs, and poetry.

Anacostia Museum/Smithsonian Institution
http://www.si.edu/archives/historic/anacost.htm

This is the home page of the Center for African American History and Culture of the Smithsonian Institution, which is expected to become a major repository of information. Explore its many avenues.

Abraham Lincoln Online
http://www.netins.net/showcase/creative/lincoln.html

This is a well-organized, high-quality site that will lead to substantial material about Abraham Lincoln and his era. Discussions among Lincoln scholars can be accessed in the Mailbag section.

Gilder Lehrman Institute of American History
http://www.digitalhistory.uh.edu/index.cfm?

Click on the links to various articles presented through this website to read outstanding, first-hand accounts of slavery in America through the period of Reconstruction.

Secession Era Editorials Project
http://history.furman.edu/~benson/docs/dsmenu.htm

Newspaper editorials of the 1800s regarding events leading up to secession are presented on this Furman University site. When complete, this distinctive project will offer additional features that include mapping, statistical tools, and text analysis.

UNIT 1

The New Land

Unit Selections

1. **America's First Immigrants,** Evan Hadingham
2. **1491,** Charles C. Mann
3. **A Desperate Trek across America,** Andrés Reséndez
4. **Brave New World: The Watercolors That John White Produced in 1585 Gave England Its First Startling Glimpse of America,** Abigail Tucker
5. **Champlain among the Mohawk, 1609: A Soldier-Humanist Fights a War for Peace in North America,** David Hackett Fischer
6. **The Birth of America: Struggling from One Peril to the Next, the Jamestown Settlers Planted the Seeds of the Nation's Spirit,** Lewis Lord
7. **Strangers in a New Land: Henry Hudson's First American Adventure,** Peter C. Mancall
8. **Blessed and Bedeviled,** Helen Mondloch
9. **The Real Pirates of the Caribbean,** *USA Today*
10. **Wilderness Ordeal,** John F. Ross

Key Points to Consider

- What new evidence is there that Native Americans may have come to the Western Hemisphere at a much earlier time than previously thought?

- Discuss Samuel de Champlain's plan to create a French Empire in the new world. Why did it ultimately fail?

- Analyze the problems faced by the early settlers in Jamestown and how they attempted to cope. In what ways did they "plant the seeds of the nation's spirit"?

- Analyze the Salem witch trials of 1692. What attitudes and beliefs led to these persecutions?

- Why did piracy in the Caribbean prove so lucrative in the eighteenth century? From which groups were these pirates drawn? In what ways could piracy be considered an "equal opportunity" occupation?

- The expedition led by Major Robert Rogers against the French during the French and Indian War was a relatively small operation. Why was it so significant and what implications did it have for France's Indian allies?

Student Website

www.mhhe.com/cls

Internet References

Early America
http://earlyamerica.com/earlyamerica/index.html

1492: An Ongoing Voyage/Library of Congress
http://lcweb.loc.gov/exhibits/1492

The Mayflower Web Page
http://www.mayflowerhistory.com

Europeans had been fascinated with the "New World" long before they were able to mount expeditions to actually go there. Artists and writers imagined all sorts of exotic plants and animals and depicted human inhabitants as ranging from the most brutal savages to races of highly advanced peoples. These latter were reputed to have constructed cities of great splendor, where fabulous treasures of precious metals and jewels lay for the taking. The "age of exploration" had to await the sufficient accumulation of capital to finance expeditions and the advanced technology to make them feasible. Motives were mixed for undertaking such ventures: the desire to explore the unknown, national rivalries, the quest for routes to the Far East, the desire to convert the heathens to Christianity, and pure greed. Spain and Portugal led the way, followed by France and England.

The "new world," of course, was new only to Europeans. The inhabitants had lived here for a long time without even knowing (let alone caring) that Europe existed. Estimates are that there were from 80 to 100 million people living in the Western Hemisphere at the time the explorations began. In the region that became the United States there were no powerful empires such as those developed by the Aztecs in Mexico or the Incas in Peru. There were, however, fairly sophisticated settlements such as the small town of Cahokia, located near present-day St. Louis, Missouri. European incursions proved catastrophic for peoples of whatever stage of civilization. Not only did some of the explorers treat indigenous peoples with great brutality, they brought with them a variety of deadly diseases against which natives had no defenses. The expansion of Europe, therefore, came at the expense of millions of unfortunates in the new world.

For years the conventional wisdom was that what we call "Native Americans" emigrated here from Asia across the Bering land bridge to Alaska. The article, "America's First Immigrants," shows that this view has been challenged by archaeologists who have found a settlement dating from at least 1,000 years before this migration was supposed to have occurred. "1491" discusses population estimates and what is known about their societies and suggests that they had a far larger impact on the environment than previously suspected. Much has been written about the Spanish "Conquistadors," and their frequently brutal treatment of indigenous peoples. "A Desperate Trek across America" tells the story of one Spanish expedition to seize Florida that was devastated and how a few survived.

The English arrived late in the process. Some of them were searching for precious metals and jewels, as had their Spanish counterparts. Others came to settle permanently, either to escape religious persecution or merely to build new lives for themselves. The article "Brave New World: The Watercolors That John White Produced in 1585 Gave England Its First Startling Glimpse of America" points out that White's watercolors, though frequently inaccurate, provided the English with an attractive view of the "New World" that helped stimulate emigration.

"The Birth of America" describes the harrowing experiences of those who settled Jamestown in 1607. They had to cope with climate, disease, Indians, and struggles among themselves. "Champlain among the Mohawks, 1609" tells of an individual's

AMERICA BEFORE COLUMBUS.

COPYRIGHT, 1893, BY GEBBIE & CO.

CHAMPLAIN EXPLORING THE CANADIAN WILDERNESS.

Library of Congress. LC-USZ62-3019

efforts to create a "New France" that would live in harmony with the Indians. Champlain never was able to bring about peace among the warring tribes. At about the same time Dutch explorer Henry Hudson journeyed to the New World, trying to find the legendary "Northwest Passage" to Asia. He failed, of course, but explored what became known as Hudson River.

The idea that witches existed was commonly held in New England during the seventeenth century, as it was elsewhere. The Salem witch trials have received great attention by historians, who differ among themselves as to the roots of this phenomenon. "Blessed and Bedeviled" examines commonly held beliefs at the time that led to the persecution of more than 150 people.

First discovered in 1984, the wreck of the pirate ship *Whydah* has since yielded a mine of artifacts as well as treasure chests of jewels and precious metals. Originally built as a slave ship, the *Whydah* was captured by a band of pirates led by Captain "Black Sam" Bellamy and became a very successful marauder. "This is a story of the making of America," the author writes, "a true story more powerful than fiction."

In 1759, in the midst of the French and Indian War, Captain Robert Rogers led a bold British expedition against the French in the Lake Champlain area. A small force of only 150 men, Rogers's troops suffered terrible hardships on their way to the target and during their retreat. The significance of this raid lay not in the number of enemy killed, but in serving notice on France's Indian allies that they could not rely on their European ally for protection.

America's First Immigrants

You were probably taught that the hemisphere's first people came from Siberia across a long-gone land bridge. Now a sea route looks increasingly likely, from Asia or even Europe.

EVAN HADINGHAM

About four miles from the tiny cattle town of Florence, Texas, a narrow dirt road winds across parched limestone, through juniper, prickly pear and stunted oaks, and drops down to a creek. A lush parkland of shade trees offers welcome relief from the 100-degree heat of summer. Running beside the creek for almost half a mile is a swath of chipped, gray stone flakes and soil blackened by cooking fires—thousands of years of cooking fires. This blackened earth, covering 40 acres and almost six feet thick in places, marks a settlement dating back as far as the last ice age 13,000 years ago, when mammoths, giant sloths and saber-toothed cats roamed the North American wilderness.

Since archaeologists began working here systematically seven years ago, they have amassed an astonishing collection of early prehistoric artifacts—nearly half a million so far. Among these are large, stone spearheads skillfully flaked on both sides to give an elegant, leaf-shaped appearance. These projectiles, found by archaeologists throughout North America and as far south as Costa Rica, are known as Clovis points, and their makers, who lived roughly 12,500 to 13,500 years ago, are known as Clovis people, after the town in New Mexico near where the first such point was identified some seven decades ago.

A visit to the Gault site—named after the family who owned the land when the site was first investigated in 1929—along the cottonwood- and walnut-shaded creek in central Texas raises two monumental questions. The first, of course, is, Who were these people? The emerging answer is that they were not simple-minded big-game hunters as they have often been depicted. Rather, they led a less nomadic and more sophisticated life than previously believed.

The second question—Where did they come from?—lies at the center of one of archaeology's most contentious debates. The standard view holds that Clovis people were the first to enter the Americas, migrating from Siberia 13,500 years ago by a now-submerged land bridge across the Bering Strait. This view has been challenged recently by a wide range of discoveries, including an astonishingly well-preserved site in South America predating the supposed migration by at least 1,000 years.

Researchers delving into the origins question have sought to make sense of archaeological finds far and wide, from Canada, California and Chile; from Siberia; and even, most controversially, from France and Spain. The possibility that the first people in the Americas came from Europe is the boldest proposal among a host of new ideas. According to University of Texas at Austin archaeologist Michael Collins, the chief excavator of the Gault site, "you couldn't have a more exciting time to be involved in the whole issue of the peopling of the Americas. You can't write a paper on it and get it published before it's out of date. Surprising new finds keep rocking the boat and launching fresh waves of debate."

In 1932, an American archaeologist identified distinctive spearheads associated with mammoth skeletons near Clovis, New Mexico. The discovery supported an emerging realization that humans lived with now-extinct ice age creatures in North America.

For prehistoric people, one of the chief attractions of the Gault site was a knobby outcrop of a creamy white rock called chert, which conceals a fine, gray, glasslike interior. If struck expertly with a stone or antler tool, the rock fractures in predictable ways, yielding a Clovis point. In the end, each spearhead has distinctive grooves, or "flutes," at the base of each face and was fastened to a wooden shaft with sinew and resin.

Ancient pollen and soil clues tell archaeologists that the climate in Clovis-era Texas was cooler, drier and more tolerable than today's summertime cauldron. Vast herds of mammoths, bison, horses and antelope ranged on the grasslands southeast of Gault, and deer and turkeys inhabited the plateau to the west. Along the creek, based on bones found at the site, Clovis hunters also preyed on frogs, birds, turtles and other small animals.

This abundance of food, coupled with the exceptional quality of the chert, drew people to Gault in large numbers. Unlike the majority of Clovis sites, which are mostly the remains of temporary camps, Gault appears to have been inhabited over long periods and thus contradicts the standard view that Clovis people were always highly mobile, nomadic hunters. Michael Collins says that of the vast quantity of artifacts found at the site, many are tool fragments, left behind by people who'd stuck around long enough to not only break their tools but also to salvage and rework them. The researchers also unearthed a seven by seven foot square of gravel—perhaps the floor of a house—and a possible well, both signs of more than a fleeting presence.

Another clue was concealed on a 13,000-year-old Clovis blade about the size of a dinner knife. Under a magnifying lens, the blade's edge is glossy, rounded and smooth. Marilyn Shoberg, a stone tool analyst on the Gault team who has experimented with replicas, says the blade's polish probably came from cutting grass. This grass could have been used for basketry, bedding, or thatching to make roofs for huts.

Among the most unusual and tantalizing finds at the Gault site are a hundred or so fragments of limestone covered with lightly scratched patterns. Some resemble nets or basketry, while a few could be simple outlines of plants or animals. Although only a dozen can be securely dated to Clovis times, these enigmatic rocks are among the very few surviving artworks from ice age America.

"What this site tells us is that Clovis folks were not specialized mammoth hunters constantly wandering over the landscape," says Collins. "They exploited a variety of animals, they had tools for gathering plants and working wood, stone and hide, and they stayed through the useful life of those tools. All these things are contrary to what you'd expect if they were highly nomadic, dedicated big-game hunters." Yet this unexpected complexity sheds only a feeble glimmer on the more contentious issue of where the Clovis people came from and how they got here.

In the old scenario, still popular in classrooms and picture books, fur-clad hunters in the waning moments of the last ice age, when so much seawater was locked up in the polar ice caps that the sea level was as much as 300 feet lower than today, ventured across a land bridge from Siberia to Alaska. Then, pursuing big game, the hunters trekked south through present-day Canada. They passed down a narrow, 1,000-mile-long treeless corridor bounded by the towering walls of retreating ice sheets until they reached the Great Plains, which teemed with prey. The human population exploded, and the hunters soon drove into extinction some 35 genera of big animals (see box on page 6). All of these were supposedly dispatched by the Clovis point, a Stone Age weapon of mass destruction.

Digging at the Gault site in central Texas, according to project director Michael Collins, has almost doubled the number of Clovis artifacts excavated in North America. Researchers there have also uncovered evidence of ice age art.

For more than half a century, this plausible, "big-game" theory carried with it an appealing, heroic image. As James Adovasio of Mercyhurst College puts it in his book *The First Americans,* it was as if the ice sheets had parted "like the Red Sea for some Clovis Moses to lead his intrepid band of spear-toting, mammoth-slaying wayfarers to the south." But recent discoveries are indicating that almost everything about the theory could be wrong. For one thing, the latest studies show that the ice-free corridor didn't exist until around 12,000 years ago—too late to have served as the route for the very first people to come to America.

Clovis people buried caches of tools. Some stashed points were crafted from exotic stone; others seem too big and thin to have functioned as weapons. One cache was found with a child's bones, suggesting that burying tools could be a ritual act.

Perhaps the strongest ammunition against the old scenario comes from Monte Verde, an archaeological site on a remote terrace, which is today some 40 miles from the Pacific in southern Chile. Here, about 14,500 years ago, a hunting-and-gathering band lived year-round beside a creek in a long, oval hide tent, partitioned with logs. Archaeologist Tom Dillehay of Vanderbilt University began probing Monte Verde in 1977, unearthing the surface of the ancient encampment, complete with wood, plants and even remains of food, all preserved under a layer of waterlogged peat. Dillehay recovered three human footprints, two chunks of uneaten mastodon meat and possibly even traces of herbal medicine (indicated by nonfood plants still used by healers in the Andes). The dating of these extraordinary finds, at least 1,000 years before the earliest Clovis sites in North America, aroused skepticism for two decades until, in 1997, a group of leading archaeologists inspected the site and vindicated Dillehay's meticulous work.

No such triumph has emerged for any of the dozen or so sites in North America claimed to predate Clovis. But among the most intriguing is a rock overhang in Pennsylvania called Meadowcroft, where a 30-year campaign of excavation suggests that hunters may have reached the Northeast 3,000 or 4,000 years before the Clovis era.

Saber-toothed cats prowled North America for millions of years. For some reason, they died out about 13,000 years ago.

Meanwhile, genetics studies are pointing even more strongly to an early entry into the continent. By analyzing the mitochondrial DNA of living Native Americans, Douglas Wallace, a geneticist at the University of California at Irvine, and his colleagues have identified five distinct lineages that stretch back like family trees. Mitochondria are the cells' energy factories. Their DNA changes very little from one generation to the next, altered only by tiny variations that creep in at a steady and predictable rate. By counting the number of these variations in related lineages, Wallace's team can estimate their ages. When the team applied this technique to the DNA of Native Americans, they reached the stunning conclusion that there were at least four separate waves of prehistoric migration into the Americas, the earliest well over 20,000 years ago.

If the first Americans did arrive well before the oldest known Clovis settlements, how did they get here? The most radical theory for the peopling of the New World argues that Stone Age mariners journeyed from Europe around the southern fringes of the great ice sheets in the North Atlantic. Many archaeologists greet this idea with head-shaking scorn, but the proposition is getting harder to dismiss outright.

Dennis Stanford, a Clovis expert at the Smithsonian Institution's Department of Anthropology who delights in prodding his colleagues with unconventional thinking, was a longtime supporter of the land bridge scenario. Then, with the end of the cold war came the chance to visit archaeological sites and museums in Siberia—museums that should have been filled with tools that were predecessors of the Clovis point. "The result was a big disappointment," says Stanford. "What we found was nothing like we expected, and I was surprised that the technologies were so different." Instead of a single leaf-shaped Clovis spearhead, ice age Siberian hunters made projectiles that were bristling with rows of tiny razor-like blades embedded in wooden shafts. To Stanford, that meant no Siberian hunters armed with Clovis technology had walked to the Americas.

Meanwhile, Bruce Bradley, a prehistoric stone tool specialist at Britain's University of Exeter, had noticed a strong resemblance between Clovis points and weapons from ice age Europe. But the idea that the two cultures might be directly connected was heretical. "It certainly wasn't part of the scientific process at that point," Bradley says. "There was no possibility, forget it, don't even think about it." Bradley eventually pursued it to the storerooms of the Musée National de Préhistoire in Les Eyzies-de-Tayac in southwest France, where he pored through boxes of local prehistoric stone tools and waste flakes. "I was absolutely flabbergasted," he recalls. "If somebody had brought out a box of this stuff in the United States and set it down in front of me, I'd have said, 'Man, where did you get all that great Clovis stuff?'" But the material was the work of a culture called the Solutrean that thrived in southwest France and northern Spain during the coldest spell of the ice age, from around 24,000 to 19,000 years ago.

Thousands of years before their successors created the masterworks of Lascaux and Altamira, Solutrean-age artists began painting vivid murals in the depths of caves such as Cougnac and Cosquer. They made delicate, eyed sewing needles out of bone, enabling them to stitch tightfitting skin garments to repel the cold. They devised the *atlatl,* or spear thrower, a hooked bone or wood handle that extends the reach of the hunter's arm to multiply throwing power. But their most distinctive creation was a stone spearhead shaped like a laurel leaf.

Apart from the absence of a fluted base, the Solutrean laurel leaf strongly resembles the Clovis point and was made using the same, highly skillful flaking technique. Both Clovis and Solutrean stone crafters practiced controlled overshot flaking, which involved trimming one edge by striking a flake off the opposite side, a virtuoso feat of handiwork rarely seen in other prehistoric cultures. To Bradley, "there had to be some sort of historic connection" between the Solutrean and Clovis peoples.

Dennis Stanford and Bruce Bradley say that similarities between Clovis and Solutrean finds are overwhelming.

Critics of the theory point to a yawning gap between the two peoples: roughly 5,000 years divide the end of Solutrean culture and the emergence of Clovis. But Stanford and Bradley say that recent claims of pre-Clovis sites in the southeastern United States may bridge the time gap. In the mid-1990s at Cactus Hill, the remains of an ancient sand dune overlooking the Nottoway River on Virginia's coastal plain, project director Joseph McAvoy dug down a few inches beneath a Clovis layer and uncovered simple stone blades and projectile points associated with a hearth, radiocarbon dated to some 17,000 to 19,000 years ago. This startlingly early date has drawn skeptical fire, but the site's age was recently confirmed by an independent dating technique. Stanford and Bradley suggest that the early people at Cactus Hill were Clovis forerunners who had not yet developed the full-blown Clovis style. They are convinced that many more sites like Cactus Hill will turn up on the East Coast. But the burning question is, Did these ice age Virginians invent the Clovis point all by themselves, or were they descendants of Solutreans who brought the point with them from Europe?

Many archaeologists ridicule the notion that people made an arduous, 3,000-mile journey during the bleakest period of the ice age, when the Atlantic would have been much colder and stormier than today. Stanford believes that traditional Inuit technology suggests otherwise; he has witnessed traditional seagoing skills among Inupiat communities in Barrow, Alaska. Inupiat hunters still build large skin-covered canoes, or *umiaks,* which enable them to catch seals, walrus and other sea

Hunted to Extinction?

At the end of the last ice age, 35 genera of big animals, or "megafauna," went extinct in the Americas, including mammoths, mastodons, giant ground sloths, giant beavers, horses, short-faced bears and saber-toothed cats. Archaeologists have argued for decades that the arrival of hunters wielding Clovis spear points at around the same time was no coincidence. Clovis hunters pursued big game—their signature stone points are found with the bones of mammoths and mastodons at 14 kill sites in North America. Experiments carried out with replica spears thrust into the corpses of circus elephants indicate that the Clovis point could have penetrated a mammoth's hide. And computer simulations suggest that large, slow-breeding animals could have easily been wiped out by hunting as the human population expanded.

But humans might not be entirely to blame. The rapidly cycling climate at the end of the ice age may have changed the distribution of plants that the big herbivores grazed on, leading to a population crash among meat-eating predators too. New research on DNA fragments recovered from ice age bison bones suggests that some species were suffering a slow decline in diversity—probably caused by dwindling populations—long before any Clovis hunters showed up. Indigenous horses are now thought to have died out in Alaska about 500 years before the Clovis era. For mammoths and other beasts who did meet their demise during the Clovis times, many experts believe that a combination of factors—climate change plus pressure from human hunters—drove them into oblivion.

Amid all the debate, one point is clear: the Clovis hunter wasn't as macho as people once thought. Bones at the Gault site in central Texas reveal that the hunters there were feeding on less daunting prey—frogs, birds, turtles and antelope—as well as mammoth, mastodon and bison. As the late, renowned archaeologist Richard (Scotty) MacNeish is said to have remarked, "Each Clovis generation probably killed one mammoth, then spent the rest of their lives talking about it."

and medium-sized game with a similar, limited range of raw materials—stone, bone, ivory, antler, wood and sinew. They're going to come up with similar solutions."

More tellingly, in Straus' view, is that he can find little evidence of seafaring technology in the Solutrean sites he has dug in northern Spain. Although rising sea levels have drowned sites on the ice age coastline, Straus has investigated surviving inland cave sites no more than a couple of hours' walk from the beach. "There's no evidence of deep-sea fishing," says Straus, "no evidence of marine mammal hunting, and consequently no evidence, even indirect, for their possession of seaworthy boats."

And David Meltzer, an archaeologist at Southern Methodist University and a critic of the European-origins idea, is struck more by the differences between the Solutrean and Clovis cultures than their similarities—particularly the near-absence of art and personal ornaments from Clovis. Still, he says, the controversy is good for the field. "In the process of either killing or curing" the theory, "we will have learned a whole lot more about the archaeological record, and we'll all come out smarter than we went in."

Besides crossing the land bridge from Asia and traveling to ice age America from Europe by boat, a third possible entryway is a sea route down the west coast. Using maritime skills later perfected by the Inuit, prehistoric south Asians might have spread gradually around the northern rim of the Pacific in small skin-covered boats. They skirt the southern edge of the Bering land bridge and paddle down the coast of Alaska, dodging calving glaciers and icebergs as they pursue seals and other marine mammals. They keep going all the way to the beaches of Central and South America. They arrive at Monte Verde, inland from the Chilean coast, some 14,500 years ago. Each new generation claims fresh hunting grounds a few miles beyond the last, and in a matter of centuries these first immigrants have populated the entire west coast of the Americas. Soon the hunters start moving inland and, in the north, their descendants become the Clovis people.

Clovis people may well have reached North America via sea route. Seals and other marine prey may have sustained them until they found New World hunting grounds.

Many archaeologists now accept the west coast theory as a likely solution to the origin of the earliest Americans. On Prince of Wales Island in southeastern Alaska, inside the aptly named On Your Knees Cave, University of South Dakota paleontologist Timothy Heaton and University of Colorado at Boulder archaeologist E. James Dixon recovered an accumulation of animal bones from the last ice age. When mile-high ice sheets still straddled the interior of the continent 17,000 years ago, ringed seals, foxes and seabirds made their home on the island. "Humans could easily have survived there," Heaton says.

The ultimate evidence for the western sea route would be the discovery of pre-Clovis human remains on the coast. No

mammals that abound along the frozen edges of the pack ice. When twilight arrives or storms threaten, the hunters pull their boats up on the ice and camp beneath them. Ronald Brower of the Inupiat Heritage Center in Barrow says, "There's nothing that would have prevented . . . people from crossing the Atlantic into the Americas 19,000 years ago. It would be a perfectly normal situation from my perspective."

A different critique of the out-of-Europe theory dismisses the resemblance between Solutrean and Clovis points. Many archaeologists suggest that similarities between Clovis and Solutrean artifacts are coincidental, the result of what they call convergence. "These were people faced with similar problems," says Solutrean expert Lawrence Straus of the University of New Mexico. "And the problems involved hunting large-

such luck. Dixon and Heaton have found human jaw fragments and other remains in the On Your Knees Cave, but those date to about 11,000 years ago—too recent to establish the theory. And what may be the oldest-known human remains in North America—leg bones found on Santa Rosa Island, off the California coast—are from 13,000 years ago, the heart of the Clovis era. Still, those remains hint that by then people were plying the waters along the Pacific Coast.

If the trail of the very earliest Americans remains elusive, so, too, does the origin of the Clovis point. "Although the technology needed to produce a Clovis point was found among other cultures during the ice age," says Ken Tankersley of Northern Kentucky University, "the actual point itself is unique to the Americas, suggesting that it was invented here in the New World." If so, the spearhead would be the first great American invention—the Stone Age equivalent of the Swiss Army Knife, a trademark tool that would be widely imitated. The demand for the weapon and the high-quality stone it required probably encouraged Clovis people to begin long-distance trading and social exchanges. The spearhead may also have delivered a new level of hunting proficiency and this, in turn, would have fueled a population spurt, giving Clovis people their lasting presence in the archaeological record.

Sheltering from the broiling heat under the cottonwoods at Gault, Michael Collins told me of his conviction that the Clovis people who flocked to the shady creek were not pioneers but had profited from a long line of forebears. "Clovis represents the end product of centuries, if not millennia, of learning how to live in North American environments," he said. "The Clovis culture is too widespread, is found in too many environments, and has too much evidence for diverse activities to be the leavings of people just coming into the country." Collins reminded me that his team has investigated less than 10 percent of the enormous site. And archaeologists have barely scratched the surface of a handful of other Gault-size, Clovis-era sites—Williamsburg, in Virginia, for instance, or Shoop, in Pennsylvania. "One thing you can be sure," he said, beaming, "there'll be great new discoveries just around the corner."

EVAN HADINGHAM is the senior science editor of the PBS series NOVA and the author of books on prehistory.

1491

Before it became the New World, the Western Hemisphere was vastly more populous and sophisticated than has been thought—an altogether more salubrious place to live at the time than, say, Europe. New evidence of both the extent of the population and its agricultural advancement leads to a remarkable conjecture: the Amazon rain forest may be largely a human artifact.

CHARLES C. MANN

The plane took off in weather that was surprisingly cool for north-central Bolivia and flew east, toward the Brazilian border. In a few minutes the roads and houses disappeared, and the only evidence of human settlement was the cattle scattered over the savannah like jimmies on ice cream. Then they, too, disappeared. By that time the archaeologists had their cameras out and were clicking away in delight.

Below us was the Beni, a Bolivian province about the size of Illinois and Indiana put together, and nearly as flat. For almost half the year rain and snowmelt from the mountains to the south and west cover the land with an irregular, slowly moving skin of water that eventually ends up in the province's northern rivers, which are sub-subtributaries of the Amazon. The rest of the year the water dries up and the bright-green vastness turns into something that resembles a desert. This peculiar, remote, watery plain was what had drawn the researchers' attention, and not just because it was one of the few places on earth inhabited by people who might never have seen Westerners with cameras.

Clark Erickson and William Balée, the archaeologists, sat up front. Erickson is based at the University of Pennsylvania; he works in concert with a Bolivian archaeologist, whose seat in the plane I usurped that day. Balée is at Tulane University, in New Orleans. He is actually an anthropologist, but as native peoples have vanished, the distinction between anthropologists and archaeologists has blurred. The two men differ in build, temperament, and scholarly proclivity, but they pressed their faces to the windows with identical enthusiasm.

Indians were here in greater numbers than previously thought, and they imposed their will on the landscape. Columbus set foot in a hemisphere thoroughly dominated by humankind.

Dappled across the grasslands below was an archipelago of forest islands, many of them startlingly round and hundreds of acres across. Each island rose ten or thirty or sixty feet above the floodplain, allowing trees to grow that would otherwise never survive the water. The forests were linked by raised berms, as straight as a rifle shot and up to three miles long. It is Erickson's belief that this entire landscape—30,000 square miles of forest mounds surrounded by raised fields and linked by causeways—was constructed by a complex, populous society more than 2,000 years ago. Balée, newer to the Beni, leaned toward this view but was not yet ready to commit himself.

Erickson and Balée belong to a cohort of scholars that has radically challenged conventional notions of what the Western Hemisphere was like before Columbus. When I went to high school, in the 1970s, I was taught that Indians came to the Americas across the Bering Strait about 12,000 years ago, that they lived for the most part in small, isolated groups, and that they had so little impact on their environment that even after millennia of habitation it remained mostly wilderness. My son picked up the same ideas at his schools. One way to summarize the views of people like Erickson and Balée would be to say that in their opinion this picture of Indian life is wrong in almost every aspect. Indians were here far longer than previously thought, these researchers believe, and in much greater numbers. And they were so successful at imposing their will on the landscape that in 1492 Columbus set foot in a hemisphere thoroughly dominated by humankind.

Given the charged relations between white societies and native peoples, inquiry into Indian culture and history is inevitably contentious. But the recent scholarship is especially controversial. To begin with, some researchers—many but not all from an older generation—deride the new theories as fantasies arising from an almost willful misinterpretation of data and a perverse kind of political correctness. "I have seen no evidence that large numbers of people ever lived in the Beni," says Betty

J. Meggers, of the Smithsonian Institution. "Claiming otherwise is just wishful thinking." Similar criticisms apply to many of the new scholarly claims about Indians, according to Dean R. Snow, an anthropologist at Pennsylvania State University. The problem is that "you can make the meager evidence from the ethnohistorical record tell you anything you want," he says. "It's really easy to kid yourself."

More important are the implications of the new theories for today's ecological battles. Much of the environmental movements is animated, consciously or not, by what William Denevan, a geographer at the University of Wisconsin, calls, polemically, "the pristine myth"—the belief that the Americas in 1491 were an almost unmarked, even Edenic land, "untrammeled by man," in the words of the Wilderness Act of 1964, one of the nation's first and most important environmental laws. As the University of Wisconsin historian William Cronon has written, restoring this long-ago, putatively natural state is, in the view of environmentalists, a task that society is morally bound to undertake. Yet if the new view is correct and the work of humankind was pervasive, where does that leave efforts to restore nature?

The Beni is a case in point. In addition to building up the Beni mounds for houses and gardens, Erickson says, the Indians trapped fish in the seasonally flooded grassland. Indeed, he says, they fashioned dense zigzagging networks of earthen fish weirs between the causeways. To keep the habitat clear of unwanted trees and undergrowth, they regularly set huge areas on fire. Over the centuries the burning created an intricate ecosystem of fire-adapted plant species dependent on native pyrophilia. The current inhabitants of the Beni still burn, although now it is to maintain the savannah for cattle. When we flew over the areas, the dry season had just begun, but mile-long lines of flame were already on the march. In the charred areas behind the fires were the blackened spikes of trees—many of them one assumes, of the varieties that activists fight to save in other parts of Amazonia.

After we landed, I asked Balée, Should we let people keep burning the Beni? Or should we let the trees invade and create a verdant tropical forest in the grasslands, even if one had not existed here for millennia?

Balée laughed. "You're trying to trap me, aren't you?" he said.

Like a Club between the Eyes

According to family lore, my great-grandmother's great-grandmother's great-grandfather was the first white person hanged in America. His name was John Billington. He came on the *Mayflower*, which anchored off the coast of Massachusetts on November 9, 1620. Billington was not a Puritan; within six months of arrival he also became the first white person in America to be tried for complaining about the police. "He is a knave," William Bradford, the colony's governor, wrote to Billington, "and so will live and die." What one historian called Billington's "troublesome career" ended in 1630, when he was hanged for murder. My family has always said that he was framed—but we *would* say that, wouldn't we?

A few years ago it occurred to me that my ancestor and everyone else in the colony had voluntarily enlisted in a venture that brought them to New England without food or shelter six weeks before winter. Half the 102 people on the *Mayflower* made it through to spring, which to me was amazing. How, I wondered, did they survive?

In his history of Plymouth Colony, Bradford provided the answer: by robbing Indian houses and graves. The *Mayflower* first hove to at Cape Cod. An armed company staggered out. Eventually it found a recently deserted Indian settlement. The newcomers—hungry, cold, sick—dug up graves and ransacked houses, looking for underground stashes of corn. "And sure it was God's good providence that we found this corn," Bradford wrote, "for else we know not how we should have done." (He felt uneasy about the thievery, though.) When the colonists came to Plymouth, a month later, they set up shop in another deserted Indian village. All through the coastal forest the Indians had "died on heapes, as they lay in their houses," the English trader Thomas Morton noted. "And the bones and skulls upon the several places of their habitations made such a spectacle" that to Morton the Massachusetts woods seemed to be "a new found Golgotha"—the hill of executions in Roman Jerusalem.

To the Pilgrims' astonishment, one of the corpses they exhumed on Cape Cod had blond hair. A French ship had been wrecked there several years earlier. The Patuxet Indians imprisoned a few survivors. One of them supposedly learned enough of the local language to inform his captors that God would destroy them for their misdeeds. The Patuxet scoffed at the threat. But the Europeans carried a disease, and they bequeathed it to their jailers. The epidemic (probably of viral hepatitis, according to a study by Arthur E. Spiess, an archaeologist at the Maine Historic Preservation Commission, and Bruce D. Spiess, the director of clinical research at the Medical College of Virginia) took years to exhaust itself and may have killed 90 percent of the people in coastal New England. It made huge differences to American history. "The good hand of God favored our beginnings," Bradford mused, by "sweeping away great multitudes of the natives . . . that he might make room for us."

By the time my ancestor set sail on the *Mayflower*, Europeans had been visiting New England for more than a hundred years. English, French, Italian, Spanish, and Portuguese mariners regularly plied the coastline, trading what they could, occasionally kidnapping the inhabitants for slaves. New England, the Europeans saw, was thickly settled and well defended. In 1605 and 1606 Samuel de Champlain visited Cape Cod, hoping to establish a French base. He abandoned the idea. Too many people already lived there. A year later Sir Ferdinando Gorges—British despite his name—tried to establish an English community in southern Maine. It had more founders than Plymouth and seems to have been better organized. Confronted by numerous well-armed local Indians, the settlers abandoned the project within months. The Indians at Plymouth would surely have been an equal obstacle to my ancestor and his ramshackle expedition had disease not intervened.

Faced with such stories, historians have long wondered how many people lived in the Americas at the time of contact. "Debated since Columbus attempted a partial census on Hispaniola in 1496," William Denevan has written, this "remains one of the great inquiries of history." (In 1976 Denevan assembled and edited an entire book on the subject, *The Native Population of the Americas in 1492.*) The first scholarly estimate of the indigenous population was made in 1910 by James Mooney, a distinguished ethnographer at the Smithsonian Institution. Combing through old documents, he concluded that in 1491 North America had 1.15 million inhabitants. Mooney's glittering reputation ensured that most subsequent researchers accepted his figure uncritically.

That changed in 1966, when Henry F. Dobyns published "Estimating Aboriginal American Population: An Appraisal of Techniques With a New Hemispheric Estimate," in the journal *Current Anthropology*. Despite the carefully neutral title, his argument was thunderous, its impact long-lasting. In the view of James Wilson, the author of *The Earth Shall Weep* (1998), a history of indigenous Americans, Dobyns's colleagues "are still struggling to get out of the crater that paper left in anthropology." Not only anthropologists were affected. Dobyns's estimate proved to be one of the opening rounds in today's culture wars.

Dobyns began his exploration of pre-Columbian Indian demography in the early 1950s, when he was a graduate student. At the invitation of a friend, he spent a few months in northern Mexico, which is full of Spanish-era missions. There he poked through the crumbling leather-bound ledgers in which Jesuits recorded local births and deaths. Right away he noticed how many more deaths there were. The Spaniards arrived, and then Indians died—in huge numbers at incredible rates. It hit him, Dobyns told me recently, "like a club right between the eyes."

It took Dobyns eleven years to obtain his Ph.D. Along the way he joined a rural-development project in Peru, which until colonial times was the seat of the Incan empire. Remembering what he had seen at the northern fringe of the Spanish conquest, Dobyns decided to compare it with figures for the south. He burrowed into the papers of the Lima cathedral and read apologetic Spanish histories. The Indians in Peru, Dobyns concluded, had faced plagues from the day the conquistadors showed up—in fact, before then: smallpox arrived around 1525, seven years ahead of the Spanish. Brought to Mexico apparently by a single sick Spaniard, it swept south and eliminated more than half the population of the Incan empire. Smallpox claimed the Incan dictator Huayna Capac and much of his family, setting off a calamitous war of succession. So complete was the chaos that Francisco Pizarro was able to seize an empire the size of Spain and Italy combined with a force of 168 men.

Smallpox was only the first epidemic. Typhus (probably) in 1546, influenza and smallpox together in 1558, smallpox again in 1589, diphtheria in 1614, measles in 1618—all ravaged the remains of Incan culture. Dobyns was the first social scientist to piece together this awful picture, and he naturally rushed his findings into print. Hardly anyone paid attention. But Dobyns was already working on a second, related question: If all those people died, how many had been living there to begin with? Before Columbus, Dobyns calculated, the Western Hemisphere held ninety to 112 million people. Another way of saying this is that in 1491 more people lived in the Americas than in Europe.

His argument was simple but horrific. It is well known that Native Americans had no experience with many European diseases and were therefore immunologically unprepared—"virgin soil," in the metaphor of epidemiologists. What Dobyns realized was that such diseases could have swept from the coastlines initially visited by Europeans to inland areas controlled by Indians who had never seen a white person. The first whites to explore many parts of the Americas may therefore have encountered places that were already depopulated. Indeed, Dobyns argued, they must have done so.

Peru was one example, the Pacific Northwest another. In 1792 the British navigator George Vancouver led the first European expedition to survey Puget Sound. He found a vast charnel house: human remains "promiscuously scattered about the beach, in great numbers." Smallpox, Vancouver's crew discovered, had preceded them. Its few survivors, second lieutenant Peter Puget noted, were "most terribly pitted . . . indeed many have lost their Eyes." In *Pox Americana* (2001), Elizabeth Fenn, a historian at George Washington University, contends that the disaster on the northwest coast was but a small part of a continental pandemic that erupted near Boston in 1774 and cut down Indians from Mexico to Alaska.

Because smallpox was not endemic in the Americas, colonials, too, had not acquired any immunity. The virus, an equal-opportunity killer, swept through the Continental Army and stopped the drive into Quebec. The American Revolution would be lost, Washington and other rebel leaders feared, if the contagion did to the colonists what it had done to the Indians. "The small Pox! The small Pox!" John Adams wrote to his wife, Abigail. "What shall We do with it?" In retrospect, Fenn says, "One of George Washington's most brilliant moves was to inoculate the army against smallpox during the Valley Forge winter of '78." Without inoculation smallpox could easily have given the United States back to the British.

So many epidemics occurred in the Americas, Dobyns argued, that the old data used by Mooney and his successors represented population nadirs. From the few cases in which before-and-after totals are known with relative certainty, Dobyns estimated that in the first 130 years of contact about 95 percent of the people in the Americas died—the worst demographic calamity in recorded history.

Dobyns's ideas were quickly attacked as politically motivated, a push from the hate-America crowd to inflate the toll of imperialism. The attacks continue to this day. "No question about it, some people want those higher numbers," says Shepard Krech III, a Brown University anthropologist who is the author of *The Ecological Indian* (1999). These people, he says, were thrilled when Dobyns revisited the subject in a book, *Their Numbers Become Thinned* (1983)—and revised his own estimates upward. Perhaps Dobyns's most vehement critic is David Henige, a bibliographer of Africana at the University of Wisconsin, whose *Numbers from Nowhere* (1998) is a landmark in the literature of demographic fulmination. "Suspect in 1966, it is no less suspect nowadays," Henige wrote of Dobyns's work. "If anything, it is worse."

When Henige wrote *Numbers From Nowhere,* the fight about pre-Columbian populations had already consumed forests' worth of trees; his bibliography is ninety pages long. And the dispute shows no sign of abating. More and more people have jumped in. This is partly because the subject is inherently fascinating. But more likely the increased interest in the debate is due to the growing realization of the high political and ecological stakes.

Inventing by the Millions

On May 30, 1539, Hernando de Soto landed his private army near Tampa Bay, in Florida. Soto, as he was called, was a novel figure: half warrior, half venture capitalist. He had grown very rich very young by becoming a market leader in the nascent trade for Indian slaves. The profits had helped to fund Pizarro's seizure of the Incan empire, which had made Soto wealthier still. Looking quite literally for new worlds to conquer, he persuaded the Spanish Crown to let him loose in North America. He spent one fortune to make another. He came to Florida with 200 horses, 600 soldiers, and 300 pigs.

From today's perspective, it is difficult to imagine the ethical system that would justify Soto's actions. For four years his force, looking for gold, wandered through what is now Florida, Georgia, North and South Carolina, Tennessee, Alabama, Mississippi, Arkansas, and Texas, wrecking almost everything it touched. The inhabitants often fought back vigorously, but they had never before encountered an army with horses and guns. Soto died of fever with his expedition in ruins; along the way his men had managed to rape, torture, enslave, and kill countless Indians. But the worst thing the Spaniards did, some researchers say, was entirely without malice—bring the pigs.

According to Charles Hudson, an anthropologist at the University of Georgia who spent fifteen years reconstructing the path of the expedition, Soto crossed the Mississippi a few miles downstream from the present site of Memphis. It was a nervous passage: the Spaniards were watched by several thousand Indian warriors. Utterly without fear, Soto brushed past the Indian force into what is now eastern Arkansas, through thickly settled land—"very well peopled with large towns," one of his men later recalled, "two or three of which were to be seen from one town." Eventually the Spaniards approached a cluster of small cities, each protected by earthen walls, sizeable moats, and deadeye archers. In his usual fashion, Soto brazenly marched in, stole food, and marched out.

After Soto left, no Europeans visited this part of the Mississippi Valley for more than a century. Early in 1682 whites appeared again, this time Frenchmen in canoes. One of them was Réné-Robert Cavelier, Sieur de la Salle. The French passed through the area where Soto had found cities cheek by jowl. It was deserted—La Salle didn't see an Indian village for 200 miles. About fifty settlements existed in this strip of the Mississippi when Soto showed up, according to Anne Ramenofsky, an anthropologist at the University of New Mexico. By La Salle's time the number had shrunk to perhaps ten, some probably inhabited by recent immigrants. Soto "had a privileged glimpse" of an Indian world, Hudson says. "The window opened and slammed shut. When the French came in and the record opened up again, it was a transformed reality. A civilization crumbled. The question is, how did this happen?"

Swine alone can disseminate anthrax, brucellosis, leptospirosis, trichinosis, and tuberculosis. Only a few of Hernando de Soto's pigs would have had to wander off to infect the forest.

The question is even more complex than it may seem. Disaster of this magnitude suggests epidemic disease. In the view of Ramenofsky and Patricia Galloway, an anthropologist at the University of Texas, the source of the contagion was very likely not Soto's army but its ambulatory meat locker: his 300 pigs. Soto's force itself was too small to be an effective biological weapon. Sicknesses like measles and smallpox would have burned through his 600 soldiers long before they reached the Mississippi. But the same would not have held true for the pigs, which multiplied rapidly and were able to transmit their diseases to wildlife in the surrounding forest. When human beings and domesticated animals live close together, they trade microbes with abandon. Over time mutation spawns new diseases: Avian influenza becomes human influenza, bovine rinderpest becomes measles. Unlike Europeans, Indians did not live in close quarters with animals—they domesticated only the dog, the llama, the alpaca, the guinea pig, and here and there, the turkey and the Muscovy duck. In some ways this is not surprising: the New World had fewer animal candidates for taming than the Old. Moreover, few Indians carry the gene that permits adults to digest lactose, a form of sugar abundant in milk. Non-milk-drinkers, one imagines, would be less likely to work at domesticating milk-giving animals. But this is guesswork. The fact is that what scientists call zoonotic disease was little known in the Americas. Swine alone can disseminate anthrax, brucellosis, leptospirosis, taeniasis, trichinosis, and tuberculosis. Pigs breed exuberantly and can transmit diseases to deer and turkeys. Only a few of Soto's pigs would have had to wander off to infect the forest.

Indeed, the calamity wrought by Soto apparently extended across the whole Southeast. The Coosa city-states, in western Georgia, and the Caddoan-speaking civilization, centered on the Texas-Arkansas border, disintegrated soon after Soto appeared. The Caddo had had a taste for monumental architecture: public plazas, ceremonial platforms, mausoleums. After Soto's army left, notes Timothy K. Perttula, an archaeological consultant in Austin, Texas, the Caddo stopped building community centers and began digging community cemeteries. Between Soto's and La Salle's visits, Perttula believes, the Caddoan population fell from about 200,000 to about 8,500—a drop of nearly 96 percent. In the eighteenth century the tally shrank further, to 1,400. An equivalent loss today in the population of New York City would reduce it to 56,000—not enough to fill Yankee Stadium. "That's one reason whites think of Indians as nomadic hunters," says Russell Thornton, an anthropologist at the University of California at Los Angeles. "Everything else—all the heavily populated urbanized societies—was wiped out."

Could a few pigs truly wreak this much destruction? Such apocalyptic scenarios invite skepticism. As a rule, viruses, microbes, and parasites are rarely lethal on so wide a scale—a pest that wipes out its host species does not have a bright evolutionary future. In its worst outbreak, from 1347 to 1351, the European Black Death claimed only a third of its victims. (The rest survived, though they were often disfigured or crippled by its effects.) The Indians in Soto's path, if Dobyns, Ramenofsky, and Perttula are correct, endured losses that were incomprehensibly greater.

One reason is that Indians were fresh territory for many plagues, not just one. Smallpox, typhoid, bubonic plague, influenza, mumps, measles, whooping cough—all rained down on the Americas in the century after Columbus. (Cholera, malaria, and scarlet fever came later.) Having little experience with epidemic diseases, Indians had no knowledge of how to combat them. In contrast, Europeans were well versed in the brutal logic of quarantine. They boarded up houses in which plague appeared and fled to the countryside. In Indian New England, Neal Salisbury, a historian at Smith college, wrote in *Manitou and Providence* (1982), family and friends gathered with the shaman at the sufferer's bedside to wait out the illness—a practice that "could only have served to spread the disease more rapidly."

Indigenous biochemistry may also have played a role. The immune system constantly scans the body for molecules that it can recognize as foreign—molecules belonging to an invading virus, for instance. No one's immune system can identify all foreign presences. Roughly speaking, an individual's set of defensive tools is known as his MHC type. Because many bacteria and viruses mutate easily, they usually attack in the form of several slightly different strains. Pathogens win when MHC types miss some of the strains and the immune system is not stimulated to act. Most human groups contain many MHC types; a strain that slips by one person's defenses will be nailed by the defenses of the next. But, according to Francis L. Black, an epidemiologist at Yale University, Indians are characterized by unusually homogeneous MHC types. One out of three South American Indians have similar MHC types; among Africans the corresponding figure is one in 200. The cause is a matter for Darwinian speculation, the effects less so.

In 1966 Dobyns's insistence on the role of disease was a shock to his colleagues. Today the impact of European pathogens on the New World is almost undisputed. Nonetheless, the fight over Indian numbers continues with undiminished fervor. Estimates of the population of North America in 1491 disagree by an order of magnitude—from 18 million, Dobyns's revised figure, to 1.8 million, calculated by Douglas H. Ubelaker, an anthropologist at the Smithsonian. To some "high counters," as David Henige calls them, the low counters' refusal to relinquish the vision of an empty continent is irrational or worse. "Non-Indian 'experts' always want to minimize the size of aboriginal populations," says Lenore Stiffarm, a Native American-education specialist at the University of Saskatchewan. The smaller the numbers of Indians, she believes, the easier it is to regard the continent as having been up for grabs. "It's perfectly acceptable to move into unoccupied land," Stiffarm says. "And land with only a few 'savages' is the next best thing."

"Most of the arguments for the very large numbers have been theoretical," Ubelaker says in defense of low counters. "When you try to marry the theoretical arguments to the data that are available on individual groups in different regions, it's hard to find support for those numbers." Archaeologists, he says, keep searching for the settlements in which those millions of people supposedly lived, with little success. "As more and more excavation is done, one would expect to see more evidence for dense populations than has thus far emerged." Dean Snow, the Pennsylvania State anthropologist, examined Colonial-era Mohawk Iroquois sites and found "no support for the notion that ubiquitous pandemics swept the region." In his view, asserting that the continent was filled with people who left no trace is like looking at an empty bank account and claiming that it must once have held millions of dollars.

The low counters are also troubled by the Dobynsian procedure for recovering original population numbers: applying an assumed death rate, usually 95 percent, to the observed population nadir. Ubelaker believes that the lowest point for Indians in North America was around 1900, when their numbers fell to about half a million. Assuming a 95 percent death rate, the pre-contact population would have been 10 million. Go up one percent, to a 96 percent death rate, and the figure jumps to 12.5 million—arithmetically creating more than two million people from a tiny increase in mortality rates. At 98 percent the number bounds to 25 million. Minute changes in baseline assumptions produce wildly different results.

"It's an absolutely unanswerable question on which tens of thousands of words have been spent to no purpose," Henige says. In 1976 he sat in on a seminar by William Denevan, the Wisconsin geographer. An "epiphanic moment" occurred when he read shortly afterward that scholars had "uncovered" the existence of eight million people in Hispaniola. *Can you just invent millions of people?* he wondered. "We can make of the historical record that there was depopulation and movement of people from internecine warfare and diseases," he says. "But as for how much, who knows? When we start putting numbers to something like that—applying large figures like ninety-five percent—we're saying things we shouldn't say. The number implies a level of knowledge that's impossible."

Nonetheless, one must try—or so Denevan believes. In his estimation the high counters (though not the highest counters) seem to be winning the argument, at least for now. No definitive data exist, he says, but the majority of the extant evidentiary scraps support their side. Even Henige is no low counter. When I asked him what he thought the population of the Americas was before Columbus, he insisted that any answer would be speculation and made me promise not to print what he was going to say next. Then he named a figure that forty years ago would have caused a commotion.

To Elizabeth Fenn, the smallpox historian, the squabble over numbers obscures a central fact. Whether one million or 10 million or 100 million died, she believes, the pall of sorrow that engulfed the hemisphere was immeasurable. Languages, prayers, hopes, habits, and dreams—entire ways of life hissed away like steam. The Spanish and the Portuguese lacked the germ theory of disease and could not explain what was happening (let alone stop it). Nor can we explain it; the ruin was too long ago and too all-encompassing. In the long run, Fenn says, the consequential finding is not that many people died but that many people once lived. The Americas were filled with a stunningly diverse assortment of peoples who had knocked about the continents for millennia. "You have to wonder," Fenn says. "What were all those people *up* to in all that time?"

Buffalo Farm

In 1810 Henry Brackenridge came to Cahokia, in what is now southwest Illinois, just across the Mississippi from St. Louis. Born close to the frontier, Brackenridge was a budding adventure writer; his *Views of Louisiana,* published three years later, was a kind of nineteenth-century *Into Thin Air,* with terrific adventure but without tragedy. Brackenridge had an eye for archaeology, and he had heard that Cahokia was worth a visit. When he got there, trudging along the desolate Cahokia River, he was "struck with a degree of astonishment." Rising from the muddy bottomland was a "stupendous pile of earth," vaster than the Great Pyramid at Giza. Around it were more than a hundred smaller mounds, covering an area of five square miles. At the time, the area was almost uninhabited. One can only imagine what passed through Brackenridge's mind as he walked alone to the ruins of the biggest Indian city north of the Rio Grande.

To Brackenridge, it seemed clear that Cahokia and the many other ruins in the Midwest had been constructed by Indians. It was not so clear to everyone else. Nineteenth-century writers attributed them to, among others, the Vikings, the Chinese, the "Hindoos," the ancient Greeks, the ancient Egyptians, lost tribes of Israelites, and even straying bands of Welsh. (This last claim was surprisingly widespread; when Lewis and Clark surveyed the Missouri, Jefferson told them to keep an eye out for errant bands of Welsh-speaking white Indians.) The historian George Bancroft, dean of his profession, was a dissenter: the earthworks, he wrote in 1840, were purely natural formations.

Bancroft changed his mind about Cahokia, but not about Indians. To the end of his days he regarded them as "feeble barbarians, destitute of commerce and of political connection." His characterization lasted, largely unchanged, for more than a century. Samuel Eliot Morison, the winner of two Pulitzer Prizes, closed his monumental *European Discovery of America* (1974) with the observation that Native Americans expected only "short and brutish lives, void of hope for any future." As late as 1987 *American History: A Survey,* a standard high school textbook by three well-known historians, described the Americas before Columbus as "empty of mankind and its works." The story of Europeans in the New World, the book explained, "is the story of the creation of a civilization where none existed."

Alfred Crosby, a historian at the University of Texas, came to other conclusions. Crosby's *The Columbian Exchange: Biological Consequences of 1492* caused almost as much of a stir when it was published, in 1972, as Henry Dobyns's calculation of Indian numbers six years earlier, though in different circles. Crosby was a standard names-and-battles historian who became frustrated by the random contingency of political events. "Some trivial thing happens and you have this guy winning the presidency instead of that guy," he says. He decided to go deeper. After he finished his manuscript, it sat on his shelf—he couldn't find a publisher willing to be associated with his new ideas. It took him three years to persuade a small editorial house to put it out. *The Columbian Exchange* has been in print ever since; a companion, *Ecological Imperialism: The Biological Expansion of Europe, 900–1900,* appeared in 1986.

Human history, in Crosby's interpretation, is marked by two world-altering centers of invention: the Middle East and central Mexico, where Indian groups independently created nearly all of the Neolithic innovations, writing included. The Neolithic Revolution began in the Middle East about 10,000 years ago. In the next few millennia humankind invented the wheel, the metal tool, and agriculture. The Sumerians eventually put these inventions together, added writing, and became the world's first civilization. Afterward Sumeria's heirs in Europe and Asia frantically copied one another's happiest discoveries; innovations ricocheted from one corner of Eurasia to another, stimulating technological progress. Native Americans, who had crossed to Alaska before Sumeria, missed out on the bounty. "They had to do everything on their own," Crosby says. Remarkably, they succeeded.

When Columbus appeared in the Caribbean, the descendants of the world's two Neolithic civilizations collided, with overwhelming consequences for both. American Neolithic development occurred later than that of the Middle East, possibly because the Indians needed more time to build up the requisite population density. Without beasts of burden they could not capitalize on the wheel (for individual workers on uneven terrain skids are nearly as effective as carts for hauling), and they never developed steel. But in agriculture they handily outstripped the children of Sumeria. Every tomato in Italy, every potato in Ireland, and every hot pepper in Thailand came from this hemisphere. Worldwide, more than half the crops grown today were initially developed in the Americas.

Maize, as corn is called in the rest of the world, was a triumph with global implications. Indians developed an extraordinary number of maize varieties for different growing conditions, which meant that the crop could and did spread throughout the planet. Central and Southern Europeans became particularly dependent on it; maize was the staple of Serbia, Romania, and Moldavia by the nineteenth century. Indian crops dramatically reduced hunger, Crosby says, which led to an Old World population boom.

In the Aztec capital Tenochtitlán the Spaniards gawped like hayseeds at the side streets, ornately carved buildings, and markets bright with goods from hundreds of miles away.

Along with peanuts and manioc, maize came to Africa and transformed agriculture there, too. "The probability is that the population of Africa was greatly increased because of maize and other American Indian crops," Crosby says. "Those extra people helped make the slave trade possible." Maize conquered Africa at the time when introduced diseases were leveling Indian societies. The Spanish, the Portuguese, and the British were alarmed by the death rate among Indians, because they wanted to exploit them as workers. Faced with a labor shortage, the Europeans turned their eyes to Africa. The continent's quarrelsome societies helped slave traders to siphon off millions of people. The maize-fed population boom, Crosby believes, let the awful trade continue without pumping the well dry.

Back home in the Americas, Indian agriculture long sustained some of the world's largest cities. The Aztec capital of Tenochtitlán dazzled Hernán Cortés in 1519; it was bigger than Paris, Europe's greatest metropolis. The Spaniards gawped like hayseeds at the wide streets, ornately carved buildings, and markets bright with goods from hundreds of miles away. They had never before seen a city with botanical gardens, for the excellent reason that none existed in Europe. The same novelty attended the force of a thousand men that kept the crowded streets immaculate. (Streets that weren't ankle-deep in sewage! The conquistadors had never heard of such a thing.) Central America was not the only locus of prosperity. Thousands of miles north, John Smith, of Pocahontas fame, visited Massachusetts in 1614, before it was emptied by disease, and declared that the land was "so planted with Gardens and Corne fields, and so well inhabited with a goodly, strong and well proportioned people . . . [that] I would rather live here than any where."

Smith was promoting colonization, and so had reason to exaggerate. But he also knew the hunger, sickness, and oppression of European life. France—"by any standards a privileged country," according to its great historian, Fernand Braudel—experienced seven nationwide famines in the fifteenth century and thirteen in the sixteenth. Disease was hunger's constant companion. During epidemics in London the dead were heaped onto carts "like common dung" (the simile is Daniel Defoe's) and trundled through the streets. The infant death rate in London orphanages, according to one contemporary source, was 88 percent. Governments were harsh, the rule of law arbitrary. The gibbets poking up in the background of so many old paintings were, Braudel observed, "merely a realistic detail."

The Earth Shall Weep, James Wilson's history of Indian America, puts the comparison bluntly: "the western hemisphere was larger, richer, and more populous than Europe." Much of it was freer, too. Europeans, accustomed to the serfdom that thrived from Naples to the Baltic Sea, were puzzled and alarmed by the democratic spirit and respect for human rights in many Indian societies, especially those in North America. In theory, the sachems of New England Indian groups were absolute monarchs. In practice, the colonial leader Roger Williams wrote, "they will not conclude of ought . . . unto which the people are averse."

Pre-1492 America wasn't a disease-free paradise, Dobyns says, although in his "exuberance as a writer," he told me recently, he once made that claim. Indians had ailments of their own, notably parasites, tuberculosis, and anemia. The daily grind was wearing; life-spans in America were only as long as or a little longer than those in Europe, if the evidence of indigenous graveyards is to be believed. Nor was it a political utopia—the Inca, for instance, invented refinements to totalitarian rule that would have intrigued Stalin. Inveterate practitioners of what the historian Francis Jennings described as "state terrorism practiced horrifically on a huge scale," the Inca ruled so cruelly that one can speculate that their surviving subjects might actually have been better off under Spanish rule.

I asked seven anthropologists, archaeologists, and historians if they would rather have been a typical Indian or a typical European in 1491. Every one chose to be an Indian.

I asked seven anthropologists, archaeologists, and historians if they would rather have been a typical Indian or a typical European in 1491. None was delighted by the question, because it required judging the past by the standards of today—a fallacy disparaged as "presentism" by social scientists. But every one chose to be an Indian. Some early colonists gave the same answer. Horrifying the leaders of Jamestown and Plymouth, scores of English ran off to live with the Indians. My ancestor shared their desire, which is what led to the trumped-up murder charges against him—or that's what my grandfather told me, anyway.

As for the Indians, evidence suggests that they often viewed Europeans with disdain. The Hurons, a chagrined missionary reported, thought the French possessed "little intelligence in comparison to themselves." Europeans, Indians said, were physically weak, sexually untrustworthy, atrociously ugly, and just plain dirty. (Spaniards, who seldom if ever bathed, were amazed by the Aztec desire for personal cleanliness.) A Jesuit reported that the "Savages" were disgusted by handkerchiefs: "They say, we place what is unclean in a fine white piece of linen, and put it away in our pockets as something very precious, while they throw it upon the ground." The Micmac scoffed at the notion of French superiority. If Christian civilization was so wonderful, why were its inhabitants leaving?

Like people everywhere, Indians survived by cleverly exploiting their environment. Europeans tended to manage land by breaking it into fragments for farmers and herders. Indians often worked on such a grand scale that the scope of their ambition can be hard to grasp. They created small plots, as Europeans did (about 1.5 million acres of terraces still exist in the Peruvian Andes), but they also reshaped entire landscapes to suit their purposes. A principal tool was fire, used to keep down underbrush and create the open, grassy conditions favorable for game. Rather than domesticating animals for meat, Indians retooled whole ecosystems to grow bumper crops of elk, deer, and bison. The first white settlers in Ohio found forests as open as English parks—they could drive carriages through the woods. Along the Hudson River the annual fall burning lit up the banks for miles on end; so flashy was the show that the Dutch in New Amsterdam boated upriver to goggle at the blaze like children at fireworks. In North America, Indian torches had their biggest impact on the Midwestern prairie, much or most of which was created and maintained by fire. Millennia of exuberant burning shaped the plains into vast buffalo farms. When Indian societies disintegrated, forest invaded savannah in Wisconsin, Illinois, Kansas, Nebraska, and the Texas Hill Country. Is it possible that the Indians changed the Americas more than the invading Europeans did? "The answer is probably yes for most regions for the next 250 years or so" after Columbus. William Denevan wrote, "and for some regions right up to the present time."

Amazonia has become the emblem of vanishing wilderness—an admonitory image of untouched Nature. But the rain forest itself may be a cultural artifact—that is, an artificial object.

When scholars first began increasing their estimates of the ecological impact of Indian civilization, they met with considerable resistance from anthropologists and archaeologists. Over time the consensus in the human sciences changed. Under Denevan's direction, Oxford University Press has just issued the third volume of a huge catalogue of the "cultivated landscapes" of the Americas. This sort of phrase still provokes vehement objection—but the main dissenters are now ecologists and environmentalists. The disagreement is encapsulated by Amazonia, which has become *the* emblem of vanishing wilderness—an admonitory image of untouched Nature. Yet recently a growing number of researchers have come to believe that Indian societies had an enormous environmental impact on the jungle. Indeed, some anthropologists have called the Amazon forest itself a cultural artifact—that is, an artificial object.

Green Prisons

Northern visitors' first reaction to the storied Amazon rain forest is often disappointment. Ecotourist brochures evoke the immensity of Amazonia but rarely dwell on its extreme flatness. In the river's first 2,900 miles the vertical drop is only 500 feet. The river oozes like a huge runnel of dirty metal through a landscape utterly devoid of the romantic crags, arroyos, and heights that signify wilderness and natural spectacle to most North Americans. Even the animals are invisible, although sometimes one can hear the bellow of monkey choruses. To the untutored eye—mine, for instance—the forest seems to stretch out in a monstrous green tangle as flat and incomprehensible as a printed circuit board.

The area east of the lower-Amazon town of Santarém is an exception. A series of sandstone ridges several hundred feet high reach down from the north, halting almost at the water's edge. Their tops stand drunkenly above the jungle like old tombstones. Many of the caves in the buttes are splattered with ancient petroglyphs—renditions of hands, stars, frogs, and human figures, all reminiscent of Miró, in overlapping red and yellow and brown. In recent years one of these caves, La Caverna da Pedra Pintada (Painted Rock Cave), has drawn attention in archaeological circles.

Wide and shallow and well lit, Painted Rock Cave is less thronged with bats than some of the other caves. The arched entrance is twenty feet high and lined with rock paintings. Out front is a sunny natural patio suitable for picnicking, edged by a few big rocks. People lived in this cave more than 11,000 years ago. They had no agriculture yet, and instead ate fish and fruit and built fires. During a recent visit I ate a sandwich atop a particularly inviting rock and looked over the forest below. The first Amazonians, though, must have done more or less the same thing.

In college I took an introductory anthropology class in which I read *Amazonia: Man and Culture in a Counterfeit Paradise* (1971), perhaps the most influential book ever written about the Amazon, and one that deeply impressed me at the time. Written by Betty J. Meggers, the Smithsonian archaeologist, *Amazonia* says that the apparent lushness of the rain forest is a sham. The soils are poor and can't hold nutrients—the jungle flora exists only because it snatches up everything worthwhile before it leaches away in the rain. Agriculture, which depends on extracting the wealth of the soil, therefore faces inherent ecological limitations in the wet desert of Amazonia.

As a result, Meggers argued, Indian villages were forced to remain small—any report of "more than a few hundred" people in permanent settlements, she told me recently, "makes my alarm bells go off." Bigger, more complex societies would inevitably overtax the forest soils, laying waste to their own foundations. Beginning in 1948 Meggers and her late husband, Clifford Evans, excavated a chiefdom on Marajó, an island twice the size of New Jersey that sits like a gigantic stopper in the mouth of the Amazon. The Marajóara, they concluded, were failed offshoots of a sophisticated culture in the Andes. Transplanted to the lush trap of the Amazon, the culture choked and died.

Green activists saw the implication: development in tropical forests destroys both the forests and their developers. Meggers's account had enormous public impact—*Amazonia* is one of the wellsprings of the campaign to save rain forests.

Then Anna C. Roosevelt, the curator of archaeology at Chicago's Field Museum of Natural History, re-excavated Marajó. Her complete report, *Moundbuilders of the Amazon* (1991), was like the anti-matter version of *Amazonia*. Marajó, she argued, was "one of the outstanding indigenous cultural achievements of the New World," a powerhouse that lasted for more than a thousand years, had "possibly well over 100,000" inhabitants, and covered thousands of square miles. Rather than damaging the forest, Marajó's "earth construction" and "large, dense populations" had *improved* it: the most luxuriant and diverse growth was on the mounds formerly occupied by the Marajóara. "If you listened to Meggers's theory, these places should have been ruined," Roosevelt says.

Meggers scoffed at Roosevelt's "extravagant claims," "polemical tone," and "defamatory remarks." Roosevelt, Meggers argued, had committed the beginner's error of mistaking a site that had been occupied many times by small, unstable groups for a single, long-lasting society. "[Archaeological remains] build up on areas of half a kilometer or so," she told me, "because [shifting Indian groups] don't land exactly on the same spot. The decorated types of pottery don't change much over time, so you can pick up a bunch of chips and say, 'Oh, look, it was all one big site!' Unless you know what you're doing, of course." Centuries after the conquistadors, "the myth of El Dorado is being revived by archaeologists," Meggers wrote last fall in the journal *Latin American Antiquity,* referring to the persistent Spanish delusion that cities of gold existed in the jungle.

The dispute grew bitter and personal; inevitable in a contemporary academic context, it has featured vituperative references to colonialism, elitism, and employment by the CIA. Meanwhile, Roosevelt's team investigated Painted Rock Cave. On the floor of the cave what looked to me like nothing in particular turned out to be an ancient midden: a refuse heap. The archaeologists slowly scraped away sediment, traveling backward in time with every inch. When the traces of human occupation vanished, they kept digging. ("You always go a meter past sterile," Roosevelt says.) A few inches below they struck the charcoal-rich dirt that signifies human habitation—a culture, Roosevelt said later, that wasn't supposed to be there.

For many millennia the cave's inhabitants hunted and gathered for food. But by about 4000 years ago they were growing crops—perhaps as many as 140 of them, according to Charles R. Clement, an anthropological botanist at the Brazilian National Institute for Amazonian Research. Unlike Europeans, who planted mainly annual crops, the Indians, he says, centered their agriculture on the Amazon's unbelievably diverse assortment of trees: fruits, nuts, and palms. "It's tremendously difficult to clear fields with stone tools," Clement says. "If you can plant trees, you get twenty years of productivity out of your work instead of two or three."

Planting their orchards, the first Amazonians transformed large swaths of the river basin into something more pleasing to human beings. In a widely cited article from 1989, William Balée, the Tulane anthropologist, cautiously estimated that about 12 percent of the nonflooded Amazon forest was of anthropogenic origin—directly or indirectly created by human beings. In some circles this is now seen as a conservative position. "I basically think it's all human-created," Clement told me in Brazil. He argues that Indians changed the assortment and density of species throughout the region. So does Clark Erickson, the University of Pennsylvania archaeologist, who told me in Bolivia that the lowland tropical forests of South America are among the finest works of art on the planet. "Some of my colleagues would say that's pretty radical," he said, smiling mischievously. According to Peter Stahl, an anthropologist at the State University of New York at Binghamton, "lots" of botanists believe that "what the eco-imagery would like to picture as a pristine, untouched Urwelt [primeval world] in fact has been managed by people for millennia." The phrase "built

environment," Erickson says, "applies to most, if not all, Neotropical landscapes."

"Landscape" in this case is meant exactly—Amazonian Indians literally created the ground beneath their feet. According to William I. Woods, a soil geographer at Southern Illinois University, ecologists' claims about terrible Amazonian land were based on very little data. In the late 1990s Woods and others began careful measurements in the lower Amazon. They indeed found lots of inhospitable terrain. But they also discovered swaths of *terra preta*—rich, fertile "black earth" that anthropologists increasingly believe was created by human beings.

Terra preta, Woods guesses, covers at least 10 percent of Amazonia, an area the size of France. It has amazing properties, he says. Tropical rain doesn't leach nutrients from *terra preta* fields; instead the soil, so to speak, fights back. Not far from Painted Rock Cave is a 300-acre area with a two-foot layer of *terra preta* quarried by locals for potting soil. The bottom third of the layer is never removed, workers there explain, because over time it will re-create the original soil layer in its initial thickness. The reason, scientists suspect, is that *terra preta* is generated by a special suite of microorganisms that resists depletion. "Apparently," Woods and the Wisconsin geographer Joseph M. McCann argued in a presentation last summer, "at some threshold level . . . dark earth attains the capacity to perpetuate—even *regenerate* itself—thus behaving more like a living 'super'-organism than an inert material."

In as yet unpublished research the archaeologists Eduardo Neves, of the University of São Paulo; Michael Heckenberger, of the University of Florida; and other colleagues examined *terra preta* in the upper Xingu, a huge southern tributary of the Amazon. Not all Xingu cultures left behind this living earth, they discovered. But the ones that did generated it rapidly—suggesting to Woods that *terra preta* was created deliberately. In a process reminiscent of dropping microorganism-rich starter into plain dough to create sourdough bread, Amazonian peoples, he believes, inoculated bad soil with a transforming bacterial charge. Not every group of Indians there did this, but quite a few did, and over an extended period of time.

When Woods told me this, I was so amazed that I almost dropped the phone. I ceased to be articulate for a moment and said things like "wow" and "gosh." Woods chuckled at my reaction, probably because he understood what was passing through my mind. Faced with an ecological problem, I was thinking, the Indians *fixed* it. They were in the process of terraforming the Amazon when Columbus showed up and ruined everything.

Scientists should study the microorganisms in *terra preta,* Woods told me, to find out how they work. If that could be learned, maybe some version of Amazonian dark earth could be used to improve the vast expanses of bad soil that cripple agriculture in Africa—a final gift from the people who brought us tomatoes, corn, and the immense grasslands of the Great Plains.

"Betty Meggers would just die if she heard me saying this," Woods told me. "Deep down her fear is that this data will be misused." Indeed, Meggers's recent *Latin American Antiquity* article charged that archaeologists who say the Amazon can support agriculture are effectively telling "developers [that they] are entitled to operate without restraint." Resuscitating the myth of El Dorado, in her view, "makes us accomplices in the accelerating pace of environmental degradation." Doubtless there is something to this—although, as some of her critics responded in the same issue of the journal, it is difficult to imagine greedy plutocrats "perusing the pages of *Latin American Antiquity* before deciding to rev up the chain saws." But the new picture doesn't automatically legitimize paving the forest. Instead it suggests that for a long time big chunks of Amazonia were used nondestructively by clever people who knew tricks we have yet to learn.

Environmentalists want to preserve as much of the world's land as possible in a putatively intact state. But "intact" may turn out to mean "run by human beings for human purposes."

I visited Painted Rock Cave during the river's annual flood, when it wells up over its banks and creeps inland for miles. Farmers in the floodplain build houses and barns on stilts and watch pink dolphins sport from their doorsteps. Ecotourists take shortcuts by driving motorboats through the drowned forests. Guys in dories chase after them, trying to sell sacks of incredibly good fruit.

All of this is described as "wilderness" in the tourist brochures. It's not, if researchers like Roosevelt are correct. Indeed, they believe that fewer people may be living there now than in 1491. Yet when my boat glided into the trees, the forest shut out the sky like the closing of an umbrella. Within a few hundred years the human presence seemed to vanish. I felt alone and small, but in a way that was curiously like feeling exalted. If that place was not wilderness, how should I think of it? Since the fate of the forest is in our hands, what should be our goal for its future?

Novel Shores

Hernando de Soto's expedition stomped through the Southeast for four years and apparently never saw bison. More than a century later, when French explorers came down the Mississippi, they saw "a solitude unrelieved by the faintest trace of man," the nineteenth-century historian Francis Parkman wrote. Instead the French encountered bison, "grazing in herds on the great prairies which then bordered the river."

To Charles Kay, the reason for the buffalo's sudden emergence is obvious. Kay is a wildlife ecologist in the political-science department at Utah State University. In ecological terms, he says, the Indians were the "keystone species" of American ecosystems. A keystone species, according to the Harvard biologist Edward O. Wilson, is a species "that affects the survival and abundance of many other species." Keystone species have a disproportionate impact on their ecosystems. Removing them,

Wilson adds, "results in a relatively significant shift in the composition of the [ecological] community."

When disease swept Indians from the land, Kay says, what happened was exactly that. The ecological ancient régime collapsed, and strange new phenomena emerged. In a way this is unsurprising; for better or worse, humankind is a keystone species everywhere. Among these phenomena was a population explosion in the species that the Indians had kept down by hunting. After disease killed off the Indians, Kay believes, buffalo vastly extended their range. Their numbers more than sextupled. The same occurred with elk and mule deer. "If the elk were here in great numbers all this time, the archaeological sites should be chock-full of elk bones," Kay says. "But the archaeologists will tell you the elk weren't there." On the evidence of middens the number of elk jumped about 500 years ago.

Passenger pigeons may be another example. The epitome of natural American abundance, they flew in such great masses that the first colonists were stupefied by the sight. As a boy, the explorer Henry Brackenridge saw flocks "ten miles in width, by one hundred and twenty in length." For hours the birds darkened the sky from horizon to horizon. According to Thomas Neumann, a consulting archaeologist to Lilburn, Georgia, passenger pigeons "were incredibly dumb and always roosted in vast hordes, so they were very easy to harvest." Because they were readily caught and good to eat, Neumann says, archaeological digs should find many pigeon bones in the pre-Columbian strata of Indian middens. But they aren't there. The mobs of birds in the history books, he says, were "outbreak populations—always a symptom of an extraordinarily disrupted ecological system."

Throughout eastern North America the open landscape seen by the first Europeans quickly filled in with forest. According to William Cronon, of the University of Wisconsin, later colonists began complaining about how hard it was to get around. (Eventually, of course, they stripped New England almost bare of trees.) When Europeans moved west, they were preceded by two waves: one of disease, the other of ecological disturbance. The former crested with fearsome rapidity; the later sometimes took more than a century to quiet down. Far from destroying pristine wilderness, European settlers bloodily *created* it. By 1800 the hemisphere was chockablock with new wilderness. If "forest primeval" means a woodland unsullied by the human presence, William Denevan has written, there was much more of it in the late eighteenth century than in the early sixteenth.

Cronon's *Changes in the Land: Indians, Colonists, and the Ecology of New England* (1983) belongs on the same shelf as works by Crosby and Dobyns. But it was not until one of his articles was excerpted in *The New York Times* in 1995 that people outside the social sciences began to understand the implications of this view of Indian history. Environmentalists and ecologists vigorously attacked the anti-wilderness scenario, which they described as infected by postmodern philosophy. A small academic brouhaha ensued, complete with hundreds of footnotes. It precipitated *Reinventing Nature?* (1995), one of the few academic critiques of postmodernist philosophy written largely by biologists. *The Great New Wilderness Debate*

(1998), another lengthy book on the subject, was edited by two philosophers who earnestly identified themselves as "Euro-American men [whose] cultural legacy is patriarchal Western civilization in its current postcolonial, globally hegemonic form."

It is easy to tweak academics for opaque, self-protective language like this. Nonetheless, their concerns were quite justified. Crediting Indians with the role of keystone species has implications for the way the current Euro-American members of that keystone species manage the forests, watersheds, and endangered species of America. Because a third of the United States is owned by the federal government, the issue inevitably has political ramifications. In Amazonia, fabled storehouse of biodiversity, the stakes are global.

Guided by the pristine myth, mainstream environmentalists want to preserve as much of the world's land as possible in a putatively intact state. But "intact," if the new research is correct, means "run by human beings for human purposes." Environmentalists dislike this, because it seems to mean that anything goes. In a sense they are correct. Native Americans managed the continent as they saw fit. Modern nations must do the same. If they want to return as much of the landscape as possible to its 1491 state, they will have to find it within themselves to create the world's largest garden.

A Desperate Trek across America

Andrés Reséndez

The 250 starving Spanish adventurers dubbed the shallow estuary near their campsite the "Bay of Horses," because every third day they killed yet another draft animal, roasted it, and consumed the flesh. Fifty men had already died of disease, injury, and starvation. What was worse, after having walked the length of Florida without finding gold, those still alive had lost contact with their ships. They were stranded in an alien continent.

"We were in such straits that anything that had some semblance of a solution seemed good to us," wrote Álvar Núñez Cabeza de Vaca, the expedition's royal treasurer, in one of the most harrowing survival stories ever told. "I refrain here from telling this at greater length because each one can imagine for himself what could happen in a land so strange."

Indeed, Cabeza de Vaca and the other leaders of the ill-fated venture had agreed to a desperate gamble: to trade their most effective weapons against the Indians—horses and firearms—for five makeshift vessels that might or might not be capable of carrying them to safety. Eating the horses gave them time to build the rafts. To make nails and saws, they threw their crossbows, along with stirrups and spurs, into an improvised forge.

Like past conquistadors, Cabeza de Vaca and his men had relied on their breastplates, horses, and lethal weapons to keep the Indians at bay. Such overwhelming technological advantages meant they often did not even bother to negotiate, instead simply imposing their will. By sacrificing the very tools of their supremacy, they would now have to face the New World fully exposed to its perils and hold on only by their wits.

The expedition had unraveled with frightening speed. Just months earlier, the hopeful adventurers had embarked from Cuba in four ships and a brigantine and made landfall near present day Tampa Bay, intending to take possession of Florida in the name of His Most Catholic Majesty. Caught up in the excitement and rush to explore, the commander rashly divided the expedition, ordering the captains to take their ships on an exploration of the coast, while the men and the horses were put ashore. They agreed to meet just a few miles north of the debarkation point. But the interminable and confusing coast of Florida prevented the two parties from making contact.

With their jury-rigged saws they cut down trees, dragged them to the beach, lashed them together with the tails and manes of their dead horses, and fashioned sails from their tattered shirts. After five or six weeks, they slaughtered their last horse, then dragged the 15-ton rafts into the water. Fifty men crowded aboard each craft, the fifth commanded by Cabeza de Vaca. "And so greatly can necessity prevail," he observed, "that it made us risk going in this manner and placing ourselves in a sea so treacherous, and without any one of us who went having any knowledge of the art of navigation." The rafts floated only a few inches above the waterline; the waves would wash over the men as they traveled.

Little did the men on the rafts know that they were embarking on an eight-year adventure that would ultimately take their few survivors across the entire continent. After several weeks, storms separated the flotilla. Tormented by extreme hunger and drenched by the splashing of the waves, they were on the brink of death. "The people began to faint in such a manner that when the sun set," Cabeza de Vaca would recall, "all those who came in my raft were fallen on top of one another in it, so close to death that few were conscious." Only the helmsman and Cabeza de Vaca took turns steering the raft: "Two hours into the night, the helmsman told me that I should take charge of the raft, because he was in such condition that he thought he would die that very night." Near dawn, Cabeza de Vaca heard the surf, and later that day they landed.

While most of the men survived the harrowing monthlong passage across the Gulf, eventually washing up on the coast of what is now Texas, many more perished of exposure and hunger that winter, some even resorting to cannibalism. Fewer still withstood enslavement at the hands of the natives in the vicinity of Galveston Bay. Ultimately, only four—Cabeza de Vaca, two other Spaniards in commanding positions, and an African slave named Estebanico—would escape their Indian masters after six years of toil. As slaves, Cabeza de Vaca and his companions were forced to cope with native North America on its own terms, bridging two worlds that had remained apart for 12,000 years or more. They lived by their wits, coming to terms with half a dozen native languages and making sense of societies that other Europeans could not even begin to fathom.

Incredibly, the four castaways used this knowledge to refashion themselves into medicine men. As Cabeza de Vaca would explain it: "we made the sign of the cross over them and blew on them and recited a Pater Noster and an Ave Maria; and then we prayed as best we could to God Our Lord to give them health and inspire them to give us good treatment." In one instance he revived a man who appeared to be dead. At the Indians' insistence, all four survivors performed curing ceremonies. And thus many natives came to believe that these four strange-looking beings were able to manipulate the power of nature.

This real or imagined gifts of healing enabled the four survivors to move unimpeded, their reputation preceding them wherever they went. Nor were their actions a mere charade to win food and respect. They believed that their curative abilities went somehow much deeper: they came to see their incredible suffering odyssey as a test to which God had subjected them before revealing the true purpose of their existence. They viewed their sufferings as mortifications of the flesh, their beatings and extreme hunger akin to those of flagellants who inflicted torment upon themselves or of monks who fasted nigh unto death.

Once, alone and unable to find his party's camp, Cabeza de Vaca wandered in the woods naked in dread of the approaching chill of night. "But it pleased God that I found a tree aflame, and warmed by its fire I endured the cold that night." For five days he nursed that fire, before finally finding his companions.

Cabeza de Vaca wandered in the woods naked and alone, dreading the approach of night.

The four wanderers were no longer mere castaways; they had become explorers once again. Yet theirs was a most peculiar expedition. Four naked and unarmed outsiders were led by hundreds, even thousands, of Indians. They were fed, protected, and passed off as though prized possessions from one indigenous group to the next. They became the first outsiders to behold what would become the American Southwest and northern Mexico, the first non-natives to describe this enormous land and its peoples.

By the time the four reemerged from the continental interior and reached the Pacific Coast, they had been so utterly transformed by the experience that fellow Europeans could hardly recognize them. A posse of Spanish slavers operating in what is now northwestern Mexico spotted potential prey: 13 Indians walking barefoot and clad in skins. On closer inspection, some of the details did not seem quite right. One was a black man. Could he be an Indian or an African emerging from the heart of the continent? Another member of the party appeared to be a haggard white man with hair hanging down to his waist and a beard reaching to his chest.

When Cabeza de Vaca addressed them in perfect Spanish, the slavers were "so astonished," he wrote, "that they neither talked to me nor managed to ask me anything," but bent themselves on rounding up the Indian escort. But Cabeza de Vaca and his companions would not allow it. No longer did the castaways view their companions as mere chattels, the rightful prize of Christian conquest.

Perhaps no one understood their transformation more than the Indians themselves, who were unable to believe that Cabeza de Vaca and his three companions belonged to the same race as the slavers. The Indians had observed, he later wrote, that "we cured the sick, and they [the Spanish slavers] killed those who were well; that we came naked and barefoot, and they went about dressed and on horses and with lances; and that we did not covet anything but rather, everything they gave us we later returned and remained with nothing, and that the others had no other objective but to steal everything they found and did not give anything to anyone."

Cabeza de Vaca went back to Spain, attached himself to the court of Charles V, and was able to present his ideas of a humane colonization of the New World. After years of lobbying, he was dispatched to South America, where he attempted to carry out his plans, alas with little success. He spent the last years of his life in his native Andalusia, reminiscing about his adventures in another world.

Brave New World

The Watercolors That John White Produced in 1585 Gave England Its First Startling Glimpse of America

Abigail Tucker

John white wasn't the most exacting painter that 16th-century England had to offer, or so his watercolors of the New World suggest. His diamondback terrapin has six toes instead of five; one of his native women, the wife of a powerful chief, has two right feet; his study of a scorpion looks cramped and rushed. In historical context, though, these quibbles seem unimportant: no Englishman had ever painted America before. White was burdened with unveiling a whole new realm.

In the 1580s, England had yet to establish a permanent colonial foothold in the Western Hemisphere, while Spain's settlements in Central and South America were thriving. Sir Walter Raleigh sponsored a series of exploratory, and extraordinarily perilous, voyages to the coast of present-day North Carolina (then called Virginia, for the "Virgin Queen" Elizabeth) to drum up support for a colony among British investors. White, a gentleman-artist, braved skirmishes with Spanish ships and hurricanes to go along on five voyages between 1584 and 1590, including a 1585 expedition to found a colony on Roanoke Island off the Carolina coast. He would eventually become the governor of a second, doomed colony the British established there, but in 1585 he was commissioned to "drawe to life" the area's natural bounty and inhabitants. Who lived there, people back at court wanted to know; what did they look like; and what did they eat? This last question was vital, because Europe had recently entered a mini ice age and crops were suffering. Many of White's watercolors serve as a kind of pictorial menu. His scene of the local Algonquians fishing shows an enticing array of catches, including catfish, crab and sturgeon; other paintings dwell on cooking methods and corn cultivation.

"The message was: "Come to this place where everything is neat and tidy and there is food everywhere!" says Deborah Harkness, a science historian at the University of Southern California who studied White's watercolors and has written a book on Elizabethan London.

Occasionally, though, White seems to have been captivated by less digestible fare. He painted a magnificent watercolor study of a tiger swallowtail butterfly, and on a stop for provisions in the West Indies he rendered a "flye which in the night semeth a flame of fyer"—a firefly. These oddities, as much as his more practical illustrations, lodged in the Elizabethan imagination: engravings based on them were published in 1590, kindling interest in England's distant claims.

Today White's dozens of watercolors—the only surviving visual record of the land and peoples encountered by England's first settlers in America—remain vital documents for colonial scholars, who rejoiced when the works were exhibited earlier this year by the North Carolina Museum of History in Raleigh, the Yale Center for British Art in New Haven, Connecticut, and the Jamestown Settlement in Virginia. Owned by the British Museum, White's originals must be kept in storage, away from the damaging effects of light, for decades at a time; their transatlantic visit was a rarity.

Little is known about White's background. We do, however, know he married Thomasine Cooper in 1566 and they had at least two children. Before the 1585 expedition he may have been employed in Queen Elizabeth's Office of Revels, and he was almost certainly a gentleman—well educated and well connected; watercolor was considered a genteel medium, far more refined than oil. White sketched in graphite pencil and colored with indigo, vermilion and ground gold and silver leaf, among other pigments.

It's unclear when he actually completed his iconic American series, but he made his observations in the summer of 1585. After crossing the Atlantic, his ship stopped briefly in the West Indies, where White saw (and at some point painted)—in addition to the firefly—plantains, pineapples, flamingos and other curiosities. Soon afterward the explorers sailed north to the Carolina coast.

As they built a crude fort on Roanoke, White went on excursions and began depicting the native Algonquian peoples. He detailed their ceremonies, ossuaries and meals of hulled corn. He carefully rendered the puma tail dangling from one chief's apron and a medicine man's pouch of tobacco or herbs. "White was documenting an unknown population," says Peter Mancall, an early American historian at the University of Southern California who delivered the opening lecture for the Yale exhibition. "He was trying to show how women carried their children, what a sorcerer looked like, how they fished."

White's iconic image of an Algonquian chief (his jewelry, long bow, feathers and puma tail signal his wealth and status) came to symbolize all North American Indians at the time of early contact with Europeans.

White's charge was to "drawe to life" the New World's natural bounty and native inhabitants. He detailed the Algonquians' villages, ceremonies, and attire. He showed how they fished, how they ate (hulled corn) and what a sorcerer looked like.

But White probably also tweaked his Algonquian portraits. The swaggering poses are borrowed from European painting conventions, and one chief carries a gigantic bow that, according to the catalog, "would have reminded any English person looking at it of the similarity between English soldiers and Indian warriors." Other scenes, posed or not, were likely painted with investors in mind. An Algonquian chief, for instance, wears a large copper pendant, signaling that the precious metal was to be found in the New World. Scholars believe this may be Wingina, the "King of Roanoke," who was beheaded not long after White's 1585 visit because an English commander saw him as a threat. (Indeed, the chief probably did not appreciate the colonists' demands on his village's food stores.) On paper, however, the chief's expression is pleasant, perhaps even amused. There is almost no evidence of any English presence

in the watercolors. Though tensions with the Indians had started to mount, White portrays an untouched world. This may have been a practical decision on his part: the British already knew what colonists looked like. But, in light of the Algonquians' eventual fate (they would soon be decimated by what they called "invisible bullets"—white men's diseases), the absence of any Europeans is also ominous. The only discernible sign of their arrival in Roanoke is a tiny figure in the arms of an Algonquian girl: a doll in Elizabethan costume.

The girl "is looking up at her mother as if to say, 'Is this someone I could meet or even possibly be?'" says Joyce Chaplin, an American history professor at Harvard University who wrote an essay for the exhibition catalog. "It's very poignant."

White's paintings and the text accompanying them (written by Thomas Harriot, a scientist also on the 1585 voyage) are virtually all that remain of that time and place. After presenting his paintings in England to an unknown patron, possibly Raleigh or the queen, White returned to Roanoke in 1587 as governor, bringing with him more than a hundred men, women and children. Their supplies quickly ran out, and White, leaving members of his own family on the island, returned to England for assistance. But English relations with the great sea power Spain had deteriorated, and as the Armada threatened, he was unable to get back to Roanoke until 1590. By then, the English settlers had vanished, and the mystery of the "Lost Colony" was born. It's still unclear whether the settlers died or moved south to assimilate with a friendly native village. At any rate, because of rough seas, the approaching hurricane season and damage to his ship, White was able to search for the colonists for only about a day and never learned the fate of his daughter, Elinor, his son-in-law, Ananias Dare, and his granddaughter, Virginia, the first English child born in North America.

Such hardships, British Museum curator Kim Sloan writes in the show's catalog, lead one to wonder "what drove this man even to begin, never mind persist in, an enterprise that lost him his family, his wealth and very nearly his life." White's own last years are also lost to history: the final record of his life is a letter from 1593 to Richard Hakluyt (an English author who wrote about voyages to America), in which White sums up his last trip—"as lucklesse to many, as sinister to my selfe."

Today some of the plants and animals White painted, including a glaring loggerhead turtle, are threatened. Even the watercolors themselves are in precarious condition, which is why the British Museum displays them only once every few decades. In the mid-19th century they sustained heavy water damage in a Sotheby's auction house fire. Chemical changes in the silver pigments have turned them black, and other colors are mere shadows of what they once were.

The originals were engraved and copied countless times, and versions showed up in everything from costume books to encyclopedias of insects. The paintings of Indians became so entrenched in the English consciousness that they were difficult to displace. Generations of British historians used White's illustrations to describe Native Americans, even those from other regions. Later painters, including the 18th-century natural history artist Mark Catesby, modeled their works on versions of White's watercolors.

Britain did not establish a permanent colony until Jamestown in 1607, nearly two decades after white left America for the last time. Jamestown was a settlement of businessmen: there was no gentleman-artist on hand to immortalize the native people there. In fact, the next major set of American Indian portraits would not appear until George Catlin painted the peoples of the Great Plains more than 200 years later.

Magazine staff writer **ABIGAIL TUCKER** reported on rare color photographs from the Korean War in the November issue.

Champlain among the Mohawk, 1609

A Soldier-Humanist Fights a War for Peace in North America

DAVID HACKETT FISCHER

A few generations ago, American colonial history centered on a single narrative that flowed from Jamestown in 1607 to the Declaration of Independence in 1776. Today early American history has blossomed into a braided narrative with many story lines.

A starting point might be four small beginnings, far apart in space but close in time. On April 26, 1607, Capt. John Smith and his comrades founded Jamestown in Virginia. Four months later, in mid-August 1607, Capt. George Popham established a New England colony near Pemaquid in Maine. The following year, during the spring and summer of 1608, Spanish colonists, led by Capt. Martínez de Montoya, built a permanent settlement at Santa Fe in the region they called New Mexico. And on July 3, 1608, Capt. Samuel de Champlain founded the first permanent colony in New France at Quebec. The stories that began to unfold at these places shaped much of modern North America.

One of the most interesting of those small beginnings was New France. For more than 30 years the central figure was the extraordinary Champlain. He left six fascinating books of travels, filled with many superb maps and illustrations. His writings tell much about his actions but little about the man, and nearly nothing about his inner life.

Champlain came from Brouage, a little town on the Bay of Biscay on the Atlantic coast of France. A busy place in his youth, it served as the center of a lucrative salt trade. Today this small seaport lies quietly a mile from the sea. Born around 1570 and probably baptized Protestant, he grew up in a prosperous maritime family and was schooled by his father, who had risen through the ranks from seaman, pilot, and master to captain, merchant, and ship owner. Champlain came of age in a dark period, when horrific wars of religion had shattered France.

The United States has experienced one civil war, in which 600,000 people died over four years. The French people suffered nine civil wars of religion in nearly 40 years (1562–98). More than 2 million died, and atrocities beyond description occurred. Champlain fought in the largest of these wars, following an extraordinary leader who would become Henry IV, founder of the Bourbon dynasty. The king became the young Champlain's mentor, model, patron, and friend. Both men converted to Catholicism but always defended toleration for Protestants.

War was their profession. While always keeping a soldier's creed of honor, duty, courage, and loyalty to a larger cause, their feelings about war changed with the horrors they encountered. These veteran campaigners came to hate war for its cruelly, destruction, and terrible waste. They knew, however, that some of the world's evils overshadow even war. In a world of cruelty and violence, they dedicated themselves to fighting for peace and humanity.

Henry and his army won their last great struggle in 1598, giving France the Peace of Vervins and toleration under the Edict of Nantes. Henry next set his sights on bringing a general peace to Europe. Soon a web of peace treaties opened the Atlantic to commerce and made North America accessible for those many colonial beginnings in 1607 and 1608. It was a pivot point in American history.

The king was deeply interested in America, particularly the large area labeled on world maps as Nova Francia, after voyages of Jacques Cartier in the 16th century. Henry intended to turn that geographical expression into an empire called la Nouvelle France. Champlain got a new job.

He had already begun to serve the king as a secret agent. In 1599 he traveled through Spanish America on a long espionage mission. Upon its completion, Champlain delivered a long report called a *Bref discours* that outlined the strengths and resources of the Spanish empire in detail. Champlain found the people he variously called *Indiens* or *sauvages* fascinating. Impressed by their high intelligence, he was shocked by the cruelty and violence they had suffered under the Spanish. To illustrate the report, Champlain added his own luminous watercolors of their sufferings: Indians burned alive for heresy; Indians cudgeled on the orders of priests for not attending mass; Indians and African slaves compelled to dive to lethal depths in the pearl fisheries of Margarita Island off the coast of Venezuela. Altogether the *Bref discours* was a report on how not to found an empire in America.

Impressed with the report, King Henry gave Champlain a pension and the assignment to work with other experts in the basement of the Louvre on the colonization of North America.

Champlain closely studied the history of earlier French settlements, which had all ended in disaster. He also traveled to the Atlantic ports of France, interviewing fishermen who knew about America and the dangerous waters of the North Atlantic. He composed what he called his *grand dessein* for France in North America, a plan in large part based on a dream of peace and humanity, of amity and concord among the peoples of Europe and America.

Champlain pulled many others into his grand design, moving in a number of circles, all of which revolved around Henry IV. One consisted of the men who would go eventually with him to America: Pierre Dugua, the sieur de Mons; Marc Lescarbot; Jean de Poutrincourt; and François Gravé du Pont, a grizzled mariner from Saint-Malo whom he called Pont-Gravé. His friends at court formed another circle: Pierre Jeannin, several Sillerys and Brularts, and his old commander, the Comte de Cossé-Brissac, who offered advice and urgent support.

These men all shared a common bond as Christian humanists. While a few were Protestants, most embraced the literal Catholic idea of a universal faith. Men of learning, they were full of curiosity about the world and all its peoples. In their broad spirit of humanity, they had inherited the values of the Renaissance; in time, their work would inspire the Enlightenment. In a difficult time, they kept the idea of humanism alive; in doing so, they became important world figures.

Together they carefully prepared for a new sort of European presence in America, one that stressed peaceful cohabitation with the Indians, trading actively, and exploring the continent together. Pont-Gravé made a voyage in 1602 and persuaded Indian leaders to allow two young Montagnais "princes," as the Pont-Gravé called them, to come to France, learn the language, and serve as translators. In 1603 they all sailed to the St. Lawrence on a voyage of reconnaissance, arriving on May 26, 1603, at the little port of Tadoussac near the Saguenay River. Champlain and Pont-Gravé looked across the river and saw a huge gathering of Indians from many nations, including Montagnais, Algonquian, and Etchemin, the latter being Champlain's name for the nations living in what is now the state of Maine.

The two Frenchmen and the young Montagnais translators crossed the river, walked unarmed into the camp, and were invited to join a *tabagie,* or tobacco feast. Champlain, Pont-Gravé, and the representatives of these many Indian nations talked together through the night and into the next day. The informal alliance they formed would last for many generations, and the legacy of this first *tabagie* still lives on. All were warriors in search of peace, who were open and candid, learned to respect each other's vital interests, and created an alliance founded on cohabitation, trade, and mutual support against attacks by others.

After this beginning, other voyages followed. Champlain helped to found French settlements on the St. Croix River in 1604, in Acadia (now Nova Scotia) in 1605–6, and at Quebec. He explored the country, met with many other Indian nations, and forged alliances with more than 50 of them—more than any European leader of his time.

Champlain's special pattern of relating with the Indians made the history of New France fundamentally different than those of New Spain, New England, New Netherland, and Virginia. The Spanish conquistadors sought to subjugate the Indians. The English pushed the Indians away, built a big "pale" in Virginia, and forbade Indians from crossing it unless they presented a special passport. Only the French established a consistent policy of peaceful cohabitation, and something of its spirit persists in North America to this day.

A MAJOR THREAT to Champlain's design for New France was incessant warfare among the Indian nations in the St. Lawrence Valley. Much of it pitted the Iroquois League, and especially the Mohawk nation, against the Algonquian and Montagnais to the north, the Huron to the west, and the Etchemin to the east. As long as it continued, there could be no peace in the St. Lawrence Valley, no security for trade, and no hope for the dream of American Indians and Europeans living together in peace.

Champlain believed that a major cause of war was fear, and his remedy was to seek peace through diplomacy. To that end he had built alliances among the Montagnais, Algonquian, Huron, and other nations. But the Iroquois League proved difficult to work with. One historian of the Iroquois observes that by the start of the 17th century they were "at odds with all their neighbors—Algonquin and Huron to the north, Mahican on the east, and Susquehannock to the south." Many Indian nations in the Northeast were at war with some of their neighbors. The Iroquois, however, were at war with nearly all of theirs. They had a reputation for skill in war, among many warrior nations; they were also known for cruelty in a cruel world.

In 1608 Champlain had promised to aid the Indian nations of the St. Lawrence Valley when the Iroquois attacked them. At the same time, he understood that the Iroquois were victims as well as aggressors, so he sent peace feelers through a captive Mohawk woman. These overtures accomplished nothing. Mohawk war parties continued to attack the St. Lawrence Indians.

After a long and difficult winter of 1608 and 1609 in Quebec, Champlain decided that peace could be achieved only by concerted military action against the Mohawk. He did not intend a war of conquest. Instead he envisioned that a coalition of Montagnais, Algonquian, and Huron, with French support, might deliver one or two sharp blows that could deter future Mohawk attacks by raising the cost of their raiding to the north.

When Champlain met Pont-Gravé at Tadoussac on June 7, he laid out a bold plan for "certain explorations in the interior" and made clear his intention to enter "the country of the Iroquois" with "our allies the Montagnais." Both men knew that this plan would mean a fight with some of the most formidable warriors in North America. It was an act of breathtaking audacity, considering the small size of Champlain's force. But what Champlain lacked in mass, he made up in acceleration. He also had the early firearm known as the arquebus, and the Mohawk did not. The sieur de Mons had sent him a few good men who were trained in the use of that difficult weapon. Champlain also had many Indian allies with hundreds of warriors.

ON JUNE 28, 1609, Champlain set out from Quebec with a party of French soldiers and hundreds of Indian warriors. A week later they entered "the country of the Iroquois." Champlain and his party paddled their canoes south from the St. Lawrence Valley up the river of the Iroquois, known today as the Richelieu River. He wrote, "No Christians but ourselves had ever penetrated this place." Eventually most of the French and Indians decided to turn back, daunted by what lay ahead, but Champlain pressed on with a war party of only 60 Indians and two Frenchmen at his side. It was a courageous decision. Others would have called it foolhardy to the point of madness.

Champlain and his allies made a portage of about a mile around the rapids on the Richelieu, well into Iroquois country. At the end of each day, the expedition built a semicircular fort on the edge of the river. Some took bark from trees to make wigwams, while others felled big trees to make an abatis of tangled branches around their camp, leaving only the riverbank open as a line of retreat. They sent forward a party of three canoes and nine men to search four or six miles ahead. The scouts found nothing, and all retired for the night. This was one of the first occasions when European soldiers traveled with a large Indian war party in North America.

Intent on battling the Mohawk, who threatened his grand plans for peace in the region, Champlain traveled south from Quebec in the summer of 1609, coming across the beautiful lake that he would give his name to. Here Champlain, two French soldiers, and his Indian allies confronted a powerful Mohawk party and defeated them convincingly with the aid of Hudson's wheelock arquebus, an early muzzle loading firearm.

On July 14, 1609, they reached the large lake from which the river flowed. Champlain exercised his right to name it Lake Champlain on his map, as he and his two French companions may have been the first Europeans to see it. He reckoned its length at 80 to 100 leagues, and later amended his estimate to 50 or 60 land leagues, which is roughly correct. He explored both sides of the lake, saw the Green Mountains of Vermont to the east, and to the west sighted the Adirondacks, which are visible from the eastern shore. On the many maps created by Champlain, this lake was the only place where he put his name on the land.

As they moved further south, tensions mounted. On the evening of July 29, 1609, they approached the lake's southern end; on their right they passed a low peninsula with willow trees and a sandy beach below a steep eroded bank. Beyond the beach Champlain saw a promontory projecting into the water. His Indian allies knew it well. The Iroquois called it "the meeting place of two waters": *tekontató:ken* or, to European ears, Ticonderoga. The name came from two big, beautiful lakes. Lake George to the south and west was 200 feet above Lake Champlain, draining into it from a height greater than Niagara Falls. The water flowed downward through a run of falls and

rapids that the French called a *chute,* entering Lake Champlain at Ticonderoga. For many generations past and to come, Ticonderoga served as one of the most strategic locations in North America, a key to anyone who wanted to control the long chain of lakes and rivers running from the St. Lawrence to the Hudson. For the Mohawk, it was also a sacred and magical place.

In the night of July 29, as Champlain's party rounded the promontory of Ticonderoga, their bow paddlers saw shadows stirring on the water ahead of them. As they stared intently into the darkness, the shadows began to assume an earthly form. They were boats of strange appearance, larger than northern birch-bark canoes, and filled with men. The Indians instantly identified them: Mohawk!

Each group sighted the other at about the same time. Both taken by surprise, they turned away and moved in opposite directions. "We retreated into the middle of the lake," Champlain later wrote. The Mohawk landed on a sand beach between the promontory of Ticonderoga and Willow Point to the north, where a fringe of willow trees still flourishes near the water's edge, and built a small fort or barricade.

Champlain and his allies remained afloat on the lake and lashed their canoes together with poles so as not to become separated in the night. "We were on the water," he wrote, "within bow-shot of their barricades." Songs and cries pierced the night. The Mohawk shouted insults at their enemies. "Our side was not lacking in repartee," Champlain recalled. As dawn approached, both sides prepared for battle. In the darkness before first light, Champlain's Indian allies paddled around the promontory and landed in a secluded spot where they were not under observation. "My companions and I were always kept carefully out of sight, lying flat in the canoes," he wrote. His allies sent scouts ahead to watch the Mohawk fort. The rest assembled in their fighting formation and moved forward toward the Mohawk barricade.

The three Frenchmen remained carefully hidden behind them. Each prepared his weapon, a short-barreled, shoulder-fired arquebus à rouet, Champlain's highly developed wheel-lock weapon that did not require a smoldering matchlock, which might have betrayed their position. Champlain dangerously overloaded his arquebus with four balls. On Cape Cod in 1605, his weapon had exploded in his hands and nearly killed him. But overloading was highly effective in close combat, so he accepted the risk.

At first light the Mohawk warriors mustered quickly and came out of the fort, many of them wearing wooden armor that was proof against stone arrowheads. Both forces assembled in close formation on opposite sides of a clearing between the water and the woods.

Champlain peered through the ranks of his allies and studied the Mohawk as they emerged from their barricade. He counted 200 warriors, "strong and robust men in their appearance," and he watched as "they advanced slowly to meet us with a gravity and assurance that I greatly admired." The Mohawk were in tight ranks—a disciplined close-order forest phalanx that had defeated many foes. Their wooden armor and shields covered their bodies. In the front were two Mohawks, each wearing three high feathers above their heads. Champlain's Indians told him that the men with the big feathers were chiefs, and "I was to do what I could to kill them."

Champlain's Indian allies were now about 200 yards from the Mohawk, and they began to move forward also in close formation. Once again Champlain kept behind them, remaining invisible to the other side. On Champlain's orders, the other two Frenchmen slipped into the forest and crept forward around the right flank of the Mohawk.

When they were about 50 yards from their enemy, Champlain's allies parted. Champlain strode forward alone until 30 yards from the enemy. The Mohawk stopped in amazement and studied this astonishing figure who wore a burnished steel cuirass and helmet that glittered in the golden light of the morning sun. Then a Mohawk leader raised his bow.

Champlain tells us, "I put my arquebus against my cheek and aimed straight at one of the chiefs." As the Mohawk drew their bowstrings, Champlain fired. There was a mighty crash and a cloud of white smoke. Two chiefs fell dead, and another warrior was mortally wounded—three men brought down by one shot. Champlain's Indian allies raised a great shout, so loud that "one could not have heard the thunder."

The Mohawk were stunned and "greatly frightened." Even so, they fought back bravely. Both sides fired clouds of arrows, and Champlain reloaded his weapon. As he did so, his two French companions emerged on the edge of the forest. They appear to have been veteran fighters—skilled arquebusiers and highly disciplined soldiers. Using the trees for cover, they knelt side by side, steadied their weapons, and took aim. "As I was reloading my arquebus," Champlain wrote, "one of my companions fired a shot from the woods." This second blow was delivered into the flank of the Mohawk formation, and it had a devastating effect. A third chief went down. The tight Mohawk formation shuddered in a strange way and sudenly came apart. "It astonished them so much that, seeing their chiefs dead, they lost courage, took to their heels, and abandoned the field and their fort, fleeing into the depth of the forest." Champlain led his Indian allies in a headlong charge. "I pursued them, and laid low still more of them."

Many historians have criticized Champlain for going to war with the Iroquois. Some have written that he initiated hostilities that would continue for two centuries. In the late 20th century, ethnohistorians studying this question came to a different conclusion. They agreed that he did not start these wars, but that the fighting had been going on between the Mohawk and their neighbors to the north long before he arrived.

Further, Iroquois ethnologist William N. Fenton writes, "Nineteenth-century historians to the contrary, this incident did not precipitate a hundred years of Mohawk vengeance against New France." It put a stop to major fighting between the Mohawk and the French for a generation. An ethnologist of the Huron agrees. Bruce Trigger writes of the two battles: "This was the last time that the Mohawks were a serious threat along the St. Lawrence River until the 1630s. Having suffered serious losses in two successive encounters, they avoided armed Frenchmen."

After the battles at Ticonderoga and the Rivière des Iroquois, the Mohawk made several peace overtures to the French. Champlain, however, could not find a way to make lasting peace with the Iroquois without alienating the Montagnais, Algonquian, and Huron. Even so, he hoped for a modus vivendi between the French and the Mohawk, and he achieved it. A fragile quasi peace was won by force of arms, and it continued for a generation, until 1634. The leaders who followed Champlain in Quebec and Paris (also in Boston, Philadelphia, Williamsburg, and London) were unable to keep it going. They used too much force or too little. Champlain's policy effected a middle way of peace through the carefully calibrated use of limited force. We are only beginning to understand how he did it.

From *Chaplain's Dream* by David Hackett Fischer, (Simon & Schuster, 2008). Copyright © 2008 by David Hackett Fischer. Reprinted by permission of Simon & Schuster.

The Birth of America

Struggling from One Peril to the Next, the Jamestown Settlers Planted the Seeds of the Nation's Spirit

Lewis Lord

"Virginia, Earth's only Paradise!" So declared Michael Drayton, poet laureate of England, in a merry ballad marking the departure of three ships crammed with men anticipating fast fortunes in the New World. The prospective colonists set sail from London just before Christmas of 1606, bound for the Chesapeake Bay. It was the last Christmas most of them would ever know.

By the following August, when their Jamestown settlement was barely three months old, almost every day brought a new death.

September found half of those 105 original settlers in their graves. "Our men were destroyed with cruell diseases such as Swellings, Flixes, Burning Fevers, and by warres," a survivor reported, "but for the most part they died of meere famine."

Thirteen years before the Mayflower brought Pilgrims to Massachusetts, the Virginia colony served as England's toehold on a continent eventually inhabited and governed mostly by English-speaking people. History books list Jamestown, founded in 1607, as America's first permanent English settlement, and its 400th anniversary will be celebrated this year with festivals, exhibits, and commemorative coins, plus a springtime visit by Queen Elizabeth II. But that success in Virginia was not the piece of cake it first was billed to be. For years, Jamestown was a deadly fiasco, periodically in peril and ultimately revived and enriched by cultivation of a habit-forming weed and the toil of indentured whites and enslaved blacks.

In Europe's race to colonize the New World, England started late. For nearly a century after 1492, the English watched with envy as Spain dominated much of the hemisphere that Columbus discovered. In 1587, two decades after the Spanish settled St. Augustine in Florida, the English abandoned their insular ways and planted 110 men, women, and children on Roanoke Island off present-day North Carolina. When a supply ship returned later, all were gone. Even now, no one knows what became of that "Lost Colony."

Sir Walter Raleigh, the favorite courtier of Elizabeth I, reportedly lost 40,000 pounds on the venture. His reward, granted in advance, was knighthood and the Virgin Queen's permission to name the new land Virginia, in her honor. They envisioned Virginia as every place north of Mexico that the English could take and occupy.

Despite the costs and setbacks, pressures mounted for another expedition. English traders imagined colonists producing wine and olive oil, harvesting timber, and uncovering gold. Others saw Virginia as an ideal home for the poor. England's population was rising rapidly, but jobs were stagnant. Ministers noted that God ordered man to multiply and fill the Earth. What better place to do so than the vast and—as they perceived it—empty continent across the sea?

Pacific path. In 1606, several well-to-do Englishmen laid plans for what would become the Jamestown colony. With the blessings of James I, Elizabeth's successor, they formed the Virginia Company, a joint stock company in which investors, known as "adventurers," bought stock worth $3,000 a share in today's currency.

Encouraging investors and settlers alike was the popular notion that there existed on America's Atlantic coast a river within reach of the Pacific—the fabled short cut to Asia sought by Columbus and countless other explorers. Other Englishmen who bet their money or their lives may have seen the London play *Eastward Ho!* describing customs across the sea. It reported native Virginians gathering diamonds by the seashore and using chamber pots of pure gold.

In December of 1606, colonists and crew members squeezed into their three tiny ships docked in London. Within days of departure, men were bickering and seasick from storms and winds that left the Susan Constant, the Godspeed, and the Discovery anchored a month in the English Channel.

Collegiality remained in short supply as the expedition entered the Atlantic. On the flagship Susan Constant, an outspoken commoner named John Smith annoyed a higher-up and was accused of plotting insurrection. He was confined below deck, sentenced to death at the age of 27 once on shore.

Secret seven. On a stop at Nevis in the West Indies, Smith's foes stood ready to hang him. But the skipper delayed the execution, wanting more evidence before giving his passenger the rope. The young captain's luck improved further when the expedition entered the Chesapeake. The four-month ocean crossing ended with the voyagers dropping anchor on April 26, 1607, near the windswept dunes of a Virginia site they called Cape Henry. There the ship commanders opened a sealed box and pulled out a secret document: the company's instructions for starting a colony.

Read aloud was a list identifying seven members of a ruling council, the settlers who would run the colony. The first six names belonged to men of social prominence. The seventh was the bumptious prisoner in the hold. Unknowingly, someone in London had saved the man who, as much as anyone, would save Jamestown.

The company's other instructions could have been penned by a modern PR executive. Among the do's and don'ts: "Have Great Care not to Offend the naturals [the American Indians]." Don't show fear, weakness, or sickness. And, to keep investors investing and settlers settling, never mention anything unpleasant in letters sent home.

For the moment, there was nothing unpleasant to report. One man who went ashore marveled at the "faire meddowes and goodly tall Trees." But for the next 15 years, the English blundered their way from one calamity to another, beginning with the choice of where to settle. Seeking a spot easy to defend, the colonists picked a marshy peninsula 2 miles long and a mile wide that jutted into the river they named the James, 50 miles southeast of present-day Richmond. They erected a trading post, a storehouse, and a church, sprinkled the grounds with tents made of tattered sailcloth, and named the creation James Town.

No one sensed the lethal implications of the low site with its brackish water and mosquito-thick swamps. Nor did the settlers realize how much food had spoiled in the overlong voyage from London. Had they known, they might have used those days in May to plant a garden instead of scratching for gold. Nor did anyone dig a well, even though every low tide was "full of slime and filth." That summer half the colony died. "God (being angrie with us) plagued us with such famin and sicknes that the living were scarce able to bury the dead," Smith later wrote.

In the captain's view, God was "angrie" because too few of the settlers were willing to work. A third of the colonists were "gentlemen" who, by definition, did no manual labor. Some of the Jamestown gents no doubt did grab a shovel or ax, but many, in Smith's words, did nothing but "complain, curse, and despaire."

Faulty notions. All along, the danger of Indian attack competed with disease and hunger as the No. 1 threat to the colony's survival. On their first night in Virginia, two colonists were wounded by arrows shot by painted warriors hiding behind the Cape Henry dunes. Days later, however, colonists and Indians were dining together on corn bread and water, seemingly confirming the English notion that the natives lacked only a civilizing influence. Thus the settlement that sprouted at Jamestown did so without a protective wall of logs around it. Yet, within a month, hundreds of Indians attacked the outpost, killing two settlers. A strong wall was built quickly, forming a triangular fort.

The American Indians, the English believed, would quit being "savages"—their usual word for Indians—once they learned English manners. But Smith was convinced that Englishmen, too, had a lot to learn: The natives, he wrote, were "our enemies, whom we neither knew nor understood." The English even thought Indians were born white, with skin darkened by paints and dyes.

The Indians likewise guessed wrong about the English. Initially, they did not deem the settlers a threat. Powhatan, the region's powerful chief, expected the intruders to either die off or leave. When their numbers were small, he seemed pleased to swap furs and food for pots and tools. But as ship after ship brought new settlers, including a few women, the chief sensed ominous change. "Your coming hither is not for trade," he suspected, "but to invade my people, and possess my country."

Neither side felt secure. Some mornings found the Indians bringing corn to the settlement. On other days, they peppered the fort with arrows and picked off settlers who ventured outside its walls. In one instance, seven settlers in a boat spotted several native women on a riverbank. When the squaws returned their smiles, the men scrambled onto land, only to be confronted by warriors who had been hiding. Six of the seven managed to rush back to the boat. The straggler was stripped naked and tied to a stake, around which a fire was set. His tormentors used mussel shells to saw off his fingers and toes and skin him. He died as they danced around the flames.

Another ambush landed Smith in the most famous predicament of his life. While ashore during a trip up the Chickahominy River, he was surrounded and captured by hundreds of warriors.

Christmas of 1607 found him being led from village to village as a showpiece. Finally he was brought to a large lodge where a man in a raccoon-skin robe with the tails still attached was sitting. The man was Powhatan, chief of a confederacy of two dozen tribes and 200 villages spread over much of what is now eastern Virginia.

Smith in time would give two very different accounts of what occurred next. The first version, written soon after the event, had the two men discussing their intentions. The chief invited the captain "to live with him upon his river" and engage in trade, Smith wrote, and "this request I promised to performe." Smith, according to this account, then was set free. No role was mentioned for Powhatan's daughter Pocahontas, then 10 or 11 years old.

In the more celebrated record, penned many years later, Smith's head was placed on a stone and men with clubs were told "to beate out his braines." But "Pocahontas the King's dearest daughter . . . got his head in her armes, and laid her owne upon his to save him from death: whereat the Emperour was contented he should live."

Whatever Pocahontas's role, her father declared Smith his friend and set him free. That friendship, for a while, strengthened Smith's ability to barter for the food that time and again kept Jamestown from going under. With an eye on the benefits of trade, Powhatan seemed to crave peace. "Why should you take by force from us that which you can obtain by love?" the chief asked during one of the several visits Smith would make in the months ahead. "Why should you destroy us who have provided you with food?"

But the relationship between captain and chief was fickle. Whenever they met, Powhatan asked Smith to prove his friendship by leaving his pistol outside. Smith, wary of being overtaken, insisted it's OK for a friend to come armed. At one point, over the objections of Smith, the English gave Powhatan a copper crown. They were delighted when he allowed it to be placed on his head, because it meant he now was a subject of King James. Once the proud chief recognized the symbolism, he ordered another of his intermittent cutoffs in trade.

And kindness, Smith believed, was not to be wasted on savages. After his men beat back a waterborne ambush, he ordered the attackers' canoes destroyed. He relented when the Indians agreed to deliver 400 baskets of corn at harvest time. When they failed to keep their word, Smith started burning their houses. The natives quickly complied.

From his legendary close call at Powhatan's place, Smith returned to Jamestown and instantly found his life again at risk. For letting settlers be ambushed and killed, council leaders had decided he too should die. Suddenly, a supply ship from London arrived. Its commander, Christopher Newport, the same skipper who had saved Smith's neck in the West Indies, took charge and set the captain free.

No free meals. Five days after Newport's relief ship brought 80 fresh settlers into the colony, one of the newcomers accidentally set a fire that raced from one thatched structure to another, destroying almost the entire village plus the new provisions. Again, food from the Indians helped the settlers hang on till the next supply vessel appeared in the spring.

Summer 1608 found the colonists sick, lame, and complaining about the "silly president," the vain John Ratcliffe, for whom a presidential palace was being built. When Ratcliffe's term expired in September, Smith took over. He promptly scrapped the palace and dispensed a dose of military discipline. "He that will not worke shall not eate," Smith declared as he set the indolent to cutting timber and sawing boards for shelters that would help the colony endure the hard winter. Any toiler who cursed risked the penalty of cold water poured down his sleeve.

Fears of another disaster erupted with the discovery that the entire corn supply had been ruined, either from rotting or by rats. Smith halted all work in Jamestown and divided the colonists into three groups. He sent one bunch upriver to hunt game until the next supply ship arrived. Another went downriver to live on fish. The largest group got by on oysters from the Chesapeake shore.

But nothing Smith could do would give the Virginia Company what it wanted most: gold and a route to the Orient. That summer, the company ordered a new charter with "one able and absolute governor"—not a turn-taking president—serving as Jamestown's boss. Smith was demoted to running a remote lookout garrison. But before that change took effect, an accidental gunpowder explosion burned him so badly that he took a boat to England in October 1609, never to return.

Along with the leadership shakeup came a nine-ship expedition to Virginia, the largest yet, with 500 settlers on board. Since the new governor, Lord De La Warr (for whom Delaware is named), was not ready to leave, a deputy took command. Off the West Indies, a hurricane struck, sinking one ship. Seven of the eight remaining vessels limped into Jamestown just before Smith left for London.

As for the eighth ship, Sea Venture, Shakespeare would write his *Tempest* from accounts of its bout with the hurricane. For months, the flagship lay wrecked on Bermuda. From its ruin, survivors jury-rigged a new vessel. The deputy governor, Thomas Gates, was on board in May 1610 as it sailed up the Chesapeake Bay. What he found was one of American history's most dreadful horrors.

Survivors called it "the Starving Time." Sensing weakness after Smith's departure, Powhatan had told his subjects to withhold corn. Food dwindled to nothing that winter, and diseases broke out. The famished ate horses and dogs, then cats and rats, and finally the leather of their boots. One man killed, salted, and ate his wife. Of the 500 colonists alive when Smith left in the fall, barely 60 lasted into spring.

Gates decided to shut the settlement and ship everyone to England. They were 15 miles down the James when up the river came a rowboat with wondrous news: The governor, Lord De La Warr, en route from England with 150 men and ample supplies, was in the bay. Three days after it perished, the Jamestown colony was alive again.

His lordship took a whiff of the town he revived, declared it "unwholesome," and ordered a cleanup. Yet troubles persisted. Like many, De La Warr took sick almost as soon as he arrived. Ten months later, he fled to England in search of a cure.

When his successor, Sir Thomas Dale, reached Jamestown in May 1611, the colonists were at "their daily and usuall workes, bowling in the streetes." To eradicate such idleness, the company imposed a severe set of rules solemnly entitled Lawes Divine, Morall and Martiall. The draconian regulations had drumbeats starting and ending each workday, with whippings for latecomers and early quitters. A single incident of blasphemy merited the lash. A second meant a needle through the tongue, and a third meant death. Execution was prescribed for thieves, runaways, and adulterers. Dale enforced the rules mercilessly, even having a pregnant seamstress lashed for making shirts too short.

Far more useful was Dale's decision to junk what amounted to communism. Since Jamestown's start, all land was held and worked in common, with rations distributed evenly from a central storehouse. There was no incentive for an individual to work harder. Dale assigned colonists plots and let them grow for their own benefit.

It was on one of those 3-acre plots that John Rolfe tinkered with tobacco and transformed Jamestown. The English regarded the tobacco grown in Virginia as much too coarse to compete in the growing world market with the sweet-tasting leaf the Spanish raised in the West Indies. Rolfe took Indies seed, combined it in 1612 with the local variety, and produced a leaf that was smooth to smoke and easy to raise.

In 1614, he sent his first shipment to England. Soon, London was importing tens of thousands of pounds of Virginia leaf a year. Virtually every clearing in the colony was planted with tobacco.

Rolfe also made a decision in his personal life that helped ease Jamestown's relationship with the Indians, which had deteriorated since Smith's exit. In dealing with natives, Smith relied on threats and an occasional hut-burning to show toughness. His successors favored massacres. In one nighttime attack, the English killed 15 men, burned their village, and captured and murdered their queen and her children. Indians responded with attacks of their own. Amid the strife, the English took a hostage—not an ordinary hostage, but Powhatan's daughter Pocahontas. The Indian attacks subsided. While the princess remained in custody, Rolfe got Dale's permission to marry her. In April 1614—the year he first sent tobacco to London—Rolfe and Pocahontas wed in the Jamestown church. In deference to his daughter, the chief would fight no more.

Thanks to Rolfe's tobacco and Powhatan's peace, Jamestown began to thrive, as did England's newer settlements along the

James. The colony's population doubled in 1619 when more than 1,200 settlers came ashore. Many paid their way and got 50 acres in return. But most were indentured servants who worked payless for years in exchange for eventual freedom and a share of profits or a piece of land. Ninety were "young and uncorrupt maids," sent as wives for settlers.

That year, amid the sudden prosperity, popular government made its start. The company told its governor to abolish arbitrary rule, usher in English common law and due process, and form a representative assembly. Paradoxically, that also was the year a ship docked at Jamestown with 20 men and women from Africa—the beginning of the slave trade.

When Powhatan died in 1618, the "married peace" died as well. His subjects were retreating to the west, yielding their cornfields to the tobacco-driven colonists. The new chief, Opechancanough, decided the English had encroached enough. On Good Friday of March 1622, his warriors surprised and massacred 347 settlers. The survivors swore to "destroy them who sought to destroy us." Armies of Englishmen torched Indian villages and cornfields and killed hundreds of men, women, and children. The eradication campaign would continue off and on for decades. By century's end, only a few hundred Indians remained in a region once inhabited by tens of thousands.

The Good Friday massacre also spelled the end of the Virginia Company. In 1624, James I dissolved the company and turned Virginia into a crown colony.

No longer were the settlers mere laborers toiling for a stock company. They became free citizens with power to seek landed estates for themselves and their heirs. From calamities and despair emerged a permanent colony, sustaining the aspirations of an early Jamestown ballad: "Wee hope to plant a nation / Where none before hath stood."

Elsewhere . . . Trouble in the Melting Pot

In 1626, the Dutch West India Company landed the whole island of Manhattan for just $24. Of course, there has never been a bargain in Manhattan that came without a catch. While the Dutch thought they'd bought the island, the Indians thought they'd merely sold rights to *share* it. New Netherland—with towns called Lang Eylant, Breuckelen, and Staten Eylant—prospered nevertheless, cashing in on Europeans' appetite for beaver hats and its budding slave trade. By 1664, slaves made up as much as one fifth of the population of what would become New York. Colonists also hailed from Germany, Scandinavia, and France. The melting-pot-to-be was not without troubles: Slave trade aside, director-general Peter Stuyvesant also suppressed Jews and had Quakers beaten.

Elsewhere . . . Idealism on Cape Cod

Thanksgiving and cranberry sauce were not the legacy the Pilgrims set out to leave when they landed on Cape Cod in November 1620. Communalism and godliness would have been more their speed; to avoid the materialism they'd detested in England, the Pilgrims determined to share work and land in the close quarters of a single tight-knit village. But the idealism quickly derailed as reality set in: In the village, soil was subpar, but when the Pilgrims dispersed to private farms, they found better land—and more of it. Unlike Jamestown colonists, Plymouth residents interpreted England's dominion flexibly, keeping the laws they liked (bestiality remained a crime) and relinquishing those they didn't (in England, the oldest son inherited all the land, but in Plymouth, his brothers got some, too).

Elsewhere . . . Mapping New France

It took Samuel de Champlain 29 trips across the Atlantic to found and secure the city of Quebec, and all he got for his trouble was what looked at first like the wimpiest of the European colonies: In 1627, Quebec (founded in 1608) had only 55 settlers, who had cleared only $1^1/_2$ acres of land. England had dissidents, but the French liked their country too much to leave. Lacking a regular influx of residents, Quebec distinguished itself in other ways. Champlain, who had first found the natives grotesque, eventually began joining them on the warpath; he even was given three Indian girls as a sign of friendship. The relationship paid off: What New France lacked in colonists, it made up for in cartographic knowledge; New France's holdings arced from Quebec down to New Orleans.

Elsewhere . . . A 40-Year Head Start

The first continuously settled American colony began as an act of war. In 1564, the French threatened Spain's monopoly in the Americas by founding a fort on the coast of Florida, smack in the middle of Spain's shipping route. Philip II was determined to fight back—with a whole new colony. So fleet captain Pedro Menéndez de Avilés marshaled craftsmen, professionals, and families. English pirates, disease, and the lack of a sound economy hurt. But then, profit was never St. Augustine's purpose. It was meant to be a military post and a center for religious conversions. Yet friars' prayers could not compete with English guns, and governors could not block an attack by Francis Drake in 1585. Spain gave St. Augustine to the United States in 1821.

Strangers in a New Land
Henry Hudson's First American Adventure

PETER C. MANCALL

On September 3, 1609, Henry Hudson and the English and Dutch men on the 80-ton *Halve Maen (Half Moon)* came within sight of the coastline where New York meets New Jersey today. The view of the sandy white beach backed by forest must have appeared Edenic to the perhaps 20 gaunt and exhausted men, who had endured most of the past five months crammed inside the 85-foot vessel, savaged by storms, frigid weather, and an oppressive diet.

It was, Hudson would later observe, "as pleasant a land as one need tread upon" with abundant supplies of "timber suitable for shipbuilding, and for making large casks or vats." The tall oak trees were a sure index of rich soil, while the waters yielded mullet, salmon, and a ray so large that it took four men to haul it onboard. But to these hardened men, something else lay beyond the trees that filled their dreams and made the costs of exploration well worth it.

Hudson and all European explorers of the 16th and 17th centuries knew that fame and immense riches would accrue to whomever found a quick new route to the vast markets of spices and silks in East Asia and the southwest Pacific. For almost a century, the English had sought a shortcut that would not only bring glory to their realm but also abet the larger Protestant mission of rescuing Christendom from the thrall of Rome. Of course, Hudson's backers had other goals too, above all the enormous fortunes that would reward control of the East Asia trade. The English East India Company, organized only a few years earlier, was already getting ships out of the Spice Islands laden with pepper, cinnamon, cloves, and nutmeg. But they had to follow the long course from India around Africa for thousands of miles, exposed to Barbary pirate slavers. Hudson realized that an Arctic passage—despite its icebergs, barren country, and enigmatic and menacing inhabitants—could cut the distance and time substantially. A man of few words but of evident ambition and significant experience, he could have become as famous as Sir Francis Drake and buried his obscure origins under fame and wealth.

Two years earlier, he had led a mission that he hoped would take him over the top of the world, past the pole toward East Asia. This was the first of four voyages that made him one of the most intrepid and important explorers of his age—even as he failed in his quest for a way through ice to the lands of the sun, and even though his final voyage ended in mutiny, mystery, and quite possibly murder.

"Very Civill," Henry Hudson called the Indians who greeted him just north of New York's Staten Island in Septemper 1609. Not knowing what to expect, Hudson probably donned half armor when meeting Lenape Indians, forebears of Chief Lapowinsa, who was painted by Gustavus Hesselius in 1735.

The Europeans on the *Halve Maen* soon found that they were not alone in this paradise. They first met the natives the day after they cast anchor; having made land in the ancestral territory of the Delaware (also known as the Lenape), which the local Munsee called Lenapehoking or "the Land of the People." The ship's chronicler and first mate, Robert Juet, reported that the Munsee seemed happy to see the newcomers and willingly offered green tobacco in exchange for beads and knives. The Europeans found them "very civill" and marveled at their large supply of maize. On September 5 some of the crew ventured ashore in shallow-drafting rowboats known as shallops to fraternize and receive more tobacco. Some of the Indians ventured over to the *Halve Maen,* where they offered currants and hemp. Despite these peaceful exchanges, the English and Dutch men remained suspicious. They had perhaps heard tales traded around the docks at home of the unpredictability of America's native peoples.

On September 6 Hudson sent a party ashore to scout. They found meadows of plentiful flowers and grasses, as well as tall, fragrant trees. As they returned at dusk amid a rain storm, 26 Munsee paddled toward them in two canoes and attacked, wounding three of the five sailors. One of them, John Coleman, probably a veteran of Hudson's earlier failed East Indies mission two years before, took an arrow in his throat and died. Just as suddenly, the raiders then pulled away, leaving the survivors to bury Coleman in weary puzzlement. They named a point of land for him and maintained a watch the entire night. They returned at dawn to the *Halve Maen.* Encounters remained tense over the next few days, until the Europeans decided that they had rested long enough. It was time to explore the broad river that they hoped might lead them through the interior to the fabled Northwest Passage water route through North America.

Even after Coleman's death, Hudson and his crew continued to trade with the Indians, frequently accepting the hospitality of these Algonquian peoples as they sailed up the river that one day would bear his name. But they also grew increasingly suspicious of the locals, scrutinizing each group before allowing some aboard and keeping an eye out for the villain who had murdered their shipmate.

Hudson's 1609 voyage to the New World aboard the *Halve Maen* was hampered not just by the tight quarters, but also by the inability of navigators of the time to measure longitude, a geographic notation indicating east/west measurement. Hudson relied on traditional navigational tools such as a magnetic compass and dividers for measuring charted distances between two points. Just 64 years later, Hugo Allard published "New and Most Exact Map of All New Netherland," which included an inset of the Dutch colony New Amsterdam, which one day would become New York City.

When Hudson had left Amsterdam on April 4, he had no plan to cross the Atlantic. In 1607 and 1608 he had led English expeditions seeking a water route to the Spice Islands of the "South Sea," as Europeans then referred to the Pacific Ocean. Little is known about Hudson's early life, though it is possible that he had lived earlier in a small town along a rock-strewn edge of the Northumberland coast. His family had in all likelihood been involved in long-distance trade, which could have helped him gain command of the *Hopewell* in 1607, the year he first appears with certainty in the historical record. On the initial voyage he hoped to find a way across the North Pole, but he turned back when ice blocked his passage. The next year he aimed for the Northeast Passage above Scandinavia and Russia, which Europeans believed led to the Pacific. His ship could not get past Novaya Zemlya, the typically frozen archipelago that separates the Barents and the Kara seas.

Despite these setbacks, Hudson had gained a reputation as a skilled seaman who bravely ventured into little-known waters and returned with ship intact and his crew alive. His skills attracted European merchants eager to find a shortcut to the Spice Islands that avoided the slow 10,000-mile journey overland from the southwest Pacific to western Europe, or the yet longer (if faster) 20,000-mile sea route pioneered earlier by the Portuguese. Both itineraries posed costly dangers. Caravans could be raided on land, and pirates preyed on ships. Whoever found a northern route could bring spices back faster and, in theory, with less risk.

The Dutch fascination with the Northeast Passage was no passing fad. In the 1590s Willem Barentsz (known as William

Barents to the English) had made three efforts to break through to the Pacific. He survived the first two attempts but perished on the third after months trapped in the ice, only a few of his men surviving to tell the dismal story.

In 1609 the recently organized Dutch East India Company sent Hudson to follow Barentsz's trail. He complied by sailing to the northeast, but, as one of his contemporaries put it, he "found the sea as full of ice as he had found it in the preceding year, so that they lost all hope of effecting anything during the season"; some Dutch sailors, accustomed to the temperate East Indies, found the bitter cold unbearable. Hudson offered the choice between sailing westward toward the 40th parallel, to a point where the English Capt. John Smith (who had journeyed to Jamestown in 1607) had suggested that an opening to the Pacific might be found, or sailing north through the Davis Strait, along the west coast of Greenland, toward what Europeans believed to be an ice-free polar sea. The men opted for the mid-Atlantic route and better weather.

Coleman's death had confirmed the crew's misgivings. Thereafter, even peaceful meetings with the Americans were fraught with suspicions. On September 9 the Europeans, fearful of two warrior-filled canoes, tried unsuccessfully to capture several of the locals. Three days later they faced the largest group of Algonquians they had yet encountered when 28 canoes carrying men, women, and children paddled toward the ship. Juet believed that the Americans had come "to betray us." Hudson refused to allow any Indians aboard. Nonetheless, the *Halve Maen* anchored and sent scouts ashore to trade, the sailors being especially interested in beans and oysters. The next day, after the *Halve Maen* had moved another four miles upriver and anchored again, more Indians arrived to barter oysters, pumpkins, maize, and tobacco for what Juet called "trifles," which presumably included goods manufactured in Europe that would have been novel to the Americans. Over the next several days the ship sailed deeper into the valley. The sailors continued to trade for goods ranging from grapes to beaver and otter pelts, but they remained always on guard.

They came to realize that they had ventured into the midst of a network of communities. Juet did not provide the names of these groups, but in all likelihood the *Halve Maen* had sailed into the Catskills territory of the Mahican. To find out whether these Indians "had any treacherie in them," Hudson and Juet planned to invite some onboard, get them drunk on aquavit and wine, and see how they behaved. The Indians had never been drunk before, but their conduct impressed the English favorably, and soon the crew established peaceful relations with other locals. The Indians, according to Juet, treated Hudson with "reverence."

By late September the *Halve Maen* had ventured as far as it could up the once-wide river, probably near modern-day Albany. A small group dispatched to take soundings upstream returned with news that the river was narrowing; only 25 miles farther inland, it was a mere seven feet deep. Hudson realized that this could not be the Northwest Passage. By September 24 they had turned the ship and begun to retrace their route.

Hudson had failed again, but at least he could report to his Dutch investors on the potential profits of these lands. As the *Halve Maen* descended the river, the crew paid careful attention to the landscape, especially what covered it: fertile fields and forests thick with oak, walnut, chestnut, yew, and "trees of sweet wood in great abundance, and great store of Slate for houses, and other good stones." They traded and ate with the same peoples they had encountered on their journey upriver, a generally positive experience that convinced some of the men that the valley would be a good place to settle. "This is a very pleasant place to build a towne on," Juet wrote, in the first recorded reference to colonization by anyone associated with Hudson. The sailors believed that the nearby mountains might bear valuable minerals, especially when the Indians gave them stones strong enough to cut through steel or iron.

But just as the Europeans let down their guard and perhaps contemplated coexistence with the Indians, another crisis flared. On October 1 the crew hosted visitors whom Juet identified only as the "people of the Mountaynes," who seemed not to have encountered the *Halve Maen* or its crew earlier. The Europeans purchased some small skins from them, some of whom remained onboard. Juet wrote that one Indian, not among the trading party, paddled his canoe so close that eventually he leapt onto the rudder of the *Halve Maen* and climbed into the window of the cabin, where he stole Juet's pillow, two bandoliers, and two shirts. This was the kind of treachery that the Europeans had always feared, and they reacted swiftly. A sailor shot the thief dead, his comrades plunging into the river. The English gave chase in a shallop. One Indian grabbed hold of the boat and tried to overturn it. The ship's cook chopped off his hand with a sword, leaving him to drown. The others swam away. Deciding that they had seen enough, the Europeans returned to their ship and hurried downstream.

A group paddled out in two canoes, discharging arrows.

By then word of the hostilities had quite likely passed ahead of them and roused other communities. A group that had previously traded with the sailors, including one man who had actually been a guest aboard, paddled out in two canoes, discharging arrows. An English fusillade killed two or three of them. In response over 100 men ashore volleyed arrows upon the ship. Again the sailors returned fire. Juet deployed a light cannon, called a falcon, which killed three Indians, while others of the ship's company dropped three or four more with muskets.

When the skirmish abated, the *Halve Maen* sailed away, soon reaching a place the locals called Mannahata. They met with no other Americans or further violence. On October 4 the ship reached the river's mouth and headed homeward.

Hudson began his return journey pondering a dilemma. Should he head to Amsterdam to admit failure or hatch a new plan, turn the ship, and try again? After six months at sea and two opposite attempts to find a passage to the East Indies, he had had no luck northeast or northwest. His crew also debated their destination, the Dutch arguing for setting a northward course to Newfoundland, passing the winter there, and launching another search for the Northwest Passage in the spring. Giving in to English opinions, Hudson judged such a course unwise. "He was afraid of the mutinous crew," Emanuel van Meteren, the Dutch consul in London, later reported, "who had sometime savagely threatened him." Mutiny was bad enough, but food could run out over the long, dark winter, leaving his crew dead or in such debility that they could neither carry on nor return to Europe.

Hudson offered an alternate plan. The ship could winter in Ireland and then proceed to Dartmouth in early spring to prepare for the next year's search. If he could launch an expedition into the North Atlantic by mid-March, sail northwest, and hunt whales until mid-May, he would have a whole summer to seek the open northern waters before the winter ice closed the way again.

But for reasons no one bothered to document, the *Halve Maen* instead sailed eastward, reaching Dartmouth on November 7. Soon Hudson was back in London, where he spent the winter regaling others about his journey for the Dutch, his crew's inability to suffer the cold at the start of the trip toward the Northeast Passage, his tour of the North American coast, and the journey up the wide river. He probably described the bounty of that country of tall timber and furbearing creatures, its fish-thick rivers, and its potential for settlement. If he mentioned his adventures with the natives of that territory, we have no record of it. Juet left the only surviving full account of the *Halve Maen*'s repeated encounters with the Algonquians, their curious trading habits, their strange gear, and their mysterious hostilities. A fragment from Hudson's account briefly described how the Indians lived and included his opinion that they "appear to be a friendly people, but have a great propensity to steal, and are exceedingly adroit in carrying away whatever they take a fancy to." Despite that harsh judgment, Hudson mentioned to an associate of Sir Robert Cecil, the first Earl of Salisbury, that he planned to return soon to the American coast.

True to his word, he set sail the following year, this time to find the passage further north. But the troubles he had found in 1609 paled in comparison to what faced him now. At least he had survived the trip to Manhattan and up the river that now bears his name. But he never came back from the American Arctic, succumbing, like poor John Coleman, to unpredictable violence. In Hudson's case, though, the assault came from his own mutinous crew, who abandoned him, his 17-year-old son, and several other sailors. Those who got home eventually found themselves being prosecuted for murder.

Hudson was in all likelihood not the first European to lay eyes on what became New York. That honor, such as it was, belongs to the Italian explorer Giovanni da Verrazzano, who sailed into the harbor in 1524, though he never ventured upriver as Hudson did. But Hudson, English captain of the Dutch-owned *Halve Maen,* was the first to report on that rich country and thus encourage Dutch colonization. Juet's report, published in 1625, added to the growing body of travel literature that inspired the English to seek permanent outposts on the North American mainland. In 1664 they wrested control of New York from the Dutch, keeping it until their last soldiers sailed homeward in 1783 from the new republic. By then the Munsee and other Algonquians whose ancestors had both hosted and confronted Hudson's crew no longer controlled the harbor, the sweet-smelling forests of the Hudson Valley, or the rich fishing grounds—a future that Hudson, who dreamt of seaways far to the north of Manna-hata and Munsee territory, could not have imagined.

Blessed and Bedeviled

Tales of remarkable providences in puritan New England.

HELEN MONDLOCH

On October 31, 2001, Massachusetts Gov. Jane Swift signed a bill exonerating the last five souls convicted of witchcraft during the infamous Salem witch trials of 1692. Rectifying a few of history's wrongs on this Halloween day, the governor's conciliatory gesture was arguably ill-timed, given the frivolous revelry associated with this annual celebration of superstition and frights. In the real-life horror of the witch scare, at least 150 people were imprisoned, including a four-year-old girl who was confined for months to a stone dungeon. Twenty-three men and women, all of whom have now been cleared of their crimes, were hanged or died in prison, and one man was pressed (crushed) to death for his refusal to stand trial.

In probing the underpinnings of this tragic and incredible chapter of American history, New England observers past and present have agreed that the nascent Massachusetts Bay Colony provided a fertile ground for the devil's plagues. Among others, folklore scholar Richard Dorson, author of *America in Legend and American Folklore,* has argued that the frenzy culminating in the witch-hunt was fueled by legends that flourished among the Puritans, a populace that imagined itself both blessed and bedeviled. Of key importance was belief in phenomena called "providences" (more commonly called "remarkable providences"). These were visible, often terrifying, signs of God's will that forged themselves onto the fabric of daily life.

As Dorson explains, "Since, in the Puritan and Reformation concept, God willed every event from the black plague to the sparrow's fall, all events held meaning for errant man." The providences brought rewards or protection for the Lord's followers (generally the Puritans themselves) or vengeance upon His enemies. Sprung from European roots and embraced by intellectuals and common folk alike, they became the subject of a passionate story tradition that enlarged and dramatized events in the manner of all oral legends.

The pursuit of providences was greatly reinforced by those who felt compelled to record their occurrence, including John Winthrop, longtime theocratic governor of Massachusetts Bay Colony. Two prominent New England ministers, Increase Mather and his son Cotton, became the most zealous popularizers of such tales. In 1684 the elder Mather set forth guidelines for their documentation in *An Essay for the Recording of Illustri-*

ous Providences, a study that Cotton Mather would later extend in his own works. The Essay defined "illustrious" providences as the most extraordinary of divinely ordained episodes: "tempests, floods, earthquakes, thunders as are unusual, strange apparitions, or whatever else shall happen that is prodigious." The directives for recording the providences—a duty over which the elder Mather would preside in order to preserve the stories for all posterity—are likened by Dorson to methods observed by modern folklore collectors.

The flip side of the providences were the witchcrafts of the devil, who poised himself with a special vengeance against this citadel of God's elect. Where faith and fear converged, the tales of remarkable providences heightened both.

A 'City upon a Hill'

In his *Book of New England Legends and Folklore in Prose and Poetry* (1901), Samuel Adams Drake called New England "the child of a superstitious mother." Dorson acknowledges that folk legends in the colonies were "for the most part carbon copies of the folklore in Tudor and Stuart England." But in grafting themselves onto a New World setting, says Dorson, the old beliefs took on a special intensity in the realm of the Puritans.

Many have credited the Mathers with projecting and magnifying this Puritan zeal. Writing at the turn of the last century, historian Samuel McChord Crothers, quoted in B.A. Botkin's *Treasury of New England Folklore,* captured the fervency of the younger Mather, who became a principal driver of the witch-hunt:

> Even Cotton Mather could not avoid a tone of pious boastfulness when he narrated the doings of New England . . .
>
> . . . New England had the most remarkable providences, the most remarkable painful preachers, the most remarkable heresies, the most remarkable witches. Even the local devils were in his judgment more enterprising than those of the old country. They had to be in order to be a match for the New England saints.

Perhaps we can gain the proper perspective on the Puritans' passion when we consider the enormous pains they undertook to escape persecution in England and establish their new covenant across the sea. Upholding that covenant was now critical, as evidenced in the lofty proclamations of a sermon delivered in 1630 by John Winthrop. Excerpted in Frances Hill's *Salem Witch Trials Reader,* the governor's words resound with poignant irony given the events that rocked Salem sixty-two years later: "We shall be as a City upon a Hill, the eyes of all people . . . upon us; so if we shall deal falsely with our God in this work we have undertaken and to cause Him to withdraw His present help from us, we shall be made a story . . . through the world . . . and . . . we shall shame the faces of . . . God's worthy servants, and cause their prayers to be turned into curses upon us."

Clearly, the task of maintaining this sinless "City upon a Hill" wrought insecurity among the Puritans, and so, says Dorson, they "searched the providences for continued evidence of God's favor or wrath." As he reveals, popular legends spurred their confidence: "Marvelous escapes from shipwreck, Indian captivity, or starvation reassured the elect that the Lord was guarding their fortunes under His watchful eye."

Cotton Mather recorded many such episodes in his 1702 chronicle titled *Magnalia Christi Americana: The Ecclesiastical History of New England.* In one renowned tale, a spectral ship appeared to an ecstatic crowd of believers in New Haven harbor in 1647. Six months earlier the heavily freighted vessel was presumed lost, after it had sailed from that harbor and never returned. According to Mather's account, quoted by Botkin, the community lost "the best part of their tradable estates . . . and sundry of their eminent persons." Mather quotes an eyewitness who believed that God had now "condescended" to present the ship's ghostly image as a means of comforting the afflicted souls of the mourners, for whom this remarkable providence affirmed not only their fallen friends' state of grace but also their own.

The Puritans also gleaned affirmation from providences in which the Lord exacted harsh punishments on the enemies of His elect. According to Dorson, the Puritans apparently relished most these tales of divine judgment. Those scourged in the tales included Indians, Quakers, and anyone else deemed blasphemous or profane. In the *Magnalia,* Cotton Mather correlates providential offenses to the Ten Commandments. He cites the destruction of the Narragansett Indian nation by a group of white settlers as retribution for the Indians' foul contempt for the Gospel. Oral legends also relayed the fate of Mary Dyer, a Quaker who was sent to the gallows around 1659; Dyer was said to have given birth to a monster, a common curse meted out to nefarious women. Even members of the elect might be struck down by plague or fatal lightning bolts for lapses ranging from the omission of prayer to adultery and murder. The *Magnalia* narrates the doom suffered by various "heretics" who quarreled with village ministers or voted to cut their salaries.

In addition to these ancient themes of reward and punishment, the providence tales incorporated a host of familiar spectacles from an Old World tradition, including apparitions, wild tempests, and corpses that communicated with blood—all magnanimous instruments of an angry but just Lord. Like the spectral ship, apparitions offered hope and solved mysteries; the apparition of a murder victim often disclosed the identity of his killer, a belief that came into play during the witch trials. The age-old notion that a corpse bleeds at the murderer's touch also surfaced abundantly in the tales.

Increase Mather devoted a whole chapter of his *Essay* to thunder and lightning, perceiving in them signs of God's consternation over the advent of secularism in Massachusetts Bay Colony. Mather declared that thunder and lightning had been observed ever since "the English did first settle these American deserts," but warned that only in recent years had they wrought "fatal and fearful slaughters . . . among us." In the *Magnalia,* Cotton Mather, too, expounded on thunder, a phenomenon that the Harvard scholar and scientist, quoted in Dorson, astutely attributed to the "laws of matter and motion [and] . . . divers weighty clouds" in collision; lightning, he postulated, derived from "subtil and sulphureos vapours." Like his erudite father, however, Cotton maintained that God was the omnipotent "first mover" of these and other natural forces.

Tales of Witchcraft

Dorson explains that "providences issued from God and witchcrafts from the devil, and they marked the tide of battle between the forces of Christ and the minions of Satan." Tales of witchery had their own illustrious elements, including menacing poltergeists, enchantments, and innocent creatures who became possessed and tormented by wicked sorcerers.

He and others have argued that the widely circulated tales of remarkable providences, wherein the Puritans sealed their identity of chosenness, created a fertile climate for witch tales and the witch-hunt. According to Dorson, "Other Protestants in New York and Virginia, and the Roman Catholics in Maryland, spoke of witchery, but the neurotic intensity of the New England witch scare . . . grew from the providential aura the Puritans gave their colonial enterprise."

Cotton Mather himself, quoted in Dorson, described the devil's vengeful plot to "destroy the kingdom of our Lord Jesus Christ" in this region that had once been "the Devil's territories" (that is, inhabited by Indians). Both Mathers were implicated as early as the mid-eighteenth-century for promoting bloodlust over witchcraft with their recordings of providence tales. Thomas Hutchinson, governor of Massachusetts Bay in 1771–74, lamented the witch debacle in his *History of the Colony of Massachusetts Bay* (1765). According to Hill, who refers to the governor as a "man of the Enlightenment," Hutchinson's chronicle suggests "that there was widespread disapproval of hanging witches until the *Illustrious Providences and Memorable Providences* [Cotton's later work] . . . changed the climate of opinion."

Providence lore undoubtedly played a part in the actions of those who spearheaded the witch scare with their clamorous cries of demonic possession. The trouble began in January 1692 when two girls, Betty Parris, the nine-year-old daughter of Salem Village minister Samuel Parris, and her cousin Abigail Williams, age eleven, began experiencing spells of bizarre behavior. In these alarming episodes, the girls convulsed and ranted incoherently. Within a month other neighborhood girls began having similar spells; soon they all began accusing various members of the community of bewitching them.

The cause of these disturbing bouts—which would continue for ten months, until the last of the condemned was pulled down from the gallows—has been the topic of much scholarly speculation and simplistic analysis. Some have theorized, at least as an initiating factor, that the girls suffered from temporary mental illness engendered by eating ergot-infected rye (a theory to which the growing conditions and agricultural practices of the time lend credence, according to Hill). Others have postulated a conspiracy theory incorporating the fierce factionalism that emerged in large part over arguments related to the Reverend Parris' salary and living arrangements.

The most prevalent theory suggests that the girls' hysteria grew from feelings of paranoia and guilt at having dabbled in fortune-telling and other occult practices with Tituba, a native of Barbados who served as the Parris family's slave (and who later confessed, albeit under dubious circumstances, to having engaged in such activities with her young charges). Perhaps one falsehood led to another as the girls struggled to cover up their forbidden deeds; perhaps one or another girl actually believed, for a period, that she had been bewitched; perchance the girls also were pressured by their elders, who were eager to avoid scandal, to reveal the cause of their afflictions. Quite possibly, too, some combination of these factors set into motion the outbursts and subsequent accusations. In any case, as Hill argues, the girls very likely started out as victims of "human suggestibility" and at some point later became perpetrators of fraud.

This view is supported by the fact that the girls had been reared abundantly on tales of providences and demonic possession. In his popular *Memorable Providences,* quoted by Hill, Mather provided a detailed description of four children who suffered "strange fits, beyond those that attend an epilepsy," as a result of a wicked washerwoman's sorcery. In addition, Hill reveals that Puritans young and old "devoured" sensational pamphlets describing similar demonic episodes, a fact that is hardly surprising, she says, since secular reading was prohibited. In his account of the witch trials, Governor Hutchinson charges that the similarities between these well-known accounts of demonic possession and those of the "supposed bewitched at Salem . . . is so exact, as to leave no room to doubt the stories had been read by the New England persons themselves, or had been told to them by others who had read them."

One case in particular demonstrates the far-reaching influence of the providence legends: that of Giles Corey, who suffered an excruciating death by pressing for his refusal to stand trial for witchcraft. According to Dorson, as the executions mounted with dreadful fury, the fatal torture of this "sturdy, uncowed farmer" aroused the people's sympathy. Some wondered whether his only crime had been his stubborn silence. Public opinion shifted, however, thanks to the actions of Thomas Putnam, a prominent citizen and the father of twelve-year-old Anne Putnam, one of the principal accusers.

The elder Putnam wrote a letter to Samuel Sewall, one of the trial judges who would later become a famous diarist. The letter reported that on the previous night, Anne had witnessed the apparition of a man who had lived with Giles Corey seventeen years earlier. This "Natural Fool"—perhaps a mentally disabled man—had died suddenly in Corey's house; his ghost now claimed that Corey had murdered him by pressing him to death, causing "clodders of blood about his heart." The apparition reported, moreover, that Corey had escaped punishment for his crime by signing a pact with the devil, whose protective powers were now being usurped by a God who meted out His just desserts—that is, a ghastly punishment precisely matching the crime. Hence, Putnam's letter, now filed by Cotton Mather as an official court document, helped sanctify Corey's execution in the eyes of the citizenry.

By the fall of 1692 the witch crisis had begun to die down. Hill explains that the girls had apparently "overreached themselves by naming as witches several prominent people, including Lady Phipps, the wife of the governor." As the executions began drawing public criticism, Phipps dissolved the witch court and later granted reprieves to the remaining accused. Twelve years later, a sullen Anne Putnam, now twenty-four years old, stood before the congregation in Salem Village Church while the minister read aloud her apology, quoted in Hill, for the "great delusion of Satan" that had caused her to "bring upon . . . this land the guilt of innocent blood."

A Dark Legacy

With his strangely circular reasoning, Mather, reflecting on the witch crisis in a 1697 chronicle excerpted by Hill, shaped the tragedies into one great remarkable providence. Oblivious to any possibility of delusion or fraud, he attributed the calamities to God's wrath on New England, ignited by the "little sorceries" practiced by its youth as well as the "grosser" witchcrafts of those condemned: "Although these diabolical divinations are more ordinarily committed perhaps all over the world than they are in the country of New England, yet, that being a country devoted unto the worship and the service of the Lord Jesus Christ above the rest of the world, He signaled His vengeance against such extraordinary dispensations, as have not often been seen in other places."

While post-Enlightenment scholars have generally dismissed Mather's arguments as the rantings of a self-righteous fanatic, his thoughts and actions have left their mark on us. In 1953, the "Red Scare" of the McCarthy era inspired playwright Arthur Miller to re-create the Salem witch-hunt in *The Crucible.* Miller remarked in a 1996 *New Yorker* article, quoted by Hill, that the play's enduring relevance lies in its core subject: "human sacrifice to the furies of fanaticism and paranoia that goes on repeating itself forever."

In our own time, such furies seem painfully present. The era of remarkable providences leaves as its dark legacy a number of lessons not easily reckoned. Now, as the world grapples with the bane of terrorism, Hill's analysis of the Salem trials strikes a contemporary nerve: "The more a group idealizes itself, its own values, and its god, the more it persecutes both other groups and the dissenters in its midst."

Today the American government is repeatedly challenged to implement policies that will prevent the current conflict from turning into a witch-hunt. Moreover, our democratic principles still face the perennial threat of an arrogant religious impulse that has never totally died out. Even now, those among us who boldly stake their claim to the mind of God—like the self-appointed prophets who construed the events of last September 11 as a kind of remarkable providence—risk the resurrection of demons similar to the forces that once ravaged a New England community. The calamities of 1692 entreat us to conquer those demons by loving our neighbor and consigning the will of Providence to the realm of mystery.

Additional Readings

B.A. Botkin, ed., *A Treasury of New England Folklore,* Crown Publishers, Inc., New York, 1967.

Richard Dorson, *American Folklore,* University of Chicago Press, Chicage, 1967.

——, *America in Legend: Folklore from the Colonial Period to the Present,* Pantheon Books, New York, 1973.

Samual Adams Drake, *A Book of New England Legends and Folklore in Prose and Poetry,* Little, Brown, 1901.

Frances Hill, *The Salem Witch Trials Reader,* DeCapo Press, Boston, 2000.

Increase Mather, *An Essay for the Recording of Remarkable Providences,* Scholars' Facsimiles and Reprints, Inc., Delmar, N.Y., 1977. Reprint of the 1684 edition printed by J. Green for J. Browning, Boston.

HELEN MONDLOCH is a freelance writer and frequent contributor to the Culture section.

The Real Pirates of the Caribbean

This is a story of the making of America—a true story more powerful than fiction.

The classical age of piracy comes to life in "The Untold Story of the *Whydah* from Slave Ship to Pirate Ship," an interactive exhibition that has more than 200 artifacts on display, including everyday objects, personal items, and treasures from the first fully authenticated pirate ship ever to be discovered in U.S. waters. "Real Pirates" tells the true story of the *Whydah*—named after the West African trading town of Ouidah—a ship that sank off the coast of Cape Cod, Mass., nearly 300 years ago. Showcased are treasure chests of gold coins and jewelry, as well as technically advanced weaponry of the time—18th-century cannons, pistols, and swords. These artifacts painstakingly were recovered from the ocean floor over the last 25 years and form the core of this exhibition.

"This isn't fantasy—it is the real pirates' treasure that bears witness to this ship's fate," points out Scott Demel, head of Collections Management at The Field Museum.

Visitors are provided with an unprecedented glimpse into the unique economical, political, and social circumstances of the early 18th-century Caribbean. Highlighted in the multimedia galleries are compelling true stories of the diverse people whose lives converged on the *Whydah* before its demise. Visitors can get a sense of everyday life aboard the *Whydah* and meet Capt. "Black Sam" Bellamy, one of the boldest and most successful pirates of his day. Continue on the journey with Bellamy as he sails, looting dozens of ships before a violent storm sank the storied vessel.

"This unique and extraordinary exhibit defines the best of exploration," indicates Terry Garcia, National Geographic's executive vice president of Mission Programs. "From an archaeological perspective, we have the discovery of the shipwreck, its excavation, and the process by which it was authenticated. From a cultural perspective, we explore the rich history of the Caribbean trade routes during the 18th century and the inextricable link between the slave trade and piracy. This is the first time that this amazing story, with all of its interconnected layers and characters, will be presented in such an engaging format."

Museum-goers can hoist a pirate flag, tie sailing knots, and enter the ship as the pirates did, by ducking through a large wooden door and going "below deck" in a life-size replica of the ship's stern. "Real Pirates" personally relates to patrons by sharing the stories of four members of the *Whydah* crew—people who ended up on the same pirate ship for very different reasons—such as John King, the youngest-known pirate onboard; he was believed to be under 11 years old at the time of the shipwreck. King's piracy began when the ship he was traveling on with his mother was captured by Capt. Bellamy and he joined the pirate crew.

The three-masted, 300-ton *Whydah* was built as a slave ship in London in 1715 and embodied the most advanced oceangoing technology of the day. She was easy to maneuver, unusually fast, and, to protect her cargo, heavily armed and ready for battle. She was built to transport human captives from the west coast of Africa to the Caribbean—but only made one such voyage before being captured by pirates in February 1717. Soon after the ship's slaves were sold in the Caribbean, the *Whydah* was captured near the Bahamas by Bellamy. His crew quickly hoisted the Jolly Roger, signaling to others that the slave ship now was a pirate ship. On April 26, 1717, the *Whydah,* heavy with loot from more than 50 captured ships, sank during a powerful Nor'easter storm. All but two of the 146 people onboard died.

"This was a unique period in our history," proclaims Jeffrey Bolster, professor of Early American and Caribbean History at the University of New Hampshire and a member of an advisory panel composed of academic and other scholarly specialists who assisted exhibition organizers. "Through the cache of artifacts, we see a world generally undisclosed, one in which the Caribbean was the economic center and values were very different, an era before civil rights, before individual liberties, and before democracy was institutionalized. Without the slave trade and the wealth of the region, piracy would not have existed. This is a story of the making of America—a true story more powerful than fiction."

In 1984, the ship was located by underwater explorer Barry Clifford following years of searching. After more than two decades, Clifford still is actively excavating the wreck site and continues to bring gold and silver to the surface, as well as everyday items that shed light on this tumultuous period of American and world history.

To start their re-created journey on the *Whydah,* visitors are treated to an introductory video narrated by actor Louis Gossett Jr. Here, they are presented with a historical background of piracy in the 18th century and the stories of Capt. Bellamy and Clifford.

Story of the *Whydah*

In the early 1700s, most of the English slave trade was controlled by the Royal African Company—and its need for transport vessels was high. Commissioned in London as an independent ship in 1715, the *Whydah* was considered state-of-the-art and was built to be sailed at speeds of 13 knots. To this day, no one knows exactly who owned her, but it is thought that the *Whydah* was run by a consortium of businessmen—each putting up money to build her and each taking a profit once she sailed and transported slaves from Africa to the Caribbean.

Real Pirates: Fact vs. Fiction

Myth: Pirates wore eye patches due to battle scars.

Fact: The image of the maimed pirate was popularized through Robert Luis Stevenson's *Treasure Island,* and it unintentionally expressed an important truth: seafaring was a terribly dangerous line of work. Sailors routinely lost eyes, hands, and legs to flying splinters and chunks of wood in naval battles and to accidents onboard ship (shifting cargo, falling gear, etc.)

Myth: A pirate captain acted like a dictator in running his ship and crew.

Fact: Pirates actually operated on a fairly democratic system of government, where all crew mates were equal, no matter what their background, age, race, or religion. In fact, a pirate ship would elect its captain through a vote. Other matters, such as where the ship might sail, such as whether to engage in battle or put into port, also would be decided by a vote, with the majority ruling. Captains could—and did—influence voting by expressing their opinions, but votes still carried the day, sometimes in opposition to elected captains and officers.

Myth: "Walking the plank" was a typical form of punishment.

Fact: Very little evidence exists to support the notion that pirates made victims "walk the plank" as common punishment. The few depictions that show this practice are from the 1820s and beyond, but no evidence of plank-walking exists from the 18th century's Age of Piracy. The idea of walking the plank was introduced to society in 1887 in a *Harper's Weekly* article on buccaneers and again propelled into pop culture with J.M. Barrie's stage production of "Peter Pan" in the early 20th century.

Myth: A pirate crew was comprised mostly of thieves, vagrants, and men without any real skill.

Fact: Pirates typically were former sailors. There also were a number of craftsmen and a smaller number of adventurers. These communities of sailors generally were skilled. Many pirate ships also employed an onboard surgeon, considered a highly valued shipmate. In addition to the surgeon, a pirate ship crew normally included a carpenter, an artillery master, a navigator, and a pilot.

Myth: The parrot became the signature pet of pirates because of its ability to fly and seek out other ships or dry land.

Fact: Both sailors and pirates had pets onboard their ships, including dogs, cats, monkeys, and parrots. In truth, many seafaring people did acquire parrots, less for the bird's abilities than as a symbol of their cosmopolitanism—they had traveled to the ends of the Earth and they wanted to show off a bit.

Myth: Pirates were all middle-aged white men.

Fact: Historians have cited that pirates came from many countries and that nearly 30% were of African descent. It may be surprising to know that some pirate crews also included women and young children.

The *Whydah* possessed an arsenal of weaponry for defense against warships and pirates. In 1716, she set out on her maiden voyage.

The Caribbean and the New World Economy

At that time, the Caribbean was a dynamic trading center. A trade route map outlining the Atlantic world of the early 1700s is featured in this section. Imagine the amount of ship traffic—fleets carrying firearms and liquor from Europe, gold and ivory from Africa, sugar and tobacco from the Caribbean and South America, and gold and silver from Spanish mines in Peru and Mexico. All these items and more moved across this vast commercial expanse every day.

The biggest fortune to be made was in the slave trade. Several maps, illustrations, and artifacts explain in detail how the slave trade worked. Most of the soon-to-be slaves were prisoners of war or victims of local conflict. With so much money dependent on the slave trade, enslaving enemies became a motivation for going to war. African merchants marched captives along trade routes to the coast, selling them to Europeans—sometimes one or two at a time, sometimes by the dozen. Artifacts include shackles and an iron bar used as a "trade iron"—in exchange for human captives, purchasers would pay in ivory, gold, or cowrie shells (a form of African currency).

Museum-goers learn about the "Middle Passage," the voyage between the African coast and the Caribbean slave markets. Captives on a slave ship were held in hot, foul-smelling spaces so small they could only crouch or lie down. An average Atlantic crossing took eight to 12 weeks and many Africans died—some from disease, others from poor diet or lack of food. When the ship finally reached the Caribbean, captives were given medical attention and briefly allowed to recuperate. As soon as they were considered "refreshed"—recovered enough to be put on sale—they were auctioned off in slave markets. Olaudah Equiano's story is highlighted here. A former slave, Equiano published his autobiography in England in 1789. Equiano's book was the earliest firsthand account of the slave trade by a former slave.

Pirates

Visitors next come face-to-face with the famous pirate Bart Roberts, also known as Black Bart. He was considered by some to be the most successful pirate of his time, as well as a fancy dresser, as many pirate captains of that period were. Featured are fashionable items, including a silver lapel pin, shoe buckles, buttons, and copper cufflinks—all authentic pirate artifacts recovered from the *Whydah.*

Patrons then come upon a tavern scene with a crackling fire where two pirates ponder over the ship's "Articles" that describe in detail the code of conduct expected of every pirate, including how to dress and how bringing women aboard is forbidden. Everyone who joined a pirate crew was required to sign the ship's Articles. Soon-to-be pirates also swore an oath of loyalty to the crew and agreed never to betray or cheat their shipmates.

This section also tells Bellamy's fascinating story. The commanding officer of the captured *Whydah,* Bellamy was an experienced sailor from a poor family and had little to lose when he chose a life of piracy. Quickly, he became one of the most successful pirates of his day, looting dozens of ships in a year's time before finally capturing the *Whydah* in 1717. Visitors can pore over a legend detailing an accurate account of Bellamy's pirating journey through Honduras, Panama, and the Caribbean.

Capture of the *Whydah*

Bellamy chased the ship for three days before capturing her in the central Bahamas. After boarding the ship and forcing off the merchant crew, Bellamy spent days refitting the vessel from a slave ship to a pirate ship. There is a painstakingly-detailed scale model of the *Whydah* and a computerized virtual tour of the ship that looks into the configuration of the spaces below deck.

Cannons were kept loaded at all times to ward off attack. Three cannons are on display, along with a 10-step explanation of how to fire one. (It took four to six men to operate one mounted cannon.) Also shown are recovered weapons, such as sword pieces, pistols, and grenades, along with interactive kiosks where individuals can attempt to tie a pirate knot and hoist the Jolly Roger. It is here where onlookers are introduced to three more members of the *Whydah* crew who ended up on the same pirate ship for very different reasons. They are:

- Hendrick Quintor, who was of African and Dutch descent and turned pirate when the Spanish brigantine he sailed on was captured. Although little is known about the lives of most black pirates, piracy did offer black men an opportunity to participate on an equal footing, and some achieved leadership positions. The *Whydah* had at least 30 crew members of African descent; the famous pirate Blackbeard's crew was 60% black.
- John Julian was a 16-year-old Miskito Indian from southeastern Central America. Julian was a pilot of the *Whydah,* navigating the ship out of difficult waterways or hiding it in secluded spots during frequent pursuits.
- John King was no older than 11, the youngest known pirate onboard the *Whydah.* According to legend, when the ship he was traveling on with his mother was captured by Bellamy, young John insisted on joining the crew.

Board the *Whydah*

Next, patrons board a life-size partial re-creation of the ship. First stop is the captain's cabin. These were Capt. Bellamy's private quarters—it is a small space and features replicas of the types of personal items he used in everyday life. Passengers then proceed "below deck" to the crew's quarters, which is crowded and cramped. These dioramas show how pirates led their daily lives aboard the ship. Authentic artifacts in this gallery include a tea kettle in which the pirates boiled water for cooking. In the early 1700s, stored water upon a ship quickly stank and squirmed with organisms, so pirates rarely drank it. Instead, they consumed anything else they could get their hands on—with rum being their first choice. In addition, sailors of the 18th century were responsible for their personal utensils and dishes, and pirates were no exception. The table setting seen here is inscribed with the initials of the pirate owner. These men ate well—even better than sailors of that time. Their meals included food and drink from looted ships as well as fish, turtles, and birds caught in their free time.

Some pirates were hardcore gamblers. Tokens used on this ship to compete in games such as backgammon, cards, or dice are on display. Those interested can delve deeper into the various roles and responsibilities pirates had aboard the ship: learning about the quartermaster (or purser), a position given only to those able to read and write. The ship's carpenter is seen here as well. He did not just refit the ship; when there was no doctor aboard, the carpenter doubled as the ship's surgeon.

Treasure

This section showcases a portion of the thousands of silver and gold coins from all over the world. When the ship sank, she was carrying booty plundered from more than 50 ships. There was a fortune onboard in gold and silver, jewelry from Africa, as well as elephant tusks, sugar, and other commodities. Visitors are welcomed to touch a few pieces of real pirate treasure—actual coins recovered from the *Whydah* shipwreck. Folklore has led many to believe pirates buried their treasure in the sand. As witnessed by the wealth in this gallery, the historical record does not support the legend.

Loss of the *Whydah*

This part of the exhibition focuses on the powerful Nor'easter that downed the ship—a large-scale video re-creates the violent storm. When it hit, the ship was a mere 500 feet from the beach, but the ocean's bitter temperature was cold enough to kill even the most skilled swimmers. Only two of the 146 people (130 pirates and 16 prisoners) aboard survived—and they faced a storm of controversy from the public awaiting them onshore.

Pirate's Fate

Both survivors soon were captured by authorities after stopping off at a tavern for an ill-advised drink. Seven months later, the men were found guilty of piracy and robbery and were hung on the harbor in Charleston, the tide lapping at their feet as they swayed from the gallows. On display here is a gibbet, a device not used to execute, but rather to display dead pirates. Authorities thought it was a good warning for those seeking a life of lawlessness.

During the Golden Age of Piracy, there were more than 2,000 pirates operating throughout the Caribbean and along the North American coast. Throughout the *Whydah*'s short lifetime, the British Navy never captured a single pirate ship.

Discovery and Recovery

In this final gallery, visitors can examine the recovery and conservation efforts led by Clifford and his staff. Shown is a sample of the devices Clifford's team uses underwater and in their laboratory on land. Onlookers can see firsthand the techniques and technologies employed to examine items recovered from the ocean floor, including concretions—a conglomerate of rock, sand, and clay that have formed around metal artifacts. Some concretions constantly are sprayed with water to preserve the artifacts within; others rest inside water tanks. If exposed to outside elements, the artifact could be lost forever. The original ship's bell (inscribed "Whydah Gally 1716"), for instance, is submerged in a large cylinder of water in order to preserve it. When the bell was found, it was the key to authenticating the shipwreck as that of the *Whydah.*

This time-consuming conservation takes many steps and, therefore, it can be several months before an artifact is removed safely from a concretion. An explanation of the conservation process and a demonstration of how digital X-ray technology and CT scans are used in underwater exploration are featured.

"Real Pirates: The Untold Story of the *Whydah* from Slave Ship to Pirate Ship," organized by National Geographic and Arts and Exhibitions International, is on view Feb. 27-Oct. 25 at The Field Museum, Chicago.

Wilderness Ordeal

Two hundred and fifty years ago, Major Robert Rogers and his rangers launched a daring wilderness raid against an enemy village, but paid a steep price.

JOHN F. ROSS

A dozen miles north of the British fort of Crown Point on the eastern shore of Lake Champlain, amid the button-bush, bulrush, and cattail wetlands that crowded Otter Creek's delta, Maj. Robert Rogers glassed down the lake for the lateen sails of a patrolling enemy French sloop or schooner. Pulled into hiding within the marsh lay 17 whaleboats, each bearing eight oars and provisions for a month. It was Saturday, September 15, 1759, in the midst of the French and Indian War, the titanic struggle between the French and British empires for dominion over North America.

Rogers's nearly 200 handpicked men waited patiently. His glass disclosed one sloop, then another, tacking smartly within the lake's close confines. Soon a schooner joined them. Had Rogers not pulled his craft inshore, these warships would have made short work of their small flotilla.

In the coming days, the expedition, which had just set out from Crown Point, would undergo perhaps the most grueling ordeal ever recorded in North American history, and in so enduring and surviving its members would write a new chapter in the roster of special operations. The British commander in North America, Jeffery Amherst, had finally approved Rogers's long-nurtured plan to make a bold and unprecedented strike against the village of Saint-François, 150 miles north as the crow flies into Canada. Since the early years of the 18th century, the Abenaki of Saint-François, strongly encouraged by the French, had launched dozens of terrorizing raids against British colonial settlements on the frontier. By playing the enemy's own game of waging fast, surprising, and destructive small-unit warfare, Rogers was gambling that he could take the heart out of the Indians' will to continue their alliance with the French—a bold wager indeed. No British ground expeditionary force in 70 years of colonial wars had even contemplated a long-range lunge of such operational scope or strategic intent.

Rogers intended to row 75 miles north from Crown Point to the lake's northeastern headwaters at Missisquoi Bay. That evening, no clouds or fog masked the waning quarter-moon, and so his impatient rangers had to wait again.

The next day Rogers noticed that a couple dozen men showed telltale signs of measles. With a full-blown epidemic on his hands not two days into the expedition, Rogers allowed the disease no further time to take its toll, posting 41 men, mostly invalids, under a minimum escort of healthy rangers, back to Crown Point within 48 hours of setting out.

Amherst's orders to Rogers had dictated: "You will march and attack the enemy's settlements on the south side of the river St. Lawrence, in such a manner as you shall judge most effectual to disgrace the enemy, and for the success and honour of his Majesty's arms. . . . Take your revenge, but don't forget that tho' those villains have dastardly and promiscuously murdered the women and children of all ages, it is my orders that no women or children are killed."

That day, the French flotilla dropped past their position of concealment toward Crown Point. The whaleboats hurriedly resumed their tortuous journey north, hugging the eastern shore. The long train of boats each kept close to the next, following the 25th of Rogers's 28 rules of warrior conduct—North America's first war manual—that he had written to help the British survive brutal wilderness warfare against highly experienced French and Indian adversaries. The rule not only prevented dangerous straggling but also made mutual assistance possible in the event that gummed seams burst or a westerly surge broadsided and capsized part of the column.

In the morning hours of September 23 the tired men pulled into the northern confines of Missisquoi Bay. A cold rain had pounded the open boats all night, soaking the woolen blankets wrapped around heads and shoulders. In strict silence, the men dragged the boats ashore and unloaded their supplies; then they overturned the craft and covered them with brush.

One hundred and fifty men in 17 boats could only be so quiet. Despite the insistent patter of rain, a small party of keen-eared Abenaki hunters hurrying for the warmth and brandy of the French fort at Île aux Noix, some 10 miles to the northwest, heard some unmistakably human sounds and hurried yet faster.

Unaware of this shadowy passage, the rangers had tucked at least a week's cache of provisions into the boats for their return journey. Rogers posted two Indian rangers to lie watch; should the enemy discover them, they were "with all possible speed to follow on my track, and give me intelligence." The raiders' destination still lay 72 miles away; they would have to wind as much as a third more of that distance to follow any practical path.

The small command moved directly east and away from Île aux Noix out into the gently undulating hardwood forest of what is now southern Quebec. While it still comprised a few more than 150 men, the force had already lost much of the Indian ranger complement and two of its three regular officers. Amherst had required Rogers to pick his men from the entire army, not just the rangers. As was often the case over the course of his military career, Rogers was struggling to build coherent working order among a disparate group. Time and again he strove to mold frontier individualists into effective battle formations by communicating effectively with unlettered pioneer Scots-Irish, praying Indians, British regulars, and flat-footed coast provincials. He trained his men rigorously and taught them extraordinary practical skills. Above all, he treated them in a challengingly respectful and equal spirit, taught them to overcome dread, and created a collective mystique. In doing so, Rogers innovated and codified a particularly modern—and American—brand of warfare still taught to special forces today and used in critical situations the world over.

As the men pressed ever deeper into the north country that first day, a French bateau patrol chanced upon a British oar floating in Missisquoi Bay—a discovery that, complemented by the Abenaki report, persuaded the French commandant at Île aux Noix, François-Charles de Bourlamaque, to dispatch 40 men under his best partisan leaders, the veteran ensigns La Durantaye and Langy, whose formidable force had nearly annihilated Rogers's at the desperate Battle on Snowshoes. In short order the French discovered the well-masked whaleboats, took tomahawks to most of the hulls, and then burned the remains to ensure that no enemy could reconstruct that means of return.

The discovery spurred Bourlamaque into a frenzy of activity. A sizable party heading north from Missisquoi Bay would have few logical targets—most likely Chambly, Yamaska, or Saint-François, Indian villages that acted as a sort of defensive perimeter for Canadian France. He immediately sent a courier to warn the authorities in Montréal and the governor of Trois-Rivières, 22 miles northeast of Saint-François, that Yamaska and Saint-François should be reinforced. He then moved nearly 400 men to the whaleboat landing. The trap was baited: the raiders would meet a warm reception in the north if the frontier garrison did not catch them first. Should they attempt to come back by way of Missisquoi Bay, they would be thrusting their heads yet deeper into a noose.

Oblivious to these mounting perils, Rogers and his men crossed the Rivière aux Brochets (near present-day Frelighsburg) and swung northeast. One or two days later, the mud-bespattered and gasping look-outs overtook the column, crying out the password and then articulating Rogers's worst fears: 200 French and Indians lay in ambush at the whaleboat rendezvous, while another 200 had picked up the trail. All chance of returning via Lake Champlain was gone. "This unlucky circumstance . . . put us into some consternation," wrote Rogers.

In an officers' council of war, he sketched out a desperate plan, which he acknowledged stood a good chance of failure. After ravaging Saint-François, the rangers would pass eastward by way of Lake Memphremagog, and then south to the Connecticut River valley and Fort No. 4, the northernmost British outpost on the river. He calculated that starvation would nevertheless overtake them long before they reached the fort (that way to safety being a good hundred miles longer than the Champlain passage), and so he planned to summon a relief party from No. 4 to rendezvous 60 miles up the Connecticut at the west-bank infall of the Wells River. Hard though the prospect was, the officers voted to push on.

Rogers charged 1st Lt. Andrew McMullen, who had gone lame, to carry an outline of the Wells plan to Amherst, "that being the way I should return, if at all." McMullen left shortly thereafter at the head of six rangers.

On they struggled north-northeast through the spruce bogs that laced southern Quebec. As the men forded cold, dark water the color of long-steeped tea, each step proved treacherous. Submerged unseen branches, roots, and logs ripped at moccasins and stubbed now-numb toes. Sleep proved difficult because "we had no way to secure ourselves from the water." They cut saplings and laid them down, overlaid by boughs and leaves "in Form of a raft" or "a kind of hammocks" on which they could grab a few hours of dreamless rest.

For nine days they trudged, beginning before dark and camping well after dusk, gaining less than 10 miles a day however great their effort. In the pervasive wet and cold, toenails dropped off, and despite the best efforts to keep feet dry, the first signs of trench foot became painfully manifest. And the tannin-rich water also induced painful stomach cramps.

Yet Rogers's plan worked. La Durantaye's 200 pursuers could not keep going against the bogs and frigid weather with Rogers's head start. Quitting the drowned lands, they swung westward over dry ground, then drove north, intending to catch the invaders as they emerged from this difficult country.

Between the spruce wetlands and the northward-running Richelieu River flows the Yamaska, a natural water highway and marker through the forest that led directly to the Abenaki village of Saint-Michel d'Yamaska, known to the English as Wigwam Martinique, some half-dozen miles south of where that river falls into the St. Lawrence. None of the French or Indians could imagine that an alien raiding party might venture through this wilderness without keeping to its course—which made Wigwam Martinique the logical target.

Should such a force veer northeast toward Saint-François, it would have to cross the river of the same name. And nine days after leaving their boats, Rogers's exhausted column indeed came upon that treacherous, rain-swollen watercourse, remarkably within a dozen miles of their target. They would have to wade across the several-hundred-yard-wide river—a task, Rogers wrote, that would be "attended with no small difficulty, the water being five feet deep, and the current swift." Realizing that fires to dry wet clothes, a necessity in the chill fall weather, could announce their presence, Rogers told his lieutenants to have the men strip and bundle their clothes into their packs and carry them as high as possible on their necks and shoulders.

Rogers motioned forward the corps's tallest man; he would step sideways into the river, facing upstream. Another large man behind him grabbed his waist, and behind him another, forming a human chain. Slowly they sidestepped across the torrent, occasionally losing purchase on the slippery and unsecured rocks. At times the current broke a man's grip and threatened to send the hard-pressed line spilling downriver behind him. But somehow they held on and made it across.

The northern shore, soft but firm underfoot, proved a godsend to the shivering force. After several hours of marching with the sun drawing close to the horizon, Rogers shinnied up a tree and spotted smoke from cooking fires to the northwest, only five or six miles distant. That evening they closed to within two and a half miles of Saint-François.

As the gray light began to kiss the tall riverbank pines half an hour before sunrise, shadowy figures filed silently to crouch by front doors and alongside the embankment paths leading to the water. The struggling dawn revealed the grisly presence of some 600 or 700 scalps swaying in the light breeze atop trophy poles; some even hung above the white-painted Jesuit church.

For nine days Rogers and his rangers slogged north through spruce bogs that ripped moccasins and twisted ankles.

Almost predictably, a musket discharged by accident, precipitating the attack. Yet Rogers's men worked with grim efficiency, bursting down doors, and "shot some as they lay in bed, while others attempting to flee by back Ways, were tomahawked or run thro' with Bayonets," reported the *Boston Gazette* with dispassionate relish. The tribe's tradition says that some warriors defended the thick-walled council house to the death. "The major, who was never known to be idle in such an Affair, was in every Part of the Engagement encouraging his Men and giving Directions," declared the *New-York Gazette*.

Some dozen villagers fled down the embankment toward their beached canoes, but "about forty of my people pursued them, who destroyed such as attempted to make their escape that way, and sunk both them and their boats." Oral tradition reports that the early sun caught the hat ornament of Abenaki elder Obomsawin just short of the farther shore, and a sharpshooter struck him dead. The disorienting fusillade and clamoring burst upon the Indians as though their winged spirit Bmola had swept through the village on an ill wind.

In a quarter of an hour or so the action ended, the attack "done with so much alacrity by both the officers and men, that the enemy had not time to recover themselves, or take arms for their own defense, till they were chiefly destroyed." A chief's two young sons had fallen to their knees crying "Quarter!" the only word they knew in English. The clamor subsided, and a handful of rangers stood with hot gun barrels and bloody bayonets and tomahawks, half incredulous at their success and braced against a counterattack that never came. Several emerged from the French church, one brandishing a 10-pound silver statue of the Madonna over his head in triumph. Inside they had torn tapestries from the walls and trampled the Host underfoot.

A little after sunrise, Rogers ordered all but three corncribs torched. Now some of the villagers hiding in the cellars or lofts streamed out, the women and children joining a small huddle of terrified prisoners; but others chose to die in the flames. The rangers heard fierce death chants from within.

The prisoners claimed that a 300-man enemy party lay in wait only four miles distant. Rogers ordered his men to stuff their packs with corn and warned against filling valuable space with loot, but many did not listen. They would pay for their greed.

On the afternoon of October 5, the day after Saint-François burned, 38-year-old Jean-Daniel Dumas and 60 French Canadian militiamen from Trois-Rivières, 16 miles to the northeast, dogtrotted into the ruined town. Some of the dead lay prepared for burial, rolled full-length in bark bound with cord. A wild-eyed figure in a heavy black wool cassock ran up to the belated rescuers. The settlement's curé, Father Pierre-Joseph-Antoine Roubaud, could barely contain his fury at those who had defiled his church and burnt his parsonage. One detail of Roubaud's tirade stopped Dumas short. The priest repeated that the rangers had carried off Nanamaghemet, or Marie-Jeanne Gill, the wife of the white chief Jean-Louis Gill of Saint-François, and their two sons, Antoine and Sabbatis.

This complicated matters. While his own small force could catch up fairly easily with Rogers, Dumas now had to move with unusual care for fear of putting the hostages at grave risk. Dumas was no stranger to battle or strategic raiding; his savvy leadership and quick thinking had turned certain defeat into a stunning victory when Braddock's army had knocked into them outside Fort Duquesne in 1755. A skilled orchestrator of Indian warfare, Dumas had long bedeviled British settlements.

The bitter surviving Abenaki braves needed little encouragement to go with Dumas. The women were already at work grinding dried corn and forming the flour into bear-grease cakes. Unlike barely digestible raw dried corn, sagamite was a perfect food for traveling.

Rogers's party, now swelled by six Abenaki women and boys and five newly unbound prisoners, had pushed southeast, paralleling the river but this time a mile more distant, so as to avoid hunting parties returning home. The men packed their cheeks with kernels of dried corn, letting their saliva soften the hard grain, the better to chew and digest it. At their infrequent halts they spat the mulch into their canteens for further soaking.

By the third or fourth day, after plodding some 30 miles, the strained command found the topography beginning to grow uneven and rugged as they entered the western flanks of the Appalachians. Rogers kept off game trails, so the going proved hard—dipping into ravines, negotiating the canopies of large blowdowns, pushing up steep inclines. Three weeks on the march with only a few hours' respite at Saint-François were starting to take their toll on speed and fitness. Long drenching downpours did little to improve morale.

Rogers kept flanking parties and a strong rearguard at constant alert, assuming that a well-fed and vengeful pursuit force could not be far behind. And something else bothered him as he urged his ragged rangers along: he had seen precious little game as they threaded through the woods. While their sheer numbers might have scared off some animals, even the good hunters whom he sent out after deer and bear came back empty-handed. The column found only an occasional partridge or red squirrel.

His men weakening by the hour, Rogers reviewed the options. Near present-day Sherbourne his officers urged that the party be split up to make hunting easier. Even though Rogers had envisioned reaching Lake Memphremagog, just a dozen miles to the southwest, from whence they could find an easier way to the Connecticut River, he agreed. The food situation was dire.

Rogers had struck a devil's bargain. Divided, the rangers lost the advantage of numbers they would have had against almost any force likely on their trail, even while they gained the ability to move faster, more silently, and less obtrusively. Would he regret this decision? All now depended on whether McMullen had made it through to Crown Point and arranged for reprovisioning on the Wells River.

Rogers split his command into "Small Companies," each of less than 20 men, excepting his own. An experienced officer would direct each group, each carrying a compass. Rogers would take the least effective and sickliest, his group and most of the others heading toward the rendezvous on the Wells. Those led by Capt. Joseph Waite, Ens. Elias Avery, and Lts. Abernathan Cargill and Jacob Farrington charted a course roughly similar to Rogers's, south and southeast. Ranger George Turner and William Dunbar of the 80th Light Foot decided on the risky but faster Indian war trail leading southeast to the Connecticut. Billy Phillips and Lt. Jenkins of the Massachusetts militia would each lead a party back to Crown Point, southwest through the Green Mountains.

Soon enough Dumas and his Canadians and Abenaki reached the point where Rogers's force had dispersed. His scouts quickly reviewed the signs and counted three diverging parties, not the 10 at least that had set off. Quickly dividing his own column and surging with the energy of a predator, he began to hunt rangers.

Two days after Rogers broke up his command, Dumas's men overwhelmed Dunbar and Turner's group, killing both lieutenants and five men and taking three prisoner. Eight rangers fought their way out as the Indians howled retribution, then scalped, stripped, and horribly mutilated the bodies, pitching the now unrecognizable corpses into a nearby beaver pond. Eventually the shaken survivors fell in with Rogers.

At nearly the same time, Dumas ran down Ensign Avery and his detachment but bided his time, despite his men's eagerness to strike immediately. He could see that Avery's group had gone beyond the limit of their resources, the men stumbling along, eyes fixed on the ground in front of their robotically moving feet.

On the evening of the ninth day, Dumas gave the order, and a handful of Indians plunged into the midst of the worn New Englanders. One cried out when he locked eyes with a warrior only two feet away. War whoops rent the air. Completely surprised, Corp. Frederick Curtiss and the others could not even struggle to their feet; Indian hands roughly pulled them up and long knives slashed off their blankets and leggings. The Indians and Frenchmen tied them naked to trees with tumplines, except for Ranger Ballard, whose hands and feet they bound. Then the vengeful, bereaved Indians plunged their knives into him, delighting in his screams until he died.

The French leader, surging with the energy of the predator, began to hunt the rangers.

Dumas's party then scalped Ballard, loosened the legs of the living prisoners, and set out. Sometime that evening two escaped,

Forefather of Special Operations

Robert Rogers was a large shaping influence upon what, a quarter of a millennium later, is called special operations. Ranger recruits at Fort Benning today hear Rogers's name soon enough as it rings through their orientation booklets; they learn his rules of conduct, North America's first written and truly New World war manual; and his steely presence crowns the roster of the most accomplished in the Ranger Hall of Fame on campus.

It may at first be hard to understand how the tradecraft of the modern-day special operator, parachuting into the Hindu Kush after the Taliban, or a lightning strike force pushing into the dangerous Pakistani borderland, could echo the efforts of men from a preindustrial community struggling through New England winters on hickory and deergut snowshoes. But while much has certainly changed, the basic relationship of warriors to their technologies, environments, and enemies have not: the need to use them effectively, and, in particular high-adrenaline moments, the ability to restate a problem and rework it in new, deadly effective—but above all in swift and confident—ways. The dynamics and tactics of small units aggressively penetrating hostile territory, often at night and in the teeth of extreme conditions, rely on the same critical factors for success now as then: a stress on mobility, security, surprise, and the pursuit of psychological ascendancy over an enemy.

Yet it is in the more intangible realm of raised consciousness and motivation of the extreme warrior that Rogers made his truly great and transforming changes. He stressed that the real index of a warrior was the ability to get up day after day—cold, wet, hungry, and often far worse—to march and fight again. Yet he knew as well that all sheer endurance alone could do was to get a person killed farther away from home.

He synthesized several powerful forces—the Enlightenment's new concern with understanding as an instrument of mastery, the tenets of Native American woodcraft and skill, doctrines that united war endurance to daily life, the frontiersman's gradually unfolding focus on long hunting, and the Scots-Irish immigrants' raw democratic insistence that Jack is as good as his master—into forging an elite force, leveraging intense group identification and esprit de corps into an edged tool that would change the face of warfare.

eventually falling in with Rogers's party. The next day the others came to a watercourse, probably the Saint-François, where their captors built bark canoes. On the evening of the fifth day, Curtiss walked into Saint-François and found five of his comrades lying butchered in the village center. An anonymous Frenchman wrote that "some of them fell a victim to the fury of the Indian women, notwithstanding the efforts the Canadians could make to save them."

Meanwhile Rogers and his party had worked their way southwest between Lakes Magog and Massawippi and shadowed the eastern shore of Lake Memphremagog. At every check Rogers harangued stragglers with prospects of what awaited them at the rendezvous. Soon they broke into the rugged northeastern highlands of Vermont.

Fortune had not entirely abandoned Rogers. In a marathon of their own and suffering from many ailments, McMullen's team had struggled the 100 or so miles back to Crown Point in nine days, arriving on October 3, the day before Saint-François fell. Amherst detailed Samuel Stevens, one of Burbank's New Hampshire rangers who had risen through the ranks to a lieutenancy five months earlier, to march in all haste to Fort No. 4 with a dispatch ordering its commander to furnish him with whatever was needed in the way of supplies, troops, and watercraft. Stevens would paddle up the Connecticut to the rendezvous and "there Remain with Said party, so long as You shall think there is any probability of Major Rogers returning that way."

The wreck of Rogers's command passed through great groves of American beech trees whose light gray trunks resembled elephant legs. The men grew irritable, agonizingly sensitive to cold, depressed, and simultaneously apathetic and easily offended. Game proved ever more elusive. Every so often they killed a partridge, but such small prizes could provide but little relief. The group took longer and longer breaks between marches. Many fell into listlessness, responding only mechanically to the major's still astoundingly effective commands to get up and move along. By now he was pulling out all his tricks, harvesting oyster and chicken-of-the-woods mushrooms. The men scraped the exterior bark off black birch trees and ate the mildly sweet, wintergreen-tasting inside pulp.

As hunger gnawed at their guts, they doubled over on the march to find what little ease they could. Want bit so deeply home that they resorted to roasting the Indian scalps so recently taken as trophies and boiling their leather belts and straps, chewing the tough material for any ghost of nourishment. Some ate their moccasins and the nubs of candles they carried. They boiled their powder horns and drank the thin broth.

Some of the men in Lt. George Campbell's group lost their minds and "attempted to eat their own excrements," he later told a contemporary historian. After many foodless days, the spectral column, crossing a small river, came upon the horribly mutilated bodies of Dunbar and Turner's hapless party, piled up floating among a tangle of logs in a stream running off a pond. "This was not a season for distinctions," wrote Campbell, and the men waded into the water, so ridden by hunger that they tore into the raw and rotting flesh as though it were the finest dinner they had ever eaten. Their cravings somewhat assuaged, "they carefully collected the fragments, and carried them off."

How far Rogers's own struggling band broke the last taboo remains unclear. One rarely reliable source claimed that he killed an Indian woman and cut her into pieces, although killing so useful a forager does not square with his practicality. Another ranger, one named Woods, claimed that a black soldier who had died was cut up; he himself ate the man's hand along with a trout he had caught, which "made a very good breakfast."

For all these incommunicable privations, a map that Rogers drew indicates that he had kept a clear head. On October 20, some eight days after the groups divided, he and his party encountered the steep-descending Wells River somewhere near present-day Groton. The distance from the dispersal point was some 80 miles as the crow flies, but they had been compelled to travel considerably more ground as their actual course had pulled them first southwest, then southeast. Five weeks had passed since they had left Crown Point.

On a tongue of flat alluvial grassland, formed by the Wells's confluence with the main river and cleared by generations of Indian farmers, they came upon a deserted camp, its fire still burning. The survivors, who had given everything to get here, looked at one another with incredulous eyes. McMullen had clearly gotten back with Rogers's request for resupply, but the relief—with their provisions—had decamped at most only a couple of hours before. Rogers's men fired their muskets in the air and hallooed with all the strength they could muster, but the wilderness quiet swallowed all noise, and they collapsed.

By cruel fate, the relief party—Lt. Samuel Stevens and five other men—had only just given up waiting after several days. What had prompted Stevens to abandon hope after so brief a vigil? The party did not lack for provisions. Perhaps they feared enemy patrols, or perhaps the still vastness awakened ancient terrors. Most likely, however, was that Stevens did not believe that even the great major could have pulled off so demanding a journey through such treacherous terrain, a bleak judgment so absolute that he had decided not even to cache provisions.

"Our distress upon this occasion was truly inexpressible," wrote Rogers, "our spirits, greatly depressed by the hunger and fatigues we had already suffered, now almost entirely sunk within us, seeing no resource left, nor any reasonable ground to hope that we should have escaped a most miserable death by famine." Still he pushed off to hunt, but with little effect, hampered by his own diminishing strength. The Connecticut, cold and fast, reminded the survivors hourly of the abundant food just 60 miles downriver.

He ate the man's hand along with a trout he had caught.

After six days Rogers, rested but weakening further, decided to "push as fast as possible toward No. 4, leaving the remains of my party, now unable to march further." A day or two earlier, he had gotten his men to fell uniformly sized pine trees with their tomahawks, then cut them to length to form a craft capable of supporting three men and a boy. Others of the unit dug up stringy but tough spruce roots, with which he bound the logs together near the water's edge. He selected Captain Ogden, an unnamed ranger, and the part-Indian boy Sabbatis, taken from Saint-François.

He left a Lieutenant Grant in command of the withering remnant, reiterating the importance of keeping the men somehow occupied. He had already taught Grant where to look for ground-nuts (*Apios americana*), a climbing perennial vine that carries large starchy tubers, which boiled or roasted taste like potatoes. Indians often planted them in wet ground near their settlements, and thus a good many of the Saint-François raiders probably owed their lives to the people they had set out to kill.

Solemnly pledging to return within 10 days, the major gathered his three companions and pushed off with makeshift paddles that "we had made out of small trees, or spires split and hewed."

The current bore them swiftly away; at first they spun in circles, fast learning how to keep in the midline of the river and avoid obstacles.

On the second day they nearly shot right over the roaring White Falls (near today's Wilder, Vermont), only narrowly escaping by throwing themselves into the water and thrashing ashore. The raft crashed over and broke into pieces, which the current dragged out of reach downriver. The sodden, exhausted crew worked their way around the boiling whitewater. Rogers sent Ogden and the other ranger off after red squirrels, while he and Sabbatis set about building a new raft—a challenging enough task even with adequate tools. The pair built fires around the bases of several pine trees and by sheer application brought them toppling down. Then they renewed the fire to divide the logs into roughly equal lengths.

The hunters returned with a "partridge"—either a ruffed or spruce grouse—and that scrap of sustenance gave them barely enough strength to try again. The following day, the fourth since they had set out, they bound the logs together, probably with spruce roots, again risking the river's power.

The roar of Ottauquechee Falls, 50 yards of pounding cataracts, alerted the dazed foursome just in time to make it ashore. Rogers and Ogden reviewed the situation. In his journals Rogers put it simply: they would not have been "able to make a third raft in case we had lost this one." Their only chance—a steep gamble in itself—lay in getting it down the rapids. Rogers stumbled over to a bush, probably beaked hazel, pulled out his long knife, and harvested dozens of thin, wiry stems. By knotting the ends one to another, the men slowly braided a strong rope and hitched one end to the logs.

Ogden, the other ranger, and Sabbatis stared with the nearly total apathy of the starving as their leader crabbed down the embankment to the bottom of the falls. They could no longer hear one another, but Rogers waved his arm, and Ogden pushed the raft out into the current. He kept a drag on the current's power with the hazel rope while guiding it as best as he could through the tangle of rocks. At the bottom Rogers prepared "to swim in and board it when it came down, and if possible paddle it ashore." The raft bounced, bumped, and tumbled through the rapids, remarkably without coming apart. As it drew nearer, Rogers built up what head of steam he could and jumped into the icy water, kicking toward it as hard as he could.

"I had the good fortune to succeed," he later wrote with characteristic understatement. The raft's worn-out complement then worked their way toward the shivering Rogers as he lay collapsed on the rocky shore beside the crude craft. The next morning they reboarded and once more shot downriver. Near Fort No. 4 they encountered woodcutters, who at first refused to believe that this haggard remnant could be the lead detail of a fine force that only a few weeks before had dared the wilderness. The workmen helped the survivors back to Fort No. 4, where one anonymous observer noted that the major "was scarcely able to walk after his fatigues."

At Rogers's steely insistence that a provision canoe must leave immediately, a detachment pushed off upstream within a half-hour. It reached Grant's party four days later, on exactly the promised tenth day after the rafters had pushed off. Despite his own exhaustion, Rogers coordinated other canoes to probe for survivors along the Ammonoosuc, dispatched couriers to the Sun-cook and Penacook settlements on the Merrimack with instructions to supply provisions to any rangers who might straggle in, and wrote up his report to Amherst.

All told, 63 survivors somehow made their way to Fort No. 4, and another 17 to Crown Point. Dumas's partisans and the bereft people of Saint-François had killed 18 rangers; nearly a dozen known prisoners had disappeared; and starvation had claimed some two dozen more, several during Rogers's desperate passage of the Connecticut.

Rogers calculated that he had lost three officers and 46 privates. The overall number may have been slightly higher, but clearly about a third of the 142-man command that had struck Saint-François had not returned—rather more than 50 percent of the number they had killed.

In April 1760 Rogers, still weak from the ordeal, traveled to Crown Point for the court martial of Lieutenant Stevens for "Neglect of Duty upon a Detachment to Wells's River in October last," before which he testified under oath that had Stevens "delayed but a day, or even some hours longer he would have saved the Lives of a Number of his party, who Perished in the Woods." Rogers's gaze set grimly on Stevens. By flouting his corps's prime directive of complete loyalty and never giving up on one's comrades, this weak-spined subaltern had doomed many good men to slow deaths.

The court found Stevens guilty and cashiered him "a poor reward, however," wrote Rogers, "for the distresses and anguish thereby occasioned to so many brave men, to some of which it proved fatal."

The raid's success lay not in the crude accounting of lives taken but rather in the psychology of two whole societies: it had shifted the balance of terror. None of the Indian villages or French towns along the St. Lawrence could now feel secure against overland attacks. By this time, Britain had prevailed in the French and Indian War west of the Atlantic, but the final outcome of the Seven Years' War on the European continent was still unclear. Events there might force the British to return their Canadian conquests, much as they had had to give back Louisbourg in Nova Scotia in 1745.

The brilliance of Rogers's idea of undertaking a raid of such scope lay not in any massive tactical effect but in its strategic ability to unnerve the enemy. Outmatched in troop strength and resources, the French had fought—as do all effective but outnumbered powers—by employing speed and surprise to amplify what assets they possessed. Throughout the war the only British soldier who got inside the French frame of mind was Rogers, a consummate hunter and lifelong careful student of his prey. His success lay in providing a mode of warfare that outmatched the other side in its strongest suit.

The Saint-François raid delivered a blow as bold and terrifying as the Deerfield Raid of 1704 to the psyche of the St. Lawrence frontier settlements. It also sent a clear message to all Indians allied with the French: their patrons could not protect them—and the English could move where they would.

From *American Heritage*, Summer 2009, pp. 32–43. Copyright © 2009 by John F. Ross. Reprinted by permission of the author.

UNIT 2

Revolutionary America

Unit Selections

Key Points to Consider

- Discuss Thomas Paine's pamphlet "Common Sense." What did it advocate with regard to the British, and why was it so popular?

- Why was French help so important to Americans with regard to the Revolutionary War? What role did Benjamin Franklin play in securing that help?

- Most slaves and former slaves fought on the side of the colonists during the Revolutionary War. Why did others side with the British? What incentives were there for them to do so?

- Discuss the differences between those colonists who wished to pry concessions from the British but who still wanted to remain in the empire, and those who sought nothing less than independence. How and why did the latter group prevail?

- What purposes was the Declaration of Independence meant to serve? Who were the audiences to which it was addressed?

- Analyze the article "Getting Out: The First Rule of Holes." Why was it so difficult for the British to find way of ending the conflict with the Americans?

Student Website
www.mhhe.com/cls

Internet References

The Early America Review
  http://www.earlyamerica.com/review
House of Representatives
  http://www.house.gov
National Center for Policy Analysis
  http://www.public-policy.org/web.public-policy.org/index.php
Supreme Court/Legal Information Institute
  http://supct.law.cornell.edu/supct/index.html
U.S. Senate
  http://www.senate.gov
The White House
  http://www.whitehouse.gov
The World of Benjamin Franklin
  http://www.fi.edu/franklin

We live in an age of instant communication. Our call to complain about a credit card may be answered by someone in India. Television satellites permit the simultaneous viewing of events all over the world. Imagine what it was like in the eighteenth century when it took weeks for a message to be delivered from London to one of the colonies, and weeks more to receive a reply. Under such circumstances the British understandably gave wide latitude to royal governors who were on the scene and who knew more about local conditions than could the bureaucrats at home. The fact that the American colonies were but part of the British world empire also discouraged attempts to micromanage their affairs.

According to economic theory at the time, an empire could be likened to an organism with each part functioning in such a way as to benefit the whole. The ideal role of a colony, aside from helping to defend the empire when the need arose, was to serve as a protected market for the mother country's manufactured goods and as a provider of raw material for its mills and factories. Because imperial rivalries often led to war, particular emphasis was placed on achieving self-sufficiency. An imperial power did not wish to be dependent on another empire for materials, especially those of strategic value such as shipbuilding materials that might be cut off if the two came into conflict.

With regard to the American colonies, those in the South most nearly fit the imperial model. Southern colonies produced goods such as cotton and tobacco that could not be grown in Great Britain, and Southerners were disinclined to become involved in activities that would compete with British manufactures. The New England and the middle colonies were another matter. Individuals in both areas often chafed at imperial restrictions that prevented them from purchasing products more cheaply from other countries or from engaging in manufacturing their own. What served to temper discontent among these colonists was the knowledge that they depended on the British army and navy against threats by other powers, most notably the French.

During the middle decades of the 1700s, London permitted the colonists to exercise a great deal of control over their own internal affairs so long as they played their designated economic role within the empire. This attitude, which came to be known as "benign neglect," meant that colonies for all practical purposes became nearly autonomous. The passage of time and the great distances involved combined to make British rule more of an abstraction than a day-to-day relationship. Most colonists never visited the mother country, and they might go months or years without seeing any overt signs of British authority. They came to regard this as the normal order of things.

This casual relationship was altered in 1763 when what the colonists called the French and Indian War came to an end after seven years of fighting. The peace brought two results that had enormous consequences. First, British acquisition of French possessions in North America meant that the military threat to the colonists had ended. Second, the war had been enormously costly to the British people who were suffering under staggering tax burdens. The government in London, taking the

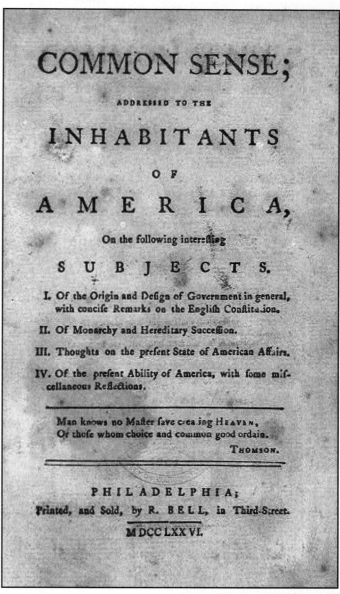

Library of Congress. LC-USZ62-10658

understandable view that the colonists ought to pay their fair share of the costs, began levying a variety of new taxes and enforcing shipping regulations that had previously been ignored. The new British crackdown represented to the colonists an unwarranted assault on the rights and privileges they had long enjoyed. Disputes over economic matters escalated into larger concerns about rights and freedoms in other areas. Many colonists who regarded themselves as loyal subjects of the crown at first looked upon the situation as a sort of family quarrel that could be smoothed out provided there was good will on both sides. When clashes escalated instead, more and more people who now regarded themselves as "Americans" began calling for independence from the motherland. Thomas Paine's pamphlet, "Common Sense," was an influential appeal for separation from the mother country. Once the Revolutionary War began, the colonists desperately needed financial and material help from the French. "Benjamin Franklin: Revolutionary Spymaster" analyzes his enormous contribution to getting that help.

"Dirty Little Secret" analyzes the relatively unknown fact that many slaves looked upon the British more as liberators than as oppressors. This article analyzes the revolution through the eyes of slaves and explains why they fought for the crown. "God and the Founders" discusses a dispute that arose at the meeting of the First Continental Congress over whether it should be opened with a prayer. The issue was resolved in such a way as to acknowledge religion without permitting it to become divisive.

Even after the early battles of the Revolutionary War, many colonists sought a negotiated settlement with Great Britain rather than to embark on the uncertain quest for independence. "The Rocky Road to Revolution" analyzes this debate and shows how those who wanted to break with the mother country triumphed. "A Day to Remember: July 4, 1776" tells how the Declaration of Independence emerged in its final form from the Second Continental Congress.

Early in the war, the French came to regard General George Washington as an ineffectual commander and sought to replace him with someone they thought would be more able. "The Baron DeKalb: Plotter or Patriot?" tells how the French tried to enlist DeKalb to help accomplish this. Instead, DeKalb become one of Washington's strongest supporters. "Getting Out: The First Rule of Holes" examines the difficulty Great Britain had in ending a seemingly endless war that was draining British resources.

The Gain from Thomas Paine

Thomas Paine, who died 200 years ago, inspired and witnessed the revolutions that gave birth to the United States and destroyed the French monarchy. A genuinely global figure, he anticipated modern ideas on human rights, atheism and rationalism. David Nash looks at his enduring impact.

DAVID NASH

At the end of President Obama's inaugural address in January 2009, he alluded to a small passage that appeared in Thomas Paine's pamphlet *Common Sense.* Faced with an American economy wracked by nervousness and self-doubt Obama noted Paine's rallying cry that galvanised and gave hope to the despairing:

> "Let it be told to the future world . . . that in the depth of winter, when nothing but hope and virtue could survive . . . that the city and the country, alarmed at one common danger, came forth to meet [this danger]."

Unique among radicals, the 200th anniversary of the death of Thomas Paine will be marked in England, in France and across the Atlantic. This is a measure of the impact of Paine's ideas both in his own country and in parts of the world that became the centre of revolutionary political change at the end of the 18th century. Paine was perhaps fortunate to live in such invigorating times and to be able to think about them so constructively. Yet what is remarkable is that his message has been capable of speaking with immediacy to each successive generation, providing radical inspiration and comfort in troubled times. This is because Paine was a persuasive author with a gift for penetrating, lucid and memorable language. However, he was also actively participating in the revolutions he wished to inspire. Both through word and deed he could justly claim "the world is my country and my religion to do good."

Thomas Paine's origins were anything but promising. He was born in Thetford in Norfolk in 1737 and was apprenticed to his father as a corset- and stay-maker, a trade that he followed intermittently. Some commentators would not let him forget this and later a number of cartoons portrayed his radicalism as an attempt forcibly to lace the English constitution in the shape of Britannia into an uncomfortable corset. After a spell in the capital, Paine embarked on a similarly lacklustre career as an excise officer. In 1768 he moved to Lewes, but debt and disillusion with this career led to his emigration to America in 1774.

Arriving in Philadelphia with a letter of introduction from Benjamin Franklin, Paine immediately began to mix with radical journalists and to make his mark. His first venture into radical journalism, as the editor of the *Pennsylvania Magazine,* was a success. The magazine focused on American colonial opposition to high-handed British policies and it flourished. From this success, Paine distilled his arguments for American independence into one of his most important pamphlets, *Common Sense*:

> . . . many strong and striking reasons may be given, to shew, that nothing can settle our affairs so expeditiously as an open and determined declaration of independence.

The pamphlet appeared in the first month of 1776 and by the end of the year had sold 150,000 copies in 56 separate editions. So impassioned was Paine that he enlisted himself in the colonists' fight for freedom, serving as aide-de-camp to an American general. He became a trusted adviser to Washington, coming to the practical and ideological defence of the colonists with a series of pamphlets under the umbrella title of *The Crisis.* These galvanised resistance and were responsible for stabilising the army's morale when it was on the point of collapse. Paine received the gratitude of the American nation and a number of states granted him pensions or gave him gifts in kind.

In the 1780s, after the defeat of the British forces and the gaining of American independence, Paine returned to England where he briefly switched his attention to scientific and engineering projects, in particular the construction of a single-span iron bridge. The movement between political science and pure science was not uncommon among Enlightenment thinkers. Just as mechanics and magnetism were mysteries of the natural world, the study of which would yield their significance, so too could similar analysis be applied to man's political instincts and relationships.

When the French Revolution ignited in 1789 Paine, though still a political animal, was initially preoccupied with other business. However, when in November 1790 Edmund Burke published *Reflections on the Revolution in France,* his shocked reaction to the violence in Paris, a response from Paine was guaranteed. Paine must have been surprised at Burke's apparent change of heart since Burke had also supported the American colonists. The two had met in 1788 and corresponded. Paine swiftly replied with what was to be his most famous and widely read work *Rights of Man,* published in early 1791. Written in an immediate and engaging style, it was spectacularly popular, selling in the region of 250,000 copies within the space of two years. Although Paine hoped for open debate, he found himself a wanted man for views that incited revolution and unrest and which threatened the established monarchical order in England. While he continued to lecture on constitutional change, government reaction was rising against him and in September 1792 he eventually fled to France, where he had been made an honorary citizen the previous month, missing the order for his arrest at Dover by some 20 minutes. In France he was feted as a defender and promoter of liberty.

"Government by kings was first introduced into the world by the Heathens . . . It was the most prosperous invention the Devil ever set foot for the promotion of idolatry"

Thomas Paine, Common Sense

Paine now took a role in the revolutionary government of France and was one of only two foreigners to be elected to the country's National Convention. He was instrumental in ensuring Louis XVI was tried but also argued against his execution. Meanwhile, in England Paine had been convicted in his absence of seditious libel and this effectively ended his relationship with the land of his birth. He also fell out of favour in his adopted country, falling victim to the factionalism and political upheavals that wracked France. He was imprisoned at the end of 1793, possibly on the fabricated grounds that he was an enemy alien. Indeed, several Americans in post-revolutionary Paris petitioned for Paine's release on the grounds that he was an American citizen and was deserving of that country's protection. Narrowly escaping execution when others imprisoned with him went to the guillotine, his American connections eventually saved him and he was freed with the help of the American ambassador James Monroe on November 4th, 1794. Within a few years Paine was rehabilitated by the Convention and was voted a pension.

During the troubled early years of the 1790s Paine wrote another of his most enduring works, *The Age of Reason.* This was intended to undermine the pretensions of established religion and the structures associated with it.

Paine eventually returned to America in 1802 to discover that he was no longer a hero. He had quarrelled with Washington and this was remembered by those who revered the country's first president after his death in 1799. Paine's anti-Christian views were also extremely unpopular and were more readily recalled than his earlier exertions for the young republic. His last years were characterised by ill-health exacerbated by his periods of imprisonment. His mood was not helped by a series of small slights and the refusal of financial support which he took to be poor recompense for all he had done for the cause of American freedom. He died in 1809 a somewhat bitter man. Even his

dying wish to be interred in a Quaker cemetery was refused. His funeral was a miserable affair and he was mourned by a tiny group of friends and two African-Americans who wanted to pay tribute to one of the few founding fathers of the United States who had argued against slavery.

Paine's story might have belonged solely to the 18th century were it not for the importance of his ideas, the captivating nature of his writing and its dramatic appeal. Paine's skill at producing political tracts for specific purposes was aided by his ability to write quickly when the mood took him. He was also adept at creating memorable phrases that enlivened his major works, ensuring them a wide audience. Paine's fame and legacy largely rests on the ideas and concepts conveyed in his three central works *Common Sense, Rights of Man* and *The Age of Reason.* In a sense these represent a fitting trio since each was written in one of the three countries whose welfare preoccupied his life: America, Britain and France, and each addressed the particular problems those countries faced at a historic moment in time.

Common Sense conveys a breathless energy and appetite for change. In its first few pages Paine urges the American people to form a government from scratch, a chance almost without precedent, which the colonists should grasp with both hands since it was likely this would be their best opportunity. The fact that this would lead to conflict and a swift call to arms was a dramatic consequence that should be recognised:

> By referring the matter from argument to arms, a new era for politics is struck; a new method of thinking hath arisen. All plans, proposals . . . are like the almanacks of the last year, which though proper then, are superseded and useless now.

Paine argued that the American colonists had right and justice on their side in their struggle for independence. He also suggested that the colonies could afford such a break with Britain since they were prosperous and economically independent. However, he did not simply offer these as arguments for freedom, but went further to ask Americans to think about what they wished to do with their independence once they had gained it. Paine demonstrated that American freedom was wholly justified since the ancient, corrupt and privilege-ridden British monarchy had dispensed with fairness and justice in favour of coercing the colonies into submission.

By seeking independence the colonies could cast off such tyranny and look forward to the creation of a new society that would be governed by properly elected and accountable representatives of the people. Paine sketched the form this government might take and also suggested crucial social reforms to promote and sustain the common good. This blend of radical political ideals with concrete schemes for reforms of everyday life was a theme he would return to. Nonetheless, his immediate intention in *Common Sense* was to show how a break with the forms of organisation of the old world was essential. In so doing he unashamedly urged republican thinking: "Government by kings was first introduced into the world by Heathens," he wrote, "from whom the children of Israel copied the custom. It was the most prosperous invention the Devil ever set on foot for the promotion of idolatry." Individuals were not protected or

Edmund Burke before Marie Antoinette, 1790 satire (Library of Congress)

When Paine came to write in defence of English liberty his thoughts upon the subject were able to be couched as replies and refutations to the arguments presented in Burke's *Reflections*. Outraged and alarmed by the consequences of the French Revolution, Burke argued for a retention of what was antique, tried and tested. The destruction of the apparatus of the *ancien régime* clearly alarmed those who felt civilisation itself would be compromised in France and beyond. Burke argued that the English constitution was robust and should be defended because it had stood the test of time and had conveyed benefits upon its citizens. It operated through a system of checks and balances that always represented a control on each area of government, ensuring against overmighty subjects or tyrannical kings.

Burke argued this system had evolved organically and had thus been able to incorporate gradual change and newly developing interests. Moreover, it was capable of recognising that those who had a stake in the welfare of society were those best able to govern and those most likely to govern justly and for the benefit of the community. Burke focused upon the Glorious Revolution of 1688 as a dramatic illustration of his case. The tyrannical James II had been persuaded to abdicate in favour of the reforming William of Orange. Not surprisingly, many have seen this as a blueprint for more modern forms of conservatism that see society protected by property ownership and trust in governing institutions.

Paine challenged Burke's arguments, suggesting that they were an overblown defence of vested interests and privileges. His anger towards Burke's position played out in a carping personal attack on his writing style in the opening sections of *Rights of Man*. Paine noted that the so-called legitimate monarchy Burke was so fond of rested on the actions of an "armed banditti" led by someone who in his own land had been known as "William the Bastard". In this Paine was stoking the radical idea of the "Norman Yoke" which posited that freeborn Englishmen had been dispossessed by the Anglo-French interlopers who had taken control of the country after the Conquest of 1066.

Rejecting Burke's view that a country's government was organic and preordained by providence, Paine saw this tradition as an intolerable burden, one which fostered what he called "Old Corruption", a conspiracy in which those who produced little or nothing defrauded those who created the nation's wealth. Paine argued instead that individuals were not born to their position in life but came into the world with certain basic, indestructible rights. These gave individuals freedom to make choices about everything, including the type of government they wished for themselves. No previous generation had any right to predetermine the nature of this government or to commit subsequent generations to its will. "Man has no property in man, neither has one generation a property in the generations that are to follow," Paine wrote.

Age of Reason has attracted attention from some rather different quarters. Paine was a vociferous opponent of organised religion, writing that "All national institutions of churches, whether Jewish, Christian or Turkish [Islamic], appear to me no other than human inventions, set up to terrify and enslave mankind, and monopolise power and profit." But he was anxious to

privileged by birth or position in the society he envisaged. He answered those who wondered where America might find its future monarch with the telling phrase "the Law is King". The accountability of people for their actions was seen as a central core of the new society, a reflection of wider Enlightenment thinking that increasingly viewed humankind in terms of the individual.

Having given the American colonists the reason to fight, *The American Crisis* offered support when their backs were against the wall:

These are times that try men's souls. The summer soldier and the sunshine patriot will shrink from the service of their country; but he that stands now, deserves the love and thanks of man and woman . . . What we obtain too cheap, we esteem too lightly; it is dearness only that gives everything its value. Heaven knows how to put a proper price upon its goods; and it would be strange indeed if so celestial an article as freedom should not be highly rated.

save the French nation from its collapse into destructive anti-clericalism and atheism. Paine stopped short of holding this extreme position, seeing instead the hand of a creator at work in the universe. Much of the *Age of Reason* explored the effect of applying rational thought to the stories and accounts of the Old and New Testaments. Paine subjected these texts to the test of reason and concluded that their claim to ultimate truth was suspect. Facts appeared implausible and the textual consistency they would require if they were the truthful word of God was lacking, inviting not belief and reverence but ridicule. Importantly for his own deism Paine's *Age of Reason* pushed God and established religion further and further apart. This was apparent in his suggestion that a moral God who had created the universe as it was bore no relation to the God portrayed in the Bible, who was by turns jealous, devious and tyrannical.

Paine's ideas did not melt away after his death. For generations, his analysis made sense and inspired confidence in those whose Christian faith was wavering. *Age of Reason* has been regularly republished in cheap editions in both Britain and the United States up until the present day.

In the first years of the 19th century political radicals latched onto Paine's attacks on "Old Corruption" and how they might dismantle the privileged aristocratic rule inherited from the 18th century. These ideas spoke to artisans and small producers and laid the foundations for 19th-century examinations of wealth and its distribution, even if Paine's analysis which attacked the landed aristocrat would later be replaced by an indictment of the capitalist.

Although Paine's critique did not fit the analysis of later Marxist socialism he had an influence on social democratic ideals. With the collapse and discredit of Marxism in the years after 1989 interest in Paine, with his undiluted focus upon individual rights surrounded by a network of enabling social mechanisms, was to some extent revived. Yet some socialists never lost sight of Paine's meritocratic messages. E.P. Thompson saw him as a great publicist of the issues associated with freedom and wove him centrally into the narrative of his 1963 classic, *The Making of the English Working Class*. Thompson also acknowledged a debt to Paine for lessons about activism and writing for a purpose.

Thompson's involvement in the Campaign for Nuclear Disarmament (CND) echoed Paine's desire to get actively involved in the politics he wrote about. Similarly Thompson's *Writing by Candlelight* (1980), in which he despaired about the superpowers' relentless arms race and diplomatic posturing, was written for a purpose. Thompson may equally have concluded that, like Paine, he was living through a "time to try men's souls".

Similarly Tony Benn throughout his parliamentary career as a radical socialist has often referred to Paine's punchy political language and his inspirational quest for accountable government. When Benn met world leaders he would ask them three questions: Who had elected them? Were such elections fair? And, finally, did the people have a chance of getting rid of them? All these sentiments echo Paine and reflect the influence of a voice that speaks across the centuries. It might even be argued that Paine created the idea of the global village where individuals co-exist as citizens; certainly he was the first to make the message of individual and natural rights traverse boundaries in what, for the 18th century, was the blink of an eye.

Further Readings

G. Claeys, *Thomas Paine: Social and Political Thought* (Unwin Hyman, 1989)

I. Dyck, *Citizen of the World: Essays on Thomas Paine* (St Martin's Press, 1988)

J. Fruchtman, *Thomas Paine: Apostle of Freedom* (Four Walls Eight Windows 1994)

J. Keane, *Tom Paine: A Political Life* (Little, Brown, 1995)

B. Kuklick, *Thomas Paine* (Ashgate 2006)

T. Paine and J. Dos Passos, *The Essential Thomas Paine* (David & Charles, 2008)

M. Philp, *Thomas Paine* (OUP 2007)

B. Vincent, *The Transatlantic Republican: Thomas Paine and the Age of Revolutions* (Penguin, 2005)

DAVID NASH is Professor of History at Oxford Brookes University and the author of *Blasphemy in the Christian World: A History* (Oxford University Press, 2007).

From *History Today,* June 2009, pp. 12–18. Copyright © 2009 by History Today, Ltd. Reprinted by permission.

Benjamin Franklin: Revolutionary Spymaster

ERIC NIDEROST

On May 5, 1775, a packet ship arrived in Philadelphia after a six-week passage across the Atlantic from England. This was a common enough occurrence, since the city's bustling waterfront along the Delaware River usually teemed with ships carrying passengers and merchandise from all over the world. The ship nestled beside a waiting dock, its gangplank enabling the weary human cargo to plant their feet on dry land.

One of the passengers was an old man accompanied by his teenage grandson. The old man's face was distinctive, though not yet the icon it was later to become. A large oval face was framed by a fringe of long gray hair that fell unbound to his shoulders. Slightly hooded blue-gray eyes peered over rectangular glasses, and a well-shaped nose hovered above a thin slash of a mouth, just now pursed in concentration as he carefully walked down the swaying gangplank.

Benjamin Franklin was coming home to his adopted city after an absence of about a decade. He was the most famous man in colonial America, honored for his many inventions and his contributions to science. Franklin was also a public figure, comfortable in the world of politics and letters. Dr. Franklin—he held an honorary degree from Scotland's prestigious University of St. Andrews—had been an agent representing colonial interests in Great Britain.

Franklin's homecoming was bittersweet. There was a growing rift between Britain and its 13 American colonies, and Franklin had devoted months of time and effort trying to repair the breach and effect reconciliation. In truth, the good doctor was a very reluctant revolutionary, at least in the beginning. He loved Britain, and harbored dreams of "that fine and noble China vase the British Empire" growing ever greater in wealth and power.

The dream was becoming a nightmare, however, and the "noble China vase" was teetering on the edge of a precipice. One more gust of political turmoil and it would fall and smash into pieces. The last couple of years in England had not been happy ones for Franklin; in fact, they had transformed him slowly from ardent Anglophile to committed revolutionary.

Franklin had once been blindly in love with Britain; now the scales fell from his eyes. His efforts at reconciliation were spurned, a British minister characterizing Franklin as "one of the bitterest and most mischievous enemies this country [Britain] had ever known." Having heard the term "American" spat out like some loathsome obscenity, Franklin, his patience ended, decided to go home. He also decided that complete independence from Britain was the best course of action.

When Franklin arrived in Philadelphia, he could not be sure of his reception. Years before, he had written to a friend that there was a possibility he would be looked on "in England of being too much an American, and in America of being too much an Englishman." Those worries evaporated the moment Franklin and his 15-year-old grandson, Temple, touched shore. People shouted his name, and there were spontaneous cheers to mark his progress. As the word spread, church bells even pealed in welcome. But the colonies were in turmoil. The First Continental Congress denied that the British Parliament had any authority to tax the colonies. That, the first Congress insisted, was exclusively the right of their own colonial assemblies. Rhetoric soon turned to bloodshed, when fighting broke out between Massachusetts farmers and British troops at Lexington and Concord.

A few days after Franklin's arrival, the Second Continental Congress met in Philadelphia in the Pennsylvania statehouse (now Independence Hall) on Chestnut Street to discuss the issues and plan a course of action. The birth of the United States was not an easy one, and it ultimately involved a long, painful and exceedingly slow gestation. In fact, it took a year, from the spring of 1775 to the summer of 1776, for a majority of congressmen to finally accept the reality of independence.

Benjamin Franklin was chosen to be one of Pennsylvania's congressional representatives only a day after his return from England. He accepted the post, but made sure that he did not reveal his true feelings on the touchy issue of independence. In the meantime, he served on several congressional committees, keeping up a pace that would have exhausted a 30-year-old, much less a man who had recently passed his 69th birthday.

Congress created a Continental Army for mutual defense and appointed George Washington, a distinguished Virginian, as its commander in chief. British troops in Boston were already besieged by American forces, and an expedition was soon organized to invade and capture Canada for the rebel cause.

While Congress deliberated, argued and occasionally dithered, questions began to arise in the minds of many members— should America seek foreign aid; would the United Colonies be better off if they entered into a foreign alliance; or should they go it alone, trusting in God and the righteousness of their cause?

Franklin, prescient as usual, foresaw the need of foreign aid. He wrote to a friend in July 1775 that Americans "have not yet applied to any foreign power for assistance, nor have we offered our commerce for friendship. Perhaps we never may; it is natural to think of it, if we are pressed."

These musings, which many felt but dared not speak aloud, took more concrete form after August 23, 1775, when King George III declared the colonies to be in open rebellion. While the majority of Congress still hesitated to make the final, irrevocable break with the mother country, it was deemed prudent to prepare for the worst.

To this end a Committee of Secret Correspondence was formed on November 29, 1775, with the mission of "corresponding with our friends in Great Britain, Ireland and other parts of the world." The last part of the sentence, "other parts of the world," seems to have been added casually, and made purposely unclear, perhaps to allay the fears of those members of Congress who still hoped for reconciliation. In reality, "other parts of the world" could only mean the rest of Europe, including Britain's hereditary enemies France and Spain.

The Committee of Secret Correspondence was, in fact, an embryonic State Department. (Its title was changed to Committee for Foreign Affairs in April 1777, once the need for secrecy had been obviated by the Declaration of Independence.) The committee's distinguished members included Franklin, Virginian Benjamin Harrison, John Jay of New York, Marylander Thomas Johnson and Pennsylvanian John Dickinson.

Benjamin Franklin quickly became the committee's most prominent member. He had many connections in Europe, and his fame abroad might open doors otherwise closed to America. Among intellectuals, he was celebrated as the "man who dared the lightning" and a true apostle of the Enlightenment. His famous experiment in the 1750s had proven beyond a doubt that lightning was indeed electricity. Franklin also created one of the first batteries, and even coined the use of the words "positive" and "negative" to describe electric charges.

Franklin immediately took up his quill, writing a flurry of letters to his still-wide circle of European friends. He entered the murky world of diplomacy and espionage literally at the stroke of a pen. Philadelphia was as yet unoccupied by British troops, but it was almost certainly occupied by British spies, so Franklin had to exercise caution. Where to begin? Charles Guillaume-Frederic Dumas was an intellectual, by some accounts a Swiss, who was living in The Hague. The Netherlands was no longer a great power, but its strategic location assured that it was a major "listening post" of European politics. In his December 9, 1775, missive, Franklin made Dumas an agent of the Committee of Secret Correspondence.

Acting as the committee's spokesman, Franklin told Dumas that America might find it necessary "to ask the aid of some foreign power." The latter's task was clear: "As you are situated at The Hague, where ambassadors from all the courts reside, you should make use of the opportunity . . . discovering, if possible, the disposition of the several courts to such assistance or alliance."

Franklin's hope of foreign aid was not as far-fetched as it may have seemed at the time. When King Louis XVI came to the throne in 1774, he appointed Charles Gravier, comte de Vergennes, as his new foreign minister. Vergennes was a career diplomat with a lifetime's worth of experience. A monarchist to the core, he did not understand the complex issues of taxation and self-government that were threatening to tear the British empire completely asunder. Vergennes was certain of only one thing—Britain's troubles might provide France with a golden opportunity for revenge.

France's defeat in the Seven Years' War was a national humiliation, and to suffer that defeat at the hands of the British only added to the disgrace. When the war ended, France was forced to surrender Canada and its vast holdings along the Mississippi River drainage. Only two small fishing islands off the south coast of Newfoundland, Saint-Pierre and Miquelon, remained of what was once a great French empire in North America.

Late in 1774 Vergennes wrote: "The quarrel between the colonies and the British government seems to grow more serious every day. . . . It may prove the most fatal blow to the authority of the metropolis [London]." The foreign minister wanted to help the struggling Americans provided, of course, that they proved themselves capable of winning. The French were not going to throw away money and possibly lives on a losing proposition.

But Vergennes needed to base his decisions on solid, reliable intelligence. Reports from America were often fragmentary and sometimes contradictory. Vergennes knew that ultimately the American revolt would be decided on the battlefield. Could an American "army of peasants" stand up to trained British regulars?

Adrien-Louis de Bonnieres de Sousastre, comte de Guines, was the French ambassador to the Court of St. James's. Though posted in England, he disliked the island kingdom and agreed with Vergennes that America could be helped and encouraged. Guines wrote, "I think it might be advantageous to us . . . to have among them [the Americans] a capable man who could judge the situation from the political and military standpoint, could foresee the course of events, and send reports by each merchant ship."

In fact, Guines had someone in mind for this mission, and lost no time sending a letter to Vergennes that lavishly praised the candidate. Chevalier Julien-Alexandre Achard de Bonvouloir was a retired officer of the elite *Régiment du Cap* who had recently returned from America, where he had established many solid contacts. Guines admitted that Bonvouloir had a handicap—he was lame—but that he was intelligent and fully capable.

Guines also noted that Bonvouloir was cost effective, willing to undertake the secret mission for 200 *louis d'or*. "If nothing is accomplished," explained the French ambassador, clinching his argument, "it is only the loss of 200 louis." The comte de Guines exaggerated many of his young protégé's attributes. Bonvouloir, 26, was the black sheep of an old Norman family who had squandered much of his inheritance. He had served in the *Régiment du Cap*, but only as a volunteer.

Bonvouloir was a "prodigal son" who desperately wished to get back into his family's good graces. He also hoped to become a commissioned army officer, and carve out a brilliant military career. Bonvouloir mainly wanted recognition, not money, for his efforts, and this was his golden opportunity to prove himself on the world stage. He was determined to succeed at any cost.

Vergennes was convinced, and a short time later Bonvouloir was given the assignment. Nobody cared that the young French noble had no espionage experience and did not even speak English. Vergennes did give the fledgling spy a detailed set of instructions, an oblique acknowledgment of his inexperience. He was to carry no written instructions, nothing that would incriminate him or the French government. Bonvouloir was to keep his eyes and ears open, recording his impressions in minute detail. Vergennes stressed that he was not to represent himself as an official agent of France, but merely as an "Antwerp merchant" with vaguely powerful "friends" back in Europe.

In keeping with his "Antwerp merchant" guise, letters would have to be full of routine business details. This was a cover, in case the missives were intercepted by British agents. The secret portions were to be written in a kind of invisible ink made of milk, which could be developed and read only when heated with a hot shovel.

Bonvouloir was not to make any commitments, but nevertheless assure the Americans of French sympathy and best wishes. As a further expression of goodwill, Bonvouloir was to tell the Americans the French had no designs on Canada. The memory of the Seven Years' War, with its devastating French and Indian raids along the frontier, was still fresh in most American minds. Americans had spent blood and treasure evicting France from Canada in the late war, and did not wish to see the French flag rising once again over Montreal and Quebec.

Once American fears were assuaged on that score, Bonvouloir was to move on, hinting that French ports would be open to trade once independence was declared. Vergennes was well aware that many Americans hesitated to break with Britain; veiled offers of French trade and assistance might tip the scales for independence.

Vergennes made it clear that the first person he wanted Bonvouloir to contact was Benjamin Franklin. Franklin's scientific writings were well known in France, and the doctor himself had visited Paris in the 1760s. Franklin was a man of influence, tact and intelligence, and also sat on several important congressional committees. The Philadelphia printer would be the perfect conduit to express France's encouragement to a vacillating Congress.

Bonvouloir set sail for America on September 8, 1775. Unfortunately his ship was buffeted by autumnal gales, storms so severe the journey took twice as long as usual. "I had a frightful passage," he wrote. "I had one hundred days at sea, twenty times I thought I should perish; I was reduced to two biscuits a day . . . a little salt beef and stale water."

Once ashore, Bonvouloir's next question was how to make contact with Benjamin Franklin. Franklin was a great man, and busier than usual during those hectic and tumultuous times. Bonvouloir had no credentials, no official status. He did not even have a letter of introduction, which was a common way of meeting well-known figures in those days. The chevalier did have one friend—really, just an acquaintance—who might provide the access to Franklin that Bonvouloir desperately needed.

Francis Daymon was a merchant who had been born in Paris and immigrated to Philadelphia, where he married an American woman. He spoke English well, and supplemented his income by tutoring people in French. Above all he was a part-time librarian with Franklin's Library Company. Franklin had hired Daymon, and some accounts say the Frenchman also helped Franklin brush up on his French.

The Library Company, founded by Franklin and a group of friends in 1731, was the first circulating library in America. Books were costly in the colonial period; a single tome could cost an average man a month's salary. The Library Company allowed subscribers to pool their money and buy books for the benefit of all. By 1770 the library boasted some 2,033 volumes, and the number grew every day.

Space was at a premium, so the Library Company moved into the second floor of Carpenter's Hall by 1774. Carpenter's Hall was a classic specimen of Georgian architecture, formed in the shape of a Greek cross and crowned by a shining white cupola. It had been the site of the First Continental Congress, and many delegates had borrowed books from the Library Company's upstairs holdings. Daymon took care of the collection, recorded who took out the books and who returned them, and did shelving and other related chores.

Bonvouloir contacted Daymon and dropped enough hints to give the librarian some idea—however vague—of his mission. Daymon told Bonvouloir he would do what he could, and he proved a man of his word. When the librarian told Franklin about the encounter, the latter was naturally suspicious. Bonvouloir might well prove a double agent, or even an out-and-out British spy. Traitors to the Crown were hanged. If Franklin and the Secret Committee spoke too freely to this man, they might end up with a noose around their necks. With all the danger involved, it was ironic that the name Bonvouloir meant "goodwill" in English.

Franklin, after some further deliberation, felt the potential benefits more than justified the risks. It was clear that next year's campaign was going to be crucial for the American cause. Help was needed, and needed soon. In spite of Bonvouloir's fervent disavowals, it was clear he was acting on the orders of the French government. The French may have been slow, tentative and perhaps even irritating, but they were finally showing signs of abandoning their official neutrality. Bonvouloir's mission was a significant first step in that direction.

It was agreed that members of the Committee of Secret Correspondence would meet with Bonvouloir, but only under conditions of utmost discretion. Carpenter's Hall was chosen for the nighttime rendezvous. The meeting would involve only four men: Franklin, fellow committee member Jay, Francis Daymon and the mysterious Frenchman. It was best to keep participants to an absolute minimum; a larger group would only attract unwanted attention.

Daymon was needed to act as an interpreter. Franklin knew how to read French, having taught himself the rudiments of the language as early as the 1730s. He also knew how to speak a little French, but he was far from fluent at the time, and it was important that no misunderstandings arise due to mistranslation.

As things turned out, there were three long meetings with the French agent, all occurring between December 18 and 27, 1775.

The first meeting set the pattern for the rest. One chilly night Franklin slipped on a cloak and walked to Carpenter's Hall. It was agreed that each participant would go to the rendezvous separately, using different routes, and strictly under the cover of darkness.

Franklin's great brick house on High Street was only about a block from the hall, so he didn't have far to go. It was ironic that, thanks to Franklin, Philadelphia boasted the best lighted streets in the country. Four-sided lamps, designed by Franklin himself, hung suspended from tall poles and gave out a strong glow. Under those street lamps, his bulky silhouette easily could be seen as he trudged through the frigid streets.

Once Franklin showed up—the last to arrive by some accounts—Daymon led the party up the stairs to the second floor by the light of a flickering candle. He had already made sure that the building's shutters were tightly fastened, lest any telltale beam of light betray the fact that Carpenter's Hall was not empty. The stairs bore an uncanny resemblance to the kind seen on scaffolds. For all these men knew, this might be a dress rehearsal for a climb of a more sinister kind.

The second floor of Carpenter's Hall was divided into two large rooms. The east room housed the Library Company's books, while the west room was home to its many scientific devices and equipment. In 1774 the west room was described as a "handsome Appartment [sic]" where "apparatus is deposited and directors meet." Cluttered as the west room was with telescopes, air pumps and electrical devices, the east room was a logical place to conduct the secret talks. It was, after all, where the library directors met.

John Jay later recalled Bonvouloir as an "elderly, lame gentleman, having the appearance of an old, wounded French officer." It's a curious description, because the chevalier was in his mid-20s at the time. He did have a game leg, but nothing else fits. Jay's story does conjure up yet another intriguing possibility—that Bonvouloir was in disguise.

The chevalier de Bonvouloir rigidly adhered to his instructions. "I made them no offer," he proudly recalled later, "absolutely none." But Franklin and Jay assumed—correctly—that he was a French agent, and acted accordingly. Apparently Franklin took the lead in the discussions, and though the tone was friendly, Bonvouloir was put on the defensive.

"These affairs are so delicate," he admitted, "that with all the goodwill possible, I tremble as I advance." Franklin and Jay cut to the chase. They wanted to know if France would aid America, and at what price. The chevalier said that yes, France might come to the rebels' aid, but he did not know what the condition would be.

Franklin apparently asked if France was favorable to the American cause. Bonvouloir pleaded ignorance, explaining he was only a "private citizen." When pressed, the chevalier opined that France did wish them well. Benjamin Franklin knew that few American officers had training in European warfare. When the Frenchman was asked if his country might supply two good military engineers, Bonvouloir was evasive, but promised to forward the request to friends back home.

America was rich in a variety of natural resources, but poor in gold or silver specie to pay for arms. Franklin queried Bonvouloir about the possibility of obtaining arms and munitions in exchange for American commercial goods. Once again the chevalier gave a conditional assent, but stressed the French government would not take part in such transactions. Instead, business would be conducted by private French merchants.

The meetings concluded on an upbeat note. In spite of Bonvouloir's attempts at evasion, it was clear that France was indeed interested in helping the American cause. This was encouraging to Franklin and Jay.

As soon as the last session was over, the chevalier quickly sent messages back to France as instructed. On December 28, Bonvouloir penned an account of both the clandestine encounters at Carpenter's Hall and his impressions of the general situation. Many of his statements are exaggerations, the narrative peppered with facts that sound plausible but are ultimately false. There is no deliberate attempt to deceive his superiors; it's obvious from the tone that Bonvouloir believes what he is saying. Much of the report is a product of a fevered imagination desperate to achieve success.

The evidence is circumstantial, but Franklin's own "fingerprints" seemed to be all over Bonvouloir's report. Ben Franklin was a skilled propagandist, and it looks as if he filled the Frenchman's head with facts and figures to suggest America was in a better position than it really was. Some of Bonvouloir's statements bear suspicious similarities to some of Franklin's own letters to foreign friends that year.

Bonvouloir saw the budding Revolution in a favorable light, as when he boldly states, "The Confederates [Americans] are preparing themselves extensively for the coming spring." This sounds much like Franklin's letter of December 9, 1775, when the printer speaks glowingly of how "our artificers are also every where busy in fabricating small arms, casting cannon, etc."

The French emissary reported: "Everyone here is a soldier, the troops are well clothed, well paid and well armed. They have more than 50,000 regular soldiers and an even larger number of volunteers who do not wish to be paid. . . . Nothing shocks or frightens them, you can count on that. Independency is a certainty for 1776."

This, of course, was a wild exaggeration. Washington's Continental Army never had more than 18,000 to 20,000 men at a time, and usually the figures were much lower. The troops were badly paid, often badly clothed, especially in winter, and had to endure periods of sickness and semi-starvation. Ironically, the only one of Bonvouloir's predictions that proved accurate was that America would declare its independence from Britain.

The Secret Committee of Correspondence was encouraged by the chevalier de Bonvouloir's clandestine visits, so much so that on March 2, 1776, they appointed Connecticut lawyer and revolutionary leader Silas Deane as a special envoy to negotiate with the French government.

On the French side, Bonvouloir swallowed the committee's propaganda hook, line and sinker. When his wildly positive report reached France on February 27, 1776, it gave Vergennes more ammunition to persuade King Louis XVI to aid the rebellious colonies. France and Spain were not ready for open hostilities, but it was secretly agreed by both parties that the rebellion must be kept alive as long as possible.

Meanwhile, another pro-American Frenchman was enlisted as a middleman between the two nations. Pierre Augustin Caron de Beaumarchais was a flamboyant man of many talents, author of the play *Barber of Seville* and later *Marriage of Figaro*. Among his other accomplishments, he was a French spy, passionately devoted to the American cause. In April 1776, Vergennes wrote to Beaumarchais: "We will secretly give you one million *livres*. We will try to obtain an equal sum from Spain. [He did.] With these two millions you will establish a commercial firm and . . . supply the Americans with arms, munitions, equipment. . . ." Once the funds were in hand, a dummy company—Hortalez & Cie—was set up to funnel arms and supplies to America. While still maintaining a precarious neutrality, France was now fully committed to providing substantial aid to the insurgent Americans.

The chevalier de Bonvouloir soon faded into obscurity. He stayed on in America for about a year, but accomplished little of consequence. After some wrangling he managed to get a commission in the French navy, sailed to India in his ship and died there in 1783.

After independence was declared, Franklin sailed for France on October 27, 1776, as a member of a commission authorized by Congress to negotiate a commercial treaty with Louis XVI's government. In 1778 Franklin signed a Franco-American Treaty of Alliance. Thus, from those first furtive winter meetings at Carpenter's Hall in Philadelphia three years earlier, aided by Franklin's wise guidance and diplomacy, emerged massive French moral, monetary, material and eventually direct military support for the American colonial cause.

Dirty Little Secret

To see the Revolutionary War through the eyes of slaves is to better understand why so many of them fought for the crown.

SIMON SCHAMA

Ten years after the surrender of George III's army to General Washington at Yorktown, a man known as British Freedom was hanging on in North America. Along with a few hundred other souls, he was scratching a living from the stingy soil around Preston, a few miles northeast of Halifax, Nova Scotia. Like most of the Preston people, British Freedom was black and had come from a warmer place. Now he was a hardscrabbler stuck in a wind-whipped corner of the world between the blue spruce forest and the sea. But he was luckier than most.

British Freedom had title to 40 acres, and another one and a half of what the lawyers' clerks in Halifax were pleased to call a "town lot." It didn't look like much of a town, though, just a dirt clearing with rough cabins at the center and a few chickens strutting around and maybe a mud-caked hog or two. Some of the people who had managed to get a team of oxen to clear the land of bald gray rocks grew patches of beans and corn and cabbages, which they carted to market in Halifax along with building lumber. But even those who prospered—by Preston standards—took themselves off every so often into the wilderness to shoot some birch partridge, or tried their luck on the saltwater ponds south of the village.

What were they doing there? Not just surviving. British Freedom and the rest of the villagers were clinging to more than a scrap of Nova Scotia; they were clinging to a promise. Some of them even had that promise printed and signed by officers of the British Army on behalf of the king himself, that the bearer so-and-so was at liberty to go wherever he or she pleased and take up whatever occupation he or she chose. That meant something for people who had been slaves. And the king's word was surely a bond. In return for their loyal service in the late American war, they were to be granted two gifts of unimaginably precious worth: their freedom and their acres.

It was, they told themselves, no more than their due. They had done perilous, dirty, exhausting work. They had been spies amid the Americans; guides through the Georgia swamps; pilots taking ships over treacherous sandbars; sappers on the ramparts of Charleston as French cannonballs took off the limbs of the men beside them. They had dug trenches; buried bodies blistered with the pox; powdered the officers' wigs and, marching smartly drummed the regiments in and out of disaster. The women had cooked and laundered and nursed the sick; dabbed at the holes on soldiers' bodies; and tried to keep their children from harm. Some of them had fought. There had been black dragoons in South Carolina; waterborne gangs of black partisans for the king on the Hudson River; bands of black guerrillas who would descend on Patriot farms in New Jersey and take whatever they could, even white American prisoners.

So they were owed. They had been given their liberty, and some of them got land. But the soil was thin and strewn with boulders, and the blacks had no way, most of them, to clear and work it unless they hired themselves or their families out to the white Loyalists. That meant more cooking and laundering; more waiting on tables and shaving pink chins; more hammering rocks for roads and bridges. And still they were in debt, so grievously that some complained their liberty was no true liberty at all but just another kind of slavery in all but name.

But names counted. British Freedom's name said something important: that he was no longer negotiable property. For all its bleak hardships, Preston was not a Georgia plantation. Other Prestonians—Decimus Murphy, Caesar Smith—had evidently kept their slave names as they had made the passage to liberty. But British Freedom must have been born, or bought, as someone else. He may have shaken off that name, like his leg irons, on one of the 81 sailings out of New York in 1783, which had taken 30,000 Loyalists, black and white, to Nova Scotia, for no one called British Freedom is listed in the Book of Negroes, which recorded those who, as free men and women, were at liberty to go where they wished. It is also possible that British Freedom could have found his way to Nova Scotia in one of the earlier Loyalist evacuations—from Boston in 1776 or from Charleston in 1782. In the frightening months between the end of the war and the departure of the British fleets, as American planters were attempting to locate the whereabouts of escaped slaves, many of them changed their names to avoid identification. British Freedom may just have gone one step further in giving himself an alias that was also a patriotic boast.

Whichever route he had taken, and whatever trials he was enduring, British Freedom's choice of name proclaims something startling: a belief that it was the British monarchy rather than the new American republic that was more likely to deliver Africans from slavery. Although Thomas Jefferson, in the Declaration of Independence, had blamed "the Christian King" George III for the institution of slavery in America, blacks like British Freedom did not see the king that way at all. On the contrary, he was their enemy's enemy and thus their friend, emancipator and guardian.

Tens of thousands of African-Americans clung to the sentimental notion of a British freedom even when they knew that the English were far from being saints in respect to slavery. Until 1800, when its courts decisively ruled the institution illegal, there were slaves, as well as free blacks, in Nova Scotia, and there were hundreds of thousands more in the British Caribbean. Nonetheless, in 1829 one of the first militant African-American emancipationists, David Walker, wrote from Boston in his Appeal to the Coloured Citizens of the World that the "English" were "the best friends the coloured people have upon earth. Though they have oppressed us a little and have colonies now in the West Indies which oppress us sorely—Yet notwithstanding [the English] have done one hundred times more for the melioration of our condition, than all the other nations of the earth put together." White Americans, on the other hand, with their posturing religiosity and their hollow cant of freedom, he consigned to the lowest reaches of hypocritical infamy.

Whether the British deserved this reputation as the most racially broadminded among nations and empires is, to say the least, debatable. But during the Revolutionary War there is no question that tens of thousands of Africans, enslaved in the American South, did look to Britain as their deliverer, to the point where they were ready to risk life and limb to reach the lines of the royal army. To give this astounding fact its due means being obliged to tell the story of Anglo-American conflict, both during the Revolution and after, in a freshly complicated way.

To be sure, there were also many blacks who gave the Patriots the benefit of the doubt when they listened and read of their war as a war for liberty. If there was a British Freedom, there was also a Dick Freedom—and a Jeffery Liberty—fighting in a Connecticut regiment on the American side. Blacks fought and died for the American cause at Concord, Bunker Hill, Rhode Island and finally at Yorktown (where they were put in the front line-whether as a tribute to their courage or as expendable sacrifices is not clear). At the Battle of Monmouth in New Jersey, black troops on both sides fought each other. But until the British aggressively recruited slaves in 1775 and 1776, state assemblies, even in the North, as well as the multistate Continental Congress, flinched from their enlistment. In February 1776 Congress instructed Washington that, while free Negroes might be retained, no more should be enlisted. Slaves, of course, were to be excluded from the Continental Army set up by Congress.

By contrast, the proclamation of John Murray; Lord Dunmore, the last Colonial governor of Virginia, from HMS William on November 7, 1775, unequivocally promised outright liberty to all slaves escaping from Rebel plantations, reaching British lines and serving in some capacity with the army. The promise was made from military rather than humanitarian motives, and for every British Freedom who lived to see it kept, there were many more who would be unconscionably betrayed. Yet from opportunist tactics, some good might still arise. Dunmore's words, sanctioned by the British government and reiterated by Generals William Howe and Henry Clinton (who extended the definition of those entitled to liberty to black women and children), took wing in the world of the slaves, and they themselves took off, in their tens of thousands, shortly after.

Seeing the Revolutionary War through the eyes of enslaved blacks turns its meaning upside down. In Georgia, the Carolinas and much of Virginia, the vaunted war for liberty was, from the spring of 1775 to the late summer of 1776, a war for the perpetuation of servitude. The contortions of logic were so perverse, yet so habitual, that George Washington could describe Dunmore as "that arch traitor to the rights of humanity" for promising to free slaves and indentured servants.

Henry Melchior Muhlenberg, a Pennsylvania Lutheran pastor, knew what he was talking about when he wrote that the black population "secretly wished the British army might win, for then all Negro slaves will gain their freedom. It is said that this sentiment is universal among all the Negroes in America." And every so often truth broke through the armor of Patriot casuistry. In December 1775, Lund Washington wrote to his cousin George of both blacks and indentured servants, who were departing from the Washington properties at speed, that "there is not a man of them but would leave us if they believ'd they could make there [sic] escape . . . Liberty is sweet."

The founding fathers were themselves candid about the extent of the disappearance of their slaves, not least because so many of them experienced serious personal losses. Thomas Jefferson, who had seen his own attempt to incorporate a paragraph attacking slavery in the Declaration of Independence stricken out by Congress, lost 30 of his own during the few weeks in the spring of 1781, when Lord Cornwallis' troops were not far from his home, Monticello. He believed—and the judgment of most modern historians concurs—that at least 30,000 slaves had escaped from Virginia plantations in attempts to reach the British lines. The same went for the rest of the South.

The story of this mass flight, aptly characterized by historian Gary Nash as the Revolutionary War's "dirty little secret," is shocking in the best sense, in that it forces an honest and overdue rethinking of the war as involving, at its core, a third party. This third party of African-Americans, moreover, accounted for 20 percent of the entire population of 2.5 million Colonists, rising in Virginia to as much as 40 percent. When it came to the blacks caught up in their struggle, neither side, British nor American, behaved very well. But in the end, as British Freedom and multitudes like him appreciated, it was the royal, rather than the republican, road that seemed to offer a surer chance of liberty. Although the history that unfolded from the entanglement between black desperation and British paternalism would often prove to be bitterly tragic, it was, nonetheless, a formative moment in the history of African-American freedom.

It was among the Loyalist Africans that some of the earliest free Baptist and Methodist churches were created in and near Shelburne, Nova Scotia; there too that the first whites to be converted by a black preacher were baptized in those red rivers by the charismatic minister David George. The first schools expressly for free black children were opened in the Loyalist diaspora of Nova Scotia, where they were taught by black teachers like Catherine Abernathy in Preston and Stephen Blucke in Birchtown. In Sierra Leone, where more than a thousand of the "Nova Scotians" ended up after journeying back across the Atlantic, this time as persons not property, the American blacks experienced for the first time (and all too ephemerally) a meaningful degree of local law and self-government. It was another first when an elected black constable, the ex-slave Simon Proof, administered a flogging to a white sailor found guilty of dereliction of duty.

The history of black loyalism, however, is much more than a catalog of "firsts." The story also gives the lie to the stereotype of the Africans as passive, credulous pawns of American or British strategy. Whether they opted for the Patriot or for the Loyalist side, many of the blacks, illiterate or not, knew exactly what they were doing, even if they could never have anticipated the magnitude of the perils, misfortunes and deceits that would result from their decision. Often, their choice was determined by a judgment of whether, sooner or later, a free America would be forced to honor the Declaration of Independence's principle that the birthright of all men was liberty and equality; or whether (in the South especially), with the spectacle of runaways being hunted down and sent to labor in lead mines or saltpeter works, fine sounding promises were likely to be indefinitely deferred. It was not a good sign when enlistment incentives offered to white recruits in Georgia and South Carolina included a bounty of a free slave at the end of the war.

Throughout 1773 and 1774 the tempo of reported runaways gathered ominous momentum from New York to Georgia. Escapes were now imagined to be the prelude to a concerted rising. In New York concern about illicit "assemblies" of Negroes was so serious that instructions were issued to apprehend any blacks appearing in any sort of numbers after dark. To the jumpier Americans it did not bear contemplating what might happen should the slaves, especially in the Southern plantation Colonies, take it into their head that the vaunted liberties of Old England somehow applied to them. In the Virginia Gazette, one of many advertisements offering rewards for the recapture of runaways mentioned a Gabriel Jones and his wife, said to be on their way to the coast to board a ship for England, "where they imagine they will be free (a Notion now prevalent among the Negroes greatly to the vexation and prejudice of their Masters)."

Now where could slaves get such absurd ideas? Another advertisement supplies the answer. One Bacchus, it seems, in Augusta County, Georgia, ran away, leading his master to believe that he too might head for a port, there "to board a vessel for Great Britain from the knowledge he has of the late determination of the Somerset case."

What was this? Did slaves read law reports? How could it be that a judgment rendered in June 1772 by Lord. Chief Justice Mansfield in the court of the King's Bench in the case of a runaway African, James Somerset, recaptured by his master, could light a fire in the plantations?

Mansfield had set Somerset free, but had taken pains not to make a general ruling on the legality of slavery in England. However, the "Negro frolicks" in London celebrating the court decision had swept legal niceties aside. Across the Atlantic word spread, and spread quickly, that slavery had been outlawed in Britain. In 1774 a pamphlet written under the name "Freeman," published in Philadelphia, told American slaves that they could have liberty merely by "setting foot on that happy Territory where slavery is forbidden to perch." Before the Patriots knew it, the birds had already begun to fly the coop.

SIMON SCHAMA is university professor of art history and history at Columbia.

God and the Founders

Battles over faith and freedom may seem never-ending, but a new book, '*American Gospel,*' argues that history illuminates how religion can shape the nation without dividing it.

Jon Meacham

America's first fight was over faith. As the Founding Fathers gathered for the inaugural session of the Continental Congress on Tuesday, September 6, 1774, at Carpenters' Hall in Philadelphia, Thomas Cushing, a lawyer from Boston, moved that the delegates begin with a prayer. Both John Jay of New York and John Rutledge, a rich lawyer-planter from South Carolina, objected. Their reasoning, John Adams wrote his wife, Abigail, was that "because we were so divided in religious sentiments"—the Congress included Episcopalians, Congregationalists, Presbyterians, and others—"we could not join in the same act of worship." The objection had the power to set a secular tone in public life at the outset of the American political experience.

Things could have gone either way. Samuel Adams of Boston spoke up. "Mr. S. Adams arose and said he was no bigot, and could hear a prayer from a gentleman of piety and virtue who was at the same time a friend to his country," wrote John Adams. "He was a stranger in Philadelphia, but had heard that Mr. Duche (Dushay they pronounce it) deserved that character, and therefore he moved that Mr. Duche, an Episcopal clergyman, might be desired to read prayers to the Congress tomorrow morning." Then, in a declarative nine-word sentence, John Adams recorded the birth of what Benjamin Franklin called America's public religion: "The motion was seconded and passed in the affirmative."

The next morning the Reverend Duche appeared, dressed in clerical garb. As it happened, the psalm assigned to be read that day by Episcopalians was the 35th. The delegates had heard rumors—later proved to be unfounded—that the British were storming Boston; everything seemed to be hanging in the balance. In the hall, with the Continental Army under attack from the world's mightiest empire, the priest read from the psalm: " 'Plead my cause, O Lord, with them that strive with me: fight against them that fight against me.' "

Fight against them that fight against me: John Adams was at once stunned and moved. "I never saw a greater effect upon an audience," he told Abigail. "It seemed as if Heaven had ordained that Psalm to be read on that morning." Adams long tingled from the moment—the close quarters of the room, the mental vision in every delegate's head of the patriots supposedly facing fire to the north, and, with Duche's words, the summoning of divine blessing and guidance on what they believed to be the cause of freedom.

As it was in the beginning, so it has been since: an American acknowledgment of God in the public sphere, with men of good will struggling to be reverent yet tolerant and ecumenical. That the Founding Fathers debated whether to open the American saga with prayer is wonderfully fitting, for their conflicts are our conflicts, their dilemmas our dilemmas. Largely faithful, they knew religious wars had long been a destructive force in the lives of nations, and they had no wish to repeat the mistakes of the world they were rebelling against. And yet they bowed their heads.

More than two centuries on, as millions of Americans observe Passover and commemorate Easter next week, the role of faith in public life is a subject of particularly pitched debate. From stem cells and science to the Supreme Court, from foreign policy and the 2008 presidential campaign to evangelical "Justice Sundays," the question of God and politics generates much heat but little light. Some Americans think the country has strayed too far from God; others fear that religious zealots (from the White House to the school board) are waging holy war on American liberty; and many, if not most, seem to believe that we are a nation hopelessly divided between believers and secularists.

History suggests, though, that there is hope, for we have been fighting these battles from our earliest days and yet the American experiment endures.

However dominant in terms of numbers, Christianity is only a thread in the American tapestry—it is not the whole tapestry. The God who is spoken of and called on and prayed to in the public sphere is an essential character in the American drama, but He is not specifically God the Father or the God of Abraham. The right's contention that we are a "Christian nation" that has fallen from pure origins and can achieve redemption by some kind of return to Christian values is based on wishful thinking, not convincing historical argument. Writing to the Hebrew Congregation in Newport, Rhode Island, in 1790, George Washington assured his Jewish countrymen that the American government "gives to bigotry no sanction." In a treaty with the Muslim nation of Tripoli initiated by Washington, completed by John Adams, and ratified by the Senate in 1797, we declared "the Government of the United States is not, in any sense, founded on the Christian religion. . . ." The Founders also knew the nation would grow ever more diverse; in Virginia, Thomas Jefferson's bill for religious freedom was "meant to comprehend, within the mantle of its protection, the Jew and the Gentile, the Christian and the Mahometan, the Hindoo and infidel of every denomination." And thank God— or, if you choose, thank the Founders—that it did indeed.

In Jefferson's words, 'The God who gave us life gave us liberty'—including the liberty to believe or not to believe.

Understanding the past may help us move forward. When the subject is faith in the public square, secularists reflexively point to the Jeffersonian "wall of separation between church and state" as though the conversation should end there; many conservative Christians defend their forays into the political arena by citing the Founders, as though Washington, Adams, Jefferson, and Franklin were cheerful Christian soldiers. Yet to claim that religion has only recently become a political force in the United States is uninformed and unhistorical; in practice, the "wall" of separation is not a very tall one. Equally wrong-headed is the tendency of conservative believers to portray the Founding Fathers as apostles in knee britches.

The great good news about America—the American gospel, if you will—is that religion shapes the life of the nation without strangling it. Driven by a sense of providence and an acute appreciation of the fallibility of humankind, the Founders made a nation in which faith should not be singled out for special help or particular harm. The balance between the promise of the Declaration of Independence, with its evocation of divine origins and destiny, and the practicalities of the Constitution, with its checks on extremism, remains the most brilliant of American successes.

The Founding Fathers and presidents down the ages have believed in a God who brought forth the heavens and the earth, and who gave humankind the liberty to believe in Him or not, to love Him or not, to obey Him or not. God had created man with free will, for love coerced is no love at all, only submission. That is why the religious should be on the front lines of defending freedom of religion.

Our finest hours—the Revolutionary War, abolition, the expansion of the rights of women, hot and cold wars against terror and tyranny, Martin Luther King Jr.'s battle against Jim Crow—can partly be traced to religious ideas about liberty, justice, and charity. Yet theology and scripture have also been used to justify our worst hours—from enslaving people based on the color of their skin to treating women as second-class citizens.

Still, Jefferson's Declaration of independence grounded America's most fundamental human rights in the divine, as the gift of "Nature's God." The most unconventional of believers, Jefferson was no conservative Christian; he once went through the Gospels with a razor to excise the parts he found implausible. ("I am of a sect by myself, as far as I know," he remarked.) And yet he believed that "the God who gave us life gave us liberty at the same time," and to Jefferson, the "Creator" invested the individual with rights no human power could ever take away. The Founders, however, resolutely refused to evoke sectarian—specifically Christian—imagery: the God of the Declaration is largely the God of Deism, an Enlightenment-era vision of the divine in which the Lord is a Creator figure who works in the world through providence. The Founding Fathers rejected an attempt to rewrite the Preamble of the Constitution to say the nation was dependent on God, and from the Lincoln administration forward presidents and Congresses refused to support a "Christian Amendment" that would have acknowledged Jesus to be the "Ruler among the nations."

At the same time, the early American leaders were not absolute secularists. They wanted God in American public life, but in a way that was unifying, not divisive. They were politicians and philosophers, sages and warriors, churchmen and doubters. While Jefferson edited the Gospels, Franklin rendered the Lord's Prayer into the 18th-century vernacular, but his piety had its limits: he recalled falling asleep in a Quaker meeting house on his first day in Philadelphia. All were devoted to liberty, but most kept slaves. All were devoted to virtue, but many led complex—the religious would say sinful—private lives.

The Founders understood that theocracy was tyranny, but they did not feel they could—or should—try to banish religion from public life altogether. Washington improvised "So help me, God" at the conclusion of the first presidential oath and kissed the Bible on which he had sworn it. Abraham Lincoln issued the Emancipation Proclamation, he privately told his cabinet, because he had struck a deal with "my Maker" that he would free the slaves if the Union forces triumphed at Antietam. The only public statement Franklin D. Roosevelt made on D-Day 1944 was to read a prayer he had written drawing on the 1928 Episcopal Book of Common Prayer. John Kennedy said that "on earth, God's work must truly be our own," and Ronald Reagan was not afraid to say that he saw the world as a struggle between light and dark, calling the Soviet empire "the focus of evil in the modern world." George W. Bush credits Billy Graham with saving him from a life of drift and drink, and once said that Christ was his favorite philosopher.

Sectarian language, however, can be risky. In a sermon preached on the day George Washington left Philadelphia to take command of the Continental Army, an Episcopal priest said: "Religion and liberty must flourish or fall together in America. We pray that both may be perpetual." The battle to preserve faith and freedom has been a long one, and rages still: keeping religion and politics in proper balance requires eternal vigilance.

Our best chance of summoning what Lincoln called "the better angels of our nature" may lie in recovering the true sense and spirit of the Founding era and its leaders, for they emerged from a time of trial with a moral creed which, while imperfect, averted the worst experiences of other nations. In that history lies our hope.

The Rocky Road to Revolution

While most members of Congress sought a negotiated settlement with England, independence advocates bided their time.

JOHN FERLING

We hold these truths to be self-evident, that all men are created equal, that they are endowed by their Creator with certain unalienable Rights, that among these are Life, Liberty and the pursuit of Happiness—That to secure these rights, Governments are instituted among Men, deriving their just powers from the consent of the governed . . .

Laboring at his desk in the midst of a Philadelphia heat wave in June 1776, Thomas Jefferson hastened to complete a pressing assignment. A Congressional committee, recognizing his "happy talent for composition," had given the 33-year-old Jefferson responsibility for drafting a declaration of independence, a document that Congress needed almost immediately. Jefferson, one of Virginia's seven delegates to the Second Continental Congress, worked in his two-room apartment on the second floor of a tradesman's house at Market and Seventh streets, a heavily trafficked corner. He rose before sunrise to write and, after the day's long Congressional session, he returned to his lodging to take up his pen again at night. Toward the end of his life, Jefferson would say that his purpose had been to "place before mankind the common sense of the subject." Congress, he recalled, required an "expression of the American mind."

Jefferson well knew that America was at a defining moment in its history. Independence would sever ties with a long colonial past and propel the 13 states—and the new American nation to which they would belong—into an extremely uncertain future. Jefferson also knew that Congress wanted the declaration completed by July 1, less than three weeks after he was given the assignment.

No one appreciated better than he the irony in the sudden desire for haste. Jefferson had been prepared to declare independence perhaps as much as a year earlier, from the moment that war against the mother country erupted on April 19, 1775. Yet Congress had refused. In the 14 months since American blood had been shed at Lexington and Concord, American soldiers had also died at Bunker Hill, in the siege of Boston, and during an ill-fated invasion of Canada. In addition, the Royal Navy had bombarded and burned American towns, and the colonists' commerce had been nearly shut down by a British blockade. Still, Congress had not declared independence.

But not even Jefferson, passionate advocate of independence that he was, fully grasped the importance of the document he was preparing. Nor did his colleague, John Adams of Massachusetts, who had masterminded the arduous struggle within Congress to declare independence. Focused single-mindedly on that contentious undertaking, Adams regarded the actual statement itself as a mere formality—he would call it "a theatrical show"—a necessary instrument of propaganda. Jefferson, for his part, said little about his accomplishment. Not long after his work was completed, he would depart Philadelphia to return to his responsibilities in the Virginia legislature. Still, he was more than mildly vexed that Congress had made revisions—or "mutilations," as he put it—to the language of his original draft. Historians now agree that Congress' alterations and excisions enhanced the Declaration's power. Jefferson's magisterial opening passage, and indeed, much of his original language, actually survived intact.

Today, the passage of time has dulled our memory of the extent to which many Americans, including a majority in the Continental Congress, were, for a very long period, reluctant to break ties completely and irrevocably with Britain. The creation of the document we have come to regard as the seminal expression of revolutionary ardor was by no means inevitable. More than two-and-a-quarter centuries after the Declaration was signed, this eloquent assertion of individual rights, reinstalled last September in a state-of-the-art glass encasement at the National Archives in Washington, D.C., can be assessed in all of its complexity—as the product of the protracted political debate that preceded its formulation.

By the summer of 1776, the patience of many congressmen had been sorely tried by bitter wrangling over the question of whether or not to declare independence. Many of the legislators thought it nonsensical to fight a war for any purpose other than independence, yet others disagreed. For month after bloody month Congress had sat on its hands, prompting John Adams to exclaim early in 1776 that America was caught "between Hawk and Buzzard," fighting a war it could not win unless it declared independence from Britain, thereby prompting England's enemies, most prominently France, to aid in the struggle.

America's war with the mother country had commenced when a British army of nearly 900 men, acting on orders from London, had marched from Boston to Concord, intending to destroy a colonial arsenal and, if possible, capture ringleaders John Hancock and Samuel Adams. The Second Continental Congress, which assembled in Philadelphia just three weeks later, had barely been gaveled to order when John Rutledge of South Carolina, a 35-year-old lawyer from Charleston, raised the critical question: "Do We aim at independancy? or do We only ask for a Restoration of Rights & putting of Us on Our old footing [as subjects of the crown]?" It would take Congress 14 months to answer that question.

Congress quickly divided into two factions. One felt that the British actions at Lexington and Concord in April required nothing less than a clean break from the motherland; they believed colonists would always be second-class citizens in the British Empire. This faction would have declared independence in May or June 1775. But a second faction, which comprised a substantial majority in Congress, yearned to be reconciled with Britain. These delegates believed in waging war only to compel London to accept America's terms—Rutledge's "old footing"—to return to the way things were before Parliament tried to tax Americans and claim unlimited jurisdiction over them.

Opposition to Parliament had been growing since it enacted the first American tax, the Stamp Act of 1765. At the First Continental Congress, which met in Philadelphia in September 1774, some delegates wanted to force repeal of it and other repressive measures through a trade embargo. A more conservative faction had pushed for a compromise to provide American representation in Parliament. In the end, Congress adopted the trade boycott, and war had come. "Nothing," wrote John Adams, "but Fortitude, Vigour, and Perseverance can save Us."

Most who had attended the First Continental Congress now sat in the Second, where they were joined by several fresh faces. For instance, Hancock, who had escaped capture at Lexington thanks to Paul Revere's timely warning, was now a member of the Massachusetts delegation. Sixty-nine-year-old Benjamin Franklin, who had just returned to Philadelphia after a decade in London, had been named a delegate from Pennsylvania. Gone were those from the First Continental Congress who refused to countenance a war against Britain, prompting Richard Henry Lee of Virginia to observe that a "perfect unanimity" existed in the Second Continental Congress, at least on the war issue.

John Adams concurred that a "military Spirit" that was "truly amazing" had seized the land. Militiamen were "as thick as Bees," he said, marching and drilling everywhere, including in the steamy streets outside the Pennsylvania State House where Congress met. His cousin, Samuel Adams, believed an equally militant spirit gripped Congress and that every member was committed to "the Defence and Support of American Liberty." The Adams cousins soon discovered, however, that while all in Congress supported the war, sentiment for severing ties with Britain was strong only in New England and Virginia. Reconciliationists prevailed everywhere else.

John Adams counseled patience. "We must Suffer People to take their own Way," he asserted in June 1775, even though that path might not be the "Speedyest and Surest." He understood that to push too hard for independence was to risk driving conservative Americans back into Britain's arms. Thus, for most of 1775, the pro-independence faction never spoke openly of a break with Britain. Adams likened America to that of "a large Fleet sailing under Convoy. The fleetest Sailors must wait for the dullest and slowest." For the foreseeable future, he lamented, "Progress must be slow."

But Adams was confident that those who favored reconciliation would be driven inexorably toward independence. In time, he believed, they would discover that London would never give in to America's demands. Furthermore, he expected that war would transform the colonists' deep-seated love for Britain into enmity, necessitating a final break.

Reconciliationists were strongest in the Middle Atlantic colonies (New York, New Jersey, Pennsylvania, Maryland and Delaware) and in South Carolina, all of which had long since been drawn into the economic web of the Atlantic world. Before the war, the products of the backcountry—furs, hides and lumber—as well as grain, had moved through New York and Philadelphia to markets in the Caribbean and England. Charleston exported indigo and rice. In return, English-manufactured goods entered the colonies through these ports. Business had flourished during most of the 18th century; in recent years Philadelphia's merchants had routinely enjoyed annual profits of more than 10 percent.

The great merchants in Philadelphia and New York, who constituted a powerful political force, had other compelling reasons for remaining within the empire. Many relied upon credit supplied by English bankers. The protection afforded to trans-atlantic trade by the Royal Navy minimized insurance and other overhead costs. Independence, Philadelphia merchant Thomas Clifford asserted in 1775, would "assuredly prove unprofitable." The "advantages of security and stability," said another, "lie with . . . remaining in the empire."

And there was fear of the unknown. Some in Congress spoke of a break with Britain as a "leap in the dark," while others likened it to being cast adrift on "an Unknown Ocean." To be sure, many things *could* miscarry should America try to go it alone. After all, its army was composed of untried soldiers led, for the most part, by inexperienced officers. It possessed neither a navy nor allies and lacked the funds to wage a lengthy conflict. The most immediate danger was that the fledgling nation might lose a war for independence. Such a defeat could unleash a series of dire consequences that, the reconciliationists believed, might be avoided only if the colonies, even in the midst of war, were to negotiate a settlement *before* breaking absolutely with Britain. The reconciliationists held that it was still possible to reach a middle ground; this view seemed, to men such as John Adams, a naive delusion. Finally, the anti-independence faction argued, losing the war might well result in retaliation, including the loss of liberties the colonists had long enjoyed.

Even victory could have drawbacks. Many felt independence could be won only with foreign assistance, which raised the specter of American dependence on a European superpower, most likely autocratic and Roman Catholic France. But Adams believed that fear of anarchy accounted for most conservative opposition to independence. More than anything, said Adams, it rendered "Independency . . . an Hobgoblin, of so frightfull Mein" to the reconciliationists.

Pennsylvania's John Dickinson soon emerged as the leader of those who sought rapprochement with Britain. Dickinson, who was 43 in 1775, had been raised on plantations in Maryland and Delaware. One of the few supporters of the war to have actually lived in England, where he had gone to study law, in London, he had not been impressed by what he found there. The English, he concluded, were intemperate and immoral; their political system was hopelessly corrupt and run by diabolical mediocrities. Returning to Philadelphia to practice law in 1757, he was soon drawn to politics.

Tall and thin, Dickinson was urbane, articulate and somewhat prickly. A patrician accustomed to having his way, he could be quick-tempered with those who opposed him. He had once brawled with a political adversary and challenged him to a duel. Early in the Second Continental Congress, following an incendiary speech by Adams, Dickinson pursued him into the State House yard and, in a venomous outburst, as recounted by Adams, demanded: "What is the reason, Mr. Adams, that you New Englandmen oppose our Measures of Reconciliation. . . . Look Ye," he threatened, "If you don't concur with Us, in our pacific System, I, and a Number of Us, will break off from you . . . and We will carry on the Opposition by ourselves in our own Way." Adams was infuriated by Dickinson's invective: the two never spoke again.

Dickinson had a distinguished record. In 1765 he had served in the Stamp Act Congress convened to protest that measure. Two years later, he published his cogent and illuminating *Letters from a Farmer in Pennsylvania,* America's most popular political tract before 1776, which assumed that Parliament, though possessed of the right to regulate trade, lacked authority to tax the colonists. That was the very stand taken by 1774's First Continental Congress, and a constitutional settlement along those lines—not independence—was what the reconciliationists hoped to achieve through war. Dickinson charged that London had launched an "inexpressibly cruel War." Its "Sword is opening our Veins," he said, compelling Americans to fight for their freedom.

But he also warned that a war for independence would be interminable. British prime minister Lord Frederick North had pledged an implacable fight to maintain "every Advantage" that Britain derived from its control of the colonies. Before any war for independence ended, Dickinson prophesied, Americans would have "tasted deeply of that bitter Cup called the Fortunes of War." Not only would they have to "wade thro Seas of Blood," but in due course, hostilities would bring on mas-

sive unemployment within the maritime trades, heinous cruelties along the frontier, slave insurrections in the South and the relentless spread of disease from armies to civilians. And even in the unlikely event independence was achieved, Dickinson argued, yet another catastrophe might well lie in store: France and Spain would destroy the infant United States. In contrast, a war for reconciliation would be short-lived. Confronted with "a bloody & tedious Contest attended with Injury to their Trade," Lord North's government would collapse. Its successor would be compelled to accept Congress' terms: American "Dependence & Subordination" on the Crown, but with it a recognition from London that Parliament's only power over the colonies was the regulation of American trade.

Given Dickinson's position as a longtime foe of Parliamentary taxation, it was only to be expected that he would emerge as a leader in Congress. Adams' rise, however, was a different story. When he became leader of the independence forces—what one contemporary observer, Dr. Benjamin Rush, described as the "first man in the House"—many were caught by surprise. Before his election to Congress in 1774, Adams was largely inexperienced in public life. He had served only one term in the Massachusetts assembly and had not even headed the Massachusetts delegation at the First Congress—cousin Sam had assumed that responsibility.

Forty years old in 1775, John Adams had grown up on a small farm just south of Boston, where his father moonlighted as a shoemaker to earn the money to send his oldest son to Harvard. Like Dickinson, Adams had practiced law, and also like him, had advanced rapidly. Within a dozen years of opening his law office, Adams maintained the heaviest caseload of any attorney in Boston. Unlike Dickinson, Adams was initially wary of the American protest against British policies, believing that the ministry had simply erred in its actions and might be expected to mend its ways. He had been converted to open support of the popular cause only in 1773.

Adams came to keenly desire a leadership role, but feared that his physical limitations—he was portly and balding—and irascible manner would frustrate his ambitions. Furthermore, he was no jovial backslapper. Gruff and argumentative, he was maladroit when it came to talking about what he regarded as the favorite topics of men: dogs, horses and women. Nevertheless, those who penetrated his churlish exterior discovered a good-natured, self-effacing and exceptionally bright individual. And he possessed the skills needed to be an effective legislator. He was tireless, a skilled debater, an incisive, if not flamboyant, orator and a trenchant thinker. He quickly won a reputation as the Congressional authority on diplomacy and political theory. His colleagues found him to be unfailingly well prepared, prudent, honest and trustworthy—in short, just the man to follow in this high-stakes endeavor.

The first issue to truly divide the Second Continental Congress arose early on. In May 1775, as it considered the creation of the Continental Army, Dickinson insisted on petitioning the king with what he characterized as a "Measure of Peace." Adams privately branded it a "Measure of

Imbecility" and raged that some delegates, at least those from the mercantile colonies of New York and Pennsylvania, were "selfish and avaricious." For those congressman, he charged, "a ship [was] dearer than" the lives of Continental soldiers. In October 1774, the First Continental Congress had petitioned the monarch; Adams feared that to do so again was to risk appearing weak. Franklin concurred. "It is a true old saying," he remarked, "that *make yourselves sheep and the wolves will eat you.*"

Nevertheless, the independence faction wanted no confrontation with Dickinson's at this crucial juncture of the war, and the Olive Branch Petition, as the peace measure was known, was approved, though only after a contentious debate over its wording. Richard Penn, a former governor of Pennsylvania, carried it to England. Franklin advised a London friend, a director of the Bank of England, that this was Britain's last hope for preventing "a total Separation" by the colonies. To another friend in England he wrote: "If you flatter yourselves with beating us into submission, you know neither the [American] people nor the country."

At about the same time, Congress created a committee to draft a "Declaration of the Causes and Necessity of Taking Up Arms." Among others, it appointed Jefferson, who had only recently joined the Virginia delegation, and Dickinson to the committee. Jefferson, who enjoyed a reputation as a facile writer, was asked to draft the document. With views similar to Adams', he produced a paper that reiterated the charges of British tyranny and harshly cataloged the ministry's "avowed course of murder and devastation." Dickinson was appalled. He feared that such a provocative statement would make a measured response to the Olive Branch Petition impossible. He demanded, and obtained, an opportunity to tone down Jefferson's draft. Dickinson's softer proclamation stipulated that "we mean not to dissolve that Union" with Britain. It was adopted in July 1775.

The reconciliationists held sway through the summer of 1775, but as hostilities unfolded and Congress was required to prosecute the war, their hold gradually weakened. By the end of 1775, Congress had issued a Continental currency, drawn up regulations applying to all militia, created a Continental post office and taken control of Indian relations. Feeling "a little of the Seafaring Inclination," as Adams put it, Congress also established an American navy and two battalions of marines. It regulated American trade, assumed responsibility for the enforcement of the embargo of British commerce, attempted to resolve intercolonial territorial disputes and even acted as the national judiciary, hearing appeals from state courts in cases that involved the seizure of British ships.

Congress additionally began to conduct foreign policy. It created a Secret Committee to contract for arms imports and a Committee of Secret Correspondence to establish contact with "our friends" throughout the world. In March 1776, Congress dispatched one of its own, Silas Deane of Connecticut, to Versailles to pursue talks with the French government. In fact, if not in name, the Second Continental Congress had become the government of an autonomous union of American provinces.

Back in November 1775, word had arrived that George III had branded the colonists rebels and traitors and had contemptuously refused to accept the Olive Branch Petition. Two months later, the full text of the king's speech to Parliament reached Philadelphia. In it the monarch unsparingly assailed those colonists who supported hostilities, charging that they were part of a "wicked" and "desperate conspiracy." In addition, he revealed his intention to obtain foreign mercenaries to help suppress the rebellion. Hancock, by now president of Congress, wryly remarked that the Crown's actions "don't look like a Reconciliation." John Adams gleefully noted that Dickinson "sinks . . . in the public opinion."

Indeed, evidence was mounting that the mood of the country was changing. Already, by the summer of 1775, when Congress began authorizing the colonies to create their own governments, supplanting those chartered by the Crown, it had taken its most radical step since the creation of the army. Dickinson and his principal ally, James Wilson of Pennsylvania, fought back. In January 1776 they proposed that Congress adopt yet another "humble & dutiful Petition" disclaiming independence to the king. This time Congress refused. Some members, such as Samuel Adams, had begun to see the reconciliationists as "Tools of a Tyrant."

Yet Congress still remained unwilling to declare independence. Had a vote been taken in early January 1776, the measure would likely have failed. On the 17th of that month, however, word reached Philadelphia of a devastating military setback, the young army's first. The news was instrumental in propelling Congress on its final journey toward independence.

As Washington's army besieged British regulars in Boston during the summer of 1775, Congress had authorized an invasion of lightly defended Canada in order to defeat British forces there. It was a troubled campaign from the start, and on December 31 disaster struck. An attack on Quebec was repulsed; 500 men, half of America's invading army, were lost: 100 were killed or wounded and another 400 taken prisoner. So much for any expectation of a short-lived war. Overnight, many in Congress came to believe that no victory would ever be possible without foreign assistance; all understood that no aid from any outside power would be forthcoming so long as America fought for the "purpose of repairing the breach [with Britain]," as Thomas Paine had observed in his incendiary pamphlet *Common Sense,* published in January 1776.

Soon after the debacle at Quebec, John Adams observed that there now existed "no Prospect, no Probability, no Possibility" of reconciliation. Late in February came still more stunning news. Congress learned that Parliament had enacted the American Prohibitory Act, shutting down all trade with the colonies and permitting seizure of colonial vessels. John Adams called the law "a Gift" to the pro-independence party. Virginia's Richard Henry Lee concurred, saying that it severed the last ties with the mother country. It was "curious," he stated, that Congress yet hesitated to declare independence when London had already "put the two Countries asunder."

As spring foliage burst forth in Philadelphia in 1776, ever larger numbers of Americans were coming round to independence. The "Sighing after Independence" in Massachusetts,

© Getty Images/Hisham F. Ibrahim

said James Warren, speaker of the colony's House of Representatives, had become nearly "Universal." By mid-May every Southern colony had authorized its delegates to vote for breaking off ties with Britain.

Within Congress, emotions ran high. "I cannot conceive what good Reason can be assignd against [independence]," Samuel Adams railed in mid-April. He exclaimed that the "Salvation of the Country depends on its being done speedily. I am anxious to have it done." John Adams maintained that had independence been declared months earlier, America's armies would already possess French arms. Elbridge Gerry, a Massachusetts delegate, complained that "timid Minds are terrified at the Word Independency," while Franklin deplored those who clutched at the "vain Hope of Reconciliation." As for General Washington, he said he believed that Congress had "long, & ardently sought for reconciliation upon honourable terms," only to be rebuffed at every turn. He had long been of the opinion that "all Connexions with a State So unjust" should be broken.

Still, the reconciliationists held out, encouraged by a passage in the Prohibitory Act that authorized the monarch to appoint commissioners to grant pardons and to receive the grievances of colonists. Dickinson and his followers viewed the appointees as peace commissioners and held out hope that they were being sent to resolve differences. Many in Congress refused to budge until they learned just what the envoys had to offer. John Adams disdainfully predicted that this was "a Bubble" and a misbegotten "Messiah that will never come." Samuel Adams said that he was "disgusted" both with the "King & his Junto," who spoke of peace while making "the most destructive Plans," and with the reconciliationists who were willing to be "Slaves" to "a Nation so lost to all Sense of Liberty and Virtue."

In May, as American newspapers published the text of Britain's treaties with several German principalities, authorizing the hiring of mercenaries, outrage toward the Crown skyrocketed. Many were now convinced, as Richard Henry Lee said, that the action proved Britain was bent "upon the absolute conquest and subduction of N. America." Nearly simultaneously, word arrived of yet more calamities in Canada. Congress had dispatched reinforcements following the failed attack in December, but smallpox and desertions soon thinned their ranks. With the arrival of British reinforcements in May, the American army commenced a long, slow retreat that lasted until mid-June. Now, said Lee, it "is not choice then but necessity that calls for Independence, as the only means by which a foreign Alliance can be obtained."

One final matter helped the slowest sailors in Congress catch up with the swiftest. Month after month had passed with no sign of the so-called peace commissioners. Then, in the spring, it was learned that, although some commissioners had been named, they had been ordered not to treat with Congress. That proved a final blow; all but the most ardent reconciliationists were persuaded that the king's envoys were coming for the sole purpose of dividing American opinion and derailing the war effort.

With the tide so turned, in mid-May, Congress declared that "every kind of authority under the . . . Crown should be totally suppressed" and instructed each colony to adopt a new government suitable for providing for the "happiness and safety of their constituents and . . . America in general." John Adams, who called this the "last Step," believed this was tantamount to a declaration of independence. Even Maryland's Thomas Stone, a foe of separation, disconsolately allowed that the "Dye is cast. The fatal Stab is given to any future Connection between this Country & Britain." Only a formal declaration of independence remained, and that could not now be long in coming.

On June 7, three weeks after Congress urged changes in the provincial governments, Lee introduced a motion for independence: "*Resolved,* That these United Colonies are, and of right ought to be, free and independent States, that they are absolved from all allegiance to the British Crown, and that all political connection between them and the State of Great Britain is, and ought to be, totally dissolved."

Congress rancorously debated Lee's motion for two days. Several reconciliationists from the Middle-Atlantic colonies made their final stand, even threatening to "secede from the Union" if Congress declared independence. But their threats and recriminations no longer frightened the majority, including Oliver Wolcott of Connecticut, who recognized that America was in the "Midst of a great Revolution . . . leading to the lasting Independancy of these Colonies." On June 11, Congress created a five-member committee to prepare a statement on independence. Adams, Franklin, Jefferson, Roger Sherman of Connecticut and Robert Livingston of New York were given until July 1 to complete their work. Once again it was to Jefferson that a panel turned, this time for the fateful task of drafting the declaration.

Jefferson and his colleagues beat the deadline by two days, submitting on June 28 a document that explained and defended independence. By July 1, the final consideration of Lee's motion to declare independence was taken up. That day's session, John Adams told a friend in a letter written early that morning, would see "the greatest Debate of all." With the outcome no longer in doubt, he said that he prayed for "the new born Republic" about to be created.

When debate began midmorning on that hot, steamy Monday, Dickinson was first on his feet to make one last speech against independence. Speaking emotionally for perhaps as much as two hours in the stifling heat of the closed room (windows were kept shut to keep spies from listening in), Dickinson reviewed the familiar arguments: America could not win the war; at best, it could fight Britain to a stalemate, and deadlocked wars often ended in partition treaties in which territory is divided among the belligerents; therefore, after all the killing, some colonies would remain part of the British Empire, while others would pass under the control of France or Spain.

It was John Adams—soon to be christened "the Atlas of Independence" by New Jersey's Richard Stockton—who rose to answer Dickinson. Striving to conceal his contempt for his adversary, Adams spoke extemporaneously in subdued tones. Once again, he reviewed the benefits of independence. Although his speech was not transcribed, he surely invoked the ideas he had expressed and the phrases he had used on many another occasion. Breaking ties with Britain, he argued, would ensure freedom from England's imperial domination; escape from the menace of British corruption; and the opportunity to create a republic based on equality of representation.

Others then took the floor. The speeches stretched past the customary 4 o'clock adjournment and into the evening. The business was "an idle Mispence of Time," Adams remarked sourly, as "nothing was Said, but what had been repeated and hackneyed in that Room an hundred Times for Six Months past." After the Congress reconvened the next morning, July 2, the delegates cast their momentous votes. Twelve states—the colonies would become states with the vote—voted for independence. Not one voted against the break with Britain. New York's delegation, which had not yet been authorized by the New York legislature to separate from the mother country, did not vote. (Dickinson and Robert Morris did not attend, and Pennsylvania cast its vote for independence by a three-to-two margin.)

Adams predicted that July 2 would ever after "be solemnized with Pomp and Parade, with Shews, Games, Sports, Guns, Bells,

Bonfires and Illuminations from one End of this Continent to the other." He was wrong, of course, for July 4, the date that Congress approved the formal Declaration of Independence, would become the commemorative day. But Adams had made one prediction that would prove tellingly correct. With the Union intact after a 15-month battle for independence, and with the step finally taken that could secure foreign assistance in America's desperate war, Adams declared he could "see the Rays of ravishing Light and Glory" that would accompany military victory.

HISTORIAN JOHN FERLING is the author of *A Leap in the Dark: The Struggle to Create the American Republic.*

March on Quebec

Dorchester Heights, Boston, September 3, 1775.

WILLARD STERNE RANDALL

On that dusty gray Sunday morning, Benedict Arnold, a newly commissioned Colonel in the Continental Army, accompanied his Commander in Chief, George Washington, and reviewed the 16,000 troops laying siege to British-held Boston. Riding a big chestnut horse and resplendent in the scarlet uniform he had designed, the forceful Arnold called for volunteers willing to undertake a bold and dangerous mission: he had persuaded Washington that, if they could move quickly, Quebec City could be taken before the British could bring reinforcement from England. He would only need independent authority and 1,000 men for a surprise attack on the enemy stronghold through the Maine woods. Men volunteered in droves.

For the march on Quebec, Arnold was inventing a new kind of unit: a light infantry regiment specially adapted to amphibious raids. During the French and Indian War, Robert Rogers' famous Rangers had conducted long-range scouts and raids across lakes, rivers, and mountains, but, living off the land, had not had to deal with the logistics of transporting substantial supplies. For all except the Rangers and small Indian raiding parties, the dense backwoods of northern New England had acted as an effective barrier to overland travel between the colonies and Canada. During that war, the total absence of roads and scarcity of trails, ineffective maps, and a topography tortured by glaciers had forced the British to launch most attacks on French Canada by sea. Even if everything went right—and things would go horribly wrong—Arnold's plan of marching and paddling 400 miles seemed next to impossible.

But Arnold was a man who embraced long odds. In joint command with Ethan Allen, he had captured Fort Ticonderoga in a daring early morning assault, then sailed up Lake Champlain and seized several British ships and a fort at Saint-Jean-sur-Richelieu in Quebec. From captured dispatches, he knew there were only 750 redcoats in all Canada.

Slimming the mass of volunteers to 1,080 men, Arnold dispatched a courier ahead to Gardiner, Maine, to commission shipwright Reuben Colburn to build 200 lightweight bateaux. From surveyor Samuel Goodrich he ordered maps for his battalion commanders, all unknowing that both men were loyalists opposed to the Revolution.

To make the maps, Arnold relied on the travel diary of British Engineer Capt. John André, who had accompanied the British march down the Kennebec from Quebec Province during the French and Indian War. As was the custom of the time, André had created two diaries: one accurate, the other bogus, to throw off any enemy using it. Arnold had somehow acquired the wrong one.

The drive on Quebec hit snags from the outset, and bureaucratic entanglements delayed departure for more than two weeks. Finally, under a heavy fog, Arnold threaded his makeshift fleet by night through the British blockade toward Maine. He soon learned to his dismay that a summerlong drought had all but dried up the Kennebec, exposing rocks and shoals. Instead of sailing upriver to Gardiner, his force would have to march along the riverbank, laboriously lining their overloaded canoes around the river's multiple hazards.

At Colburn's shipyards he received yet another shock—a meadow full of badly built bateaux, created from heavy, wet, green planks that would shrink over their even heavier oak frames, leaving open wide fissures to the water. These hastily-constructed, undersized, and overweight boats would have to be worked through 350 miles of rough water and portages on a route that would turn out to be 200 miles longer than Arnold's maps indicated. Three more days went to caulking the boats and building 20 replacements.

Leaves were already turning and temperatures plunging before Arnold could finally shove off on September 27. On every portage it took four men to carry each empty bateau, which dug hard into their shoulders as they scrambled uphill over thickly wooded dirt paths and around high waterfalls.

At Skowhegan the soldiers bullied the boats up a three-mile slope while teams of men marched alongside, bent under the weight of barrels and bearskin-wrapped bundles of provisions, covering only half the distance Arnold had anticipated. Most of the men had never poled a boat before, and so they waded and hauled the laden bateaux more than halfway up the river. One man wrote they could have been mistaken "for amphibious animals, as they were a great part of the time under water." They slept on the ground in wet uniforms, their clothing "frozen a pane of glass thick."

The next day Arnold ordered the boats ashore, emptied out the cargo, and sorted through the waterlogged supplies. The planks had leaked, the barrels filling with water. Salted meat and cod had begun to rot. Flour and peas had turned into a moldy paste. He stopped the expedition for eight days to make repairs—precious days that pushed the men further into the heart of winter.

At 4 A.M. on October 18, Arnold awakened as a wall of water roared through the river basin, stirred up by a West India hurricane. The river rose 12 feet, sweeping away most of the remaining food and gear. Seven boatloads of food, guns, gunpowder, and clothing were lost. Leaving "Camp Disaster," he saw some of his men eating candles.

On October 23 Arnold called an emergency council of war. That evening he knelt in front of the headquarters fire, raising his voice to be heard above the sputtering and hissing of the wet firewood and the coughing of the score of miserable officers from his first two battalions. Those present would later remember Arnold's eyes flashing as he acknowledged that the hardships were worse than anyone had imagined, the maps bad, and food dwindling to starvation point. Yet only one man had died, and although exhausted, the soldiers otherwise remained healthy. He continued his speech, powerfully outlining his case for pushing on to Canada, which he felt was feasible if remaining supplies were evenly divided and strictly rationed. In the face of such indomitable spirit and careful planning, the officers voted to continue the campaign.

Arnold issued a stream of orders—sending back the sick and weak, redistributing rations, and moving the strongest men forward. Runners headed downstream with orders for the second in command, Lt. Col. Roger Enos. Little did Arnold know, but Enos had called his own council of war, which had decided that the 350 men of the rear battalion would turn back to Massachusetts, taking with them most of the remaining provisions and all the medical supplies. When Arnold learned of Enos's decision three days later, he flew into a rage.

Enos's loss of nerve effectively dashed Arnold's chances of taking Quebec by surprise. Bitterly disappointed, Arnold ordered his officers to abandon the remaining bateaux to conserve the men's strength; they were now down to half a cup of flour a day, an ounce of pork, and broth made from bark. Arnold had to make a difficult decision. It was obvious that the maps had failed him and his force was likely to become hopelessly lost if not well guided. Yet his men would starve if their rations were not replenished. He decided he must go on and find food, judging it better to risk the main body becoming temporarily lost than for them to starve.

With several Indian guides and 15 soldiers, he paddled on toward Canada to seek food from the French settlements on the Chaudière River, covering 13 miles by 10 in the morning. Behind him, his men faced the dangerous mountainous borderlands called the Height of Land. The officers gave their morsels of pork to the men. Some took raw hides intended to make shoes, chopped them up, singed off the hair, boiled them, and wrung the juice into their canteens.

Day after day, what was left of Arnold's proud little army struggled, the men often stripping naked and crossing unnamed frigid lakes and rivers with their clothes wrapped around rifles held over their heads. Heavy snowfalls were now common, and the exhausted men barely had the strength to kick aside the sodden ground cover and collapse in their soaked uniforms. When they finally crossed into Canada following the Chaudière toward Quebec, they found the bateaux of their advance party shattered and scattered along riverbanks after they had plunged over 20-foot waterfalls. Men had drowned or died when they could no longer be carried.

After eight miles of trudging on November 3, the regimental doctor stopped and rubbed his eyes at "a vision of horned cattle . . . three horned cattle and two horses." Six days after racing ahead of his men and nearly losing his life in the falls, Arnold had sent back lifesaving livestock and supplies—along with the orders that anyone who had provisions left was to let the livestock pass to the rear, where the weakest lagged behind. Soon two birch-bark canoes appeared, laden with cornmeal, mutton for the sick, and even tobacco bought from the habitants. After the first real meal after many days, the restored army marched 20 miles, in all covering 30 before camping. That day and next, Arnold was in constant motion up and down the line, making sure all his men were fed.

At 10:30 P.M. on November 3, 1775, Arnold's column, down to 675 of the 1,080 men who had left Cambridge 51 days earlier—nearly 40 percent of the army lost by death and desertion—reeled like drunkards into the first French settlement, their bare feet leaving bloodstains on the snowy riverbank. "Our clothes were torn in pieces by the bushes and hung in strings," wrote one man. "Few of us had any shoes, but moccasins made of new skins—many of us without hats—and beards long and visages thin and meager. I thought we much resembled the animals which inhabit New Spain called the Ourang-outang."

Benedict Arnold was too late to take the prime prize of Quebec, now heavily reinforced by Scottish Highlanders under veteran officers, but his arrival across the St. Lawrence from the walled city boosted American morale as news of the march of "that brave little army" reached Congress and was spread by newspapers.

Arnold's report to Washington contained only praise for the men, no self-applause. The fact that only Enos's force had turned back and that every other soldier had kept on to the objective or died trying to attested to Arnold's triumphant leadership. He did not mention that he had personally covered the distance nearly three times, almost died when he narrowly missed shooting over the falls, or that he too was no less weak, bearded, and half-starved than those who had so steadily followed him.

The tribute that pleased Arnold the most came from just those men who had the most right to complain: "Our bold though inexperienced general discovered such firmness and zeal as inspired us with resolution," wrote one private. "The hardships and fatigues he encountered, he accounted as nothing in comparison with the salvation of his country."

George Washington's verdict on the expedition must have rung bitterly five years later when Arnold had found another cause: "The merit of that officer is certainly great and I heartily wish that fortune may distinguish him."

From *American Heritage*, Fall 2008, pp. 26–27. Copyright © 2008 by Willard Sterne Randall. Adapted from the book, *Benedict Arnold, Patriot and Traitor*, a finalist for the Pulitzer Prize. The author is a Professor of History at Champlain College. Reprinted by permission of the author.

A Day to Remember: July 4, 1776

CHARLES PHILLIPS

On Independence Day every year, millions of Americans turn out for myriad parades, public and backyard barbecues, concerts of patriotically stirring music and spectacular pyrotechnic displays, and they do so to celebrate the day on which we declared our independence from Great Britain.

But America did not declare its independence on July 4, 1776. That happened two days earlier, when the second Continental Congress approved a resolution stating that "these United Colonies are, and of a right ought to be, free and independent States." The resolution itself had first been introduced back on June 7, when Virginia's Richard Henry Lee rose in the sweltering heat of the Congress' Philadelphia meeting house to propose an action many delegates had been anticipating—and not a few dreading—since the opening shots of the American Revolution at Lexington and Concord.

Lee asked for a newly declared independent government, one that could form alliances and draw up a plan for confederation of the separate Colonies. The need for some such move had become increasingly clear during the last year, especially to George Washington, if for no other reason than as a rallying cry for his troops. The Virginia soldier chosen by Congress to general its Continental Army languished in New York, short of supplies, short of men and short of morale while facing the threat of a massive British offensive.

But many in Congress, some sent with express instructions against independence, were leery of Lee's proposal despite the growing sentiment for independence stirred up by such rebel rousers as Boston's Samuel Adams and the recent émigré Thomas Paine. Paine's political pamphlet, Common Sense, openly attacked King George III and quickly became a bestseller in the Colonies; Paine donated the proceeds to the Continental Congress. Lee was so closely associated with Adams that critics charged Lee with representing Massachusetts better than he did Virginia. On the night before Lee offered up his resolution, Adams boasted to friends that Lee's resolution would decide the most important issue Americans ever had faced.

Little wonder that the more conservative delegates, men such as Pennsylvania's John Dickinson and South Carolina's Edward Rutledge, balked. Treat with France? Surely. Draw up articles of confederation? Fine. But why declare independence? The Colonies, they argued, were not even sure they could achieve it. To declare their intent now would serve merely to warn the British, and hence forearm them. Dickinson wanted to postpone the discussion—forever if he could—and he managed to muster support for three weeks of delay. At the same time, Lee's faction won approval to appoint committees to spend the three weeks preparing drafts on each point of the resolution.

Sam Adams was named to the committee writing articles of confederation. His cousin, John Adams, a great talker, headed the committee drawing up a treaty with France. John Adams also was appointed to help draft a declaration of independence along with the inevitable choice, the celebrated author and internationally renowned philosopher Benjamin Franklin. Congress also assigned New York conservative Robert Livingston and Connecticut Yankee Roger Sherman to the committee but fell to arguing over a fifth member.

Southern delegates wanted one of their own to achieve balance. But many in Congress disfavored the two obvious candidates, considering Lee too radical and his fellow Virginian Benjamin Harrison too conservative. There was another Virginian, however, a 32-year-old lanky, red-haired newcomer named Thomas Jefferson, who had a reputation for learning in both literature and science. Though he seemed to shrink from public speaking, the Adamses liked him, and John pushed so effectively for Jefferson to join the committee that, when the votes were counted, he tallied more than anyone else.

Franklin's health was clearly failing, and he wouldn't be able to draft the declaration. Adams was busy with what he probably considered at the time the more important work of Grafting an alliance with France (though he would live to regret such an opinion). Neither Livingston nor Sherman evidently had the desire nor, most probably, the talent to pen the kind of document needed. To Jefferson, then, with his reputation as a fine writer, fell the task of drafting a resolution whose language, edited and approved by the committee, would be acceptable to all the delegates.

Jefferson worried about his sick wife, Martha, back home and longed to be in Virginia working on the colony's new constitution, then under debate in Williamsburg. Nevertheless, he set to work and quickly produced what, given the time constraints, was a remarkable document. A justification to the world of the action being taken by Britain's American Colonies assembled in Congress, the declaration was part bill of indictment and part philosophical assertion, the latter an incisive summary of Whig political thought.

With the document's key sentiments much inspired, say some, by such Scottish Enlightenment figures as Francis Hutcheson, and its thinking much influenced, say many, by John Locke's Two Treatises of Government, the declaration summarized common notions expressed everywhere in the Colonies in those days. Many such notions could be found in numerous local proclamations. Especially relevant, because it was on Jefferson's mind, was the language of the new Virginia constitution with its elaborate Bill of Rights penned by his cohort, George Mason. Indeed, Jefferson's assignment was to capture the sense of the current rebellion in the 13 Colonies and distill its essence into a single document.

In this, as everyone recognized, he greatly succeeded, though he did not do it alone. Despite what Jefferson himself later wrote, and John Adams, too, when age and the glory of the Revolution led them both to embroider their accounts, the committee reviewed Jefferson's work, and then he ran it past both senior members, Adams and Franklin. He incorporated suggested changes before writing a clean copy. Still, Jefferson personally was quite proud of the draft he laid before Congress on June 28, 1776.

On the first day of July, with Jefferson's manuscript at the ready, the delegates once more took up Richard Henry Lee's resolution to openly declare independence. Lee was off in Virginia, where Jefferson wished to be, so he was not there to see John Dickinson's last protest seemingly cow the Congress, before an eloquent rebuttal by a determined John Adams carried the motion. Congress on July 2 without dissent voted that the American Colonies were from that day forward free and independent states.

That evening an exultant John Adams wrote home to his wife that July 2, 1776, would "be celebrated by succeeding generations as the great anniversary festival." It was his day of triumph, as well he knew, and he imagined it "commemorated as the day of deliverance by acts of devotion to God Almighty. It ought to be solemnized with pomp and parade, with shows, games, sports, guns, bells, bonfires and illuminations from one end of the continent to the other, from this time forward forever more."

Congress immediately turned to consider Jefferson's document. It would have to serve as a sort of early version of a press release—an explanation that could be disseminated at home and around the globe by broadside and to be read aloud at gatherings. Its statements had to inspire the troops and garner public support for the action Congress had just taken. Not surprisingly, Congress paid close attention to the document's language.

The delegates took the time to spruce it up a little and edit out what they found objectionable. In general the Congress was fine with the vague sentiments of the early paragraphs that have since become the cornerstone of American democracy: "We hold these truths to be self-evident: that all men are created equal, that they are endowed by their Creator with certain unalienable rights; that among these are life, liberty, and the pursuit of happiness; that to secure these rights, governments are instituted among men, deriving their just powers from the consent of the governed" and so on.

What the delegates were more interested in, however, and what they saw as the meat of the document, were the more concrete declarations. For years, they had based their resistance to England on the belief they were not fighting a divinely chosen king, but his ministers and parliament. But during the previous 14 months the Crown had waged war on them, and King George had declared the Colonials in rebellion, that is, outside his protection. Common Sense had gotten them used to thinking of the king as that "royal brute" and this document was supposed to explain why he should be so considered. Thus Jefferson had produced a catalog of George III's tyrannies as its heart and soul.

Congress at length struck out some sentimental language in which Jefferson tried to paint the British people as brothers indifferent to American suffering and a paragraph where he ran on about the glories the two people might otherwise have realized together. But more substantive changes were especially telling. Among George's crimes, Jefferson had listed the slave trade, contending that the king had "waged a cruel war against human nature" by assaulting a "distant people" and carrying them into slavery in "another hemisphere." This was too much for Jefferson's fellow slaveholders in the South, especially South Carolina, and certain Yankee traders who had made fortunes from what Jefferson called the "execrable commerce." Together, representatives of these Southern and Yankee interests deleted the section.

For the rest, the delegates also changed a word here and there, usually improving some of the hasty writing. They worked the language of Lee's resolution into the conclusion and added a reference to the Almighty, which Jefferson would have been happier without. "And," the document now concluded, "for support of this Declaration, with a firm reliance on the protection of divine Providence, we mutually pledge to each other our lives, our fortunes, and our sacred honor."

None of this sat well with the young author. He made a copy of the declaration as he submitted it and the "mutilated" version Congress approved, and sent both to his friends and colleagues, including Richard Henry Lee, who agreed the original was superior, though most historians since have concluded otherwise.

In any case, after more than two days of sometimes-heated debate, on July 4, 1776, the Continental Congress approved the revised document that explained its declaration of independence of July 2. The approval was not immediately unanimous, since the New York delegates had to await instructions from home and did not assent until July 9. At the time of approval, Congress ordered the document "authenticated and printed," and that copies "be sent to several assemblies, conventions and committees, or councils of safety, and to the several commanding officers of the continental troops; that it be proclaimed in each of the United States, and at the head of the army." If any delegates officially signed the approved document on the glorious Fourth, they were President John Hancock and Secretary Charles Thomson.

Within days the printed document was circulated across the land. The declaration was read aloud in the yard of the Philadelphia State House to much loud cheering. When New York formally accepted the declaration, the state celebrated by releasing its debtors from prison; Baltimoreans burned George III in effigy; the citizens of Savannah, Ga., gave him an official funeral.

The carefully engrossed copy we see reproduced everywhere today, with its large handwritten calligraphy, was not ordered prepared until July 19, and it was not ready for signing until August 2. Delegates probably dropped in throughout the summer to add their names to the bottom of the document. In any event, since the proceedings were secret and the signers all in danger of their lives, the names were not broadcast.

Even before the engrossed copy was ready, and long before it was signed by all, the legends were growing—how Hancock signed the parchment so boldly that John Bull could read his name without spectacles. How Hancock remarked to Benjamin Franklin: "We must be unanimous. There must be no pulling in different ways. We must all hang together." And how Franklin replied, "Yes, we must indeed all hang together, or most assuredly we shall hang separately."

Almost from the start, confusion blurred the distinctions between the July 2 act of declaring independence, the July 4 approval of the document explaining that declaration, and the actual signing of the Declaration. That confusion might best be represented by John Trumbull's famous 1819 painting, which now hangs in the Capitol Rotunda and appears on the back of the $2 bill. Thought by most Americans to represent the signing of the Declaration of Independence, it was intended by Trumbull "to preserve the resemblance of the men who were the authors of this memorable act," not to portray a specific day or moment in our history.

The Fourth of July was not as widely celebrated during the heat of the Revolutionary War or during the period of confederation as it was afterward. It became much more popular as a national holiday in the wake of the War of 1812 and with the passing of the Revolutionary generation.

And then four score and seven years after that July 4, 1776, President Abraham Lincoln used the lofty ideas and flowing words of the Declaration as the basis for his famous Gettysburg Address to sanctify the country's sacrifices in the Civil War and, in so doing, he redefined the nation as a land of equality for all. Ever since, those early paragraphs of the Declaration, with their beautifully phrased abstractions and sentiments, have served virtually to define the American faith in secular democracy. His well-chosen remarks and our July 4 Independence Day celebrations, like Trumbull's painting, honor not a single event but, rather, the democratic process, the ideas proposed back then and the men who directly made them possible.

CHARLES PHILLIPS is the author and co-author of numerous works of history and biography. These include *What Every American Should Know About American History, The Macmillan Dictionary of Military Biography; Cops, Crooks, and Criminologists; What Everyone Should Know About the Twentieth Century, Tyrants, Dictators, and Despots;* and *The Wages of History.* Phillips has edited several multivolume historical reference works, including the *Encyclopedia of the American West, the Encyclopedia of War* and *the Encyclopedia of Historical Treaties.*

The Baron De Kalb

Plotter or Patriot?

In 1777 a Bavarian baron slipped across the Atlantic to supplant George Washington. Johann de Kalb would instead become a stalwart American ally.

Thomas Fleming

When Marie-Joseph-Paul-Yves-Roch-Gilbert du Motier, Marquis de Lafayette, arrived in South Carolina in June 1777, he intended to aid the faltering American Revolution in any way he could. The 19-year-old aristocrat and soldier was unaware, however, that his traveling companions included one whose secret mission was to depose George Washington as commander in chief of the Continental Army. That man was Baron Johann de Kalb, and his evolution from European intriguer to American military hero is one of the great stories of the Revolution.

Though a close friend and adviser to the idealistic Lafayette, de Kalb was no starry-eyed postadolescent. He was a 55-year-old professional soldier, a title to which few in the French army had better claim.

De Kalb was born in 1721 to peasant parents in the Bavarian principality of Ansbach-Beyreuth. By the age of 22 the husky 6-footer with the searching brown eyes, ample forehead and chiseled nose had somehow obtained the noble "de" before his last name. While most historians think he simply invented it, he may have acquired it from a ruler of one of the many tiny principalities and duchies into which Bavaria was divided in those days. Whatever its origin, the title could only have helped him as he set out on his military career.

As a young man he served as a lieutenant in the Löwendahl Regiment, among the best German units in the service of France. De Kalb's baptism by fire came in the War of the Austrian Succession, a dynastic brawl that began in 1740 and pitted France, Spain and Prussia against Austria and Britain. Much of the fighting took place in present-day Belgium and Holland. By the time the carnage subsided in 1748, de Kalb was a captain and adjutant of his regiment—the "officer of detail" who ran things in peacetime.

In 1756 war again exploded between France and Britain. Over the next seven tumultuous years, de Kalb rose to lieutenant colonel and assistant quartermaster general of the Army of the Upper Rhine—positions that introduced him to many powerful French businessmen and politicians and won him the friendship of Charles-François de Broglie, the most influential general in the French army. A former field commander and onetime head of King Louis XV's private diplomatic service, de Broglie helped de Kalb acquire the Order of Military Merit, adding the title "baron" to the younger man's noble "de".

In 1764 Baron de Kalb retired from the army and married Anna Elizabeth Emilie van Robais, heiress to a fortune made by Dutch cloth makers who had immigrated to France. De Kalb bought a handsome chateau near Paris and for several years was a seemingly contented civilian. But the humiliating peace the victorious British had imposed on France at the close of the Seven Years' War left de Broglie and many other professional soldiers hungry for revenge. Especially galling was the way Britain had stripped France of most of her overseas empire in North America and India.

In 1768 de Broglie persuaded Étienne François, the French chief minister, to send de Kalb to America to assess a brewing revolution that might detach the colonies from Britain; among his many talents, de Kalb spoke fluent English. In four months of travel along America's Eastern Seaboard, he learned enough to advise de Broglie that French intervention would be unwise at the moment. The colonists were indeed riled over British attempts at taxation, but most remained too hostile to Catholic France and too enamored of their English heritage to consider a French alliance.

Thanks mostly to British arrogance and stupidity, the American Revolution erupted much sooner than de Kalb predicted. But it was a chaotic affair, and after some rebel gains in 1775, the British dispatched a huge fleet and army that in 1776 wreaked havoc on General Washington and his untrained battalions.

In August 1775, de Broglie, perhaps anticipating the difficulties colonists would face in trying to throw off the British yoke unassisted, had arranged a meeting in France between Lafayette and William, Duke of Gloucester, younger brother of

King George III. During that meeting the duke expressed some sympathy with the Americans in their revolt, and an inspired Lafayette concluded his personal involvement in the revolution might aid the colonists' effort.

Resolved to stir up as much trouble as possible for the British, and believing Washington incapable of leading his troops to victory, de Broglie decided de Kalb should also journey to the colonies. His mission would be to rescue the faltering revolution by persuading the rebels to replace Washington with de Broglie as commander of the Continental Army. If de Kalb succeeded, America would become a decisive weapon in France's global power struggle with England.

To the Europeans the scheme was neither far-fetched nor venal. Foreign soldiers were common in European armies—a fact of which de Kalb himself was a prime example. Moreover, as a Freemason, de Broglie was truly sympathetic to the American cause. So was de Kalb; in late 1775 he wrote to a German friend in Philadelphia that he was ready to "devote the rest of my days in the service of your liberty and to the utmost of my ability employ my 32 years experience acquired in the military art for your advantage."

The plan hatched, de Kalb took leave from the French army and signed a contract with Silas Deane of Connecticut, whom the Americans had sent to France to buy weapons and supplies. The baron was assured a commission as a major general in the Continental Army, and de Kalb also secured commissions for 15 other lower-ranking officers he and de Broglie had chosen to facilitate the takeover.

Paris swirled with rumors of others who sought to help the sinking revolt, notably young Lafayette, France's richest nobleman. De Kalb encouraged him, and soon Lafayette, too, secured a major generalship from the ebullient Deane—a gesture that would have been unthinkable had de Kalb not pledged to mentor the young marquis. The baron remained confident his professional experience would give him the weight he needed to persuade the colonists to send for de Broglie. After several irritating delays, Lafayette bought a ship and sailed for America with de Kalb and entourage.

Arriving in the summer of 1777, the French volunteers got a frosty reception from Washington and the Continental Congress. The American commander in chief had rescued the revolutionary cause with last-ditch victories in Trenton and Princeton that winter, and rebels' confidence in him had soared. Moreover, Deane had heedlessly handed out commissions to far too many Europeans, all of who expected a general's or colonel's rank and privileges. American officers, toughened by two years of war, were loath to take orders from newcomers. Lafayette sized up the situation and volunteered to serve without pay. He would be happy, he said, to accept a place on Washington's staff as "a pupil."

De Kalb, with his three decades of military experience, would not even consider following Lafayette's example. He was about to return to France when Congress relented and again offered him a major generalship. Lafayette, who had become deeply impressed with de Kalb on their voyage to America, may have interceded with Washington on his mentor's behalf.

By the time de Kalb joined the Continental Army, Washington had lost Philadelphia and was wintering his discouraged troops at a dreary spot called Valley Forge. He gave de Kalb command of a division spearheaded by brigadier generals Ebenezer Learned and John Patterson, but even this gesture of confidence failed to change the baron's poor opinion of the American commander.

In a letter to France, de Kalb condemned Valley Forge as a "wooded wilderness, certainly one of the poorest districts in Pennsylvania; the soil thin, uncultivated and almost uninhabited, without forage and without provisions!" Worse, as far as de Kalb was concerned, "We are to lie in shanties, generals and privates." He grimly concluded, "The idea of wintering in this desert can only have been put in the head of the commanding general by an interested speculator or a disaffected man."

In letters de Kalb described Washington as "the weakest general" he had ever seen, a man who repeatedly succumbed to bad advice from Congress or aides and subordinate generals.

In other letters de Kalb described Washington as "the weakest general" he had ever seen, a man who repeatedly succumbed to bad advice from Congress or aides and subordinate generals. De Kalb and his colleagues were developing an equally low opinion of the whole American Revolution. Shortly before the Army marched to Valley Forge, gifted engineer Brig. Gen. Louis Duportail wrote to the French minister of war: "Such are the people that they move without spring or energy . . . and without a passion for the cause in which they are engaged, and in which they follow only as the hand which puts them in motion directs. There is a hundred times more enthusiasm for this revolution in any one coffeehouse at Paris than in the 13 provinces united."

Lafayette was equally shocked by the widespread lack of enthusiasm for the revolution. "When I was in Europe," the marquis told Washington in labored, recently acquired English, "I thought here almost every man was a lover of liberty and rather die free than live [a] slave.

"You can conceive my astonishment," Lafayette continued, upon discovering that many Americans professed loyalty to George III as often as devotion to the newborn republic. Having arrived under the false impression that "all good Americans were united together," Lafayette instead discovered "dissensions in Congress [and] parties who hate one another as much as the enemy itself."

Proof of this grim fact was a growing contingent in Congress that wanted to replace Washington with Maj. Gen. Horatio Gates, who had won a crucial victory at Saratoga while Washington was losing the struggle for Philadelphia. Brig. Gen. Thomas Conway, an Irish-born French officer hired by Deane, eagerly joined this intrigue, badmouthing Washington in taverns and in the halls of Congress. But the levelheaded de Kalb declined to participate, despite the opportunity to advance de Broglie as a far better candidate for supreme command.

In truth, de Kalb's opinion of Washington and the revolution he was leading had already begun to change. The Bavarian also realized the blue-blooded and imperious de Broglie would never be able to cope with the mélange of hostile congressmen, incompetent quartermasters and commissaries, and Army intriguers whipped up by the ambitious Gates and the loose-lipped Conway.

As a professional soldier, de Kalb was a lifelong student of leadership. He was also a realist. He regarded Washington as a fellow realist—a leader who didn't sit around wailing about his troops' failures and weaknesses, but rather coped with them. The tall Virginian dazzled Congress with a masterful report on the Army's problems and won the authority to choose his own quartermaster and commissary generals, who soon had the soldiers eating well. When officers by the dozen began resigning their commissions rather than endure the privations of Valley Forge, Washington demanded and got from the reluctant Congress a promise of half pay for life for the men.

Given the divided Congress and lackluster public support, de Kalb realized that without Washington the revolution would probably collapse. He wrote to de Broglie, telling him that it simply was not "practicable" to replace Washington with a foreign commander. He also wrote to Henry Laurens of South Carolina, the president of Congress and a swing figure in the "Get Washington!" game. De Kalb told Laurens the Virginian was "the only proper person" to command the Army, saying, "He does more every day than could be expected from any general in the world, under the circumstances."

De Kalb said Washington was "the only proper person" to command the Army. "He does more every day than could be expected."

When Gates and fellow conspirators offered Lafayette command of a winter invasion of Canada, the marquis insisted on de Kalb as his second; the plotters had wanted Conway. Arriving in Albany, Lafayette and de Kalb found no preparations for a serious campaign. De Kalb advised Lafayette to abandon the enterprise. The marquis did so and skewered the inept Gates and fellow conspirators in a series of savage letters to Laurens.

The purgatory of Valley Forge ended with the electrifying news that France had signed a treaty of alliance with the United States. The panicky British retreated from Philadelphia to New York and launched a terror campaign against American civilians, burning seaports in Connecticut and Massachusetts and ravaging inland towns. It was then that de Kalb,

disgusted by these tactics, became a wholehearted supporter of the American cause. But circumstances conspired to keep him out of the few battles fought in 1778 and 1779. In a letter to his wife, de Kalb complained he had yet to hear a shot fired in "this frustrating war."

In 1778 the British, discouraged by their failures in the North, shifted the war to the South. They swiftly conquered Georgia and besieged the southern Continental Army in Charleston. In a gesture of continued confidence in de Kalb, Washington gave the baron command of two veteran brigades—about 1,200 men from Delaware and Maryland—and ordered him to march to Charleston's relief. Maj. Gen. Benjamin Lincoln's garrison surrendered to the British while de Kalb and his men were en route, however, and American resistance in South Carolina evaporated.

Amid the melee, the huge, roaring de Kalb was an obvious target. Enemy bayonets found their mark, and bullets thudded home.

Congress then unilaterally chose Gates to remedy the situation, and Washington ordered de Kalb to place himself under the intriguer's command. Gates, confident he could replicate his Saratoga triumph, rushed south in July 1780 and called out 1,800 untrained militia, mostly from North Carolina, giving him about 3,200 rank and file. He christened this shaky collection of veterans and amateurs "the Grand Army." The British field commander, Lord Charles Cornwallis, marched to meet Gates' challenge with about 2,250 men, all seasoned regulars. Cornwallis' goal was to defend the major British supply base at Camden, S.C.

In the Continental Army, everything was going wrong. De Kalb's men were starving, as the rudimentary governments of North Carolina and Virginia had done nothing to supply them. Regardless, Gates astonished everyone by ordering the Army to march immediately, telling the troops they would soon be well fed. Gates was relying on written assurance from guerrilla leader Thomas Sumter, who insisted only about 700 British troops stood between the Grand Army and Camden.

De Kalb and several brigadier generals advised Gates either to retreat or circle west through Salisbury to obtain food and rum. Gates ignored them and led the Army on a more direct route through desolate pine barrens and swamps, where the men got sick eating unripe peaches and corn. After 120 exhausting miles, Gates capped his ineptitude by ordering a night march to launch a surprise attack on the British camp—the worst imaginable tactic for mostly amateur soldiers barely able to form a column.

Adding to the American disarray was another Gates brainstorm: Having no rum, he gave his men a gill of molasses at dinner. Mixed with mush and dumplings, this dessert had a catastrophic effect on the men's intestines. The night march was repeatedly disrupted as dozens of men rushed to the nearby woods to relieve themselves.

Meanwhile, Cornwallis had decided to attack the Americans.

On August 16, the two armies collided in the predawn darkness about five miles from Camden. After a brief skirmish, they withdrew to wait for sunrise. Washington had already recognized the militia's inability to withstand a British frontal assault. Ignoring those hard lessons, Gates formed a line of battle, the amateurs comprising his left wing and center. De Kalb and his veterans were on the right, with one Maryland regiment in reserve. Swamps protected the flanks of both armies.

After a brief artillery barrage and a single volley, the well-fed, well-liquored British infantry charged, bayonets lowered, screaming insults and curses. The American militiamen broke without firing a shot, abandoning guns, packs and self-respect. Gates, shouting that he would rally them, rode off in their wake and didn't look back for 60 miles. That act of cowardice left de Kalb and his veterans to cope with an inflamed, rampaging British infantry almost twice their number.

De Kalb called for the reserve, the 1st Maryland Regiment, whose general had fled the field with Gates. Assuming command, one of the unit's colonels tried to bring the regiment into line beside de Kalb's men. But the British had swarmed around the Continentals' right flank, opening a 600-foot gap. The astute Cornwallis ordered them to change front and attack the new arrivals. In a half-hour of fierce fighting, the British routed the Marylanders.

That left de Kalb and his 600 Maryland and Delaware men to fend off the entire enemy force. At first the Americans didn't just hold their own, they prevailed, in one bayonet charge capturing 50 prisoners. Then the British attacked on all sides. Bullets smashed into de Kalb's horse, sending it crashing to the swampy earth. Undeterred, he drew his sword and personally led another bayonet attack.

It was brutal hand-to-hand combat. At one point, a British saber slashed open de Kalb's head. A nearby officer bandaged the wound and begged him to leave the field. De Kalb refused and called for another counterattack. His men broke through the oncoming British, swung around and smashed into them from the rear. Amid the melee, the huge, roaring de Kalb was an obvious target. Enemy bayonets found their mark, and bullets thudded home till he was bleeding from 11 wounds.

Then came a ferocious British cavalry charge that broke the surviving American veterans and sent them fleeing into the swamps. The mortally wounded de Kalb toppled to the ground. His aide, Charles, Chevalier du Buisson, threw himself across the baron's body, shouting de Kalb's name and rank as the British infantry rushed to sink their bayonets into him one last time.

Cornwallis and his staff were riding across the chaotic battlefield and intervened. The British commander ordered de Kalb carried to his tent. The baron lived another three days, conscious until the end. He ordered du Buisson to relay his thanks and praise to the officers and men of the Delaware and Maryland regiments who had fought so well beside him. De Kalb also told one sympathetic British officer that he faced death consoled by the thought that he gave his life "as a soldier fighting for the rights of man." The ultimate professional soldier would die an American patriot.

For further reading, **THOMAS FLEMING** recommends: *General de Kalb: Lafayette's Mentor,* by A. E. Zucker, and *The Life of John Kalb,* by Friedrich Kapp.

Getting Out
The First Rule of Holes

"Know when to hold 'em, know when to fold 'em, know when to walk away, know when to run," the gambler says in a popular song. But in the aftermath of imperialism and war, walking away is not so simple. *Dissent's* editors asked several scholars and writers to look at British, French, and American exit strategies—and to pay special attention to the difficulties, above all, the need to protect friends and collaborators and to minimize violence. In these pages, the focus is on each particular case—the American colonies, the Philippines, India, Korea, Algeria, and Vietnam—but we are obviously looking toward an American withdrawal from Iraq. We will write about that in the Spring *Dissent*. EDS.

STANLEY WEINTRAUB

How does one recognize the looming inevitable? In the 1760s, the British, having defeated the French in America and expanded George III's overseas empire, saw only profit and prestige ahead. A New England cleric, the Reverend Samuel Cooper, told his congregation that the colonists were indebted "not only for their present Security and Happiness, but, perhaps for their very Being, to the paternal Care of the Monarch." The legitimacy of royal rule was little questioned. In that future seedbed of sedition, Boston, Thomas Foxcroft declared, "Above all, we owe our humble *Thanks* to his Majesty and with loyal Hearts full of joyous Gratitude, we bless the *King*, for his Paternal Goodness in sending such effectual Aids to his American Subjects . . . when we needed the Royal Protection."

Fighting a seven-year war three thousand miles from home, when travel time was measured in months, had pinched the British economy. Why not, then, have the colonists, who had been rescued from the wicked French, pay something for their own protection? It was a petty stamp tax on printed paper, a bargain fee (a quarter of what Britons at home paid) on imported tea. It would go to quartering Redcoats to keep away marauding Indians, or to inhibit revengeful "Frogs."

This imperial logic escaped its beneficiaries. Outspoken colonists resented paying anything on their own behalf, claiming lack of representation in Parliament, the tax-raising body in remote London. But that complaint was only the tip of the trade iceberg. Colonists by law could not manufacture weapons or ammunition (or much else) for their own defense. British industry at home was sustained by commercial barriers. Americans were to supply the raw materials for the making of goods they would have to buy as finished products.

Within a decade, objections about taxes, trade, and troops had plucked the gilded genie from the transatlantic bottle. Colonial farmers, craftsmen, and merchants began proposing a new concept, *liberty,* as a solution to their discontent. In Britain, complacent merchants, manufacturers, and landowners saw only ignorance, ingratitude, and greed motivating the radicalized handful of New England Yankees, who—despite a way with words—lacked arms and fighting zeal. In the seemingly tractable South, Tory planters—self-styled aristocrats—prospered alongside a noisy rabble and illiterate backwoodsmen. Samuel Johnson grumbled that deprivation of the "rights of Englishmen" was an unrealistic grievance. Americans were no less represented in Parliament than most inhabitants on his own side of the water, who lived in increasingly teeming districts excluded from seats in Parliament. Americans were "a race of convicts, and ought to be thankful for any thing we allow them short of hanging."

Did the Establishment foresee unwelcome change? Could it maintain the imperial equilibrium by granting token seats— unlikely ever to be occupied—in the House of Commons, as London was an ocean away and members unsalaried, or by prudently tucking Redcoats away in obscure barracks; or by relaxing commercial restrictions, to forestall such outrages as a Boston Tea Party; or by proposing that prosperity be shared? Could a royal symbolic presence suffice? We will never know. Instead, what were called the Coercive Acts annulled most local rights granted under colonial charters, turning over elections, appointments, and the administration of justice to Crown officials.

Henry Laurens, a political moderate from South Carolina, later to become presiding officer of the Continental Congress, warned that the colonists, who until then saw little in common, "would be animated to form . . . a Union and phalanx of resistance." In lonely opposition, a few Members of Parliament rose to urge that negotiation would have a better chance of resolving differences than coercion, although as mutual hostility grew, it became clear that any compromise short of some form of independence would not be accepted. The outgoing secretary of war, Viscount Barrington, predicted that pursuing a hard line, however popular at home, "will cost us more than we can ever gain by success." Advising conciliation, the ailing William Pitt, the Elder, now Lord Chatham, warned, "We shall be forced ultimately to retreat: let us retreat when we can, not when we must."

Royal supremacists failed the geopolitical test of maps. In the early 1770s, few recognized, as did Pitt, that the sprawling overseas colonies, more than 1,800 miles north to south, would become more populous than the mother country and would be impossible to subdue, oversee, and manage. At the start of the small-scale and unexpected rebellion, George III impatiently condemned the first risings as parricide—a conspiracy against the "parent state." He was "unalterably determined," he told a supine Parliament, many of its members bought off by the Palace, "to compel absolute submission." Yet, as Ben Franklin observed, once hostilities began in 1775, "Britain, at the expence of three millions, has killed 150 Yankees this campaign, which is [£]20,000 a head; and at Bunker's Hill . . . gained a mile of ground. . . . During the same time 60,000 children have been born in America." Anyone versed in mathematics, he posited, "will easily calculate the time and expence necessary to kill us all, and conquer our whole territory."

From the vantage point of a Cabinet office under Lord North, the Earl of Suffolk saw no reason for alarm at early reverses in Massachusetts. "The stocks are unaffected, and the respectable part of the City is in very proper sentiments." He deplored any "disinclination to persevere." Nevertheless, Edmund Burke, MP for Bristol and an outspoken, if outnumbered, critic of colonial policy, warned of "iron tears" being shed—musket shot and cannon balls fired in helpless anger. The king reminded his subjects, rather, of national honor, by which he implied international embarrassment. But behind his rhetoric lay the feared economic repercussions of losing America. "No man in my dominions desires solid peace more than I do," he claimed, "but no inclination to get out of the present difficulties can incline me to enter into the destruction of the empire." Besides, his hawkish military advisers in Whitehall, preeminent among them Lord George Germain, the micromanaging secretary for America, saw "no common sense in protracting a war of this sort. I should be for exerting the utmost force of this Kingdom to finish the rebellion in one campaign."

As Count Helmuth von Moltke would write in the next century, no strategy survives the first contact with the enemy. British generals recommended forcing the war to a conclusion, although one commander would replace another as each, in turn, failed. All were ambitious careerists, with promotions, titles, and parliamentary gratuities dancing in their heads. General John Burgoyne, who, before a shot was fired, advocated "persuasion rather than the sword," now decried diverting "British thunder" by "pitiful attentions and Quaker-like scruples." They possessed overwhelming military superiority. They were better equipped, better trained, more numerous, and more professional than the poorly equipped, ragged, undisciplined patchwork amateurs serving short enlistments and unlikely to stay on for further service. The London *Morning Post* published a list of rebel generals ostensibly ridiculed for their prewar occupations—a boat builder, a bookseller, a servant, a milkman, a jockey, a clerk. It was a covert satire on British snobbery, implying that commanders of noble birth were overmatched by officers reaching the top by merit in classless America. Misguided generalship was compounded by civilian arrogance at Whitehall. "Rarely has British strategy," Winston Churchill would write, "fallen into such a multitude of errors. Every principle of war was either violated or disregarded."

Although the British had a surplus of brass, as the war dragged on it became frustrating to fill the ranks. When it became difficult to raise more Redcoats, Parliament obstinately authorized hiring thousands of mercenaries from German statelets ("Hessians," although not all were from Hesse) and constructing warships by the dozen. The amphibious assault on Long Island and Manhattan employed an armada not surpassed in numbers until D-Day in 1944, yet in remote upstate New York in 1777, Burgoyne and his army, bereft of reinforcements, surrendered at Saratoga.

General William Howe took the rebel capital, Philadelphia, chasing George Washington into woeful winter quarters at Valley Forge. Still, Washington was winning merely by keeping his army alive while imperial overstretch took its toll. The insurgency thrived on British attrition. With more land to occupy and control than he had troops to accomplish the job, Howe scuttled back to New York the next spring, explaining later from London, once he had been replaced (and promoted), that professional soldiers lost to shot and disease would be difficult to replace from across an ocean, while the upstart Americans could recruit marginally trained militiamen close at hand. He would "never expose the troops . . . where the object is inadequate."

If the object was not worth the effort, why not abandon it? Undeterred, other generals succeeded Howe. Never numerous, local loyalist volunteers were decreasing, while further foreign hirelings were largely unaffordable under dwindling budgets, captive now to the contagion of pessimism and new parliamentary parsimony. Even the country landowners, the conservative backbone of the regime, were becoming disillusioned, as a wry "Dialogue between a Country Squire and his Tenant" suggested in the *London Gazeteer* in 1778:

Tenant: Pray, Squire, when do you think the war will end?

Squire: At Doomsday, *perhaps* sooner; but this is certain, the nation is almost ruined, and we country gentlemen are the greatest sufferers.

As an unbridled press revealed, returning casualties and the declining standards for enlistment made soldiering a grim option, largely for the jobless and the poor. "An Exact Representation of Manchester Recruits," captioning a cartoon of weird, dehumanized volunteers, illustrated the increasing national pain. "The Master of the Arses, or the Westminster Volunteers" showed six motley recruits spurred on, front and rear, by bayonet-bearing Redcoats, one inductee stumbling with a crutch and stick, another on gouty, swathed legs. "The Church Militant" satirized an equally useless dimension of belligerence. In that broadside, a group of clergy, some lean and ascetic, others stout and gross, all led by obtuse bishops, sing "O Lord Our God, Arise and Scatter Our Enemies." Desperation about the war was out in the open.

Decades later, Charles Dickens imagined a scene in *Barnaby Rudge,* in the aptly named Black Lion tavern in the late 1770s, in which the barkeep observes scornfully as a recruiting sergeant offers his spiel, "I'm told there ain't a deal of difference between a fine man and another one, when they're shot through and through."

The sergeant suggests to potential enlistees a life of wine, women, and glory, and a timid voice pipes, "Supposing you should be killed, sir?" Confidently, the Redcoat responds, "What then? Your country loves you, sir; his Majesty King George the Third loves you; your memory is honoured, revered, respected; . . . your name's wrote down at full length in a book in the War Office. Damme, gentlemen, we must all die some time or other, eh!" Pages later, the publican's son, who fell for the sales pitch and has returned from Savannah, sits quietly in the tavern with one sleeve empty. "It's been took off," his father explains, "at the defence of the Salwanners. . . . In America, where the war is." To his listeners, it is all meaningless.

While losses, prices, and taxes fueled anxiety, no effective tactics surfaced to put down the rebellion. End-the-war adherents were an increasing yet still powerless minority. Since the "experiment" of putting the Americans down was failing, the *St. James's Chronicle* editorialized, Britain should "withdraw in time with a good grace, and declare them INDEPENDENT." Although the House of Lords remained firmly behind the king, in the Commons a former general and Cabinet minister, Henry Seymour Conway, moved that "this mad war" should "no longer be pursued." The motion failed by one vote. "We are not only *patriots out of place,*" Sir George Savile, a Yorkshire MP, remarked gloomily to the Marquis of Rockingham, "but patriots *out of the opinion of the public.*" Rockingham advised waiting "till the Publick are actually convinced of the calamitous State we are in." That would come only after the futile campaigns of Earl Cornwallis in the presumably safe American South. Not many months after, Rockingham would be the first peace prime minister.

Cornwallis busied himself evading defeat, but he ran out of alternatives late in 1781, once the French intervened by land and sea. Third forces are often crucial. Uninterested in American ideals about liberty and equality, the French were determined to give the British a black eye and arrived in Yorktown before a rescue fleet from New York. Abroad, few had been listening to radicals like Josiah Tucker, an Anglican divine and amateur economist, who in a pamphlet, *Cui Bono,* called for getting out. America, he charged, had become a "millstone" round the neck of Britain. "If we ourselves have not the wisdom to cut the Rope, and let the Burthen fall off, the Americans have kindly done it for us."

As Cornwallis surrendered at Yorktown, a British band played "The World turn'd Upside Down." After further weeks of national dismay, George Germain, pushed to resign, was rewarded for his sacrifice with a viscountcy. A broadside cartoon, "Three Thousand Leagues beyond the Cannon's Reach," portrayed him satirically yet realistically as unable to direct military affairs from distant London. His office as secretary for America was soon abolished by Rockingham's reform government.

T he British had no exit strategy other than victory. Capitulation and a draft treaty negotiated in Paris the next year with the grudgingly recognized United States required evacuating troops from the few Atlantic seaports they still held and keeping faith somehow with loyalists still within British boundaries. There were also thousands of prisoners of war to be paroled, held hostage in vain by Congress for payment of their upkeep. The hard and possibly thankless decisions were left to the pragmatic last Redcoat commander, Sir Guy Carleton, who, with a mere knighthood, eyed a peerage for his services. (He would get it.) Fleets of transports would evacuate Charleston, Wilmington in North Carolina, and tightly held Savannah, taking with them prominent but angry loyalists who had to abandon their properties. Most were promised only a sailing to Halifax and resettlement in the sparsely populated Maritime Provinces. Diehards were granted six hundred very likely untillable acres; officers choosing Canada were offered fifteen hundred acres; and men in the ranks could look forward to a meager fifty. Some troops opting for further duty were sent to the West Indies to garrison sugar islands against the French.

Under occupation beyond New York and Long Island were isolated frontier posts on the Canadian border held for payment of colonial debts acknowledged in the treaty. As the financial settlements were made unwillingly and late, Forts Niagara, Oswego, Presque Isle, Mackinaw, and Detroit would not be relinquished until the mid-1790s. The Treaty of Paris called for the British departure to be accomplished "with all convenient speed," but the major remaining enclave of New York was held by Carleton until he had confirmation of acceptable guarantees for withdrawal of his troops and local loyalists. About three thousand slaves within British lines were permitted to leave with owners who certified them. Others were reclaimed by Washington's "commissioners" (for lack of documentation) as "American property," while most aged, sick, and otherwise helpless slaves were cynically abandoned to freedom as worthless for labor. Ironically, the chattels left behind were liberated for less than idealistic reasons, but Washington, after all, was a slaveholder.

For Carleton, getting out was a logistic nightmare. It had taken 479 vessels to bring the first 39,000 troops to New York in July 1776. Re-embarking the occupiers and their equipage required much more—several months and hundreds of sailings and return sailings through early December 1783, as frantic sympathizers by the thousands (29,244 evacuees from New York to gloomy Nova Scotia alone), along with their most prized goods, were assured accommodation. Few—only the wealthy elite and those closely associated with the royal government—were eligible for immigration to England, where Benedict Arnold had already arrived, to no acclaim, with his family. The British had no interest in housing, employing, or feeding their miserable and burdensome transatlantic cousins.

Humiliated, George III threatened to abdicate in favor of the playboy Prince of Wales, but prudently dropped the idea. Rather, in a rare attack of realism, the king belatedly recognized the first rule of holes: when you realize you're in one, stop digging. His second thoughts went into a draft memorandum now in the Royal Archives at Windsor. Getting out, he realized, had been the right course all along, although accomplished now for the wrong reason—defeat. "America is lost!" the king wrote. "Must we fall beneath the blow? Or have we resources to repair the mischief?"

Alternatives to the "Colonial Scheme," he contended, would sustain British power and prosperity while involving an independent American nation. "A people spread over an immense tract of fertile land, industrious because free, and rich because industrious, presently [will] become a market for the Manufactures and Commerce of the Mother Country." He conceded that the war had been "mischievous to Britain, because it created an expence of blood and treasure worth more . . . than we received

from America." The more potent Americans became, the less they would be "fit instruments to preserve British power and consequence." Investing any effort to regain hegemony over the colonies would only contribute to "the insecurity of our power." Was an empire destined to be lost worth the price to preserve it? Through the global marketplace the lost lands could still promote British prosperity. Getting out, even accepting humiliation, he argued, could be an unforeseen boon if exploited wisely.

The king's document, based on the thwarted American experience, was a remarkable prophecy. Yet George conceded that the catastrophe had so weakened him at home that he had no clout with his ministers, reactionary or radical. He put the draft aside. Future governments would pour vast resources into subjugating, yet failing to assimilate, the successor jewel in the Crown—the subcontinent of India—and millions of square miles of indigestible Africa, eventually to relinquish them all at staggering cost to the home islands. It was always foolhardy to be tempted to stay, and always too late to get out. "Mutual interest," the Reverend Tucker had opined, was "the only Tie . . . in all Times and Seasons, and this Principle will hold good, I will be bold to say, till the end of Time."

STANLEY WEINTRAUB is author of *Iron Tears: America's Battle for Freedom, Britain's Quagmire* (Free Press, 2005) and *General Washington's Christmas Farewell: A Mount Vernon Homecoming, 1783* (Plume, 2004).

UNIT 3

National Consolidation and Expansion

Unit Selections

Key Points to Consider

- Discuss the opposing visions of Alexander Hamilton and Thomas Jefferson as the new government got underway. Who tended to win out during the Washington administration?

- Why can the Louisiana Purchase be considered a "revolution"? Discuss the ramifications of this acquisition at the time and for the future course of United States history.

- Compare and contrast the status of white women and black slaves during the early Republic. White women obviously had certain advantages, but what were the similarities?

- Analyze the impact the invention of the cotton gin had on slavery with regard to working conditions and treatment of slave families.

- Manufacturing during the nation's early years moved from the home, to the shop, to the factory. How did this transition affect the status and treatment of workers?

- Andrew Jackson has been condemned for his brutal treatment of Indians. What policies did he institute than can be viewed as innovative and precursors of the modern presidency?

- William Henry Harrison's campaign in 1840 emphasized his fondness for hard cider as opposed to elitists who preferred wine and champagne. More recently, one candidate professed his love for pork rinds and another had herself photographed swigging beer from a bottle. What does this sort of pandering say about our electoral process?

Student Website
www.mhhe.com/cls

Internet References

Consortium for Political and Social Research
   http://www.icpsr.umich.edu
Department of State
   http://www.state.gov
Mystic Seaport
   http://amistad.mysticseaport.org
Social Influence Website
   http://www.workingpsychology.com/intro.html

University of Virginia Library
   http://www.lib.virginia.edu/exhibits/lewis_clark
Women in America
   http://xroads.virginia.edu/~HYPER/DETOC/FEM
Women of the West
   http://www.wowmuseum.org

The individuals who wrote the U.S. Constitution could only provide a general structure under which the government would work. Those involved in actually making the system function had to venture into uncharted territory. There were no blueprints as to exactly which body had what powers or what their relationships with one another would be. And, if disputes arose, which individual or group would act as arbiter? Officials during the first few years after 1789 were conscious that practically everything they did would be regarded as setting precedents for the future. Even such apparently trivial matters as the proper form of addressing the president caused debate. From hindsight of more than 200 years, it is difficult to appreciate how tentative they had to be in establishing this newborn government.

The most fundamental difference over the Constitution arose over whether it should be interpreted strictly or loosely. That is, should governmental powers be limited to those expressly granted in the document, or were there "implied" powers that could be exercised as long as they were not expressly prohibited? Many of the disputes were argued on principles, but the truth is that most individuals were trying to promote programs that would benefit the interests they represented.

George Washington, as first president, was a towering figure who provided a stabilizing presence during the seemingly endless squabbles. He believed that he served the entire nation, and that there was no need for political parties (he disdainfully referred to them as "factions"), which he regarded as divisive. Despite his disapproval, nascent political parties did begin to develop fairly early on in his first administration.

Washington's first Secretary of the Treasury, Alexander Hamilton, almost invariably favored those measures that would benefit the commercial and manufacturing interests of the Northeast. Secretary of State Thomas Jefferson and his ally James Madison just as often spoke for the rural and agricultural interests of the West and the South. These two groups frequently clashed over what the Constitution did or did not permit, what sources of revenue should be tapped to pay for government, and a host of other issues. The fact that Washington most often sided with Hamilton's views made him a partisan despite his wish to remain above the fray. "The Best of Enemies" analyzes the Hamilton–Jefferson struggle.

The Constitution's failure to provide for political parties led to a major crisis following the election of 1800. Aaron Burr and Thomas Jefferson ended up tied in the electoral college even though both were Republicans. There were threats of violence over this issue, and some states even threatened secession unless it was resolved satisfactorily. "Cliffhanger" examines this situation and the way it was settled.

"Fallen Timbers Broken Alliance" tells how Anthony Wayne's victory over the Native Americans in 1794 resulted in British evacuation from forts in what is now known as the Midwest, thereby opening the area for American expansion. By 1803 the United States already was a large country, stretching from the Atlantic Ocean to the Mississippi River. Some said it was too large. Propertied Easterners complained that the western migration lowered property values and raised wages, and they feared population shifts would weaken their section's influence in government.

Library of Congress. LC-B8171-152-A

Others thought that the great distances involved might cause the system to fly apart, given the primitive means of communication and transportation at the time. When Thomas Jefferson had the unexpected opportunity to double the nation's size by purchasing the huge Louisiana Territory, as discussed in "The Revolution of 1803," he altered the course of American history.

Two articles analyze the conditions under which dispossessed Americans had to live during these years. "Women in the Early Republic" argues that although a great deal of attention has been paid to the history of women in recent years, the period 1790 to 1830 has been neglected. This essay helps explain why. The invention of the cotton gin in the 1790s had an enormous impact on the institution of slavery. "The Everyday Life of Enslaved People in the Antebellum South" describes how it resulted in the large-scale migration of slaves from the Upper South to states such as Mississippi and Alabama. Working conditions in the new areas were extremely harsh and many slave families were broken apart in the process.

Manufacturing in the early years moved from the home to small shops, which in turn gave way to factories employing relatively large numbers of people. At first some owners of these factories attempted to retain customs and relationships characteristic of the earlier period. In time these efforts were abandoned and workers were treated impersonally as just another cost of production. "Liberty Is Exploitation" describes this development.

According to legend, baseball was invented by Abner Doubleday in 1839, "Play Ball!" shows that the sport had been played for a long time by then. Many decades would pass, however, before it evolved into the game as it is played today.

As president, Andrew Jackson is best known today for having forced the evacuation of Indians from southern states resulting in what has been called the "Trail of Tears." "The Change Agent" treats this issue, but goes on to show how Jackson initiated a number of policies that anticipated the modern presidency.

"The Inebriated Election of 1840" discusses a phenomenon we have frequently witnessed in U.S. politics from that time until now. Candidates, some of them wealthy and highly educated, fall all over one another trying to identify themselves with "common" folk. Unfortunately, this sort of thing at times has greater impact on elections than an individual's stand on substantive issues.

"The Awful March of the Saints" describes a 1,300-mile trek from Iowa to Salt Lake City undertaken by 2000 Mormons in 1856. The journey was made doubly difficult because, in order to save money, the Mormons pushed or pulled hastily made handcarts instead of riding in wagons pulled by animals. This article, based on an eyewitness account, details the hardships endured during the trip, which resulted in the loss of at least 200 lives.

Fallen Timbers Broken Alliance

When the new nation needed a soldier to fight Indians and build a standing army, it called on a man whose hard-charging style had earned him the nickname "Mad Anthony".

Thomas Fleming

George Washington rarely lost his temper, but when he did, the explosion was a spectacle witnesses never forgot. Among the most memorable detonations occurred on Dec. 9, 1791, when a messenger from Secretary of War Henry Knox arrived at the president's Philadelphia mansion while Washington was entertaining dinner guests.

The president's secretary, Tobias Lear, hurried into the dining room and whispered there was news from Maj. Gen. Arthur St. Clair, commander of the Western army. The previous day a newspaper had reported a rumor the army had been mauled in a clash with Indians. The president excused himself, rushed to a nearby parlor to glance at St. Clair's dispatch, then returned to the table and chatted agreeably with his guests until they departed.

Having seen the visitors out, Lear walked into the parlor to find the 59-year-old Washington in a rage, his face red and eyes wild.

"It's all over!" the president roared, his long arms flailing. "St. Clair's defeated—routed! The officers nearly all killed! [I told him when] I took leave of him, 'Beware of a surprise!' And yet, to suffer that army be cut to pieces, hacked, butchered, tomahawked, by a surprise —the very thing I guarded him against! The blood of the slain is upon him; the curse of widows and orphans; the curse of heaven!"

For another five minutes, Washington damned St. Clair, using words that appalled the genteel Lear. Breathing in rasps, Washington finally flung himself on a nearby sofa. When he spoke again, it was in a calm measured voice: "This must not go beyond this room. General St. Clair shall have justice. I will hear him without prejudice."

But Washington was already thinking beyond St. Clair, whose military career was over. The president had realized his defeat could be a blessing in a very unpleasant disguise.

Even before Washington's 1789 election, the fledgling United States had been fighting an Indian war in the vast region between the Atlantic Ocean and the Mississippi River. Though Britain had officially ceded this territory in the treaty that ended the War for Independence, British officials in Canada refused to evacuate forts in the wilderness now called the Midwest and then called the Northwest Territory. Furthermore, King George III's representatives instructed their agents and traders to encourage Indian attacks on American settlers swarming into the region.

The result of Britain's perfidy was a series of brutal frontier massacres in which Indian war parties slaughtered an estimated 1,500 American men, women and children. Settlers in Kentucky screamed for vengeance and attacked even those tribes trying to remain at peace. Washington sent envoys to negotiate the amicable cession of some of the Indians' lands, but the Miamis, Shawnees and other warlike tribes evaded or violated the agreements.

To the president's intense frustration, the United States did not have a standing army to back his diplomacy with muscle. The reason was political: At the end of the Revolutionary War, soldiers of the Continental Army had threatened to march on Congress to extract money owed them. Though Washington had managed to talk his former troops out of such rash action, Congress came to abhor the idea of an army of regulars that might pose a threat to its authority and would require unpopular taxes to support.

Washington had proposed a token peacetime force of 3,000 men, but Congress icily ignored him. The politicians refused to recruit more than the lone regiment created in 1784. If more men were needed, the cynics said, the government could hire militiamen by the day. This reliance on amateur soldiers must have infuriated Washington, who'd told Congress throughout the war that militias specialized in running for the rear at the very sight of British bayonets.

Events soon validated Washington's opinion. In 1790 America's one-regiment regular army, reinforced by some 1,000 militiamen, launched a punitive attack on a cluster of hostile Miami villages near present-day Fort Wayne, Indiana. About 100 Miamis ambushed the advance guard, and the panicked militiamen abandoned the regulars in headlong flight. The following day the Indians mauled a second American detachment. Survivors stumbled back to Fort Washington, near present-day Cincinnati, Ohio, demoralized and humiliated. Little Turtle, the Miami chieftain, became a hero in the eyes of Northwest Indians.

The setbacks persuaded Congress to authorize creation of a second regiment and the raising of 2,000 "levies" for six months' service. Though considered regulars, these soldiers were closer to militia. To command this force, Washington and Knox chose St. Clair, who had been a major general during the Revolution. But anti-army ideologues in Congress soon undermined the new commander by reducing the regulars' pay. Less than 10 percent of the men whose enlistments expired that year signed up again. When St. Clair reached Fort Washington, he found the First Regiment had dwindled to 299 men. Recruiting for the

Soldiers, Politicians, and Indian Chiefs

George Washington Long determined to establish a standing American army despite widespread political opposition, the president knew that a professional and well-trained force would be vital in the ongoing Indian wars.

Arthur St. Clair Scottish-born and notoriously head-strong, St. Clair had a total lack of regard for his enemy's abilities, a flaw that ultimately led to the worst defeat inflicted on an American army by Indian forces.

Little Turtle Among the finest Indian military commanders of the 18th century, Little Turtle was a master of both hit-and-run tactics and set-piece combat. He led the Indian force that overwhelmed St. Clair's corps on Nov. 4, 1791.

Henry Knox Chief of the Continental Army artillery during the Revolution, in 1785 Knox became the United States' first secretary of war. It was he who tapped St. Clair to command the ill-fated regiments.

Lord Dorchester An experienced military leader, as Sir Guy Carleton he'd twice been governor of Quebec. In 1786, as governor in chief of British North America, he sought to contain the expansion of American influence.

John Graves Simcoe Appointed the first lieutenant governor of Upper Canada in 1791. Simcoe was ordered by Lord Dorchester to arm and support the Indian tribes fighting American forces throughout the Northwest Territory.

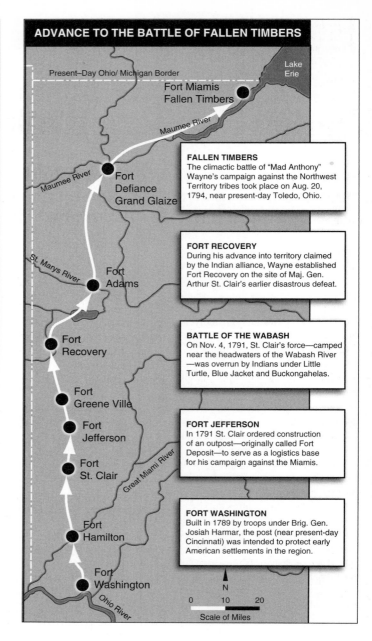

ADVANCE TO THE BATTLE OF FALLEN TIMBERS

FALLEN TIMBERS
The climactic battle of "Mad Anthony" Wayne's campaign against the Northwest Territory tribes took place on Aug. 20, 1794, near present-day Toledo, Ohio.

FORT RECOVERY
During his advance into territory claimed by the Indian alliance, Wayne established Fort Recovery on the site of Maj. Gen. Arthur St. Clair's earlier disastrous defeat.

BATTLE OF THE WABASH
On Nov. 4, 1791, St. Clair's force—camped near the headwaters of the Wabash River—was overrun by Indians under Little Turtle, Blue Jacket and Buckongahelas.

FORT JEFFERSON
In 1791 St. Clair ordered construction of an outpost—originally called Fort Deposit—to serve as a logistics base for his campaign against the Miamis.

FORT WASHINGTON
Built in 1789 by troops under Brig. Gen. Josiah Harmar, the post (near present-day Cincinnati) was intended to protect early American settlements in the region.

new Second Regiment also faltered, leaving the regulars 50 percent below their authorized strength. Saddled with his barely trained six-month levies, St. Clair was forced to call out 1,160 militiamen.

At dawn on Nov. 4, 1791, a 1,500-warrior force of Northwest Territory Indians under Little Turtle attacked St. Clair's unfortified campsite. Both militiamen and levies fled, and the attackers killed or wounded 64 officers and 807 enlisted men. In terms of casualty rate, it was the worst defeat inflicted by Indians on an American army. St. Clair managed to escape on one of the few surviving horses.

The destruction of St. Clair's force enabled Washington to browbeat a chastened Congress into authorizing four regular regiments, with three-year enlistments, plus a squadron of cavalry. As a sop to antiarmy politicians, Knox called the new force the Legion of the United States rather than the U.S. Army.

To lead the new Legion, Washington and Knox chose Pennsylvanian Anthony Wayne, a former Continental Army major general who had led the successful 1779 nighttime assault on the British fort at Stony Point, N.Y., and engineered a 1782 victory in Georgia over a much larger British army.

Wayne, whose hard-charging leadership style had earned him the nickname "Mad Anthony," was deep in debt from an ill-fated postwar venture as a Georgia rice grower and readily accepted Washington's offer. Told his army would be waiting for him in Pittsburgh, Wayne hastened there, only to find 40 morose recruits. Low pay and the prospect of facing the tomahawk-wielding "savages" who had slaughtered St. Clair's army did not attract the best and brightest. It took another 10 months for the nascent Legion to reach 1,200 men.

Wayne set about turning the illiterate farm boys and urban drifters into an army. They soon learned he was a professional soldier committed to unremitting discipline. Within five weeks in the fall of 1792, he executed seven deserters. Anyone found asleep on duty or showing "an intention to desert" got 100 lashes. Those on parade in a soiled uniform got 20 lashes. Drunk and disorderly officers were cashiered with equal ruthlessness.

To brace his tyro soldiers for the shock of war, Wayne set up mock combat. He sent one contingent into the woods with orders to imitate Indians. The chosen men stripped off their shirts and painted their bodies and faces. Then the rest of the army mounted an attack. The pseudo-Indians whooped and howled and fired blank cartridges as the attackers blasted back, roaring defiance. On the frontier, real Indians waited.

In the spring of 1793, Secretary of War Knox ordered Wayne to transport his men by boat to the disputed Northwest Territory. At Cincinnati, cheering crowds lined the banks of the Ohio River, greeting the soldiers as saviors. But the Indians, especially the warlike Miamis, were displeased with the proximity of Wayne's "legionnaires." They accused the government—still engaged in diplomatic efforts to defuse the frontier crisis—of speaking "with a double tongue."

Wayne asked the governor of Kentucky to call out 1,500 mounted militiamen. Responding militia commanders insisted they be allowed to act independently of Wayne's command. The request infuriated "Mad Anthony," who told them flatly they were in the pay of the United States and would obey his orders, or else. In an eloquent letter, Wayne warned them the Indian enemy was "a hydra," a widespread confederation hoping to cinch a chain "around the frontiers of America." The Kentuckians grudgingly agreed to obey the general.

Later that spring, news from Europe complicated matters: War had broken out between Great Britain and Revolutionary France. British officials in Canada in turn resolved to have Indian allies tie down any American forces that might invade the "14th colony" on France's behalf.

Thus prompted by the British, the Indians announced they would tolerate no Americans north of the Ohio River. American negotiators rejected the demand, given that several thousand Americans already lived on those lands under the provisions of prior treaties with individual tribes. Wayne, meanwhile, marched his army from Cincinnati 40 miles north to the American outpost at Fort Jefferson, then six miles farther into the wilderness Indians claimed was forever theirs. His soldiers built a fort that enclosed 50 acres, with huts for the enlisted men and roomier quarters for the officers. Wayne named it Fort Greene Ville, after Maj. Gen. Nathanael Greene, his closest friend in the Continental Army.

That winter Wayne confronted a stickier problem. Brig. Gen. James Wilkinson, his second in command, had overseen Fort Jefferson and other outposts in the Northwest Territory. A born liar and intriguer who sought Wayne's job, Wilkinson was also on the payroll of the Spanish government, as "Agent 13," and was hoping to make a fortune by persuading Kentucky to declare independence, backed by Spanish gold.

Wilkinson planted newspaper stories portraying Wayne as corrupt, cruel, incompetent and stupid, but "Mad Anthony" chose not to confront the disloyal subordinate and his supporters. Instead, while assuring the Indians he was willing to parley, Wayne marched eight companies of men 20 miles north to the battlefield where St. Clair's army had been butchered in 1792—the ground still littered with bones of the unburied dead. After interring the remains with military honors in a mass grave, Wayne ordered his men to build another stronghold, which he named Fort Recovery. He found the cannon St. Clair had abandoned and the Indians had buried and installed the guns in the new redoubt—an added gesture of defiance Wayne made sure the watching Indians noticed.

The Indians conferred with Lord Dorchester, the governor of Canada, who as General Guy Carleton had ably defended the colony against the Americans' 1775 invasion. Dorchester told the Indians that war between Britain and America was likely to flare up again within a year, and if the red men remained loyal to their benevolent father, George III, the Americans would be scoured from every foot of ground west of the great mountains. To prove his sincerity, Dorchester ordered Lt. Gov. John Graves Simcoe to build a fort on the Maumee River, 16 miles south of Lake Erie and well within American territory. Simcoe had commanded a Loyalist unit, the Queen's Rangers, during the Revolution and nursed a lifelong hatred of George Washington. He garrisoned the new outpost with regulars and named it Fort Miamis, in honor of Little Turtle's tribe.

The emboldened Indians decided to strike first at Wayne's Fort Recovery. On June 30, 1794, Little Turtle led an estimated 1,700 warriors through the forest. One British officer called it the most formidable Indian army in history. Their assault began with a classic ambush, as the Indians caught a 360-horse pack train in the open and annihilated it, killing a third of the soldiers in its 100-man escort. Then, whirling bloody scalps, the screaming warriors charged the fort.

It marked the first test of Wayne's 18 months of training and discipline. Fort Recovery's 250-man garrison met the assault with punishing musketry, firing buckshot and ball through loopholes as cannon flung grape into the Indian ranks. The stunned warriors sought cover behind tree stumps and sniped back for several hours, but it became apparent the fort was impregnable. The next day the attackers abandoned their siege.

The impact of failure on the fragile Indian confederacy was devastating. British agents had convinced more than 600 warriors from the Great Lakes tribes to join the attack, and its repulse prompted those warriors to pull out of the alliance and go home. An exultant Wayne hailed the victory and informed Knox that upon arrival of the 1,500 Kentucky volunteers his army would advance on the main Miami villages.

On July 29, 1794, in blazing summer heat, the Legion began its march. Ignoring his cautious aides, Wayne often rode with the advance guard to prove his confidence in their ability to repel an ambush. Each day the army set up camp well before sundown and built fortifications against a surprise attack. On August 2, after an advance of about 40 miles, Wayne paused to build a fortified supply depot.

Around 3 P.M. the following day, Wayne retired to his tent to escape the burning sun. As he rested, a massive beech tree crashed down on the tent, smashing an empty cot beside Wayne and badly bruising the general. His aides suspected Wilkinson's allies of foul play, but Wayne dismissed the incident as an unfortunate accident.

Charge the damned rascals with the bayonet!

Back east, a less overt threat to the Legion's existence was emerging. To finance the army, Secretary of the Treasury Alexander Hamilton had persuaded Congress to levy a tax on whiskey. But whiskey making was a main revenue source among many small farmers, and the excise had infuriated people in western Pennsylvania and elsewhere along the frontier. On July 15, 1794, a riot erupted in Pittsburgh. A mob burned the house and barn of John Neville, the federal tax collector for the district, and fought a pitched battle with responding soldiers. The rioters talked wildly of seceding from the United States, and several suggested seeking help from the British in Canada. Washington promptly condemned the rebellion and called out 13,000 militiamen to suppress it.

It became increasingly clear that the future of the United States might well depend on the success of Wayne's army. Resuming its march, the Legion built a passable road as it advanced. On August 8 it reached one of its objectives, the Miami settlement of Grand Glaize, comprising hundreds of cabins surrounded by fields of corn, beans and other crops.

To Wayne's surprise, the Indians had abandoned this prize without a fight. He called the settlement "the grand emporium of the hostile

Indians of the West" and began building another fortification, dubbed Fort Defiance. In the meantime, his soldiers filled their knapsacks and wagons with fresh produce, trampling the rest and burning the cabins. They left a wasteland.

The Indian retreat signaled growing disarray in their ranks. In late July, Little Turtle had gone to Detroit to extract from the British a promise of military support—specifically infantry and artillery. All he got were vague promises. Upon hearing of Wayne's razing of Grand Glaize, the British did dispatch two infantry companies to Fort Miamis but issued no orders to support the Indians in battle.

At a hastily convened Indian council, Little Turtle dismayed everyone by urging peace negotiations with Wayne. The war chiefs of the Shawnees, Ottawas and other tribes scornfully dismissed him. So Little Turtle turned over command of the army to Blue Jacket, a tall Shawnee known for his fancy clothes and hatred of white men. He had 1,300 warriors at his disposal, plus 70 Canadian militiamen mustered by Simcoe.

On August 20, a day of rain showers and oppressive humidity, Wayne's army trudged up the Maumee Valley toward Fort Miamis, laboring across deep ravines and through thick woods. The Americans marched in three columns, with 150 Kentucky cavalry and a 74-man advance guard of select troops. Cavalry guarded both flanks and the rear. Wayne was in agony from an attack of gout, but he thrust the pain aside and rode at the head of the left column.

Ahead, muskets barked here and there, followed by a volley, as breathless messengers arrived to report contact with the Indians. Blue Jacket had chosen to fight in a tornado-ravaged section of the forest, where hundreds of felled trees wove a massive tangle. The site, a few miles south of present-day Toledo, was known among the Indians as Fallen Timbers. To Blue Jacket, it seemed an ideal battlefield, a position cavalry could not penetrate and infantry would find difficult to attack in a compact mass, wielding the much-feared bayonet.

The opening Indian volley killed the leaders of the advance guard, and the Americans fell back, firing as they retreated, not a few turning to run. Anticipating a harvest of scalps, Ottawas and Potawatomis in the center of the Indian line charged from the tangled timber. But they collided with the main body of Wayne's army amid tall grass and open forest, where American marksmanship came into play.

Wayne ordered the cavalry under Captain Robert MisCampbell to out-flank the Indians. Taking only a single troop, he charged across a deep ravine into a cluster of Indians, one of whom sprang up and shot the captain in the chest, scattering the rest of the troop.

Back with the infantry, Wayne formed two lines and brought his artillery to bear with grapeshot and canister. For a few minutes the battle seesawed wildly, as the Indians sought to outflank the Legion. Some of the hottest fighting fell to the vaunted company of Vermonters known as the Green Mountain Boys. They lost seven men but stood their ground, in turn killing several Wyandotte chiefs and the commander of the Canadian militia company.

"Charge the damned rascals with the bayone!" Wayne roared, and his men sprang into action. On the right, under Wilkinson's command, the Indians took one look at the oncoming "long knives" and ran. On the left, the Canadian militia met the charge with "a most heavy fire."

(It is in this section archaeologists have reaped a gristly harvest of spent musket and rifle balls and uniform buttons, attesting to the ferocious combat.)

A company of Kentucky militia then hit the enemy from the flank, breaking their line. As the Canadians and Indians fled across open ground, Wayne's Kentucky horsemen ruthlessly rode them down. Mounting a rock to rally his men, an Ottawa war chief toppled to the ground in mid-sentence, shot through the heart by one of Wayne's riflemen. Other war chiefs also fell; Little Turtle was carried from the field, streaming blood, and flung onto a horse bound for Fort Miamis.

The British bastion now became the Indians' last hope. They would find refuge there with their English brothers and perhaps fight the long knives another day. But when they reached the fort, they found the gates shut and British soldiers on the ramparts waving them away. The illusion that had fueled their defiance came crashing down, and the Indians fled north, a routed rabble.

Within an hour, the Battle of Fallen Timbers was over. American casualties tallied 33 dead and about 100 wounded. Indian losses were thought to be about 40. Wilkinson, still trying to undermine Wayne, sneered that it was more a skirmish than a battle. But the humiliating rout and collapse of the British-Indian alliance transcended numbers.

Two months after the battle, Washington's militia army marched into western Pennsylvania to stamp out the Whiskey Rebellion. Had Wayne's army failed at Fallen Timbers, the inflamed westerners might have assumed the feckless federal government could be defied with impunity, and the British might have been encouraged to ship the rebels guns and ammunition. Instead, the king's men watched glumly from Canada as cowed rebel leaders surrendered before the federal government's show of overwhelming force.

Back in Philadelphia, news of the victory at Fallen Timbers had triggered celebrations. The president urged Congress to congratulate the Legion and its commander. The surly Jeffersonians agreed to praise the Kentucky militiamen and their brigadier general but claimed it was inappropriate for the congress of a republic to recognize a regular army general. Washington made sure Wayne received his personal congratulations. The irked ideologues tried to dismantle the Legion, but the president had too much political momentum. He insisted on a bill to establish a regular army and eventually got one. Signing it was surely one of the most satisfying moments of his presidency.

At Fort Greene Ville, Wayne negotiated an August 1795 treaty with the Indians that opened all of Ohio and much of Indiana to American settlement. A few months later the British government agreed to evacuate all its forts on American territory, and within a decade there were more than 40,000 settlers in Ohio. As the frontier retreated farther west, it became increasingly clear Anthony Wayne's victory at Fallen Timbers represented a turning point in American history.

For further reading, **THOMAS FLEMING** recommends: *Bayonets in the Wilderness: Anthony Wayne's Legion in the Old Northwest,* by Alan D. Gaff, and *Anthony Wayne: Soldier of the Early Republic,* by Paul David Nelson.

From *Military History,* August/September 2009, pp. 36–43. Copyright © 2009 by Weider History Group. Reprinted by permission.

The Best of Enemies

Jefferson was visionary and crafty. In Hamilton, he met his match. How the rivalry lives on.

Ron Chernow

On March 21, 1790, Thomas Jefferson belatedly arrived in New York City to assume his duties as the first Secretary of State after a five-year ministerial stint in Paris. Tall and lanky, with a freckled complexion and auburn hair, Jefferson, 46, was taken aback by the adulation being heaped upon the new Treasury Secretary, Alexander Hamilton, who had streaked to prominence in his absence. Few people knew that Jefferson had authored the Declaration of Independence, which had yet to become holy writ for Americans. Instead, the Virginian was eclipsed by the 35-year-old wunderkind from the Caribbean, who was a lowly artillery captain in New York when Jefferson composed the famous document. Despite his murky background as an illegitimate orphan, the self-invented Hamilton was trim and elegant, carried himself with an erect military bearing and had a mind that worked with dazzling speed. At first, Hamilton and Jefferson socialized on easy terms, with little inkling that they were destined to become mortal foes. But their clash inside George Washington's first Cabinet proved so fierce that it would spawn the two-party system in America. It also produced two divergent visions of the country's future that divide Americans to the present day.

For Hamilton, the first Treasury Secretary, the supreme threat to liberty arose from insufficient government power. To avert that, he advocated a vigorous central government marked by a strong President, an independent judiciary and a liberal reading of the Constitution. As the first Secretary of State, Jefferson believed that liberty was jeopardized by concentrated federal power, which he tried to restrict through a narrow construction of the Constitution. He favored states' rights, a central role for Congress and a comparatively weak judiciary.

At first glance, Hamilton might seem the more formidable figure in that classic matchup. He took office with an ardent faith in the new national government. He had attended the Constitutional Convention, penned the bulk of the Federalist papers to secure passage of the new charter and spearheaded ratification efforts in New York State. He therefore set to work at Treasury with more unrestrained gusto than Jefferson—who had monitored the Constitutional Convention from his post in Paris—did at State. Jefferson's enthusiasm for the new political order was tepid at best, and when Washington crafted the first government in 1789, Jefferson didn't grasp the levers of power with quite the same glee as Hamilton, who had no ideological inhibitions about shoring up federal power.

Hamilton—brilliant, brash and charming—had the self-reliant reflexes of someone who had always had to live by his wits. His overwhelming intelligence petrified Jefferson and his followers. As an orator, Hamilton could speak extemporaneously for hours on end. As a writer, he could crank out 5,000- or 10,000-word memos overnight. Jefferson never underrated his foe's copious talents. At one point, a worried Jefferson confided to his comrade James Madison that Hamilton was a one-man army, "a host within himself."

Despite Jefferson's policy battles, there was a playful side to his politics. On New Year's Day 1802, supporters in Cheshire, Mass., sent him, as a gift, a mammoth cheese that measured more than 4 ft. in diameter and 17 in. in height and weighed 1,235 lbs. President Jefferson took the pungent present in good humor. Reportedly, he stood in the White House doorway, arms outstretched, waiting for the cheese's delivery. The smelly gift was served to guests for at least a year, perhaps more.

Whether in person or on paper, Hamilton served up his opinions promiscuously. He had a true zest for debate and never left anyone guessing where he stood. Jefferson, more than a decade older, had the quiet, courtly manner of a Virginia planter. He was emphatic in his views—Hamilton labeled him "an atheist in religion and a *fanatic in politics*"—but shrank from open conflict. Jefferson, a diffident speaker, mumbled his way through his rare speeches in a soft, almost inaudible voice and reserved his most scathing strictures for private correspondence.

The epic battle between these two Olympian figures began not long after Jefferson came to New York City to assume his State Department duties in March 1790. By then Hamilton was in the thick of a contentious campaign to retire massive debt inherited from the Revolution. America had suspended principal and interest payments on its obligations, which had traded as low as 15¢ on the dollar. In an audacious scheme to restore public credit, Hamilton planned to pay off that debt at face value, causing the securities to soar from depressed levels. Jefferson and Madison thought the original holders of those securities—many of them war veterans—should profit from that appreciation even if they had already sold their paper to traders at depressed prices. Hamilton thought it would be impractical to track them down. With an eye on future U.S. capital markets, he wanted to enshrine the cardinal principle that current owners of securities incurred all profits and losses, even if that meant windfall gains for rapacious speculators who had only recently bought the securities.

That skirmish over Hamilton's public credit plan was part of a broader tussle over the U.S.'s economic future. Jefferson was fond of summoning up idyllic scenes of an agrarian America peopled by sturdy yeoman farmers. That poetic vision neglected the underlying reality of large slave plantations in the South. Jefferson was a fine populist on paper but not in everyday life, and his defense of Virginia interests was inextricably bound up with slavery. Hamilton—derided as a pseudo aristocrat, an elitist, a crypto-monarchist—was a passionate abolitionist with a far more expansive economic vision. He conceded that agriculture would persist for decades as an essential component of the economy. But at the same time he wanted to foster the rudiments of a modern economy—trade, commerce, banks, stock exchanges, factories and corporations—to enlarge economic opportunity. Hamilton dreamed of a meritocracy, not an aristocracy, while Jefferson retained the landed gentry's disdain for the vulgar realities of trade, commerce and finance. And he was determined to undermine Hamilton's juggernaut.

Because we celebrate Jefferson for his sonorous words in the Declaration of Independence—Hamilton never matched Jefferson's gift for writing ringing passages that were at once poetic and inspirational—we sometimes overlook Jefferson's consummate skills as a practicing politician. A master of subtle, artful indirection, he was able to marshal his forces without divulging his generalship. After Hamilton persuaded President Washington to create the Bank of the United States, the country's first central bank, Jefferson was aghast at what he construed as a breach of the Constitution and a perilous expansion of federal power. Along with Madison, he recruited the poet Philip Freneau to launch an opposition paper called the *National Gazette*. To subsidize the paper covertly, he hired Freneau as a State Department translator. Hamilton was shocked by such flagrant disloyalty from a member of Washington's Cabinet, especially when Freneau began to mount withering assaults on Hamilton and even Washington. Never one to suffer in silence, Hamilton retaliated in a blizzard of newspaper articles published under Roman pseudonyms. The backbiting between Hamilton and Jefferson grew so acrimonious that Washington had to exhort both men to desist.

Instead, the feud worsened. In early 1793, a Virginia Congressman named William Branch Giles began to harry Hamilton with resolutions ordering him to produce, on short deadlines, stupendous amounts of Treasury data. With prodigious bursts of energy, Hamilton complied with those inhuman demands, foiling his opponents. Jefferson then committed an unthinkable act. He secretly drafted a series of anti-Hamilton resolutions for Giles, including one that read, "Resolved, That the Secretary of the Treasury has been guilty of maladministration in the duties of his office and should, in the opinion of Congress, be removed from his office by the President of the United States." The resolution was voted down, and the effort to oust Hamilton stalled. Jefferson left the Cabinet in defeat later that year.

Throughout the 1790s, the Hamilton-Jefferson feud continued to fester in both domestic and foreign affairs. Jefferson thought Hamilton was "bewitched" by the British model of governance, while Hamilton considered Jefferson a credulous apologist for the gory excesses of the French Revolution. Descended from French Huguenots on his mother's side, Hamilton was fluent in French and had served as Washington's liaison with the Marquis de Lafayette and other French aristocrats who had rallied to the Continental Army. The French Revolution immediately struck him as a bloody affair, governed by rigid, Utopian thinking. On Oct. 6, 1789, he wrote a remarkable letter to Lafayette, explaining his "foreboding of ill" about the future course of events in Paris. He cited the "vehement character" of the French people and the "reveries" of their "philosophic politicians," who wished to transform human nature. Hamilton believed that Jefferson while in Paris "drank deeply of the French philosophy in religion, in science, in politics." Indeed, more than a decade passed before Jefferson fully realized that the French Revolution wasn't a worthy sequel to the American one so much as a grotesque travesty.

According to the new book *Jefferson's Second Revolution*, by Susan Dunn, for more than a week in early July 1800, Federalist newspapers gleefully carried the (false) story that Jefferson had died. "I am much indebted to my enemies," Jefferson said, "for proving, by their recitals of my death, that I have friends."

If Jefferson and Hamilton define opposite ends of the political spectrum in U.S. history and seem to exist in perpetual conflict, the two men shared certain traits, feeding a mutual cynicism. Each scorned the other as excessively ambitious. In his secret diary, or *Anas*, Jefferson recorded a story of Hamilton praising Julius Caesar as the greatest man in history. (The tale sounds dubious, as Hamilton invariably used Caesar as shorthand for "an evil tyrant.") Hamilton repaid the favor. In one essay he likened Jefferson to "Caesar *coyly refusing* the proffered diadem" and rejecting the trappings, but "tenaciously grasping the substance of imperial domination."

Similarly, both men hid a potent hedonism behind an intellectual facade. For all their outward differences, the two politicians stumbled into the two great sex scandals of the early Republic. In 1797 a journalist named James T. Callender exposed that Hamilton, while Treasury Secretary and a married man with four children, had entered into a yearlong affair with grifter Maria Reynolds, who was 23 when it began. In a 95-page pamphlet, Hamilton confessed to the affair at what many regarded as inordinate length. He wished to show that the money he had paid to Reynolds' husband James had been for the favor of her company and not for illicit speculation in Treasury securities, as the Jeffersonians had alleged. Forever after, the Jeffersonians tagged Hamilton as "the amorous Treasury Secretary" and mocked his pretensions to superior morality.

By an extraordinary coincidence, during Jefferson's first term as President, Callender also exposed Jefferson's relationship with Sally Hemings. Callender claimed that "Dusky Sally," a.k.a. the "African Venus," was the President's slave concubine, who had borne him five children. "There is not an individual in the neighborhood of Charlottesville who does not believe the story," Callender wrote, "and not a few who know it." Jefferson never confirmed or denied Callender's story. But the likely truth of the Hemings affair was dramatically bolstered by DNA tests published in 1998, which indicated that a Jefferson male had sired at least one of Hemings' children.

The crowning irony of the stormy relations between Hamilton and Jefferson is that Hamilton helped install his longtime foe as President in 1801. Under constitutional rules then in force, the candidate with the majority of electoral votes became President; the runner-up became Vice President. That created an anomalous situation in which Jefferson, his party's presumed presidential nominee, tied with Aaron Burr, its presumed vice presidential nominee. It took 36 rounds of voting in the House

---

Hamilton

Favored a strong Federal Government
Pushed for an economy in which trade, finance and manufacturing supplemented agriculture
Feared closer relations with France and was an Anglophile
Wanted the U.S. to have a professional federal army

Jefferson

Argued strongly for states' rights
Admired farming and the simple, rural life and hoped America would remain an agrarian nation
Favored warm, fraternal relations with France and was an Anglophobe
Thought the country should rely on state militias

---

to decide the election in Jefferson's favor. Faced with the prospect of Burr as President, a man he considered unscrupulous, Hamilton not only opted for Jefferson as the lesser of two evils but also was forced into his most measured assessment of the man. Hamilton said he had long suspected that as President, Jefferson would develop a keen taste for the federal power he had deplored in opposition. He recalled that a decade earlier, in Washington's Cabinet, Jefferson had seemed like a man who knew he was destined to inherit an estate—in this case, the presidency—and didn't wish to deplete it. In fact, Jefferson, the strict constructionist, freely exercised the most sweeping powers as President. Nothing in the Constitution, for instance, permitted the Louisiana Purchase. Hamilton noted that with rueful mirth.

CHERNOW is the author of *The House of Morgan, Titan* and the recent best-selling biography *Alexander Hamilton.*

Cliffhanger

Presidential candidates Thomas Jefferson and Aaron Burr were deadlocked in the House of Representatives with no majority for either. For seven days, as they maneuvered and schemed, the fate of the young republic hung in the ballots.

JOHN FERLING

On the afternoon of September 23, 1800, Vice President Thomas Jefferson, from his Monticello home, wrote a letter to Benjamin Rush, the noted Philadelphia physician. One matter dominated Jefferson's thoughts: that year's presidential contest. Indeed, December 3, Election Day—the date on which the Electoral College would meet to vote—was only 71 days away.

Jefferson was one of four presidential candidates. As he composed his letter to Rush, Jefferson paused from time to time to gather his thoughts, all the while gazing absently through an adjacent window at the shimmering heat and the foliage, now a lusterless pale green after a long, dry summer. Though he hated leaving his hilltop plantation and believed, as he told Rush, that gaining the presidency would make him "a constant butt for every shaft of calumny which malice & falsehood could form," he nevertheless sought the office "with sincere zeal."

He had been troubled by much that had occurred in incumbent John Adams' presidency and was convinced that radicals within Adams' Federalist Party were waging war against what he called the "spirit of 1776"—goals the American people had hoped to attain through the Revolution. He had earlier characterized Federalist rule as a "reign of witches," insisting that the party was "adverse to liberty" and "calculated to undermine and demolish the republic." If the Federalists prevailed, he believed, they would destroy the states and create a national government every bit as oppressive as that which Great Britain had tried to impose on the colonists before 1776.

The "revolution . . . of 1776," Jefferson would later say, had determined the "form" of America's government; he believed the election of 1800 would decide its "principles." "I have sworn upon the altar of God eternal hostility against every form of tyranny over the mind of Man," he wrote.

Jefferson was not alone in believing that the election of 1800 was crucial. On the other side, Federalist Alexander Hamilton, who had been George Washington's secretary of treasury, believed that it was a contest to save the new nation from "the

fangs of Jefferson." Hamilton agreed with a Federalist newspaper essay that argued defeat meant "happiness, constitution and laws [faced] endless and irretrievable ruin." Federalists and Republicans appeared to agree on one thing only: that the victor in 1800 would set America's course for generations to come, perhaps forever.

Only a quarter of a century after the signing of the Declaration of Independence, the first election of the new 19th century was carried out in an era of intensely emotional partisanship among a people deeply divided over the scope of the government's authority. But it was the French Revolution that had imposed a truly hyperbolic quality upon the partisan strife.

That revolution, which had begun in 1789 and did not run its course until 1815, deeply divided Americans. Conservatives, horrified by its violence and social leveling, applauded Great Britain's efforts to stop it. The most conservative Americans, largely Federalists, appeared bent on an alliance with London that would restore the ties between America and Britain that had been severed in 1776. Jeffersonian Republicans, on the other hand, insisted that these radical conservatives wanted to turn back the clock to reinstitute much of the British colonial template. (Today's Republican Party traces its origins not to Jefferson and his allies but to the party formed in 1854–1855, which carried Lincoln to the presidency in 1860.)

A few weeks before Adams' inauguration in 1796, France, engaged in an all-consuming struggle with England for world domination, had decreed that it would not permit America to trade with Great Britain. The French Navy soon swept American ships from the seas, idling port-city workers and plunging the economy toward depression. When Adams sought to negotiate a settlement, Paris spurned his envoys.

Adams, in fact, hoped to avoid war, but found himself riding a whirlwind. The most extreme Federalists, known as Ultras, capitalized on the passions unleashed in this crisis and scored great victories in the off-year elections of 1798, taking charge of both the party and Congress. They created a provisional army and pressured Adams into putting Hamilton in charge. They passed heavy taxes to pay for the army and, with Federalist sympathizers in the press braying that "traitors must be silent," enacted the Alien and Sedition Acts, which provided jail terms and exorbitant fines for anyone who uttered or published "any false, scandalous, and malicious" statement against the United States government or its officials. While Federalists defended the Sedition Act as a necessity in the midst of a grave national crisis, Jefferson and his followers saw it as a means of silencing Republicans—and a violation of the Bill of Rights. The Sedition Act, Jefferson contended, proved there was no step, "however atrocious," the Ultras would not take.

All along, Jefferson had felt that Federalist extremists might overreach. By early 1799, Adams himself had arrived at the same conclusion. He, too, came to suspect that Hamilton and the Ultras wanted to precipitate a crisis with France. Their motivation perhaps had been to get Adams to secure an alliance with Great Britain and accept the Ultras' program in Congress. But avowing that there "is no more prospect of seeing a French Army here, than there is in Heaven," Adams refused to go along with the scheme and sent peace envoys to Paris. (Indeed, a treaty would be signed at the end of September 1800.)

It was in this bitterly partisan atmosphere that the election of 1800 was conducted. In those days, the Constitution stipulated that each of the 138 members of the Electoral College cast two votes for president, which allowed electors to cast one vote for a favorite son and a second for a candidate who actually stood a chance of winning. The Constitution also stipulated that if the candidates tied, or none received a majority of electoral votes, the House of Representatives "shall chuse by Ballot one of them for President." Unlike today, each party nominated two candidates for the presidency.

Federalist congressmen had caucused that spring and, without indicating a preference, designated Adams and South Carolina's Charles Cotesworth Pinckney as the party's choices. Adams desperately wanted to be re-elected. He was eager to see the French crisis through to a satisfactory resolution and, at age 65, believed that a defeat would mean he would be sent home to Quincy, Massachusetts, to die in obscurity. Pinckney, born into Southern aristocracy and raised in England, had been the last of the four nominees to come around in favor of American independence. Once committed, however, he served valiantly, seeing action at Brandywine, Germantown and Charleston. Following the war, he sat in the Constitutional Convention; both Washington and Adams had sent him to France on diplomatic missions.

In addition to Jefferson, Republicans chose Aaron Burr as their candidate, but designated Jefferson as the party's first choice. Jefferson had held public office intermittently since 1767, serving Virginia in its legislature and as a wartime governor, sitting in Congress, crossing to Paris in 1784 for a five-year stint that included a posting as the American minister to France, and acting as secretary of state under Washington. His second place finish in the election of 1796 had made him vice president, as was the custom until 1804. Burr, at age 44 the youngest of the candidates, had abandoned his legal studies in 1775 to enlist in the Continental Army; he had experienced the horrors of America's failed invasion of Canada and the miseries of Valley Forge. After the war he practiced law and represented New York in the U.S. Senate. In 1800, he was serving as a member of the New York legislature.

In those days, the Constitution left the manner of selecting presidential electors to the states. In 11 of the 16 states, state legislatures picked the electors; therefore, the party that controlled the state assembly garnered all that state's electoral votes. In the other five states, electors were chosen by "qualified" voters (white, male property owners in some states, white male taxpayers in others). Some states used a winner-take-all system: voters cast their ballots for the entire slate of Federalist electors or for the Republican slate. Other states split electors among districts.

Presidential candidates did not kiss babies, ride in parades or shake hands. Nor did they even make stump speeches. The candidates tried to remain above the fray, leaving campaigning to surrogates, particularly elected officials from within their parties. Adams and Jefferson each returned home when Congress adjourned in May, and neither left their home states until they returned to the new capital of Washington in November.

But for all its differences, much about the campaign of 1800 was recognizably modern. Politicians carefully weighed which procedures were most likely to advance their party's interests. Virginia, for instance, had permitted electors to be elected from districts in three previous presidential contests, but after Federalists carried 8 of 19 congressional districts in the elections of 1798, Republicans, who controlled the state assembly, switched to the winner-take-all format, virtually guaranteeing they would get every one of Virginia's 21 electoral votes in 1800. The ploy was perfectly legal, and Federalists in Massachusetts, fearing an upsurge in Republican strength, scuttled district elections—which the state had used previously—to select electors by the legislature, which they controlled.

Though the contest was played out largely in the print media, the unsparing personal attacks on the character and temperament of the nominees resembled the studied incivility to which today's candidates are accustomed on television. Adams was portrayed as a monarchist who had turned his back on republicanism; he was called senile, a poor judge of character, vain, jealous and driven by an "ungovernable temper." Pinckney was labeled a mediocrity, a man of "limited talents" who was "illy suited to the exalted station" of the presidency. Jefferson was accused of cowardice. Not only, said his critics, had he lived in luxury at Monticello while others sacrificed during the War of Independence, but he had fled like a jack rabbit when British soldiers raided Charlottesville in 1781. And he had failed egregiously as Virginia's governor, demonstrating that his "nerves are too weak to bear anxiety and difficulties." Federalists further insisted Jefferson had been transformed into a dangerous radical during his residence in France and was a "howling atheist." For his part, Burr was depicted as without principles, a man who would do anything to get his hands on power.

Also like today, the election of 1800 seemed to last forever. "Electioneering is already begun," the first lady, Abigail Adams, noted 13 months before the Electoral College was to meet. What made it such a protracted affair was that state legislatures were elected throughout the year; as these assemblies more often than not chose presidential electors, the state contests to determine them became part of the national campaign. In 1800 the greatest surprise among these contests occurred in New York, a large, crucial state that had given all 12 of its electoral votes to Adams in 1796, allowing him to eke out a three-vote victory over Jefferson.

The battle for supremacy in the New York legislature had hinged on the outcome in New York City. Thanks largely to lopsided wins in two working-class wards where many voters owned no property, the Republicans secured all 24 of New York's electoral votes for Jefferson and Burr. For Abigail Adams, that was enough to seal Adams' fate. John Dawson, a Republican congressman from Virginia, declared: "The Republic is safe. . . . The [Federalist] party are in rage & despair."

But Adams himself refused to give up hope. After all, New England, which accounted for nearly half the electoral votes needed for a majority, was solidly in his camp, and he felt certain he would win some votes elsewhere. Adams believed that if he could get South Carolina's eight votes, he would be virtually certain to garner the same number of electoral votes that had put him over the top four years earlier. And, at first, both parties were thought to have a shot at carrying the state.

When South Carolina's legislature was elected in mid-October, the final tally revealed that the assembly was about evenly divided between Federalists and Republicans—though unaffiliated representatives, all pro-Jefferson, would determine the outcome. Now Adams' hopes were fading fast. Upon hearing the news that Jefferson was assured of South Carolina's eight votes, Abigail Adams remarked to her son Thomas that the "consequence to us personally is that we retire from public life." All that remained to be determined was whether the assembly would instruct the electors to cast their second vote for Burr or Pinckney.

The various presidential electors met in their respective state capitals to vote on December 3. By law, their ballots were not to be opened and counted until February 11, but the outcome could hardly be kept secret for ten weeks. Sure enough, just nine days after the vote, Washington, D.C.'s *National Intelligencer* newspaper broke the news that neither Adams nor Pinckney had received a single South Carolina vote and, in the voting at large, Jefferson and Burr had each received 73 electoral votes. Adams had gotten 65, Pinckney 64. The House of Representatives would have to make the final decision between the two Republicans.

Adams thus became the first presidential candidate to fall victim to the notorious clause in the Constitution that counted each slave as three-fifths of one individual in calculating population used to allocate both House seats and electoral votes. Had slaves, who had no vote, not been so counted, Adams would have edged Jefferson by a vote of 63 to 61. In addition, the Federalists fell victim to the public's perception that the Republicans stood for democracy and egalitarianism, while the Federalists were seen as imperious and authoritarian.

In the House, each state would cast a single vote. If each of the 16 states voted—that is, if none abstained—9 states would elect the president. Republicans controlled eight delegations—New York, New Jersey, Pennsylvania, Virginia, North Carolina, Georgia, Kentucky and Tennessee. The Federalists held six: New Hampshire, Massachusetts, Rhode Island, Connecticut, Delaware and South Carolina. And two delegations—Maryland and Vermont—were deadlocked.

Though Jefferson and Burr had tied in the Electoral College, public opinion appeared to side with Jefferson. Not only had he been the choice of his party's nominating caucus, but he had served longer at the national level than Burr, and in a more exalted capacity. But if neither man was selected by noon on March 4, when Adams' term ended, the country would be without a chief executive until the newly elected Congress convened in December, nine months later. In the interim, the current, Federalist-dominated Congress would be in control.

Faced with such a prospect, Jefferson wrote to Burr in December. His missive was cryptic, but in it he appeared to suggest that if Burr accepted the vice presidency, he would be given greater responsibilities than previous vice presidents. Burr's response to Jefferson was reassuring. He pledged to "disclaim all competition" and spoke of "your administration."

Meanwhile, the Federalists caucused to discuss their options. Some favored tying up the proceedings in order to hold on to power for several more months. Some wanted to try to invalidate, on technical grounds, enough electoral votes to make Adams the winner. Some urged the party to throw its support to Burr, believing that, as a native of mercantile New York City, he would be more friendly than Jefferson to the Federalist economic program. Not a few insisted that the party should support Jefferson, as he was clearly the popular choice. Others, including Hamilton, who had long opposed Burr in the rough and tumble of New York City politics, thought Jefferson more trustworthy than Burr. Hamilton argued that Burr was "without Scruple," an "unprincipled . . . voluptuary" who would plunder the country. But Hamilton also urged the party to stall, in the hope of inducing Jefferson to make a deal. Hamilton proposed that in return for the Federalist votes that would make him president, Jefferson should promise to preserve the Federalist fiscal system (a properly funded national debt and the Bank), American neutrality and a strong navy, and to agree to "keeping in office all our Foederal Friends" below the cabinet level. Even Adams joined the fray, telling Jefferson that the presidency would be his "in an instant" should he accept Hamilton's terms. Jefferson declined, insisting that he "should never go into the office of President . . . with my hands tied by any conditions which should hinder me from pursuing the measures" he thought best.

In the end, the Federalists decided to back Burr. Hearing of their decision, Jefferson told Adams that any attempt "to defeat the Presidential election" would "produce resistance by force, and incalculable consequences."

Burr, who had seemed to disavow a fight for the highest office, now let it be known that he would accept the presidency if elected by the House. In Philadelphia, he met with several

Republican congressmen, allegedly telling them that he intended to fight for it.

Burr had to know that he was playing a dangerous game and risking political suicide by challenging Jefferson, his party's reigning power. The safest course would have been to acquiesce to the vice presidency. He was yet a young man, and given Jefferson's penchant for retiring to Monticello—he had done so in 1776, 1781 and 1793—there was a good chance that Burr would be his party's standard-bearer as early as 1804. But Burr also knew there was no guarantee he would live to see future elections. His mother and father had died at ages 27 and 42, respectively.

Burr's was not the only intrigue. Given the high stakes, every conceivable pressure was applied to change votes. Those in the deadlocked delegations were courted daily, but no one was lobbied more aggressively than James Bayard, Delaware's lone congressman, who held in his hands the sole determination of how his state would vote. Thirty-two years old in 1800, Bayard had practiced law in Wilmington before winning election to the House as a Federalist four years earlier. Bayard despised Virginia's Republican planters, including Jefferson, whom he saw as hypocrites who owned hundreds of slaves and lived "like feudal barons" as they played the role of "high priests of liberty." He announced he was supporting Burr.

The city of Washington awoke to a crippling snowstorm Wednesday, February 11, the day the House was to begin voting. Nevertheless, only one of the 105 House members did not make it in to Congress, and his absence would not change his delegation's tally. Voting began the moment the House was gaveled into session. When the roll call was complete, Jefferson had carried eight states, Burr six, and two deadlocked states had cast uncommitted ballots; Jefferson still needed one more vote for a majority. A second vote was held, with a similar tally, then a third. When at 3 A.M. the exhausted congressmen finally called it a day, 19 roll calls had been taken, all with the same inconclusive result.

By Saturday evening, three days later, the House had cast 33 ballots. The deadlock seemed unbreakable.

For weeks, warnings had circulated of drastic consequences if Republicans were denied the presidency. Now that danger seemed palpable. A shaken President Adams was certain the two sides had come to the "precipice" of disaster and that "a civil war was expected." There was talk that Virginia would secede if Jefferson were not elected. Some Republicans declared they would convene another constitutional convention to restructure the federal government so that it reflected the "democratical spirit of America." It was rumored that a mob had stormed the arsenal in Philadelphia and was preparing to march on Washington to drive the defeated Federalists from power. Jefferson said he could not restrain those of his supporters who threatened "a dissolution" of the Union. He told Adams that many Republicans were prepared to use force to prevent the Federalists' "legislative usurpation" of the executive branch.

In all likelihood, it was these threats that ultimately broke the deadlock. The shift occurred sometime after Saturday's

final ballot; it was Delaware's Bayard who blinked. That night, he sought out a Republican close to Jefferson, almost certainly John Nicholas, a member of Virginia's House delegation. Were Delaware to abstain, Bayard pointed out, only 15 states would ballot. With eight states already in his column, Jefferson would have a majority and the elusive victory at last. But in return, Bayard asked, would Jefferson accept the terms that the Federalists had earlier proffered? Nicholas responded, according to Bayard's later recollections, that these conditions were "very reasonable" and that he could vouch for Jefferson's acceptance.

The Federalists caucused behind doors on Sunday afternoon, February 15. When Bayard's decision to abstain was announced, it touched off a firestorm. Cries of "Traitor! Traitor!" rang down on him. Bayard himself later wrote that the "clamor was prodigious, the reproaches vehement," and that many old colleagues were "furious" with him. Two matters in particular roiled his comrades. Some were angry that Bayard had broken ranks before it was known what kind of deal, if any, Burr might have been willing to cut. Others were upset that nothing had been heard from Jefferson himself. During a second Federalist caucus that afternoon, Bayard agreed to take no action until Burr's answer was known. In addition, the caucus directed Bayard to seek absolute assurances that Jefferson would go along with the deal.

Early the next morning, Monday, February 16, according to Bayard's later testimony, Jefferson made it known through a third party that the terms demanded by the Federalists "corresponded with his views and intentions, and that we might confide in him accordingly." The bargain was struck, at least to Bayard's satisfaction. Unless Burr offered even better terms, Jefferson would be the third president of the United States.

At some point that Monday afternoon, Burr's letters arrived. What exactly he said or did not say in them—they likely were destroyed soon after they reached Washington and their contents remain a mystery—disappointed his Federalist proponents. Bayard, in a letter written that Monday, told a friend that "Burr has acted a miserable paultry part. The election was in his power." But Burr, at least according to Bayard's interpretation, and for reasons that remain unknown to history, had refused to reach an accommodation with the Federalists. That same Monday evening a dejected Theodore Sedgwick, Speaker of the House and a passionate Jefferson hater, notified friends at home: "the gigg is up."

The following day, February 17, the House gathered at noon to cast its 36th, and, as it turned out, final, vote. Bayard was true to his word: Delaware abstained, ending seven days of contention and the long electoral battle.

Bayard ultimately offered many reasons for his change of heart. On one occasion he claimed that he and the five other Federalists who had held the power to determine the election in their hands—four from Maryland and one from Vermont—had agreed to "give our votes to Mr. Jefferson" if it became clear that Burr could not win. Bayard also later insisted that he had acted from what he called "imperious necessity" to prevent a civil war or disunion. Still later he claimed to have been swayed by the public's preference for Jefferson.

Had Jefferson in fact cut a deal to secure the presidency? Ever afterward, he insisted that such allegations were "absolutely false." The historical evidence, however, suggests otherwise. Not only did many political insiders assert that Jefferson had indeed agreed to a bargain, but Bayard, in a letter dated February 17, the very day of the climactic House vote—as well as five years later, while testifying under oath in a libel suit—insisted that Jefferson had most certainly agreed to accept the Federalists' terms. In another letter written at the time, Bayard assured a Federalist officeholder, who feared losing his position in a Republican administration: "I have taken good care of you. . . . You are safe."

Even Jefferson's actions as president lend credence to the allegations. Despite having fought against the Hamiltonian economic system for nearly a decade, he acquiesced to it once in office, leaving the Bank of the United States in place and tolerating continued borrowing by the federal government. Nor did he remove most Federalist officeholders.

The mystery is not why Jefferson would deny making such an accord, but why he changed his mind after vowing never to bend. He must have concluded that he had no choice if he wished to become president by peaceful means. To permit the balloting to continue was to hazard seeing the presidency slip from his hands. Jefferson not only must have doubted the constancy of some of his supporters, but he knew that a majority of the Federalists favored Burr and were making the New Yorker the same offer they were dangling before him.

Burr's behavior is more enigmatic. He had decided to make a play for the presidency, only apparently to refuse the very terms that would have guaranteed it to him. The reasons for his action have been lost in a confounding tangle of furtive transactions and deliberately destroyed evidence. It may have been that the Federalists demanded more of him than they did of Jefferson. Or Burr may have found it unpalatable to strike a bargain with ancient enemies, including the man he would kill in a duel three years later. Burr may also have been unwilling to embrace Federalist principles that he had opposed throughout his political career.

The final mystery of the election of 1800 is whether Jefferson and his backers would have sanctioned violence had he been denied the presidency. Soon after taking office, Jefferson claimed that "there was no idea of [using] force." His remark proves little, yet during the ongoing battle in the House, he alternately spoke of acceding to the Federalists' misconduct in the hope that their behavior would ruin them, or of calling a second Constitutional Convention. He probably would have chosen one, or both, of these courses before risking bloodshed and the end of the Union.

In the days that followed the House battle, Jefferson wrote letters to several surviving signers of the Declaration of Independence to explain what he believed his election had meant. It guaranteed the triumph of the American Revolution, he said, ensuring the realization of the new "chapter in the history of man" that had been promised by Thomas Paine in 1776. In the years that followed, his thoughts often returned to the election's significance. In 1819, at age 76, he would characterize it as the "revolution of 1800," and he rejoiced to a friend in Virginia, Spencer Roane, that it had been effected peacefully "by the rational and peaceful instruments of reform, the suffrage of the people."

Historian **JOHN FERLING** is the author of *Adams vs. Jefferson: The Tumultuous Election of 1800* (Oxford University Press).

The Revolution of 1803

The Louisiana Purchase of 1803 was "the event which more than any other, after the foundation of the Government and always excepting its preservation, determined the character of our national life." So said President Theodore Roosevelt on the 100th anniversary of this momentous acquisition. As we celebrate the 200th anniversary, it's clear that the extraordinary real estate deal also shaped America's perception of its role in the world.

PETER S. ONUF

If there was one thing the United States did not seem to need in 1803, it was more land. The federal government had plenty to sell settlers in the new state of Ohio and throughout the Old Northwest (stretching from the Ohio and Mississippi rivers to the Great Lakes), as did New York, Pennsylvania, and other states. New Englanders were already complaining that the westward exodus was driving up wages and depressing real estate prices in the East.

The United States then consisted of 16 states: the original 13, strung along the Atlantic seaboard, and three recent additions on the frontier: Vermont, which had declared its independence from New York during the Revolution, was finally recognized and admitted in 1791, and Kentucky and Tennessee, carved out of the western reaches of Virginia and North Carolina in 1792 and 1796, respectively, extended the union of states as far as the Mississippi River. The entire area east of the Mississippi had been nominally secured to the United States by the Peace of Paris in 1783, though vast regions remained under the control of Indian nations and subject to the influence of various European imperial powers.

Many skeptical commentators believed that the United States was already too big and that the bonds of union would weaken and snap if new settlements spread too far and too fast. "No paper engagements" could secure the connection of East and West, Massachusetts congressman Rufus King wrote in 1786, and separatist movements and disunionist plots kept such concerns alive in subsequent years. Expansionists had a penchant for naturalistic language: At best, the "surge" or "tide" of white settlement might be channeled, but it was ultimately irresistible.

Though President Thomas Jefferson and the American negotiators who secured the Louisiana Purchase in 1803 had not even dreamed of acquiring such a vast territory, stretching from the Mississippi to the Rockies, the expansion of the United States has the retrospective feel of inevitability, however much some modern Americans may bemoan the patriotic passions and imperialistic excesses of "Manifest Destiny" and its "legacies of conquest." Indeed, it's almost impossible for us to imagine any other outcome now, or to recapture the decidedly mixed feelings of Americans about their country's expansion at the start of the 19th century.

Jefferson and his contemporaries understood that they were at a crossroads, and that the American experiment in republican self-government and the fragile federal union on which it depended could easily fail. They understood that the United States was a second-rate power, without the "energy" or military means to project—or possibly even to defend—its vital interests in a world almost constantly at war. And they understood all too well that the loyalties of their countrymen—and, if they were honest with themselves, their own loyalties—were volatile and unpredictable.

There were good reasons for such doubts about American allegiances. Facing an uncertain future, patriotic (and not so patriotic) Americans had only the dimmest sense of who or what should command their loyalty. The Union had nearly collapsed on more than one occasion, most recently during the presidential succession crisis of 1800-01, which saw a tie in the Electoral College and 36 contentious ballots in the House of Representatives before Jefferson was elevated to the presidency. During the tumultuous 1790s, rampant partisan political strife between Federalists and Jefferson's Republicans roiled the nation, and before that, under the Articles of Confederation (1781–89), the central government ground to a virtual halt and the Union almost withered away before the new constitution saved it. Of course, everyone professed to be a patriot, dedicated to preserving American independence. But what did that mean? Federalists such as Alexander Hamilton preached fealty to a powerful, consolidated central government capable of doing the people's will (as they loosely construed it); Republican oppositionists championed a strictly construed federal constitution that left power in the hands of the people's (or peoples') state governments. Each side accused the other of being subject to the corrupt influence of a foreign power: counterrevolutionary England in the case of Federalist "aristocrats" and "monocrats"; revolutionary France for Republican "Jacobins."

In Jefferson's mind, and in the minds of his many followers, the new Republican dispensation initiated by his ascension to power in "the Revolution of 1800" provided a hopeful answer to all these doubts and anxieties. Jefferson's First Inaugural Address, which the soft-spoken, 57-year-old president delivered to Congress in a nearly inaudible whisper in March 1801, seemed to his followers to herald a new epoch in American affairs. "We are all republicans, we are all federalists," he insisted in the speech. "Let us, then, unite with one heart and one mind." The president's inspiring vision of the nation's future augured, as he told the English radical Joseph Priestley, then a refugee in republican Pennsylvania, something "new under the sun."

While Jefferson's conciliatory language in the inaugural address famously helped mend the partisan breach—and, not coincidentally, helped cast Hamilton and his High Federalist minions far beyond the republican pale—it also anticipated the issues that would come to the fore during the period leading up to the Louisiana Purchase.

First, the new president addressed the issue of the nation's size. Could an expanding union of free republican states survive without jeopardizing the liberties won at such great cost by the revolutionary generation? Jefferson reassured the rising, post-revolutionary generation that it too had sufficient virtue and patriotism to make the republican experiment work and to pass on its beneficent legacy. "Entertaining a due sense of our equal right to the use of our own faculties" and "enlightened by a benign religion, professed, indeed, and practiced in various forms, yet all of them inculcating honesty, truth, temperance, gratitude, and the love of man; acknowledging and adoring an over-ruling Providence, which by all its dispensations proves that it delights in the happiness of man here and his greater happiness hereafter," Americans were bound to be "a happy and a prosperous people."

Jefferson congratulated his fellow Americans on "possessing a chosen country, with room enough for our descendants to the thousandth and thousandth generation," a vast domain that was "separated by nature and a wide ocean from the exterminating havoc of one quarter of the globe." Jefferson's vision of nationhood was inscribed on the American landscape: "An overruling Providence, which by all its dispensations proves that it delights in the happiness of man here and his greater happiness hereafter" provided this fortunate people with land enough to survive and prosper forever. But Jefferson knew that he was not offering an accurate description of the nation's current condition. Given the frenzied pace of westward settlement, it would take only a generation or two—not a thousand—to fill out the new nation's existing limits, which were still marked in the west by the Mississippi. Nor was the United States as happily insulated from Europe's "exterminating havoc" as the new president suggested. The Spanish remained in control of New Orleans, the key to the great river system that controlled the continent's heartland, and the British remained a powerful presence to the north.

Jefferson's vision of the future was, in fact, the mirror opposite of America's present situation at the onset of the 19th century. The nation was encircled by enemies and deeply divided by partisan and sectional differences. The domain the president envisioned was boundless, continentwide, a virgin land waiting to be taken up by virtuous, liberty-loving American farmers. In this providential perspective, Indian nations and European empires simply disappeared from view, and the acquisition of new territory and the expansion of the Union seemed preordained. It would take an unimaginable miracle, acquisition of the entire Louisiana territory, to begin to consummate Jefferson's inaugural promise.

Jefferson's expansionist vision also violated the accepted axioms of contemporary political science. In his *Spirit of the Laws* (1748), the great French philosopher Montesquieu taught that the republican form of government could survive only in small states, where a virtuous and vigilant citizenry could effectively monitor the exercise of power. A large state, by contrast, could be sustained only if power were concentrated in a more energetic central government; republicanism in an expanding state would give way to more "despotic," aristocratic, and monarchical regimes. This "law" of political science was commonly understood in mechanical terms: Centrifugal forces, pulling a state apart, gained momentum as territory expanded, and they could be checked only by the "energy" of strong government.

James Madison had grappled with the problem in his famous *Federalist* 10, in which he argued that an "extended republic" would "take in a greater variety of parties and interests," making it "less probable that a majority of the whole will have a common motive to invade the rights of other citizens." Modern pluralists have embraced this argument, but it was not particularly persuasive to Madison's generation—or even to Madison himself a decade later. During the struggle over ratification of the Constitution, Antifederalists effectively invoked Montesquieu's dictum against Federalist "consolidationism," and in the 1790s, Jeffersonian defenders of states' rights offered the same arguments against Hamiltonian High Federalism. And Jefferson's "Revolution of 1800," vindicating the claims of (relatively) small state-republics against an overly energetic central government, seemed to confirm Montesquieu's wisdom. Montesquieu's notion was also the basis for the popular interpretation of what had caused the rise of British tyranny in the colonies before the American Revolution.

At the same time, however, Montesquieu's logic posed a problem for Jefferson. How could he imagine a continental republic in 1801 and negotiate a land cession that doubled the country's size in 1803? To put the problem somewhat differently, how could Jefferson—who had, after all, drafted the controversial Kentucky Resolutions of 1798, which threatened state nullification of federal authority—overcome his own disunionist tendencies?

Jefferson's response in his inaugural was to call on his fellow Americans to "pursue our own federal and republican principles, our attachment to union and representative government," with "courage and confidence." In other words, a sacred regard for states' rights ("federal principles") was essential to the preservation and strength of a "union" that depended on the "attachment" of a people determined to secure its liberties ("republican principles"). This conception of states as republics would have been familiar and appealing to many Americans, but Jefferson's vision of the United States as a *powerful* nation, spreading across the continent, was breathtaking in its boldness. How could he promise Americans that they could have it both ways, that they could be secure in their liberties yet have a federal government with enough "energy" to preserve itself? How could he believe that the American government, which had only recently endured a near-fatal succession crisis and which had a pathetically small army and navy, was "the strongest Government on earth"?

Jefferson responded to these questions resoundingly by invoking—or perhaps more accurately, inventing—an American people or nation, united in devotion to common principles, and coming together over the course of succeeding generations to constitute one great family. Thus, the unity the president imagined was prospective. Divided as they might now be, Americans would soon come to realize that they were destined to be a great nation, freed from "the throes and convulsions of the ancient world" and willing to sacrifice everything in defense of their country. In Jefferson's vision of progressive continental development, the defensive vigilance of virtuous republicans, who were always ready to resist the encroachments of power from any and every source, would be transformed into a patriotic devotion to the transcendent community of an inclusive and expanding nation, "the world's best hope." "At the call of the law," Jefferson predicted, "every man . . . would fly to the standard of the law, and would meet invasions of the public order as his own personal concern."

Jefferson thus invoked an idealized vision of the American Revolution, in which patriotic citizen-soldiers rallied against British tyranny, as a model for future mobilizations against internal as well as external threats. (It was an extraordinary—and extraordinarily influential—exercise in revisionist history. More dispassionate observers, including those who, unlike Jefferson, actually had some military experience, were not inclined to give the militias much, if any, credit for winning the war.)

Jefferson's conception of the American nation imaginatively countered the centrifugal forces, the tendency toward anarchy and disunion, that republicanism authorized and unleashed. Devotion to the Union would reverse this tendency and draw Americans together, even as their private pursuits of happiness drew them to the far frontiers of their continental domain. It was a paradoxical, mystifying formulation. What seemed to be weakness—the absence of a strong central government—was, in fact, strength. Expansion did not attenuate social and political ties; rather, it secured a powerful, effective, and affective union. The imagined obliteration of all possible obstacles to the enactment of this great national story—the removal of Indians and foreigners—was the greatest mystification of all, for it disguised how the power of the federal state was to be deployed to clear the way for "nature's nation."

In retrospect, the peaceful acquisition of the Louisiana Territory, at the bargain-basement price of $15 million, seemed to conform to the expansionist scenario in Jefferson's First Inaugural Address. The United States bought land from France, just as individuals bought land from federal and state land offices, demonstrating good intentions (to be fruitful and multiply, to cultivate the earth) and their respect for property rights and the rule of law. Yet the progress of settlement was inexorable, a "natural" force, as the French wisely recognized in ceding their claims.

The threat of armed conflict was, nonetheless, never far below the surface. When the chilling news reached America in 1802 that Spain had retroceded Louisiana to France, under pressure from Napoleon Bonaparte, some Federalists agitated for a preemptive strike against New Orleans before Napoleon could land troops there and begin to carry out his plan for a reinvigorated French empire in the Western Hemisphere. As if to provide a taste of the future, Spanish authorities in New Orleans revoked the right of American traders to store goods in the city for export, thereby sending ripples of alarm and economic distress through farms and plantations of the Mississippi valley. Americans might like to think, with Jefferson, that the West was a vast land reserve for their future generations, but nature would issue a different decree if the French gained control of the Mississippi River system.

As Senator William Wells of Delaware warned the Senate in February 1803, if Napoleon were ensconced in New Orleans, "the whole of your Southern States" would be at his mercy; the French ruler would not hesitate to foment rebellion among the slaves, that "inveterate enemy in the very bosom of those States." A North Carolina congressman expected the French emperor to do even worse: "The tomahawk of the savage and the knife of the negro would confederate in the league, and there would be no interval of peace." Such a confederation—a powerful, unholy alliance of Europeans, Indians, and slaves—was the nightmarish antithesis of the Americans' own weak union. The French might even use their influence in Congress to revive the vicious party struggles that had crippled the national government during the 1790s.

Jefferson had no idea how to respond to the looming threat, beyond sending his friend and protégé James Monroe to join U.S. Minister to France Robert R. Livingston in a desperate bid to negotiate a way out of the crisis. At most, they hoped that Napoleon would sell New Orleans and the Floridas to the United States, perhaps with a view to preempting an Anglo-American alliance. Jefferson dropped a broad hint to Livingston (undoubtedly for Napoleon's edification) that if France ever took "possession of N. Orleans . . . we must marry ourselves to the British fleet and nation." For the Anglophobe Jefferson this must have been a horrible thought, even if it was a bluff. But then, happily for Jefferson—and crucially for his historical reputation—fortune intervened.

Napoleon's intentions for the New World hinged on control of Saint-Domingue (now Haiti), but a slave revolt there, led by the brilliant Toussaint L'Ouverture, complicated the emperor's plans. With a strong assist from yellow fever and other devastating diseases, the rebels fought a French expeditionary force of more than 20,000 to a standstill. Thwarted in his western design and facing the imminent resumption of war in Europe, Napoleon decided to cut his losses. In April 1803, his representative offered the entire Louisiana Territory to a surprised Livingston. By the end of the month, the negotiators had arrived at a price. For $15 million, the United States would acquire 828,000 square miles of North America, stretching from the Mississippi River to the Rocky Mountains and from the Gulf of Mexico to the Canadian border. Over time 13 states would be carved from the new lands.

When the news reached America in July, it proved a great deal more than anyone had been contemplating but was met with general jubilation. There was widespread agreement that national security depended on gaining control of the region around New Orleans; and Spanish Florida, occupying the critical area south of Georgia and the territory that the state had finally ceded to Congress in 1802, was high on southern planters' wish list of territorial acquisitions. But it was hard to imagine any immediate use for the trans-Mississippi region, notwithstanding Jefferson's inspiring rhetoric, and there was some grumbling that the negotiators had spent more than Congress had authorized. A few public figures, mostly New England Federalists, even opposed the transaction on political and constitutional grounds.

The Lewis and Clark expedition, authorized before the Purchase was completed, testifies to Americans' utter ignorance of the West in 1803. The two explorers were sent, in effect, to feel around in the dark. Perhaps, Jefferson mused, the trans-Mississippi region could be used as a kind of toxic waste dump, a place to send emancipated slaves beyond harm's way. Or, a more portentous thought, Indian nations might be relocated west of the river—an idea President Andrew Jackson later put into effect with his infamous removal policy.

What gripped most commentators as they celebrated the news of the Purchase in 1803 was simply that the Union had survived another awful crisis. They tended to see the new lands as a buffer. "The wilderness itself," Representative Joseph Nicholson of Maryland exclaimed, "will now present an almost insurmountable barrier to any nation that inclined to disturb us in that quarter." And another congressman exulted that America was now "insulated from the rest of the world."

David Ramsay, the South Carolina historian and devout Republican, offered the most full-blown paean to the future of the "chosen country" as Jefferson had envisioned it. Echoing Jefferson's First Inaugural, he asked, "What is to hinder our extension on the same liberal principles of equal rights till we have increased to twenty-seven, thirty-seven, or any other number of states that will conveniently embrace, in one happy union, the whole country from the Atlantic to the Pacific ocean, and from the lakes of Canada to the Gulf of Mexico?" In his Second Inaugural, in 1805, Jefferson himself would ask, "Who can limit the extent to which the federative principle may operate effectively?" Gone were his doubts about the uses to which the new lands could be put. "Is it not better that the opposite bank of the Mississippi should be settled by our own brethren and children, than by strangers of another family?"

Jefferson's vision of the American future has ever since provided the mythic master narrative of American history. In the western domains that Jefferson imagined as a kind of blank slate on which succeeding generations would inscribe the image of American nationhood, it would be all too easy to overlook other peoples and other possibilities. It would be all too easy as well to overlook the critical role of the state in the progress of settlement and development. When Americans looked back on events, they would confuse effects with causes: War and diplomacy eliminated rival empires and dispossessed native peoples; an activist federal state played a critical role in pacifying a "lawless" frontier by privatizing public lands and promoting economic development. In the mythic history of Jefferson's West, an irresistible westward tide of settlement appears to be its own cause, the manifest destiny of nature's nation.

Yet if the reality of power remains submerged in Jefferson's thought, it's not at any great depth. The very idea of the nation implies enormous force, the power of a people enacting the will of "an overruling Providence." In Jefferson's Declaration of Independence, Americans claimed "the separate & equal station to which the laws of nature and of nature's God entitle them." The first law of nature, the great natural law proclaimed by writers of the day, was self-preservation, and the defining moment in American history was the great mobilization of American power to secure independence in the Revolution. President Jefferson's vision of westward expansion projected that glorious struggle into the future and across the continent. It was a kind of permanent revolution, reenacting the nation's beginnings in the multiplication of new, self-governing republican states.

Born in war, Jefferson's conception of an expanding union of free states constituted a peace plan for the New World. But until it was insulated from Europe's "exterminating havoc," the new nation would remain vulnerable, unable to realize its historic destiny. By eliminating the clear and present danger of a powerful French presence at the mouth of the Mississippi, the Louisiana Purchase guaranteed the survival of the Union—for the time being, at least. By opening the West to white American settlers, it all but guaranteed that subsequent generations would see their own history in Jefferson's vision of their future, a mythic, nation-making vision yoking individual liberty and national power and promising a future of peace and security in a dangerous world. Two hundred years later, that vision remains compelling to many Americans.

PETER S. ONUF is a professor of history at the University of Virginia. His most recent book is *Jefferson's Empire: The Language of American Nationhood* (2001). Copyright © 2003 by Peter Onuf.

Women in the Early Republic

PATRICIA CLINE COHEN

The field of U.S. women's history in the early republic presents unusual opportunities and challenges for scholars and teachers. The four decades that separate 1790 from 1830 have until recently remained a relatively underworked segment of the field, being bracketed at either end by the revolutionary and the Jacksonian eras, two periods far more event-laden and therefore, frankly, easier to teach. A glance at general U.S. history survey textbooks for the high school and college markets confirms this: chapters on the Revolution introduce daughters of liberty and republican mothers and then typically drop women as a topic until the 1830s when the cult of domesticity, the Lowell mill girls, and female reformers and abolitionists take their turns briefly on the center stage. The traditional history of the intervening years of the early republic has long been framed by a narrative of political and economic events—the rise of the party system, contested elections, embargoes and the War of 1812, courts and banking, the Missouri Compromise, canals and steamboats. These events, of so masculine a cast, appeared to leave little room for attention to women.

But it was not merely an unrelentingly masculine narrative that squeezed out the women. In part, this hiatus developed because of the initial conceptualization of the field of women's history. Back in the early 1970s, an emerging generation of scholars in pursuit of women's past was naturally drawn to the mid nineteenth century, a period marked by women's social activism and the first women's rights movement. Here there were female public figures with life stories to be told, along with organizations, conventions, strikes, manifestos, and agendas to be explained. Historians were also able to recover patterns in the lives of ordinary white women, because the spread of female literacy generated abundant manuscript and printed sources. The books, periodicals, and newspapers of the period offered evidence both of real women's lives and of an all-encompassing, sentimentalized, often cloying ideology of women's proper sphere (variously called the cult of true womanhood or the cult of domesticity, terms pioneered by historians Barbara Welter and Aileen Kraditor in the 1960s). Private letters and diaries allowed more immediate access to the world of women and permitted reconstruction of daily domestic life, female friendships, and what was termed "women's culture," seen as distinctly different from the realm of men.

The revolutionary years also beckoned to early scholars, because the research questions were so compelling. How did this democratic revolution, stirred by high-minded pronouncements about the equality of all men and the civic virtue of citizens, make any difference to the place of women in the polity? Two signal books of 1980, Mary Beth Norton's *Liberty's Daughters* and Linda Kerber's *Women of the Republic,* led the way in showing the gradual politicization of women and the impact of revolutionary ideology on thinking about gender. Both books left off in the 1790s on a cautiously rising note, showing that some women were indeed beginning to claim a special female contribution to the healthy workings of the republic. Kerber coined the apt phrase "republican motherhood" to capture a sentiment promoted and widely endorsed in the 1790s: the idea that women best served the republic by becoming educated, virtuous mothers able to train their sons to be the thinking, rational citizens required by a government founded on the consent of the governed. In a bold stroke, republican motherhood incalculably advanced the cause of women's education and led to the founding of many female academies, even as it perpetuated the notion that women's most salient connection to the state was channeled through maternal duties. In short, the legacy of the revolution was mixed, one of potentialities that remained to be realized.

In contrast, the years after the 1790s and up to the Age of Jackson have been much less attended to. Let me venture to guess that most college courses in women's history skip right over it. With few timeline-worthy events to point to, and few famous women to anchor a lecture, the years understandably get short shrift, especially in a course that has to cover a lot of ground in ten or fourteen weeks. Yet the historical processes inaugurated during those early years clearly are crucial for explaining the newly evolving gender system of the later nineteenth century. I became convinced of this back in the 1980s, when I encountered the intense puzzlement of my students at the midpoint of my course. Lectures and readings would take them up through the Revolution, capped by the midterm exam; then the following week would open with the antebellum decades, leaving them to ask in bewilderment: what happened to those potentially powerful ideas about women's advancement through education? How could the stifling glorification of domesticity replace the sturdy version of woman's sphere exemplified by Abigail Adams and Mercy Otis Warren?

Texts produced for this specialized market perpetuate the problem, for they also bound over the chasm between republican motherhood and the cult of domesticity. Nancy Woloch's standard survey, *Women and the American Experience,* moves from a pair of chapters on the eighteenth century to a second pair on the early nineteenth, where the dates 1800–1860 appear in the chapter title but the content is framed by the inauguration of *Godey's Ladies Book,* founded in 1828. Sara Evans's *Born for Liberty* makes the same leap, moving from the end of the Revolution to a new chapter that starts with the 1820s. In a similar fashion, the classroom readings book edited by Mary Beth Norton and Ruth M. Alexander, *Major Problems in American Women's History,* contains no articles centrally concerned with the 1800–1830 period. And only in the very latest edition of the Linda Kerber and Jane DeHart reader, *Women's America,* has an early-nineteenth-century essay just been added, a study of sexual coercion by Sharon Bloch.

Yet during those decades, the stage was being set for the more dramatic changes in women's lives so apparent by the mid nineteenth century. The engines of change were mostly processes, rarely attributable to individual persons or discrete events, which only makes it harder to distill them for textbook presentation or locate them on a timeline. For example, the novel argument for female education first broached in the 1790s eventually led to the founding of many hundreds of public and private schools admitting girls, with inaugural dates dotted throughout the next four decades. As a result, by the 1830s literacy for white females was at an all-time high. In the field of law, important but incremental changes in some dozen states' statute codes and in legal practice slowly built up during the early national period; by the 1830s new patterns were evident in areas like divorce and tort actions for seduction. Such a transition reveals new ways of thinking about women, sexuality, and autonomy, but the piecemeal nature of the legal process thwarts easy generalization. Likewise, a slow accumulation of alterations in men's employment patterns and the gradual incursion of a wage-based economy slowly but powerfully exerted pressure on the social definitions of women's non-waged work; but it is hard to put a finger on the moment in time when those definitions actually changed. Finally, perhaps most difficult of all to explain or even to get a handle on at the level of the individual (because of thin documentation), there occurred a slow but impressive and unmistakable decline in the birth rate in the years from 1800 to 1820, kicking off a century-long descent of momentous proportions both for women's history and for all of American history.

Taken together, these trends in education, law, work, and fertility indicate that the years of the early republic set in motion large-scale forces with profound consequences for women. As subterranean social processes, they can be challenging to teach, especially to first time history students. A discussion of some pathways by which scholars have been mapping out this shadowy territory can suggest approaches for integrating the topic into the classroom.

Some scholars concentrate on women and politics, pushing beyond the 1790s' conception of republican motherhood to larger questions of the meaning of female citizenship. Linda Kerber remains at the center of this enterprise with two recent books: *Toward an Intellectual History of Women* and *No Constitutional Right to be Ladies.* In the latter book, Kerber takes up the interesting question of the obligations of citizenship (rather than the privileges, such as voting), and she locates

an 1805 lawsuit that wonderfully reveals contested notions of female citizenship in this transitional phase between republican motherhood and the cult of domesticity. The case involved the property rights of heirs of a loyalist wife who had fled America with her husband during the Revolutionary War. Was the wife a political traitor in her own right who therefore deserved to lose her dower property, confiscated by the state, or was she a mere feme covert, a legal nonperson obliged to accompany her husband? The judicial outcome was a clear victory for the common law of domestic relations: a wife could not presume to exercise political choice independent of her husband. One of the lawyers on the winning side elaborated: "If he commanded it [fleeing the country], she was bound to obey him, by a law paramount to all other laws—the law of God." The remarkable point, however, is that lawyers on the losing side were able even to frame and sustain the contrary argument—that women were political actors—up to the state supreme court.

Another teachable episode that reveals a sense of the possibilities for women opened by the Revolution—and then decidedly shut during the early republic—was the experience of suffrage in New Jersey. Between 1775 and 1807, the state constitution permitted all persons worth over fifty pounds to vote. Free blacks and single women were technically enfranchised under this provision, but not married women, who could have no independent claim to ownership of fifty pounds. Historians long regarded the provision as a fluke, a mistake by state law framers so certain of white male prerogative that they simply forgot to specify the sex and race of voters. But a recent article by Judith Apter Klinghoffer and Lois Elkis argues that it was intentional, demonstrates that some women claimed the vote, and then explains its demise in the changing political climate of the early 1800s.

Rosemarie Zagarri is at work on a book on women and politics in the 1790s, and a foretaste of her research appears in a 1998 article, "The Rights of Man and Woman in Post-Revolutionary America." A particularly accessible and highly readable book for entry-level college students is Zagarri's brief biography of a remarkable woman of the late eighteenth century, *A Woman's Dilemma: Mercy Otis Warren and the American Revolution.* The book carries Warren into her final two decades in the new republic, and in the process it illuminates the cooling receptivity of the country to talented public women. Sheila Skemp has published a concise version of the life of Judith Sargent Murray in the Bedford Books series, examining the intellectual career of the most advanced American thinker on the question of women's common humanity with men. Murray's writings, signed with the pseudonyms "Constantia" and "The Gleaner," generated considerable interest and debate in the 1790s, but a series of personal affronts and hurtful criticism caused her to withdraw from print after 1798. By the time she died in 1820, her protofeminism was nearly forgotten. Taken together, Kerber, Zagarri, and Skemp show us a remarkable array of public expressions of women's claim to near equality with men that pepper the 1790s and then disappear. One question near the top of the research agenda is to explain what restrained and subdued those ideas in the first two decades of the nineteenth century.

The history of women and religion in the early republic shows a similar pattern of eighteenth-century opportunity followed by declension. By 1800 women made up the majority of Protestant congregants, while the church hierarchy remained exclusively male. Recent work by Susan Juster finds that in some New England Baptist congregations, remarkably egalitarian practices took hold during the mid eighteenth century, only to be deliberately scaled back by the 1810s. And Catherine Brekus has brought to light over a hundred women preachers and exhorters active in the years 1740–1845, whose lives signify a startling infringement of the traditional prohibition against female public speaking and the exercise of religious authority.

One such woman, Jemina Wilkinson of Rhode Island, transformed herself into a genderless religious leader called The Universal Friend. The Friend eschewed gendered pronouns, adopted ambiguous but mostly male-style clothes, and led a group of some 250 followers into a settlement called New Jerusalem in upstate New York in the 1790s. Such unusual assertions of female leadership came in for serious criticism. Religious periodicals in the early 1800s printed frequent reminders of the biblical prohibition, "Let your women learn to keep silence in the churches." Brekus finds that not a few of the female preachers she so painstakingly resurrected were literally erased from the official records of their churches. The religious history of the early republic's Second Great Awakening encapsulates two contradictory tendencies: a rising value on women's special piety and enthusiastic participation, coupled with an ever-louder chorus of admonitions about women's God-ordained subordination to men.

One way to approach the puzzle of the early nineteenth century is to try to decipher the thoughts, feelings, and ambitions of women themselves, through a close analysis of letters and diaries. Female literacy advanced early enough in New England for Nancy Cott to undertake an extensive study of hundreds of diaries and letter collections, forming the backbone of *The Bonds of Womanhood*. Cott sorted her material into the thematic subjects of work, domesticity, education, religion, and sisterhood. One surprising finding was that many of the central ideas about women's natural piety and submissive nature—later codified by the prescriptive cult of domesticity of the 1830s—can be delineated in young girls' diaries of the century's opening decades. Glorification of domesticity as expressed by women's literary periodicals and advice books thus cannot be written off as a plot to subdue and infantilize young women who might otherwise be unruly, impertinent, or dangerously confident; in some sense, it had its origins among the young women themselves well before the 1830s.

Another study that engages in close analysis of a woman's diary is Laurel Thatcher Ulrich's superb study of a Maine midwife, *A Midwife's Tale*. Ulrich explores the mental world and daily life of a taciturn but observant, dedicated woman and meticulously reconstructs Martha Ballard's medical practice and social networks, showing along the way the gendered household economy of the Maine frontier and the courtship and sexual practices of the day.

Young women in Ballard's town in the 1790s participated in the waning years of a somewhat looser system of sexual regulation; to be pregnant and then marry—the reverse of the usual order—was not that uncommon around New England in the eighteenth century. Thirty-eight percent of the first births that Ballard delivered, in her career total of 814 deliveries, were to mothers who conceived before they were married. But in the early republic, prenuptial pregnancies began to plummet, and loss of virginity in women began to carry a terrible stigma. How such a sea change in courtship customs was inaugurated and enforced is one of the open and fascinating questions of the period of women's history. A partial look at the story in one town, Augusta, Maine—the same town Martha Ballard inhabited—is carried forward in my own book about a servant girl in Augusta, Helen Jewett, whose fall from virtue in the 1820s earned her the scorn of her employers and other townsfolk and directly set her on the path to a spectacular career in prostitution.

Ulrich's careful delineation of male and female work in Ballard's town shows us a social world where women's domestic labor intersected with men's and earned respect and value as a significant contribution to the household economy. Jeanne Boydston carries that story forward to the 1830s in *Home and Work*. Boydston presents a model analysis of how incremental changes in the nature of men's work slowly altered the value and sentiment attached to women's domestic labor. Boydston coined the phrase "the pastoralization of housework" to refer to the process by which housework lost its association with productive labor (in contrast to men's waged labor and market relations) and instead became sentimentalized as service provided as a feminine gift. Her book shows how behavior unchanged over time could mean very different things in separate eras. The housewife of 1780 and of 1820 faced much the same set of daily tasks, but the cultural meaning attached to housework had shifted and thereby rendered it invisible as work.

Finally, family law in the early republic remained mostly unchanged, with one important exception. Politicians in state after state framed new legal codes in light of republican theory and sentiment, but significantly failed to consider rewriting the rules on "Baron and Feme," as it was called, the ancient terms "lord and wife" indicating just how much reliance was placed on old legal customs that established wives as full dependents under husbands. The legal doctrine of feme covert, for example, remained in place as it had existed in English common law.

The one departure from English precedent was a significant one: state after state provided means for divorce. Norma Basch, in *Framing American Divorce,* locates the provision of divorce in the mix of Revolution-inspired legal change. Just as Americans had dissolved the bonds of empire with Britain in the Revolution, now the new states provided a way to dissolve the bonds of matrimony. Divorce was of course based on the finding of fault with one party, and it remained narrowly tied to specific offenses, but it was gender-neutral in its application and it was legally available in most states. In fact, not many couples resorted to legal divorce; the era of sharply rising divorce rates was at least another century away. But its availability and eclectic working in case after case under various state laws reveal much about the possibilities, tensions, and choices confronting women in the early republic.

The first forty years of the new nation were characterized by legal, economic, and cultural changes that shaped the lives of men and women throughout the rest of the nineteenth century.

The nature of the changes does not lend itself to the simplified history captured in a timeline, and probably for good reason we have found it most efficient to teach this period first by describing the world of the republican mother and then leaping to the world of the 1830s, comparing two different ideal-typical models. Filling in the intervening ground is an exciting task, however, and one that can be shared in the classroom with students who are prepared to think about the amorphous and complex nature of cultural change. After all, many of these same kinds of long-term trends and processes undergird the significant influences in their own lives today, where ideas about the value of work, sexuality, family life, and the relative equality of the sexes are all still contested and in flux.

Bibliography

Basch, Norma. *Framing American Divorce: From the Revolutionary Generation to the Victorians.* Berkeley: University of California Press, 1999.

Boydston, Jeanne. *Home and Work: Housework, Wages, and the Ideology of Labor in the Early Republic.* New York: Oxford University Press, 1991.

Brekus, Catherine A. *Strangers and Pilgrims: Female Preaching in America, 1740–1845.* Chapel Hill: University of North Carolina Press, 1998.

Cohen, Patricia Cline. *The Murder of Helen Jewett: The Life and Death of a Prostitute in Nineteenth-Century New York.* New York: Knopf, 1998.

Cott, Nancy F. *The Bonds of Womanhood: "Women's Sphere" in New England, 1780–1835.* New Haven: Yale University Press, 1977.

Evans, Sara M. *Born for Liberty: A History of Women in America.* New York: Free Press, 1997.

Juster, Susan. *Disorderly Women: Sexual Politics and Evangelicalism in Revolutionary New England.* Ithaca: Cornell University Press, 1994.

Kerber, Linda K. *No Constitutional Right to be Ladies: Women and the Obligations of Citizenship.* New York: Hill and Wang, 1998.

———. *Toward an Intellectual History of Women: Essays.* Chapel Hill: University of North Carolina Press, 1997.

———. *Women of the Republic: Intellect and Ideology in Revolutionary America.* Chapel Hill: University of North Carolina Press, 1980.

Kerber, Linda K. and Jane De Hart Matthews, eds. *Women's America: Refocusing the Past.* 5th ed. New York: Oxford University Press, 2000.

Klinghoffer, Judith Apter and Lois Elkis. *"'The Petticoat Electors': Women's Suffrage in New Jersey, 1776–1807."* Journal of the Early Republic 12 (1992): 159–93.

Norton, Mary Beth. *Liberty's Daughters: The Revolutionary Experience of American Women, 1750–1800.* Boston: Little, Brown, 1980.

Norton, Mary Beth and Ruth M. Alexander. *Major Problems in American Women's History.* 2d ed. Lexington, MA: D. C. Heath, 1996.

Skemp, Sheila L. *Judith Sargent Murray: A Brief Biography with Documents.* Boston: Bedford Books, 1998.

Ulrich, Laurel Thatcher. *A Midwife's Tale: The Life of Martha Ballard, Based on Her Diary, 1785–1812.* New York: Knopf, 1990.

Woloch, Nancy. *Women and the American Experienc*e. 2d edition. New York: McGraw-Hill, 1994.

Zagarri, Rosemarie. "The Rights of Man and Woman in Post-Revolutionary America." *William and Mary Quarterly* 55 (1998): 203–30.

———. *A Woman's Dilemma: Mercy Otis Warren and the American Revolution.* Wheeling, IL: Harlan Davidson, 1995.

PATRICIA CLINE COHEN has been a professor of history at the University of California at Santa Barbara for twenty-three years. She has authored two books: *A Calculating People: The Spread of Numeracy in Early America* and *The Murder of Helen Jewett: The Life and Death of a Prostitute in Nineteenth-Century New York.* She is also the co-author of a survey textbook, *The American Promise*, for which she wrote the chapters covering 1754–1840.

The Everyday Life of Enslaved People in the Antebellum South

CALVIN SCHERMERHORN

Coming of age in a nation that hungered for black labor, antebellum America's slaves were driven relentlessly to toil in fields and factories. Their bodies weakened by fatigue and hunger, wracked by chronic illnesses and injury and, in the case of women of childbearing age, strained by near constant pregnancy, daily existence often came down to an endless struggle of will and endurance. Yet that was not the sum of the challenges and tribulations that burdened black people's lives, for they lived in the shadow of an agricultural revolution. Beginning in the 1790s, short-staple cotton became a profitable commodity owing to the introduction of efficient cotton gins (which separated the sticky seeds from the valuable lint) and a growing demand from British textile mills. To take advantage of new economic opportunities, migrating masters forcibly moved hundreds of thousands of enslaved women, children, and men from the Upper South onto the cotton and sugar frontiers of Mississippi, Texas, Arkansas, Louisiana, and Alabama. This agricultural revolution rapidly changed the shape and face of a young nation. It also profoundly altered the lives of America's slaves as owners and traders separated families, parted friends, and orphaned children. Though enslaved women and men worked as hard to repair the damage done to their families and friendships as they worked for their owners—meeting, marrying, raising babies, and forming all sorts of social institutions—few could escape the human cost of agricultural and national expansion. As Virginia native Madison Jefferson later recalled, "we [had] dread constantly on our minds," never knowing "how long master might keep us, "nor into whose hands we may fall".[1]

Such fears were especially acute among slaves who lived in the upper South states of Maryland and Virginia. In these areas where much of the domestic (or internal) migration originated, owners increasingly came to value their slaves not for the work they might perform but for the cash they could bring at auction. A decline in the profitability of tobacco, combined with a steady growth in the population of slaves, encouraged such recalculation. Between 1790 and 1860 some 1.1 million enslaved people—the majority of them between the ages of 15 and 30—found themselves forced onto the roads. Often plucked away by traders called "Georgia men" and bound together in coffles, black women and men marched south and west, footsore, forlorn, and

"Auction & Negro Sales," Whitehall Street, Atlanta, 1864. Illustrating the immense human cost of slavery, auction houses such as this one wrecked families, separated friends, and orphaned children. (Image courtesy of Library of Congress, LC-DIG-cwpb-03351.)

often missing their families. Later, as the machinery of the slave market grew more elaborate, traders packed slaves into railroad cars and the holds of ships, reducing the duration of the journey though not its harmful effects. The bulk of this traffic took place in the winter, a choice that would deliver fresh workers just in time for spring planting. Some would be dispatched at one of the many auction houses that sprang up in New Orleans, Natchez, and Memphis. Others would be marched through new neighborhoods and sold away in ones or twos by the trader. About 60 percent of America's forced migrants went that way, sold by traders and mixed in with strangers. The remainder moved along with their owners, bundled together with horses, cattle, wagons, and supplies by men (and women) eagerly seeking their fortunes on the southern frontier.[2]

Given the propensity of traders and free migrants to select the strongest, the healthiest, and the most fertile of slaves for transshipment to Deep South plantations—after all, what planters wanted were slaves who could both produce and reproduce—the impact on black families was extensive. Upper South slave communities in Virginia and Maryland were especially hard hit. There, in what amounted to the headwaters of a great forced migration, as many as one half of all sales separated parents from children. One-quarter took husbands from wives[3]. Each season that passed without the sale of a friend or relative brought considerable relief, but slaves worried and prepared for the near inevitable arrival of a trader or his agent. In anticipation of such an eventuality, Henry "Box" Brown's mother took her son "upon her knee and, pointing to the forest trees which were then being stripped of their foliage by the winds of autumn, would say to me, my son, as yonder leaves are stripped from off the trees of the forest, so are the children of the slaves swept away from them by the hands of cruel tyrants".[4] Other parents tried to delay the day of forced departure, hiding their children in the woods as did North Carolina native Moses Grandy's mother, in a heartbreaking and usually futile attempt "to prevent master selling us".[5]

Planters and masters were quick to capitalize on black people's desperate efforts to keep their families intact. Recognizing a new means to wring obedience out of their laborers, sale became a way to "domesticate" those who, like Josiah Henson's father, proved immune to more conventional forms of slave discipline. Recounting how his father had been severely beaten for having intervened to protect his wife from an overseer's assault, Henson described a punishment that failed to achieve its intended effect. "My father became a different man," Henson later wrote, but not an obedient man. Despite a hundred lashes and the amputation of his right ear, he turned "morose, disobedient, and intractable." So much so that the owner gave up on the more conventional modes of control and eventually rid himself of a difficult slave by selling Henson's father to "Alabama; and neither my mother nor I, ever heard of him again".[6]

Sale as punishment was but just one of the many reasons slaves witnessed loved ones being bound away. Slaveowners frequently balanced their personal accounts and paid off their debts by selling excess slaves. Others dismembered longstanding slave families and communities when they divided their property among heirs or gave away a slave to celebrate a child's marriage. These were practices that made enslaved women and men acutely conscious of the ambitions, health, and financial condition of those who claimed to own them. "A bankruptcy, a death, or a removal, may produce a score or two of involuntary divorces," recalled Virginia native Henry Goings. Husbands and wives who belonged to different owners and who had married "abroad" suffered disproportionately from owners' changing

fortunes. Maria Perkins learned this first hand when her owner determined to sell away a number of his slaves. "Dear Husband," Maria opened her letter, "I write . . . to let you know of my distress. my master has sold [our son] albert to trader on Monday court day and myself and other child is for sale also." "I don't want a trader to get me," Maria cried, before asking her husband to approach his own master about buying Maria and the couple's remaining child.[7]

Slaves could do little, however, to slow the rushing tide of forced migration. Swept up in a current that would deposit 285,000 people on Deep South plantations in the 1830s alone, enslaved men and women soon found themselves hard at work in their new homes, creating cotton and sugar economies one field and furrow at a time. The earliest arrivals faced the worst work, much of which involved the back-breaking labor of carving plantations from forests and building the most basic features of an agricultural infrastructure. But those who arrived later had no easy time of it. Sold away from his native Virginia, J. H. Banks arrived in Alabama by rail in the 1830s to find that his new owner "had purchased a new farm, and had taken a contract to finish three miles of railroad," which he intended his slaves to build before putting them to work making cotton.[8] Viewing the fields from his drafty and ramshackle slave quarters—a cabin with "no chinking or daubing," Banks recalled seeing the toll the work took. Despite their location "in the midst of the cotton paradise," young men who were no more "than nineteen or twenty" looked easily twice their age.[9] Along the Oconee and Savannah rivers in Georgia, the Coosa and Tombigbee rivers in Alabama, and along the banks of the Tennessee and Mississippi, conditions were no better. Young women and men labored from before dawn to after dark, usually under the supervision of overseers and horse-mounted patrollers.[10] In places where "sugar wuz king," as one former Louisiana slave recalled it, the work regime pressed even harder, mirroring the volatile Caribbean slave societies that served as models for these factories in the fields. Because of the physically demanding nature of the work slaves performed on America's sugar estates, sex balances remained far out of balance. Men, planters believed, swung the heavy cane knives more effectively than did women. As a consequence, sugar plantations were characterized by disproportionately more men than women, fewer families, and birth rates that lagged behind those of other regions, where despite the trauma of forced migration, strangers gradually came to be friends, married, and had children.[11]

Labor posed plenty of dangers, but it was not the only danger inherent to slavery. There was another side to daily life in bondage, one which women and girls especially confronted. The antebellum South was a landscape characterized by sexual violence against African American women.[12] Harriet Jacobs knew this too well, having learned this particular terrain the day her owner "began to whisper foul words" into her ear.[13] Some women tried to turn the tables and use their sexuality strategically. Though a few may have succeeded, failure could exact a deadly high price. Take Eliza, for example. The concubine of a Maryland planter, Eliza had borne the man a daughter named Emily. When jealous relatives intervened, the arrangement abruptly unraveled. Carried to Washington D.C. by her master's son-in-law Eliza realized too late that she had been badly deceived. Rather than receiving her freedom as she had been promised, the finely attired and petted Eliza found herself lodged in jail and discovered that her so-called freedom paper was actually a bill of sale.[14] Mary, too, suffered grievously when a vengeful mistress sold the Alabama woman away from the baby she had borne her master. The child, only eleven months old, went to a Kentucky owner while Mary ended up in the hands of a Maryland master. Sale did not end Mary's troubles. Subjected to the sexual harassment of her new owner's son, Mary fought back, as did the slave who had been courting her. In a rage, he murdered Mary's attacker. Neighborhood slaves were forced to watch the man who had defended Mary burned alive, and Mary—in a fit of desperation—ended her own life in the waters of the Chesapeake Bay.[15]

Day-to-day life involved more than growing the South's staple crops. Besides constructing and maintaining miles of fence and out-buildings, tending owners' livestock, splitting firewood, and performing a near endless assortment of chores associated with antebellum agricultural enterprise, slaves grew a wide range of crops. In the cotton South, for example, Henry Goings recalled, "a good hand is supposed to cultivate 15 acres of cotton and 10 acres of corn," besides "potatoes and other vegetables," which were grown "for home consumption".[16] After a day sowing, weeding, chopping, or picking cotton, slaves would also often tend to their own garden patches where they would raise vegetables, keep chickens and small livestock, and sometimes even produce commodities on marginal land. In many corners of the South—particularly in or near urban centers—enslaved people became small property owners, accumulating small amounts of wealth by peddling extra eggs, homemade confections, and homegrown produce to townspeople. A few even sold small crops of cotton or tobacco back to their owners, some of whom occasionally found themselves in perpetual debt to their slaves. Others, however, promoted slaves' productive activities as a way to shift some of the burden of support from owners to the owned. Nevertheless, slaves' home enterprises produced some advantages. In creating informal economies, enslaved people developed their own concepts of property, and in rare cases, earned enough from their entrepreneurial and agricultural activities to finance their own freedom or that of a loved one.[17]

Stretching the workday into the nights exposed slaves to a different kind of risk. Again, in the words of Henry Goings—who had been born a slave in Virginia before traveling much of the cotton South with a peripatetic owner—long work days and heavy work loads "often showed themselves in fevers and other miasmatic diseases".[18] Besides aging the nation's slaves before their time, the labor regimes that produced the South's great staples exposed workers to infectious diseases like hookworm, which was endemic on some plantations. Infected slaves grew anemic, lost weight, and succumbed to infections. The sufferers' symptoms began with a dermatitis, "ground itch" or "dew poison," when the hookworm larvae penetrated the skin en route to the small intestine. A raft of other diseases also plagued slaves. Mosquitoes spread yellow fever and malaria.

Unwashed hands and undercooked meat introduced food poisoning and dysentery. Infections transmitted through exposure to soil and fecal matter (workers often went without shoes and babies went without diapers) were common and debilitating. To combat illness, enslaved people cultivated knowledge of folk remedies and sometimes used spiritual medicine. Enslaved women exchanged information on contraception and abortion and became expert midwives. But often even experienced doctors could do little. Outbreaks of viral hepatitis or cholera might tear through a neighborhood at any time, carried on occasion by coffles of the newly arrived slaves. Not surprisingly, the average life expectancy for slaves in antebellum America was just over thirty years.[19]

In addition to being sick, enslaved people were perennially hungry and ill-clothed, especially infants, toddlers, and preteens who made up over 43 percent of the enslaved population in 1820.[20] In the upper South, insufficient quantities of food complemented poor quality, as owners stinted children, reserving calories for slaves in their most productive years. Partly as a consequence, adult slaves tended to be shorter than other Americans.[21] Frederick Douglass recalled being "so pinched with hunger" as a child that he had "fought with the dog" for the "smallest crumbs".[22] Scanty clothing compounded children's problems. Virginia native John Brown recalled that youngsters "of both sexes usually run about quite naked, until they are from ten to twelve years of age".[23] Young Moses Grandy was "compelled to go into the fields and woods to work, with my naked feet cracked and bleeding from extreme cold." To warm them he would "rouse an ox or hog, and stand on the place where it had lain".[24]

Ill-health, hunger, and the raw winds of winter rarely excused slaves from their daily labors. Indeed, in a system as heavily dependent on slaves' labor as were the cotton, sugar, tobacco, and rice crops that enriched their owners—and the nation—any deviance brought summary and often severe punishment. Whips were the favored weapon of choice, falling on slaves' backs and gouging out flesh in retaliation for the smallest infractions. But virtually anything could become an instrument of discipline and control. Masters, mistresses, overseers, and agents routinely relied on sticks, pistols, knives, fists, feet, shovels, and tongs to terrorize and subdue their slaves. Hanna Fambro's mistress beat her mother to death with a broomstick. Ira Jones's aunt died of tetanus after her owner nailed her hands to a barrel.[25] When a young mother arrived late to the fields one morning, fellow slave Charles Ball recalled, the overseer "compelled her to remove her old tow linen shift, the only garment she wore, so as to expose her hips," whereupon he "gave her ten lashes, with his long whip, every touch of which brought blood, and a shriek from the sufferer".[26] Children were not spared their owners' rods. Determined that the youngest slaves mature into the most obedient slaves, masters and mistresses beat children for crying, for failing to do their chores, and sometimes for no reason at all.[27] As one survivor recalled years after the Civil War, slavery "wuz hell".[28]

Family—whether remembered or reconstructed—gave slaves the strength to continue. Whether calling on one another

A Slave Named Gordon and the Power of Historical Images

A wood engraving from *Harper's Weekly* was drawn from a widely distributed and shocking photograph of Gordon, a runaway slave, as he received a medical examination during his induction into the Union army in March 1863. Two months earlier Gordon had been severely beaten by his overseer. While recuperating, he plotted his escape. Pursued by slavecatchers, Gordon showed particular cunning by rubbing onions on his body to disorient the pack of bloodhounds that chased him. The tactic worked. Although muddy, tired, and tattered, he reached the Union encampment at Baton Rouge after covering 80 miles in ten days. Upon learning that Lincoln had recently granted African Americans the opportunity to fight in segregated units, Gordon decided to enlist. He was among the first of nearly 200,000 black Americans to fight during the Civil War.

In the coming weeks, the photographers who took the picture of Gordon's scarred back soon realized the image's potential. They mass produced and sold copies of it around the country. Within months commercial photographers in Philadelphia, Boston, New York, and London were also reproducing the image. The photograph became the latest evidence in the abolitionist outcry over the horrors of slavery. A journalist for the *New York Independent* wrote: "This photograph should be multiplied by 100,000, and scattered over the States. It tells the story in a way that even Mrs. [Harriet Beecher] Stowe [author of *Uncle Tom's Cabin* (1852)] can not approach, because it tells the story to the eye." Abolitionist William Lloyd Garrison also repeatedly referenced Gordon's story and the famous photograph in his crusade against slavery. The photograph received its widest distribution in the July 4, 1863 edition of *Harper's Weekly.* The popular magazine recounted Gordon's story of courage, fortitude, and patriotism. This effort transformed him into a symbol that inspired many free blacks in the North to enlist.

What happened to Gordon after enlisting remains murky. The *Liberator* reported that he served as a sergeant in an black regiment that fought bravely at the siege of Port Hudson, an important Confederate stronghold on the Mississippi River twenty miles north of Baton Rouge. This battle on May 27, 1863 marked the first time that black soldiers played a leading role in an assault on a major Confederate position. Their heroism was widely noted and helped convince many skeptics to accept the enlistment of African Americans into the U.S. Army. Although little more is known about Gordon, the image lives on. By influencing the national debate about slavery, and testifying to the courage displayed by African Americans in the face of terrible brutality, Gordon's photograph not only tells an important story about slavery's history, but also reveals the power of an image in the making of that history.

to stave off an overseer's blows, sharing their meals in the sooty darkness of a plantation cabin, or as Maria Perkins attempted to do, keeping the slave trader at bay, husbands and wives, parents and children, sisters and brothers found in their affective and domestic relations the means to deflect some of the worst of slavery's impositions. For many of those who were transported out of the upper, older, and seaboard South and onto cotton and sugar's new plantations, this often meant starting their families anew. one of probably hundreds of thousands of enslaved women and men who attempted to bring order out of chaos through marriage, Virginia-born Philip Joiner met and wed Henrietta when both were enslaved in south Georgia. By the Civil War, the couple had two daughters, Lucy Ann and Mary Jane, named as so many enslaved children were after grandparents and other close kin.[29]

Despite the calloused advice of owners who told grieving husbands and wives that if they wanted a spouse "so badly, stop your crying and go and find another," many resisted forming new families while their closest kin remained alive in old homes.[30] Charles Ball, for example, joined an enslaved family on his master's South Carolina plantation—sharing a roof, helping out, and contributing food to a collective table—but he never forgot the woman and children he had been made to leave behind in Maryland. As he later explained, "a firm conviction settled upon my mind, that by some means, at present incomprehensible to me, I should yet again embrace my wife, and caress my children." At length Ball did, escaping and making his way back to Maryland, where he was recaptured and reenslaved.[31]

Countless others relied solely on memory, keeping alive in their minds those heartfelt affections. These images did little to shield slaves from owners' blows, but they did remind enslaved people that they were far more than mere tools of agricultural and industrial production. They belonged not only to masters and mistresses, but also to each other. Thus it was that when Hawkins Wilson was sold away from Virginia in 1843, he carried with him a rich set of memories that kept him in mental touch with a family he hoped to see again someday. After the Civil War and emancipation, that day seemed to be fast approaching and Wilson wrote home from Texas that he was "anxious to learn about my sisters, from whom I have been separated many years—I have never heard from them since I left Virginia twenty four years ago—I am in hopes that they are still living and I am anxious to hear how they are getting on." Lest the recipient (an agent of the Bureau of Refugees, Freedmen, and Abandoned Lands) deliver his letter into the wrong hands, Wilson offered a detailed description of his family as he had last known them:

> One of my sisters belonged to Peter Coleman in Caroline County and her name was Jane—Her husband's name was Charles and he belonged to Buck Haskin and lived near John Wright's store in the same county—She had three children, Robert, Charles and Julia, when I left—Sister Martha belonged to Dr. Jefferson, who lived two miles above Wright's store—Sister Matilda belonged to Mrs. Botts, in the same county—My dear uncle Jim had a wife at Jack Langley's and his wife was named Adie and his oldest son was named buck and they all belonged to Jack

Langley—These are all my own dearest relatives and I wish to correspond with them with a view to visit them as soon as I can hear from them—My name is Hawkins Wilson and I am their brother, who was sold at Sheriff's sale.[32]

Hawkins Wilson never reconnected with his family. Neither did hundreds of thousands of other slaves, men and women whose lives had been roughly transformed by cotton's and sugar's antebellum revolutions. Whether left behind in the upper South—unsure of where their loved ones went and how they fared—or deposited among strangers on a Deep South plantation, America's last generation of slaves experienced deep and wrenching change. Many, indeed, lived their lives in near perpetual motion. Subject to repeated sales and migrations, handed off from one owner to the next, burdened with heavy demands on their labor, and haunted by the chronic terror of losing a close friend or kinsman to a trader's coffle, America's enslaved women and men struggled continuously to maintain their health, their strength, and, above all, their humanity. Theirs were day-to-day experiences that involved a hierarchy of concerns: for nourishment, for health, and for whatever security they could eke out of a system that repeatedly visited them with the incremental terrors of forced labor and enforced separations.

Notes

1. John Blassingame, *Slave Testimony: Two Centuries of Letters, Speeches, Interviews, and Autobiographies* (Baton Rouge: Louisiana State Press, 1977), 218.

2. Steven Deyle, *Carry Me Back: The Domestic Slave Trade in American Life* (New York: Oxford University Press, 2005), 288.

3. Brenda E. Stevenson, *Life in Black & White: Family and Community in the Slave South* (New York: Oxford University Press, 1996), 204–05, 223–25; Michael Tadman, *Speculators and Slaves: Masters, Traders, and Slaves in the Old South* (Madison: University of Wisconsin Press, 1996), 147.

4. Henry "Box" Brown, *Narrative of the Life of Henry Box Brown, Written by Himself* (Manchester: Lee and Glynn, 1851), 2. Available at <http://docsouth.unc.edu/neh/brownbox/brownbox. html>.

5. Moses Grandy, *Narrative of the Life of Moses Grandy, Late a Slave in the United States of America* (London: C. Gilpin, 1843), 8. Available at <http://docsouth.unc.edu/fpn/grandy/ grandy.html>.

6. Josiah Henson, *The Life of Josiah Henson, Formerly a Slave, Now an Inhabitant of Canada, as Narrated by Himself* (Boston: Arthur D. Phelps, 1849), 1–2. Available at <http://docsouth.unc. edu/neh/henson49/henson49.html>.

7. Maria Perkins to Richard Perkins, October 7, 1852, Folder 47, Box 3, U. B. Phillips Papers, Manuscripts and Archives, Yale University Library.

8. J. W. C. Pennington, *A Narrative of Events of the Life of J. H. Banks, an Escaped Slave, from the Cotton State, Alabama, in America* (Liverpool: Rourke, 1861), 48. Available at <http://docsouth.unc.edu/neh/penning/penning.html>.

9. *Ibid.,* 49, 50–51.

10. Steven F. Miller, "Plantation Labor Organization and Slave Life on the Cotton Frontier: The Alabama-Mississippi Black Belt, 1815–1840," in *Cultivation and Culture: Labor and the Shaping of Slave Life in the Americas,* Ira Berlin and Philip D. Morgan, eds. (Charlottesville: University of Virginia Press, 1993), 155–69.

11. Richard J. Follett, *The Sugar Masters: Planters and Slaves in Louisiana's Cane World, 1820–1860* (Baton Rouge: Louisiana State University Press, 2005), 11.

12. Walter Johnson, *River of Dark Dreams: Slavery, Capitalism, and Imperialism in the Mississippi Valley's Cotton Kingdom* (Cambridge: Harvard University Press, forthcoming).

13. Harriet Jacobs, *Incidents in the Life of a Slave Girl. Written by Herself,* Jean Fagan Yellin, ed. (Cambridge: Harvard University Press, 1987), 27.

14. Solomon Northup, *Twelve Years a Slave* (London: Sampson, Low, Son & Co., 1853), 50. Available at <http://docsouth.unc .edu/fpn/northup/northup.html>.

15. Jacob D. Green, *Narrative of the Life of J. D. Green, a Runaway Slave, from Kentucky, Containing an Account of His Three Escapes, in 1839, 1846, and 1848,* 16. Available at <http://docsouth.unc.edu/neh/greenjd/greenjd.html>.

16. Henry Goings, *Rambles of A Runaway from Southern Slavery* (Stratford: J. M. Robb, 1869).

17. Dylan C. Penningroth, *The Claims of Kinfolk: African American Property and Community in the Nineteenth-Century South* (Chapel Hill: University of North Carolina Press, 2003), 45–109.

18. Goings, *Rambles of A Runaway from Southern Slavery,* xx.

19. Philip R. P. Coelho and Robert A. McGuire, "Biology, Diseases, and Economics: An Epidemiological History of Slavery in the American South," *Journal of Bioeconomics 1* (November 1999): 151–90, 160; Herbert C. Covey, *African American Slave Medicine: Herbal and Non-Herbal Treatments* (New York: Rowan and Littlefield, 2007); Sharla Fett, *Doctoring the South: Southern Physicians and Everyday Medicine in the Mid-Nineteenth Century* (Chapel Hill: University of North Carolina Press, 2003); Historical Census Browser, Geospatial and Statistical Center, University of Virginia, <http://www.lib .virginia.edu/scholarslab/resources/index.html>.

20. Historical Census Browser, Geospatial and Statistical Center, University of Virginia, <http://www.lib.virginia.edu/scholarslab/ resources/index.html>.

21. Wilma King, *Stolen Childhood: Slave Youth in Nineteenth-Century America* (Bloomington: Indiana University Press, 1997); Richard H. Steckel, "Work, Disease, and Diet in the Health and Mortality of American Slaves," in *Without Consent or Contract: Technical Papers, vol. II,* Robert W. Fogel and Stanley Engerman, eds., (New York: W. W. Norton, 1992), 498–507; Marie Jenkins Schwartz, *Born in Bondage: Growing Up Enslaved in the Antebellum South* (Cambridge: Harvard University Press, 2001).

22. Frederick Douglass, *My Bondage and My Freedom. Part I.— Life as a Slave. Part II.—Life as a Freeman* (New York: Miller, Orton, and Mulligan, 1855),75. Available at <http://docsouth .unc.edu/neh/douglass55/douglass55.html>.

23. John Brown, *Slave Life in Georgia: A Narrative of the Life, Sufferings, and Escape of John Brown, A Fugitive Slave, Now in England,* L. A. Chamerovzow ed. (London, 1855), 4–5. Available at <http://docsouth.unc.edu/neh/jbrown/jbrown .html>.

24. Grandy, *Narrative,* II. Available at <http://docsouth.unc.edu/fpn/grandy/grandy.html>.

25. Thavolia Glymph, *Out of the House of Bondage: The Transformation of the Plantation Household* (Cambridge: Oxford University Press, 2008), 55–56.

26. Charles Ball, *Slavery in the United States: A Narrative of the life and Adventures of Charles Ball, a Black Man* (New York: John S. Taylor, 1837), 159. Available at <http://docsouth.unc.edu/neh/ballslavery/ball.html>.

27. Blassingame, *Slave Testimony,* 217–18.

28. Glymph, *Out of the House of Bondage,* 33.

29. Susan Eva O'Donovan, *Becoming Free in the Cotton South* (Cambridge: Harvard University Press, 2007), 42.

30. Elizabeth Keckley, *Behind the Scenes, or, Thirty years a Slave, and Four Years in the White House* (New York: G. W. Carleton & Co., 1869), 24–25. Available at <http://docsouth.unc.edu/neh/keckley/keckley.html>.

31. Ball, *Slavery in the United States,* 36, 71.

32. Ita Berlin and Leslie S. Rowland, eds., *Families and Freedom: A Documentary History of African-American Kinship in the Civil War Era* (New York: The New Press, 1997), 17–18.

CALVIN SCHERMERHORN is assistant professor of history at Arizona State University. His research and teaching focuses on American slavery, history of the American South, and nineteenth-century African American history.

From *OAH Magazine of History,* April 2009, pp. 31–36. Copyright © 2009 by Organization of American Historians. Reprinted by permission via the Copyright Clearance Center.

Liberty Is Exploitation
The Force of Tradition in Early Manufacturing

BARBARA M. TUCKER

The industrial revolution represented a watershed in American history. The transition from agriculture to manufacturing was neither an even nor an easy process. The factory floor became a contested and negotiated place, in which the very shape of the work-place depended upon the outcome of struggles between management and labor and between the demands of the factory system and traditional values observed by families. Change occurred at a different pace in various industries as production moved from the household to the workshop and then to the factory. It was the factory system, however, that had the most dramatic impact on the production process and helped to change the economic and social direction of the new nation.

In the historiography of the early republic, the rise of the factory system has received considerable scholarly attention. Beginning in the 1970s, a plethora of monographs were published on the economic and social transformation of such industries as boots and shoes, textiles, paper, and armaments. The customary concerns of economic and business historians, however, did not dominate the discussion; instead, a "new labor history" emerged. These scholars emphasized the impact of the new industrial order on the people who worked in the shops and factories that appeared between 1790 and 1860 and followed them from their workplaces to their communities, homes, churches, and social activities. Issues of paternalism, class, and gender informed their works.

Alan Dawley and Paul Faler were among the most significant innovators in this changing field. Their work on the boot and shoe industry of Lynn, Massachusetts, partly focused on the stress caused when laborers and shoe manufacturers ceased to share a common work space or ideology. This simple change in manufacturing relations profoundly affected the town of Lynn, its neighborhoods, churches, and political structure.[1]

Other scholars turned to the textile industry, in particular Thomas Dublin, who authored a work that challenged the romanticized view of the Lowell system. With eleven investors, Francis Cabot Lowell had formed the Boston Manufacturing Company in 1813. This was one of the most innovative companies organized during the early republic, a corporation characterized by professional management, large-scale production of yarn and cloth, and a unique labor force comprised of girls and women. Dublin challenged the sentimental view of labor-management relations advanced by others. He argued that the relationship between labor and management was an economic one and that the female workers recognized it as such. Whatever community of interests emerged in Waltham and later Lowell and Lawrence, Massachusetts, was among the girls and women themselves and not between labor and management. "When women workers spoke of independence," Dublin writes, "they referred at once to independence from their families and from their employers."[2] While the Lowell system embraced a new production system, its development did not overspread the entire textile industry and remained largely confined to the regions north of Boston. Throughout most of the country, cloth continued to be produced in homes and shops on hand looms. And spinning mills, not integrated corporations, supplied workers with the necessary yarn. Many of these processes were patterned after the system introduced by Samuel Slater.

Born in England and trained under the progressive factory master Jedediah Strutt, Samuel Slater brought the Arkwright system of yarn manufacturing to the United States. Around 1790 he formed a partnership with William Almy and Obadiah Brown to build a factory for the production of yarn. (Parenthetically, most accounts link Almy with Moses Brown, who placed the ad to which Slater responded. Actually, in this partnership Smith Brown, not Moses Brown, first entered the agreement and was later replaced by Obadiah Brown.) Under their arrangement, Slater built carding engines, water frames, and a carding and roving machine which he temporarily installed in a clothier's shop in nearby Pawtucket, Rhode Island, while Almy and Brown supplied the capital. Boys were hired to operate the equipment; within weeks, he doubled his labor force and eventually moved his operations to a specially built factory. Following a practice adopted in England, young children between seven and twelve years of age were employed to operate the new equipment. Initially they were drawn from local families, but as the need for workers increased. Slater turned to the apprentice system. In 1794 he advertised for "four or five active Lads, about 15 Years of Age to serve as Apprentices in the Cotton Factory."[3]

Local poor law officials answered Slater's advertisement and sent indigent boys to the mills. But apprentices proved problematic. Some resented Slater's control over them and his disciplinary style, while others were appalled by the demanding schedule that required them to work from twelve to sixteen hours a day, six days a week. They learned few skills, received room and board in lieu of wages, and were forced to attend Sunday Schools operated by Slater where they received educational training. Many ran away. By 1797 Slater noted that one Rehoboth boy ran away and another followed, and "again If it is suffered to pass, another will go tomorrow & so on until they are all gone."[4] Another form of labor had to be found.

Slater now turned to poor families throughout the area and invited them to send their children to the mill. This form of pauper labor also presented problems. Slater needed the children but not their parents, who resented Slater's control over their children and complained about the irregularity of wage payments and the lack of light and heat in the factories. Some threatened to keep their children home while others entered the factory and withdrew their children without notice, thereby stopping the machines. Slater was exasperated. He had little control over some of the complaints voiced by the parents. Almy and Brown were responsible for paying the families in cash or in kind, but often they were not able to keep their commitments. Slater protested: "You must not expect much yarn until I am better supplied with hands and money to pay them with several are out of corn and I have not a single dollar to buy any for them." The situation was not rectified and Slater again pleaded with Almy and Brown. Send "a little money if not I must unavoidably stop the mill after this week." He could not "bear to have people come round me daily if sometimes hourly and saying I have no wood nor corn nor have not had any several days. Can you expect my children to work if they have nothing to eat?[5] In desperation, he threatened to close the mill and sell the machinery.

Pauper labor was not the answer, and Slater turned to the family system. In New England the family was the basic economic unit. The householder still dominated the family economy, and he retained considerable authority within it to discipline wife and children, protect kin, lead the family in prayer, and supervise the educational and moral training of sons and daughters. Men fought and children resisted attempts by Slater to encroach on these prerogatives. To recruit and retain a labor force of children, Slater had to find common ground with householders. He had to effect some sort of compromise with parents whereby their customary values and their social and economic position within the family and the wider society would be safeguarded and respected. Slater sought to strengthen patriarchy, not challenge it. He recruited entire families to work for him, and a division of labor developed based on age and gender. Householders were brought under the control of the factory master, but they were not required to enter the factory and work alongside their children. Instead, Slater employed them in traditional jobs such as night watchman, painter, mason, and later farm hand. He strengthened their position within the family by having householders negotiate and sign contracts for the employment of their children and personally receive all wages earned by them.

Labor contracts suggest the strength and influence householders exerted over manufacturers. At the Slater and Kimball

factory, contracts usually were signed annually beginning April 1. Abel Dudley, for example, agreed to work in 1827, and he put five children in the mill: Sumner, Mary, Eliza, Abigail, and Caroline. He stipulated, however, that "Mary and Caroline have the privilege of going to school two months each one at a time and Amos is to work at 4/pr week when they are out."[6] Some contracts included other stipulations: a child was allowed to work with the mule spinner and taught his trade; either party had to give two weeks notice before quitting; householders were to receive extra pay for Sunday work. Thus, in order to recruit and retain a stable labor force, Samuel Slater struck a compromise with New England householders. If Slater respected their traditional prerogatives, they would provide him with a plentiful, tractable supply of workers. For those families who failed to adhere to this understanding. Slater had a solution. The case of Obadiah Greenhill was typical. On April 1, 1827, Greenhill placed five children from nine to seventeen years of age in Slater's factory. On October 6, the family was "Dismissed for manifesting a disposition to make disturbance in the mills amongst the help and for misconduct in general."[7]

The force of tradition that operated in the factories was extended to village, home, and church. The new factory villages Slater established reflected the needs of New England families. Slatersville was one of the first mill villages developed by Slater and served as a model for later manufacturers:

> Like many of the towns of colonial New England, it was built around a broad road that traversed the town center. The smithy, the dry goods stores, the church, and the school were on this road. Predictably, the Congregational church stood in the geographic center of the village and was surrounded by a broad common. Toward the outskirts of the village lived more than six hundred textile workers, farm laborers, merchants, and mechanics. Their homes were one- and two-story detached and semi-detached dwellings that were built parallel to the main road and separated from one another by garden plots. Each dwelling was occupied by a single family. No house stood isolated from the central community. The mill and its outbuildings . . . did not disturb the traditional sense of community. They were built at a short distance from the village and were surrounded by fenced and tilled fields belonging to the company.[8]

The family and the church were the predominant forces in the lives of many residents. Familial and religious doctrines and discipline served as the basis for a well-ordered society and also a well-run factory. Values taught in the home and the church served the needs of the factory masters.

In the nineteenth century, the home became a training ground for a generation of factory hands. The first law of childhood, the one necessary for the proper maintenance of good family government and obviously the one necessary for the proper maintenance of good order within the factory, was unquestioning obedience. All commands had to be immediately and, in fact, cheerfully obeyed. If obedience was the first law of childhood, then deference was the second. According to nineteenth-century educator Heman Humphrey, "children must early be brought under absolute parental authority, and must submit to all the rules and regulations of the family during the whole period of their minority, and even longer, if they choose to remain at home."[9] These values were reinforced by the church.

Samuel Slater was one of the first manufacturers to establish schools for factory children. Called Sunday Schools, they later were brought under the supervision of local churches. In Webster, Massachusetts—a Slater company town—the Methodist Church played a leading role in the discipline of factory children. The written tracts, hymns, and sermons found in the church advanced a familiar message: obedience, deference, industry, punctuality, and temperance. Such lessons prepared the child and adolescent operatives for salvation and also trained them to be good, obedient factory hands. The Webster Sabbath School Constitution reinforced these notions. In part it read:

> To be regular in attendance, and punctually present at the hour appointed to open school.
>
> To pay a strict and respectful attention to whatever the teacher or Superintendent shall say or request.
>
> To avoid whispering, laughing and any other Improper conduct.[10]

Manufacturers throughout New England and the Mid-Atlantic states adopted many of the features developed by Slater. Philadelphia, for example, became a center for hand-loom weaving. This occurred even after power looms had been installed in Waltham and Lowell. In the Kensington section of Philadelphia, weavers "turned out cotton cloth on hand frames in tiny red-brick cottages lined up in monotonous rows on grid-like streets." A local resident of the area observed that the "sound of these looms may be heard at all hours in garrets, cellars, and out-houses, as well as in the weavers' apartments."[11] Among these weavers a distinct culture emerged. Workers generally owned their own looms, regulated their own time, and observed traditional feasts and holidays. They were a group of especially independent and proud men. Their craft world was "a man's dominion, the weaver's prowess an element in the constitution of patriarchal family relations."[12] But by the 1840s the industry began to change. Adjacent to their dwellings, some men constructed wooden buildings or sheds, either purchased looms outright and hired weavers to operate them, or opened their sheds to weavers who brought their own equipment with them. By the Civil War, a weaver earned from $3.00 to $4.50 per week, a wage insufficient to support a family.[13] Their children often had to work in the spinning mills. Slater's efforts to preserve the patriarchy of the fathers in effect reduced their offspring to permanent children—as opposed to the apprenticeship model that implied growth and eventual maturity.

While the spinning mills that supplied yarn to the weavers of Kensington were patterned after those started by Slater, there were differences. This was especially true for the treatment of labor. In Philadelphia, where hand loom weaving persisted well into the mid-century, the treatment of young child operatives in textile mills caused a public scandal. In 1837 a Select Committee was formed by the Pennsylvania Senate to investigate conditions of labor, especially the employment of children under twelve in the state's textile mills. One adult worker, William Shaw, commented extensively on the work and treatment of children. Most of the youngest children were employed at carding and spinning and worked from twelve to fourteen hours per day. Shaw commented further: "I have known children of nine years of age to be employed at spinning[;] at carding, as young as ten years. Punishment, by whipping, is frequent; they are sometimes sent home and docked for not attending punctually." Another witness, Joseph Dean, offered similar testimony. At his factory one-third to one-half of the operatives were under the age of twelve. He described the attitudes toward the children: "The children were occasionally punished by a blow from the hand; does not know that the strap was used. . . . Males and females were provided with separate water closets, when provided at all; no pains taken on the subject: sometimes none were provided." Another witness, Robert Craig, described some of the working conditions experienced by the young workers:

> "the children must stand all the time at their work, walking backwards and forwards; the children often complain of fatigue; witness has been many of them neglect their work, from exhaustion, and seek repose in sleep; for this, they are generally punished. . . . The greatest evil, in my mind, is that the children, from nine to eleven years old, are required to carry up from one to four stories, a box of bobbins; these boxes weight about sixteen pounds; they are carried on the head."[14]

Some labor leaders and educators—Seth Luther, Horace Mann, and Henry Barnard, among others—called for an end to child labor. While legislation was passed, it failed to solve the problem. In 1842 Massachusetts declared that children under twelve could not work more than ten hours per day. Six years later Pennsylvania passed laws stating that minors could not work over ten hours a day or sixty hours per week. But by special contract, boys and girls over fourteen could work longer.[15] And then, of course, enforcement of these laws became problematic. Who was to enforce the laws and who was to be the final arbiter in determining the age of the children?

By the time child labor laws were passed, conditions within the industry had begun to change. The industry experienced several economic downturns, especially in 1829 and chronically from 1836 to 1844. Companies took the opportunity to reorganize, and Samuel Slater was no exception. In 1829 Slater feared insolvency. He had endorsed notes and was not able to pay them without first liquidating and reorganizing his holdings. He relinquished partial control of his business to his three sons and formed Samuel Slater and Sons. Other changes included the introduction of cost accounting, the employment of paid professional managers, and incorporation. The labor force was not exempt. Family labor and many of the traditional prerogatives associated with it ended. Each hand was hired, paid, assigned jobs, and disciplined by the factory manager. Young people now could contract for themselves, and this had an important impact on the family. Economically independent now, adolescents could negotiate with parents over the price of room and board, education, discipline, dress, marriage partners, and life style. Some left home and moved into boarding houses or traveled to other mill towns looking for work. If men wanted to remain with the company, they now had to enter the mills and labor alongside their women and children, suffering an implicit loss of status. This trend spread throughout the textile industry. The paternalism that once served the needs of labor and management was discarded by manufacturers; increasingly, the Slater system came to resemble Lowell.

Less expensive hands could be found, and by the 1840s French Canadian and Irish immigrants replaced many Yankee families in the mills. Factory owners no long felt compelled to accommodate adults. Next to their factories they erected multifamily tenements and boarding houses. Built side by side along a roadway, the small wooden tenements housed from three to four families plus their boarders. Rooms were small, windows were few, storage space was limited, and garden plots were eliminated altogether. Physically the tenements, boarding houses, and factory now formed a distinct unit; the factory dominated work and home life. Overcrowding occurred, health deteriorated, and mortality rates increased. Deaths from dysentery, convulsions, lung fever, delirium tremors, dropsy, erysipelas, typhus, and of course consumption or tuberculosis were recorded. In the 1840s typhus reached epidemic proportions, striking Webster, Massachusetts, first in 1843, then again in 1844 and 1846. Consumption was endemic, and children often were its victims. Indeed, child mortality rates were high, and young children even succumbed to convulsions and "teething."[16] Several possibilities could account for such infant deaths. To quiet a crying child, parents might give him or her a drug such as laudanum; some of these children could have overdosed on opiates. Or vitamin and mineral deficiencies, including a lack of calcium, magnesium, and vitamin D, might have caused convulsions and resulted in death. As two historians suggest, however, "teething is suspect because nineteenth century physicians observed that the convulsions which ravaged babies often occurred during the teething process and concluded that the sprouting of teeth was somehow responsible—hence 'teething' as a cause of death." It has been argued that the primary source of calcium for children came from mother's milk; during teething, some women ceased to breast feed children and turned to bovine milk. This abrupt shift sometimes triggered convulsions, but people mistakenly blamed the child's death on teething.[17]

By the 1850s manufacturers with clear economic interests and goals considered labor just another cost of production. Paternalism and the force of traditional social relations gave way under changing conditions. Individual hands replaced family units in the mills; manufacturers enlarged their mills and increased their labor supply. Little attention was given to the quality of life in the factory towns. Overcrowding, disease, high mortality rates, frequent labor turnover, crime, and illiteracy came to characterize life in these communities. The factories and villages of 1850 bore scant resemblance to traditional rural manufacturing communities of 1800. In the end, neither innovators such as Lowell nor conservative paternalists such as Slater had been able to prevent the transformation of factory labor into a commodity with a price—the living wage—to be set by supply and demand.

Notes

1. Alan Dawley, *Class and Community: The Industrial Revolution in Lynn* (Cambridge, MA: Harvard University Press, 1976) and Paul G. Faler, *Mechanics and Manufacturers in the Early Industrial Revolution: Lynn, Massachusetts,* 1780–1860 (Albany: State University of New York Press, 1981).

2. Thomas Dublin, *Women at Work: The Transformation of Work and Community in Lowell, Massachusetts,* 1826–1860 (New York: Columbia University Press, 1979), 95.

3. *Providence Gazette,* October 11, 1794, quoted in Brendan F. Gilbane, "A Social History of Samuel Slater's Pawtucket, 1790–1830" (Ph.D. diss., Boston University Graduate School, 1969), 247. Much of this essay is based on the author's book; see Barbara M. Tucker, *Samuel Slater and the Origins of the American Textile industry,* 1790–1860 (Ithaca, NY: Cornell University Press, 1984).

4. Ibid., 78.

5. Ibid., 84.

6. Slater and Kimball vol. 3. contract. Abel Dudley, 1827. Samuel Slater Collection. Baker Library, Harvard University, Cambridge, Massachusetts.

7. Ibid., Obadiah Greenhill, 1827.

8. Tucker, *Samuel Slater and the Origins of the American Textile Industry,* 126.

9. Heman Humphrey. *Domestic Education* (Amherst, MA; J, S. & C. Adams, 1840), 41.

10. "Constitution of the Methodist Episcopal Church Sabbath School," 1861–1863, United Church of Christ, Webster, Massachusetts.

11. Bruce Laurie. *Working People of Philadelphia,* 1800–1850 (Philadelphia: Temple University Press, 1980), IL. See also, Edwin T. Freedley. *Philadelphia and Its Manufactures: A Handbook Exhibiting the Development, Variety, and Statistics of the Manufacturing Industry of Philadelphia in* 1857 (Philadelphia: Edward Young, 1859). 253.

12. Philip Scranton, *Proprietary Capitalism: The Textile Manufacture at Philadelphia,* 1800–1885 (Cambridge: Cambridge University Press, 1983), 195.

13. Freedley, *Philadelphia and Its Manufactures,* 254.

14. Pennsylvania General Assembly. Senate, *Report of the Select Committee Appointed to Visit the Manufacturing Districts of the Commonwealth, for the Purpose of Investigating the Employment of Children in Manufactories, Mr. Peltz, Chairman.* (Harrisburg, PA: Thompson & Clark, Printers. 1838), 12–16.

15. Elizabeth Otey, *Beginnings of Child Labor Legislation in Certain States; a Comparative Study,* vol. VI of *Report on Condition of Woman and Child Wage-Earners in the United*

States. Prepared under the direction of Chas. P. Neill, Commissioner of Labor. 61st. Cong., 2nd. Sess., (Washington, DC: Government Printing Office, 1910), 207–8.

16. Tucker, *Samuel Slater and the Origins of the American Textile Industry,* 232. See also Webster, Massachusetts. Vital Statistics, Deaths. Emory Hough, November 1853 and Lewis Johnson, 1844, 1845.

17. Kenneth F. Kiple and Virginia H. Kiple, "Slave Child Mortality: Some Nutritional Answers to a Perennial Puzzle." *Journal of Social History* 10 (March 1977): 291–92. The Kiples believe that convulsions and teething as a cause of death were misunderstood. The children had tetany, a disease not recognized at the time.

BARBARA M. TUCKER is Professor of History and Director of the Center for Connecticut Studies at Eastern Connecticut State University. She is the author of *Samuel Slater and the Origins of the American Textile Industry, 1790–1860* and has published articles in such journals as *Labor History, Business History Review, Agricultural History* and *Journal of the Early Republic.*

Play Ball!

In baseball's earliest years, players beaned baserunners and often had to flout town laws prohibiting the game.

Harry Katz

The game of baseball was not always the well-ordered sport we know today, played on elegantly manicured fields bordered by crisp white lines. As historians have debunked the widely held myth that Abner Doubleday of Cooperstown, New York, invented the sport out of whole cloth in 1839, they have discovered its deeper American origins. In 1787, the same year the Constitution was written, a Worcester, Massachusetts, publisher printed *A Little Pretty Pocket Book,* the American edition of an English book for children, which included a poem and illustration dedicated to "base-ball."

Six years ago, historian John Thorn and former major league pitcher Jim Bouton poked around the Pittsfield, Massachusetts, courthouse archives and discovered a 1791 measure that set out to stop a rash of broken windows by prohibiting anyone from playing "baseball" within 80 yards of the building. Both Worcester and Cooperstown, future home of the National Baseball Hall of Fame, banned children from playing the game.

Yet despite such resistance, baseball took off in New England, New York, and the Middle Atlantic states. Members of social clubs and workers in factories—organizations that did not exist in the hinterland—typically formed the first teams. Gentlemen, or men of some means, established the first baseball clubs, because they had the time and resources to practice the sport, travel to ball fields, and furnish equipment and uniforms.

As the 19th century progressed, a large and prosperous middle class emerged in the United States. Workers increasingly had periods of leisure time and now often looked for a game of baseball. In the cities, political or commercial patrons sometimes supported larger clubs. The New York Mutuals, a working-class team in lower Manhattan, represented "Boss" Tweed's Tammany Hall, the city's Democratic political machine of the 1860s and early 1870s.

Early organized American baseball took two forms. New Englanders knew the game as "town ball" or the "Massachusetts game," which featured base paths laid out in a square instead of a diamond, and a rule allowing fielding players to put out the batter or "striker" by "soaking" him (hitting him with a thrown ball before he reached base). Town ball flourished along the eastern seaboard. A group of young men in Philadelphia, who formed the Olympic Ball Club to play town ball in 1833, may have been the first organized baseball-related team in America. In 1838 they created and published rules aptly called their "constitution."

The Knickerbocker Base Ball Club of New York, organized in the 1840s by a group of upper-middle-class Manhattan gentlemen, took town ball and developed their own rules. In 1845 Knickerbocker Alexander Joy Cartwright, Jr., a bank teller and part-time volunteer fireman, suggested that the team play scheduled games against local clubs. To govern these games, on September 23, 1845, the Knickerbockers instituted what came to be known as the "New York rules."

By the 1850s the Knickerbockers, their cross-town rivals the Gothams, and such other clubs as the Mutuals, Eckfords, Unions, and Brooklyn Atlantics played regularly before crowds that often had traveled some distance. New York's burgeoning newspaper industry championed the sport, promoting big games and glamorizing newfound stars. Transplanted Englishman and cricket booster Henry Chadwick, the country's first sportswriter, loved baseball and devised numerous innovations, including box scores and game accounts. Known even during his own lifetime as the "father of baseball," he tirelessly promoted the sport and through his singular advocacy helped solidify it as America's most popular game.

In 1857 the Knickerbockers and 15 other clubs formed the National Association of Base Ball Players (NABBP) to "promote additional interest in baseball playing" and to "regulate various matters necessary to its good government and continued respectability." Adopting the Knickerbockers' original rules, the NABBP also specified that nine men would play on each side, bases would be set 90 feet apart, and an umpire would have the power to call strikes. Players were required to catch balls barehanded, not with their caps. (Baseball gloves would not become standard until the 1880s.) In addition, no players could be paid to play, although the trend toward luring talent to join teams in return for cushy local jobs was already under way.

One year after the NABBP formed, thousands of fans paid 50 cents at Long Island's Fashion Race Course to watch the "New

York All Stars" win a two-out-of-three-game series against their Brooklyn counterparts. The series' success, along with the city's influential press and the improvements brought about by the NABBP rules, helped make the "New York rules" the national standard, superseding the "Massachusetts game" and laying the foundation for the modern sport.

The Civil War greatly accelerated baseball's popularity. Soldiers from the Northeast, already familiar with the game, cured boredom in camp by playing ball. Officers encouraged such games to foster camaraderie and improve morale. Regiments challenged one another, and friendly rivalries developed during breaks in combat.

After the war, Army servicemen and veterans spread baseball across the country. It proved an effective salve for a nation battered by years of war and shocked by the assassination of its president. Some remembered that Lincoln had enjoyed playing ball as a young legislator in Springfield, Illinois, during the 1840s. The president and his young son Tad may have viewed one of the games on a lot adjacent to the White House.

The postwar era marked baseball's first golden age. The sport had a democratizing and unifying effect then: laborers could beat gentlemen, mechanics could best attorneys, Southerners could defeat Northerners, and Baptists could battle Methodists with no hard feelings. For a while, blacks could challenge whites; men of color played on integrated teams from the lowest to the highest levels until the 1880s, when the major leagues imposed a ban that held until 1947.

In 1867 the Washington, D.C., Nationals—a crack ball club drawing on government workers, clerks, lawyers, and some veterans—traveled by train for games in Ohio, Missouri, and Illinois. A year later, several New York–based teams followed suit, sweeping through the Midwest and taking on all comers, spreading goodwill and deepening interest in the game. The year after that, the renowned Cincinnati Red Stockings, baseball's first openly professional ball club (that is, the entire starting roster, or "picked nine," received salaries), journeyed cross-country aboard the newly completed transcontinental railroad, remaining undefeated through 65 games. Its players treated like celebrities, the team traveled widely and capped their tour with lopsided victories in the San Francisco Bay Area. Each of these tours left new fans in its wake, and by the 1870s the public's thirst for baseball seemed unquenchable. For many Americans, playing and watching baseball became two of their most cherished childhood memories.

The Change Agent

Our politics are rooted in the grand, complicated presidency of Andrew Jackson.

JON MEACHAM

In late January 1861, president-elect Abraham Lincoln was at home in wintry Springfield, Ill., contemplating his course. The South was seceding, the Union in danger of dying. In search of a quiet place to work on his Inaugural Address, Lincoln walked through streets of mud and ice to his brother-in-law's brick general store, Yates & Smith, near the corner of Sixth and Adams. Lincoln had told his friend and law partner, William Herndon, that he would need some "works" to consult. "I looked for a long list, but when he went over it I was greatly surprised," Herndon recalled. Lincoln asked for Daniel Webster's "Liberty and Union, now and forever!" oration, a copy of the Constitution, Henry Clay's speech on the Compromise of 1850—and the text of Andrew Jackson's Proclamation to the People of South Carolina.

Nearly thirty years before, in the winter of 1832–33, radicals in Charleston were raising an army to defend South Carolina's right to nullify federal laws it chose not to accept—the first step, Jackson believed, toward secession, and the destruction of the Union. Gaunt but striking, with a shock of white hair, a nearly constant cough, a bullet lodged in his chest and another in his arm, Jackson, 65 years old that winter, stood 6 feet 1 and weighed 140 pounds. "I expect soon to hear that a civil war of extermination has commenced," Jackson had said, musing about arresting the Southern leaders and then hanging them. Over a midday glass of whisky in the White House with an old friend, Jackson pounded a table as he pondered the crisis. Invoking "the God of heaven," Jackson swore to crush any rebellion.

Reading Jackson's words in a small, sparsely furnished upper room, Lincoln found what needed: the example of a president who had rescued the Union from an armed clash with a hostile South. "Disunion by armed force is treason," Jackson had written, underscoring "treason." "Are you really ready to incur its guilt? . . . Fellow-citizens, the momentous case is before you. On your undivided support of your Government depends the decision of the great question it involves—whether your sacred Union will be preserved and the blessing it secures to us as one people shall be perpetuated." Jackson won. The radicals stood down. Lincoln had his precedent.

As Americans go to the polls this week, they will be adding a new chapter to the long story of the modern presidency—a story that in many ways began with a man who is at once familiar and remote: Andrew Jackson, a kind of forgotten father of his country. In Jackson we can see the best of us and the worst of us, a style of presidential leadership that is at once inspiring and cautionary, for his fights remain our fights, his strengths our strengths and his weaknesses our weaknesses. Recalled mainly, if at all, as a mindless populist whose supporters trashed the White House on his Inauguration Day or as the scourge of the Indians, the real Jackson has been largely lost. Understood properly, however, Jackson should be seen as a man who helped make us who we are. To see him fully is to see ourselves more honestly.

The new president will be assuming an office and leading a political culture largely created by Jackson. Running at the head of a national party, fighting for a mandate from the people to govern in particular ways on particular issues, depending on a circle of insiders and advisers to help guide the affairs of the country, mastering the popular media of the age in order to transmit a consistent message at a constant pace, using the veto as a political, not just a constitutional, weapon and facing difficult confirmation battles in a Washington that is at once politically and personally charged—all are features of the modern presidency that flowered during Jackson's tenure. He was also the first president to insist on the deference he thought due the chief executive as the only official elected by all the people—a distinction he believed made the White House, not Capitol Hill, the center of national power and national action.

The America of Andrew Jackson professed a love of democracy but was willing to live with inequality; aimed for social justice but was prone to racism and intolerance; believed itself one nation but was narrowly divided and fought close elections; and occasionally acted arrogantly toward other countries while craving respect from them at the same time. Jackson himself was capable of great good and great evil, of expanding democratic opportunity to some while simultaneously defending slavery and masterminding the removal of the Indians from their native lands.

Soldier, brawler, duelist, lover and politician, he was the first U.S. president to be an assassin's target—and the only one to attack his assailant.

Jackson had led the most improbable of lives. Soldier, brawler, duelist, lover and politician, he was the first American president to be the target of assassination, and the only one to attack his assailant. He was the first truly self-made man to become president. (Jackson was, to put it kindly, no scholar. When Harvard University voted to give the seventh president an honorary degree in 1833, a Massachusetts newspaper wrote that he deserved an "A.S.S." as well as an "L.L.D.") Before Jackson, it was possible to think of America without putting the people at the center of politics; after him, such a thing was inconceivable.

Orphaned at 14, Jackson never knew his own father, who died the year he was born. The Revolutionary War claimed the lives of his mother and his brothers. "I have been Tossed upon the waves of Fortune," he once wrote, and he spent his life seeking order amid chaos and authority among men. By the age of 35, the uneducated boy from the Carolina backwoods had become a practicing lawyer, a public prosecutor, a United States attorney, a delegate to the founding Tennessee Constitutional Convention, a United States congressman, a United States senator, a judge of the state Superior Court and a major general, first of the state militia and then of the United States Army.

In the glow of his victory over the British at New Orleans in 1815—as mythic a battle as Lexington and Concord—he became a fabled figure. Popular songs were written about him; the anniversary of the victory, Jan. 8, was a national occasion for Jackson banquets and Jackson parades. There were darker moments, too. He had massacred Indians in combat, fought duels, imposed martial law on New Orleans, executed deserters in his ranks and British subjects after he pre-emptively invaded Florida in 1818. He had married the love of his life, Rachel Donelson Robards, before she was divorced from her first husband. The scandal stayed with him through the decades, and he believed that the stress of the charges of adultery and bigamy killed his beloved, who died between the election and his Inauguration.

Dirty politics, populism, an outsider struggling to succeed the unpopular son of a president: there are more than a few coincidental echoes of the Age of Jackson in this season. The challenges he faced resonate in our own age. He believed the financial sector of the American economy was spoiled, corrupt and bad for the overall health of the nation, and so he destroyed, at great length, great drama and great cost, the Bank of the United States. (The country descended into financial panic shortly after he left office.) He wanted the country to be a respected force around the world, and so he was quick to send forces to confront pirates, and he engaged in an epic diplomatic battle against France when the Chamber of Deputies refused to pay money it owed the United States. He thought the American Union sacred, and so he threatened civil war to put down the radicals in South Carolina. He was convinced that church and state should remain separate, and so he resisted calls for the

formation of a "Christian party in politics," and was troubled by ministers who involved themselves in the political arena.

Jackson would not have been puzzled by a 24/7 news cycle, for politics—and the politics of celebrity and personality—was also an obsession in his era. A Scottish visitor to Albany, N.Y., in the late 1820s noted an American love of what he called "the spirit of electioneering, which seems to enter as an essential ingredient into the composition of everything." A Democratic senator in the Jackson years said, "The large masses act in politics pretty much as they do in religion. Every doctrine is with them, more or less, a matter of *faith;* received, principally, on account of their trust in the apostle."

Jackson has been explicitly raised in two contexts of late. Supporters of Sarah Palin have invoked his outsider persona— a provincial with little to no formal education, he ran against capital elites—in a bid to link her to one of the great figures in American history. The problem with the analogy is that while Jackson packaged himself as a champion of the people, he was a tremendously accomplished man with a long public record when he came to the presidency. He did not run on his inexperience, or his lack of connections in Washington. He campaigned as a sophisticated figure of Jeffersonian restoration, eager to destroy what he saw as corrupt intermediary institutions (such as the Bank of the United States and the federal establishment) in order to keep power as close to the people as possible within a strong Union. His was a complex political philosophy.

If there was one principle at the heart of Jackson's gospel, it was this, as articulated in his first annual message in 1829: *"the majority is to govern."* This was not, to say the least, the prevailing view of the American Founders, who had consciously created a republic, not a democracy. But Jackson believed that the people—the unconnected—deserved a larger role in public life, so he rewrote the script of American politics to give them one. And he did it through force of personal will. As president, Jackson said, he was the only "direct representative" of the people—congressmen came from districts, and senators were elected by state legislatures at the time—and therefore he was the most fitting tribune of the popular will. We take this vision of the presidency for granted now—that it is, in John F. Kennedy's phrase, "the vital center of action"—but before Jackson the office tended to be more subservient to Congress.

The context of Jackson's remark about the centrality of the majority was the relationship between the people and the president, which Jackson believed should be direct and uncluttered by the Electoral College or the House of Representatives. What if a majority was off on the wrong track? "Never for a moment believe that the great body of the citizens of any State or States can deliberately intend to do wrong," Jackson once said. "They may, under the influence of temporary excitement or misguided opinions, commit mistakes; they may be misled for a time by the suggestions of self-interest; but in a community so enlightened and patriotic as the people of the United States argument will soon make them sensible of their errors, and when convinced they will be ready to repair them." The task of democratic leadership was to cultivate opinion, then to marshal and manage it. He never really doubted that he could ascertain the sense of the country. Challenged once, during a credit crisis in the

Bank War, that his visitor knew more about the people than he did, Jackson cried, "The *people?* The people, sir, are with *me.*" He was right; they usually were. Huge numbers of Americans, many of them only beginning to have a significant economic stake in the future of the country, believed Jackson represented their interests against the powerful few.

Jackson references have also flourished recently because of his relentless campaign against these entrenched financial interests—perhaps a model for the 44th president as he assesses how to address the (perennial) problem of greed on Wall Street. Jackson's hatred of the Bank of the United States was epic. The keeper of federal deposits, the bank, presided over by the brilliant, vain and aristocratic Nicholas Biddle, had private shareholders who profited from the institution, which was liberal with loans and retainers to lawmakers and other public officials who might be of use to the bank. Jackson had long distrusted banks of any kind—he had had a personal run of bad luck in his early business life—and especially disliked institutions he could not control. Biddle's bank was just that: beyond Jackson's reach. And so the president ultimately decided to veto the bank's recharter. There is a strong case to be made that, in doing so, Jackson made the wrong decision for the economy, but he was more interested in the politics of the question, and in a thundering message he framed the battle in democratic terms. "It is to be regretted that the rich and powerful too often bend the acts of government to their selfish purposes," Jackson said. "If it would confine itself to equal protection, and, as Heaven does its rains, shower its favors alike on the high and the low, the rich and the poor, it would be an unqualified blessing." But since it was not an unqualified blessing, then it required men like Jackson to set things to rights. It was not easy. Sick and exhausted amid the struggle, he told Martin Van Buren, "The Bank, Mr. Van Buren, is trying to kill me, *but I will kill it.*"

He hated the bank but loved the Union. Within its bounds Americans could battle politically forever—but if it were to break apart, Jackson believed, all was lost. At the time of the crisis with South Carolina, in his Second Inaugural in March 1833, Jackson was explicit about the stakes of the moment. "The eyes of all nations are fixed on our Republic," he said. "The event of the existing crisis will be decisive in the opinion of mankind of the practicability of our federal system of government. Great is the stake placed in our hands; great is the responsibility which must rest upon the people of the United States. Let us realize the importance of the attitude in which we stand before the world. Let us exercise forbearance and firmness."

Jackson believed that "the intelligence and wisdom of our countrymen" would, in the end, provide "relief and deliverance" from the "difficulties which surround us and the dangers which threaten our institutions"—in every era. But he himself was not always intelligent or wise, and he did not always offer relief and deliverance from difficulties that faced those on the margins of American life. As a general and as president, he secured the borders, defeated South Carolina's move toward disunion and added millions of acres to the United States by taking land from Indians. He also defended slavery, thwarting abolitionist efforts, and his dealings with the Indian tribes—dealings that finally led to the Trail of Tears—were shameful. How to reconcile the champion of "the people" with a man capable of such things? Arthur Schlesinger Jr. once noted that retrospective self-righteousness was both easy and cheap. Americans have always been willing to tolerate the morally intolerable. We should condemn Jackson for his moral failings but also remember that to condemn him is in many ways to condemn ourselves—for the abandonment of the inner cities, for the failure of our healthcare system, for injustices of any kind.

The slave quarters at Jackson's home, the Hermitage, are near his tomb, a rebuke to the generations of white Americans who limited crusades for life and liberty to their own kind, and a reminder that evil can appear normal to even the best men and women of a given time. The tragedy of Jackson's life is that a man dedicated to freedom failed to see liberty as a universal, not a particular, gift. The triumph of his life is that he held together a country whose experiment in liberty ultimately extended its protections and promises to all—belatedly, but by saving the Union, Jackson kept the possibility of progress alive, a possibility that would have died had secession and separation carried the day.

Ask Obama or McCain to name his favorite president and you get a predictable answer: Abraham Lincoln for Obama and Theodore Roosevelt for McCain. George W. Bush hopes that history will remember him not as a James Buchanan but as a Harry Truman. All these more familiar heroic presidents, though, have at least one thing in common: an admiration for Andrew Jackson. "Jackson had many faults," said Theodore Roosevelt, "but he was devotedly attached to the Union, and he had no thought of fear when it came to defending his country . . . With the exception of Washington and Lincoln, no man has left a deeper mark on American history." President Roosevelt's cousin Franklin was also fascinated by Jackson. In 1941, a few months before America entered World War II, FDR equated his task with Jackson's battle to save the Union. "In his day the threat to the Federal Union came from within," FDR told the nation that spring. "In our own day the threat to our Union and our democracy is not a sectional one. It comes from a great part of the world which surrounds us, and which draws more tightly around us, day by day."

Roosevelt's successor, Harry Truman, was so absorbed by Jackson that Eddie Jacobson, Truman's partner in a failed haberdashery, once recalled that the future president was always off in a corner reading books about Jackson rather than tending to the few customers who did come in. "He wanted sincerely to look after the little fellow who had no pull," Truman said of Jackson, "and that's what a president is supposed to do." Jackson believed that, as did Truman—and as should we.

From "American Lion: Andrew Jackson in the White House" by **JON MEACHAM.** © 2008 by Jon Meacham. To be published by Random House, an imprint of the Random House Publishing Group.

The Inebriated Election of 1840

JON GRINSPAN

Picking a president based on his qualifications as a drinking buddy seems like a quintessentially contemporary act, typical of the false familiarity of 21st-century politics. Yet the linkage of booze and ballots is as old as popular democracy itself. In one of the most important elections in American history, enfranchised citizens voted not on the promise of an imaginary Budweiser with the candidate, but because of very real barrels of crisp, refreshing hard cider.

If Americans are aware of the election of 1840, they remember it because the victorious William Henry Harrison dropped dead 30 days into his first term. His opponent, Martin Van Buren, is equally arcane, though this Kinderhook, New York native's nickname—"Old Kinderhook"—helped spawn the world's most popular expression: "O.K." What many forget is the explosive popularity of the campaign and the turnout of three-quarters of eligible voters it engendered, all helped along by Harrison's association with fermented apple juice.

Although big issues were at stake in 1840, Harrison's image as a simple soldier with a taste for down-home, American cider truly excited voters. When pundits mocked his love of the humble drink, joking, "give him a barrel of cider and he will sit the remainder of his days in his log cabin," Harrison's handlers pounced. From then on Harrison frequently appeared in public clutching a ceramic flagon of cider, flamboyantly swigging the bubbly apple brew mid-speech, to prove his common nature in the face of his opponent's ostentatious love of Madeira and champagne.

Just as lattes and lagers are powerful cultural symbols today, hard cider made a strong statement in 1840. Cider was probably the most common beverage consumed by early Americans, but so banal that few mentioned it. In a rural nation dotted with orchards, many harvested their own apples and mashed, pressed, and aged them into a fermented brew both sweet and richly pungent. But by 1840 the nation was changing, and increasingly sober, evangelical, and middle-class Americans no longer drank an annual average of seven gallons of pure alcohol per adult. As society commercialized, urbanized, and industrialized, backwoods cider recalled a simpler world of New England and Midwestern pioneers.

At least as important as the actual cider was the statement made by William Henry Harrison's thirst. Though born to a wealthy Virginia family, Harrison had remade himself as a poor frontier soldier, and drinking cider—like clearing brush—trumpeted his commonness. The culture war between cider and champagne drinkers intertwined with genuine political issues, pitting Harrison's taste in alcohol against Van Buren's extreme fiscal conservatism. One Maryland newspaper declared a contest between "the hard money office-holders of the Government and the hard cider party of the people."

The Harrison campaign did more than publicize its candidate's love of cider—it dispensed hundreds of gallons of the stuff to thirsty voters. In a corrupt and unequal democracy, Americans openly asked "what their country could do for them," demanding cushy post office jobs or massive oak barrels of free cider. Though temperance types complained, "men get beastly drunk on cider" at Harrison's rowdy rallies, most voters were ecstatic. In response to slurred complaints that Van Buren's dry speeches were "all talk and no cider," his campaign distributed dark ale, turning the election into a drinking contest between "hard cider Whigs" and "porter-bottle" Democrats. Harrison-supporters joked that "Old Kinderhook" might die of "apple-plexy."

Come November, Harrison's approach worked, winning him an astounding 80 percent of the Electoral College and making him the first candidate to earn more than one million votes. Though economics, enslavement, and employment were all major issues, the election was typified by cider. In the words of one newspaper: "We have had almost eleven years experiment of a rum-and-whiskey administration. It is time for a change. Let us try the hard cider."

Change was short-lived. Harrison caught a cold, which quickly developed into pneumonia and blood-poisoning, killing him 30 days into his presidency. Yet the campaign launched the popular excitement and record voter turnouts—often helped along by free drinks—that lasted until the start of the 20th century. The inebriated election of 1840 also introduced the term "booze" to the American lexicon, named for the Philadelphia distiller E. G. Booz, who marketed his liquor in log-cabin-shaped glass bottles.

In the years after 1840, cider's star plummeted. A market flooded with cheap grain and an influx of lager-loving German immigrants helped beer eclipse the apple brew. Temperance and eventually Prohibition finally put an end to candidates' public exchange of drinks for votes.

For decades hardly any Americans drank hard cider. Yet it has enjoyed a comeback in the last few years, and not just the syrupy concoctions marketed as easy-to-drink alternatives to beer. Perhaps the best is Samuel Smith's Organic Cider, made by the British company known for its exceptional Oatmeal Stout. This simple, clear, highly carbonated cider would have been perfect for a mid-campaign fish-fry, and is dry enough to refresh on a hot summer afternoon. Doc's Draft Hard Apple Cider is a smaller-batch, more complex brew from the Hudson Valley, which elegantly combines the freshness of green apples with the funky smoothness of sheep's milk cheese.

Finally, Michigan's J.K. Scrumpy's Organic Hard Cider is a classic fall cider, as sweet, cloudy, and thick as its non-alcoholic cousin. Though far too sugary for most of the year, Scrumpy's is ideal for the crispness of high autumn, especially paired with a sharp cheddar. It would have been perfect for toasting William Henry Harrison's November 7 victory.

JON GRINSPAN is a PhD candidate in American history at the University of Virginia.

The Awful March of the Saints

David Roberts

Florence, Near Present-Day Omaha, August 1856

For 28-year-old Patience Loader, the journey so far had been chiefly exhausting. During the four weeks from July 25 to August 22, 1856, the company with which she was traveling had covered 270 miles from Iowa City to Florence, a fledgling community six miles north of where Omaha stands today.

Loader, her father, her mother, four of her younger sisters, and a younger brother were eight of some 1,865 Mormon emigrants seeking to cross the 1,300 miles from where the railroad ended in Iowa to Salt Lake City, following the trail pioneered by Brigham Young's lead company of Mormons, who in 1847 had founded their new Zion in the Great Basin. The 1856 emigrants, however, were not traveling, as had Young's party, in covered ox-wagons, but were serving instead as their own beasts of burden. From Iowa City all the way to the city of the Saints, they would push or pull wooden handcarts freighted with three months' supply of clothing, gear, and some food. Each pilgrim was strictly limited to 17 pounds of personal baggage and a meager pound of flour per day.

The "Divine Handcart Scheme," as the Latter-day Saints called it, was Brigham Young's brainchild. Its chief motive was to save money, as the prophet sought to bring as many European converts (mostly from the working-class poor of Britain and Scandinavia) to Zion—in the first instance to save their souls, but also to shore up his breakaway theocracy against an anticipated offensive by the U.S. Army, which would, in fact, take place less than two years in the future.

For Loader, as the emigrants approached Florence, the trek had taken on an ominous new cast. Her 57-year-old father, James, had been growing weaker by the day. Now his legs and feet were so badly swollen that it was hard for him to walk. During the next two months, the Loader family would find itself caught in the vortex of the greatest disaster of North American westward migration. The part-time seamstress, who had just arrived in the New World, would put down the single most vivid account of the ordeal by any of the nearly 2,000 handcart Saints.

Loader recounts how one late September evening, her father, after walking 17 miles with the help of his wife, simply said, "My dear girls, I am not able to get any wood to Make you afire." Loader saw that it pained him deeply to admit such weakness. "Never mind," she replied reassuringly, they would build him a fire and make food.

Helped by the rest of her family, she swaddled her father in quilts, pitched a tent, and carried him inside. While Loader was building a fire the next morning, "My Sister Zilpha called to Saying patience come quick our father is dieing and when I got into the tent my poor Mother and all our family four Sisters My youngst brother Robert ten years old and my brother in law John Jaques was all kneeling on the ground around him poor dear father realizing he had to leave us he was to weak to talk to us he looked on us all with tears in his eyes then he said to Mother with great diffulcuty he said you know I love My children then he closed his eyes thees was the last words he ever said." They buried him that morning without a coffin, "and the earth thown in upon his poor body oh that sounded so hard I will never forget the sound of that dirt beign shoveld anto my poor fathers boday it seemed to me that it would break every bone in his body."

Five separate handcart companies had left Iowa City that summer. The Loader family was in the fifth and last, 575 pilgrims led by Edward Martin. The company, which might have overwintered in Florence, instead set out from that last frontier outpost on August 25—fatally late in the season, as it would turn out.

The first snow fell on October 19, disastrous timing for the Martin Company, which was fording the North Platte River. The team's few oxen were forced to swim as the eight supply wagons were floated across, but the handcarts had to be pushed through the current by the terrified pilgrims. "The water was deep and very cold," wrote Loader, "and we was drifted out of the regular crossing and we came near to beign drounded the water came up to our arm pits poor Mother was standing on the bank screaming as we got near the bank I heard Mother say for Gods Sake some of you men help My poor girls."

I heard Mother say for Gods Sake some of you men help My poor girls.

Once on the far bank, the soaking wet Saints huddled against the snow and bitter wind before moving to a campsite several miles further on. The Loader children's clothing froze stiff. "It was to late to go for wood and water," recalled Loader. ". . . that night the ground was frozen to hard we was unable to drive any tent pins in as the tent was wett when we took it down in the morning it was somewhat frozen So we stretched it open the best we could and got in under it untill morning."

On October 20, the Martin Company effectively became snowbound in a wretched camp beneath the Red Buttes, a small outcropping of ruddy sandstone in what is now central Wyoming. The Martin Saints were simply too cold, hungry, and worn out to travel on.

Meanwhile, a small party of high-ranking officials, traveling fast and light in well-made carriages, had reached Salt Lake City on October 4 to deliver the shocking news that there were some 1,300 Saints still scattered along the Mormon Trail. President Young immediately launched a major rescue effort.

Loader remembered that she and her sister had had to walk nearly a mile through knee-deep snow to find firewood, and then all she could get was "green ceder," or juniper. The single repast that stuck in her memory was broth made by boiling "an old beef head," which she "chopt it in peices the best I could."

Already dozens of the Martin Saints had died. Loader described the gruesome last hours of William Whittaker: "he was in the tent with several others . . . there was a young woman sleeping and she was awoke by poor Br Whiticar eating her fingers he was dieng with hunger and cold he also eat the flesh of his own fingers that night, he died in the morning and was burid at willow Springs before we left camp."

Nineteen died in a single night at Red Buttes. Not until October 27 did an advance party of three mounted rescuers discover the marooned company. With inspired hectoring, the scouts roused the apathetic pioneers and drove them 65 miles farther west to a hollow grove defended by a granite cirque, known ever since as Martin's Cove, which was to be the company's ultimate calvary. By the end of their futile fiveday vigil, as wind and snowstorms continued to lash the cove, 56 more of the Martin Saints perished, most from the deadly cold.

Loader almost casually offers testimony to her family's fortitude among so many others' in the midst of that grim bivouac. One bitter morning, her mother implored her and her sister to arise and light a fire. Both young women said they could not get up because of the agonizing cold. "Mother sais come girls this will not do," reported Loader. "I believe I will have to dance to you and try to make you feel better poor dear Mother she started to Sing and dance to us and she slipt down as the snow was frozen and in a moment we was all up to help our dear Mother up for we was afraid she was hurt she laugh and said I thought I could soon make you all jump up if I danced to you then we found that she fell down purposely for she Knew we would all get up to see if she was hurt."

By mid-November, wagon trains had reached the survivors. Abandoning their handcarts, the Martin Saints rode the rest of the way to Salt Lake. When the last handcart pilgrims reached their promised country at the end of November, leaving between 200 and 240 of their companions on the plains of Nebraska and Wyoming—some five or six times more than had perished in the infamous Donner Party ordeal a decade earlier.

The "Divine Scheme" had disaster built into its very design, from the inevitable breakdowns of the poorly-built handcarts, to the fact that on a pound of flour (and later, less) a day per adult, the Saints would slowly starve; and to the fact that 17 pounds of gear, clothing, and bedding was not enough to keep even the hardiest pioneer safe in a Great Plains winter. Far from being the hero of the story, Brigham Young—who masterminded the plan, determined all its parameters, placed saving money over human lives, and somehow lost track of the last companies still on the plains in the autumn of 1856—must bear the lion's share of the blame for a tragedy unmatched in American annals.

Yet once they arrived in Salt Lake City, these people, made veterans in a single season, seemed only to want to get on with their lives. Loader, otherwise so vivid a memoirist, makes it clear that her first days in Salt Lake were a forlorn business, as her extended family was broken up so that various residents could take in its members as boarders. Within a few weeks she found work in her old occupation as a seamstress. Not once in her memoirs did she ask herself whether the whole desperate journey had been worth it. Nor did she leave the church (as many of the other handcart Saints, embittered by the experience, would in subsequent years).

Patience Loader lived on in Pleasant Grove, Utah, became (according to the editor of her memoir) "a well-known and popular pillar of her community," and died in 1922 at the age of 95.

UNIT 4

The Civil War and Reconstruction

Unit Selections

Key Points to Consider

- The question as to what to do about slavery was both moral and economic. Analyze the debate over emancipation that took place on the eve of the Civil War.

- The Civil War began as a struggle over national unity, but became a conflict over the institution of slavery. What were the obstacles to issuing an emancipation proclamation earlier than Lincoln did? Why did emancipation precipitate a "constitutional dilemma"?

- Analyses of emancipation usually focus on white leaders such as Lincoln. What role did blacks play? How could one author refer to this as "the greatest slave rebellion in modern history"?

- Discuss the United States government's policies toward American Indians during the nineteenth century. What role did the buffalo play in the cultures of Plains Indians? Why did Indians resist moving to reservations?

- Analyze Abraham Lincoln's performance as commander in chief of U.S. armed forces. What qualities did he possess that enabled him to successfully lead such an enormous military undertaking even though he lacked experience and schooling?

- The last article in this volume analyzes the Civil War, emancipation, and reconstruction "on the world stage." What is meant by this phrase? Why were so many people around the globe interested in what happened in the United States during these years?

Student Website
www.mhhe.com/cls

Internet References

The American Civil War
  http://sunsite.utk.edu/civil-war/warweb.html
Anacostia Museum/Smithsonian Institution
  http://www.si.edu/archives/historic/anacost.htm
Abraham Lincoln Online
  http://www.netins.net/showcase/creative/lincoln.html
Gilder Lehrman Institute of American History
  http://www.digitalhistory.uh.edu/index.cfm?
Secession Era Editorials Project
  http://history.furman.edu/~benson/docs/dsmenu.htm

Sectionalism plagued the United States from its inception. The Constitutional proviso that slaves would count as three-fifths of a person for representational purposes, for instance, or that treaties had to be passed by two-thirds majorities grew out of sectional compromises. Manufacturing and commercial interests were strong in the North. Such interests generally supported high tariffs to protect industries and the construction of turnpikes, canals, and railroads to expand domestic markets. The South, largely rural and agricultural, strongly opposed such measures. Southerners believed that tariffs cost them money and lined the pockets of Northern manufacturers. They had little interest in what were known as "internal improvements." Such differences were relatively easy to resolve because there were no moral issues involved, and matters such as tariffs aroused few emotions in the public.

The question of slavery added a different dimension. Part of the quarrel involved economic considerations. Northerners feared that the spread of slavery would discriminate against "free" farming in the west. Southerners just as adamantly believed that the institution should be allowed to exist wherever it proved feasible. "The Emancipation Question" discusses the debate conducted on the eve of the Civil War over the economic consequences of emancipation. Disputes in 1820 and again in 1850 had resulted in compromises that papered over these differences, but they had satisfied no one. As time wore on, more and more Northerners came to regard slavery as sinful, an abomination that must be stamped out. Southerners, on the other hand, grew more receptive to the idea that slavery actually was beneficial to both blacks and whites and was condoned by the Bible. Now cast in moral terms, the issue could not be resolved in the fashion of tariff disputes by splitting differences.

"Abolitionist John Doy" shows how emotional the atmosphere became during the run-up to the Civil War. It describes the turmoil and bloodshed that developed over what became known as "Bleeding Kansas." Northern "Free Soilers" were determined that the Territory of Kansas enter the Union as a free state. Southerners were just as adamant that it would be open to slavery. A preview of the Civil War occurred there.

Moderates in the two national parties, the Whigs and Democrats, had tried to keep the slavery question from tearing the country in two. Although suffering some defections, the Democrats managed to stay together until the elections of 1860. The Whigs, however, fell apart during the 1850s. The emergence of the Republican Party, with its strength almost exclusively based in the North, signaled the beginning of the end. Southerners came to regard the Republicans as the party of abolitionism. Abraham Lincoln, Republican presidential candidate in 1860, tried to assure Southerners that although he opposed the spread of slavery, he had no intentions of seeking to abolish the institution where it already existed. He was not widely believed in the South. Republican victory in 1860 seemed to them, or at least to the hotheads among them, to threaten not just slavery but the entire Southern way of life. One by one Southern states began to secede. "There Goes the South" analyzes this process and Abraham Lincoln's response to it.

Library of Congress. LC-DIG-pga-02797

Once the war got underway, many on both sides believed it would be over quickly. They were wrong. What began as a limited conflict turned into total war against resources and morale. In addition to military operations, the North with its superior navy sought to cripple the Southern economy by blockading its ports. Unable to purchase imported goods, Southerners had to live amidst shortages of all kinds.

The Civil War began as a struggle over national union, but ultimately became a conflict over the continued existence of slavery. "Lincoln and the Constitutional Dilemma of Emancipation" analyzes the many obstacles that prevented Abraham Lincoln from issuing the preliminary Emancipation Proclamation before he did. Among the most important factors in Lincoln's mind was the Constitution's protection of property rights. Although he knew he would be criticized by some for not going far enough, he also knew he would be condemned for having exceeded his executive powers. Author Edna Greene Medford argues that Lincoln satisfied himself that he was acting within his Constitutional powers. A second article about Lincoln, "Creating a Military Image," seeks to explain how this civilian "unschooled and inexperienced in war" managed to create and successfully lead the largest military establishment yet seen at the time.

Most analyses of emancipation emphasize the roles of Abraham Lincoln and well-known abolitionist leaders. In a recent book, author Steven Hahn argues that black people themselves deserve far more credit for ending slavery than was previously thought. Indeed, he regards their conduct as "the greatest slave rebellion in modern history." "A Slave's Audacious Bid for Freedom" discusses a recently discovered slave narrative written during the 1880s by a man named Wallace Turnage. Turnage produced a vivid account of slave life as well as his own heroic efforts to escape to freedom.

A struggle took place after the war ended over how the South would be reintegrated into the Union. The most important issue was what status Blacks would have in the postwar society. Moderates such as Lincoln wished to make Reconstruction as painless as possible even though this meant continued white domination of Southern states. Radical Republicans sought to grant freed people the full rights of citizenship and were willing to use force to attain this goal. Southern whites resisted "Radical Reconstruction" any way they could, and ultimately prevailed when Northern will eroded. "The American Civil War, Emancipation, and Reconstruction on the World Stage" analyzes the events of these years and writes that they "embodied struggles that would confront people on every continent."

White encroachment on Native American lands continued up to and after the Civil War. Railroads constructed after the conflict ended speeded this process. "How the West Was Lost," describes the westward expansion that disrupted and demoralized Native American tribal culture. One of the worst catastrophes for the Plains Indians was the destruction of the once-huge buffalo herds that provided them with everything from food and clothing to weapons. The Indians fought back from time to time but confronted overwhelming odds. In the end most tribes were forced onto reservations where they became little more than wards of the state. To its great discredit, the United States made and broke countless treaties with Native Americans over the years.

The Emancipation Question

A lively dialogue over the economics of slavery played out in newspapers and magazines on the eve of the Civil War.

Tom Huntington

One hundred fifty years ago on a "frigid and repulsive" January day in New York, 30-year-old William G. Sewell departed on a steamer for Barbados, the first stop on a tour of the Caribbean island colonies of the British West Indies. Doctors had recommended that the *New York Times* editor travel south because of tuberculosis. While recuperating, he would file a series of articles on a topic that would prove of enormous interest to Americans: how had the colony's islands been affected by the abolition of slavery 25 years earlier? The British West Indies had suffered its fair share of economic difficulties, and argument ensued over whether abolition had helped or harmed. The relevance to America's situation was obvious: the United States held 4 million people in bondage, and the debate over the peculiar institution's future threatened to tear the nation apart.

Sewell, a native of British Quebec, must have encountered the antislavery sentiments of his homeland, and perhaps shared them. But, as a former attorney, he used logic rather than emotion for his arguments. In an article published on April 20, 1859, he claimed that he would address fiduciary, not moral, issues. "I consider the question to be a commercial one—to be judged favorably or unfavorably by commercial rules," he wrote. He had "no sympathy with the argument of the Abolitionists, that the question of emancipation is one in which the black race are to be only considered, or that 'depreciation of property is as nothing compared with a depreciation of morality.'"

The British Empire had outlawed slavery in 1834 and phased it out over the next four years in a surprisingly peaceful transition. "Let us look at the facts," wrote Frenchman Alexis de Tocqueville in 1843: "the abolition of slavery in the nineteen English colonies has thus far not given rise to a *single* insurrection; it has not cost the life of a single man, and yet in the English colonies there are twelve times as many blacks as there are whites." However, the production of sugar, one of the staple crops of the West Indies, had fallen off since emancipation, and advocates on both sides of the debate argued over whether the end of slavery had caused the decline.

The *Times* started publishing Sewell's examination of these issues in March and continued them through the spring, summer, and fall as he reported from Barbados, St. Vincent, Grenada, Jamaica, Trinidad, and other islands. (In 1861 Sewell published an expanded version as a book titled *The Ordeal of Free Labor in the British West Indies.*)

In Barbados Sewell acknowledged that sugar exports had declined, but he reported that exports had been decreasing even under slavery, with many plantations being sold for debt or abandoned. As Sewell asserted, "[N]o Barbadian planter would hesitate in 1859 to select free labor in preference to slave labor, as in his belief the more economical system of the two."

Nor did Sewell notice that the island's black population was suffering from a surfeit of freedom. "The masses are certainly no worse than they were under Slavery; while those who had the intelligence, industry and energy to rise, *have* risen to positions of competence, independence and wealth, which they never could have enjoyed under any other than a free system," he wrote. "Poor whites," however, suffered the most under the new conditions. "Incapable themselves of undergoing the hardships of field labor beneath a tropical sun, they employed, before emancipation, one or two slaves, upon whose services they lived. Deprived of this species of maintenance and having no resources of their own, they became such a burden to the community, that the Government has been called upon to adopt some measures for their relief."

> "Whether the whites and blacks can live together on terms of equality . . . is a problem yet unsolved," wrote a *Harper's Weekly* editor on July 16, 1859, in response to a series of pro-emancipation dispatches written for the *New York Times* by correspondent William G. Sewell from the British West Indies, where slavery had been illegal since 1834.

Sewell noted changes that emancipation had brought to the islands, including the arrival of indentured servants from Asia: "coolies" intended to replace the black laborers freed by emancipation. "The law provides for their free return after they have completed the term of industrial residence for which they were indentured," wrote Sewell, who approved of the practice.

In another article Sewell quoted a letter he had received from the British governor of the West Indies. The total cost of producing a hogshead of sugar with slaves, the governor wrote, had been more than 10 pounds. With free labor, the cost dropped to less than four. "There is very little doubt—and it cannot be intelligently questioned—that Barbados, under the *régime* of Slavery, never approached her present prosperous condition; and, in comparing the present with the past, whether that comparison be made in her commercial, mechanical, agricultural, industrial or educational status, I can come to no other conclusion than that the island offers a striking example of the superior economy of the free system," Sewell concluded. His verdict: while racial tensions were high on some of the islands, and Jamaica in particular was suffering from an economic decline, emancipation was not responsible for their struggles.

The popular *Harper's Weekly* jumped into the fray on September 3 with an editorial expressing uncertainty and anxiety over the issues Sewell had raised in his articles, including a somewhat panicky account of racial unrest in Barbados that the *Times* had published on June 29. "This is the destiny of the British West Indies," the editorial ran. "This is the result of emancipation. Improverishment and decay were the first fruits; extermination of the whites will be the ripe harvest."

Papers in the South nurtured little sentiment for emancipation. In July the editor of the *Register* in Mobile even advocated the repeal of federal laws passed in 1808 that ended the African slave trade. Proslavery sentiment was a regular feature in *DeBow's Review,* an agricultural journal published in New Orleans. In June 1859 the journal ran an article by noted Virginia agriculturist Edmund Ruffin about the effects on Southern farmers of the high prices for black slaves. Every step made to end slavery in Virginia, Ruffin declared, would "be more and more calamitous to the economical, social, and political interests of this commonwealth; and the complete consummation will be one of the greatest evils to the whole of the Southern States." Ruffin believed that slavery was "one of our chief blessings, and that its removal, by any means whatever, would be an unmixed evil and a curse to the whole community."

The views in *DeBow's* stood in marked contrast to what appeared in the *New York Times,* but both publications agreed on one thing: slaves were expensive. On August 26 the *Times* listed the results of a slave auction that had taken place in Bowling Green, Missouri. "The prices were good," an editorial writer reported. "A man verging upon three score brought about $800; a girl of six upwards of $500, and a girl of thirteen nearly $1,200.

"Such statements grate harshly on Northern ears, as well they may," the editorialist continued.

"An auction sale of human beings is a specially hideous spectacle when witnessed in a country which boasts of its freedom and civilization." The writer acknowledged that such sales had once taken place in New York City. "Slavery must fall in the South as it has fallen in the North; but what state of society shall succeed Slavery in the South is a grave question, not to be determined by the rash and angry agitations of partisan politics."

When war finally came, Edmund Ruffin helped usher it in. The agriculturist and Confederate "fire-eater" traveled to Charleston, South Carolina, as hostilities appeared imminent. On April 12, 1861, when Confederate cannon took aim at the Union stronghold of Fort Sumter out in the harbor, a Southern artillery battery gave Ruffin the honor of firing one of the first shots of the Civil War.

Sewell died of his illness the following year. Ruffin survived the war, but on June 17, 1865, after hearing news of the Confederate defeat, he penned a note in which he lambasted "the perfidious, malignant and vile Yankee race," and then killed himself with a pistol shot to the head.

Abolitionist John Doy

Tempers flare and violence reigns in the pre-Civil War battleground of Kansas.

TOM HUNTINGTON

On January 25, 1859, a small wagon expedition of three whites and 13 blacks stole away from Lawrence, Kansas, on the first leg of a journey that would take the African Americans to the free state of Iowa, far from Kansas and the ever-present threat of kidnapping by slave traders. For the three white abolitionists it was a protest against those who would deny their deepest beliefs about freedom and human rights.

The wagons splashed across the Kansas River and left Lawrence behind. Twelve miles outside town, after the party had descended a small hill, about 20 armed and mounted men emerged from behind a bluff. Guns leveled, they forced the wagons to a stop and accused the white men of stealing slaves. The expedition's white leader, John Doy, jumped from his horse and confronted a man he recognized. "Where's your process?" Doy demanded. The man shoved his gun barrel into Doy's head. "Here it is," he growled.

Ever since the passage of the Kansas-Nebraska Act in 1854, the Kansas territory had been thrust into the front lines of the increasingly rancorous national debate over slavery. The act nullified the Missouri Compromise, which had forbidden the expansion of slavery north of the 36°30 N line of latitude, and legislated that settlers could determine by popular vote whether or not to allow slavery in their territories. The stakes were high, and passions became inflamed. "The fate of the South is to be decided in Kansas," declared South Carolina Rep. Preston Brooks in March 1856. Four months later Brooks bludgeoned abolitionist Sen. Charles Sumner senseless with a cane on the floor of the Senate after the latter had delivered a speech entitled, "The Crime against Kansas."

Activists on both sides converged on Kansas, each intending to help tip the scales for or against slavery. "Border ruffians," who crossed over from slave-owning Missouri, began battling with abolitionist "free soilers." The violence gave the territory a new name: "Bleeding Kansas."

John Doy, a physician from Rochester, New York, heeded the call from abolitionist societies and moved to Kansas in July 1854. A full-bearded and serious-looking man, Doy helped found the town of Lawrence and built a house on its outskirts, where his wife and nine children joined him. As a bastion of

free-soil sympathies, Lawrence became a target of proslavers, who sacked it on May 21, 1856. In retaliation, the abolitionist firebrand John Brown and his men murdered five slave owners near Pottawatomie Creek. Three months later Doy fought alongside Brown in a pitched battle at Osawatomie, 60 miles southeast of Lawrence.

Kansas became increasingly dangerous for African Americans, so on January 18, 1859, a group of Lawrence's citizens raised money to help blacks move to safety. Brown offered to take one group north to Canada and did so without incident. Doy also volunteered to help by taking another group about 60 miles northwest to the town of Holton, the first step on the road to Iowa. His passage proved less fortunate.

Among the African Americans on Doy's expedition were Wilson Hayes and Charles Smith, cooks at a Lawrence hotel. Doy knew that both of them were free men, although they had no papers. All the others had their "free papers," including William Riley, who had been kidnapped once before from Lawrence but had managed to escape.

Free or not, all 16 members of the party now found themselves in the hands of angry men bent on delivering them to slave-owning Missouri. The ambushers forced their captives on an overnight journey to Rialto Ferry, where they were put aboard a steamboat for passage across the Missouri River. On the opposite shore, an awaiting mob paraded Doy on horseback through town, beating and cursing him. One enraged man grabbed Doy by the beard and smashed his head repeatedly against a wall of the building where the prisoners were to spend the night.

The next morning John and his 25-year-old son Charles were pushed through the mob to the courthouse. The justice of the peace, who had "a face and eyes that looked as if all the milk of human kindness he ever possessed had long since soured," Doy later remembered, sent the third white man back to Kansas but ordered the Doys locked up in Platte City and put on trial for abducting slaves.

After another rough welcome in Platte City, the two Doys were thrown into a windowless cell, "an iron box, exactly eight feet square . . . and about seven feet high, furnished with a mattress on an iron bedstead, and with a horse rug and an old piece of cotton carpeting for a coverlid." The situation proved even worse for the African Americans. Hays, Smith, and Riley landed in the Platte City jail. Doy watched through the door grate as slave trader Jake Hurd brutally whipped Hays and Smith in a futile attempt to gain a confession that they were escaped slaves, then dragged them away. Riley managed to loosen the bars from his cell window and escaped back to Kansas—only to be later kidnapped once more as he was making his way to Nebraska.

Doy's counsel successfully petitioned to have the trial moved to the slightly less hostile town of St. Joseph, and the Doys bid farewell to their miserable Platte City cell on March 24. "Pale from confinement and want of light, cadaverous, emaciated, covered with vermin—for notwithstanding the clean clothes we had had the advantage of since my wife's arrival, we had not been able to free ourselves of them—with my joints swollen, my ankles, especially, so painful that I could hardly bear my weight upon them, I was weakened both in body and mind," Doy wrote.

The jail in St. Joseph was "a paradise after the cell at Platte City," and the jailer, named Brown, "proved to be a very humane man." The jury at the first trial in St. Joseph deadlocked, so the judge set Charles free and scheduled a second trial for the elder Doy on June 20. The second jury found him guilty and sentenced him to five years' hard labor. While Doy's counsel filed an appeal to the state supreme court, prosecutors planned a dozen more indictments against him on charges of stealing other slaves in the ill-fated expedition. He faced up to 65 years in prison.

But help was on its way. On the evening of July 23 a young man visited him in the jailhouse and slipped him a note reading "Be ready at midnight."

That night a storm hit St. Joseph. Amid its fury a man knocked on the jailhouse door and shouted to Brown the jailer that he had a horse thief he wanted locked up. Somewhat reluctantly, Brown went downstairs and opened the door. Two men held the alleged criminal, his hands bound. The jailer led them upstairs and opened the door to the cell. Suddenly the horse thief whipped off his bindings and one of his "captors" jammed a revolver against Brown's chest. "If you resist or try to give an alarm, you're a dead man," he warned. "We've come to take Dr. Doy home to Kansas, and we mean to do it; so you'd best be quiet."

Doy emerged from the cell, shook the jailer's hand, and left with his rescuers. He was so weak that two men needed to support him through the storm and down to the river, where boats were waiting. "By dint of hard pulling for the current of the Missouri is very strong there, we soon landed on the Kansas bank, which I had often gazed at longingly from the window of my cell," Doy wrote. His rescuers bundled their charge into a covered wagon for the 90-mile journey back to Lawrence, where Doy was "restored to my home, to my family and friends, and to the soil I love so well."

His ordeal was over, but the country's was just beginning. In October 1859 Doy's friend and fellow abolitionist John Brown led a raid on Harpers Ferry Virginia. Civil War erupted a year and a half later.

From *American Heritage*, April 17, 2009. Copyright © 2009 by American Heritage Publishing Co. Reprinted by permission.

There Goes the South

President-elect Abraham Lincoln remained strangely silent as threats of secession became a reality during the long winter before his inauguration.

H. W. BRANDS

On the eve of his victory in the 1860 presidential election, Abraham Lincoln surprised a well-wisher by declaring, "For personal considerations, I would rather have a full term in the Senate—a place in which I would feel more consciously able to discharge the duties required and where there was more chance to make a reputation and less danger of losing it—than four years of the presidency."

Lincoln's expression of 11th-hour doubt was not merely the disclaimer of a self-deprecating politician. The nearer he got to fulfilling his ambition of becoming president, the more he realized how daunting the job would be. He did his best to maintain a cheerful front as he monitored the final election returns at the Springfield, Ill., telegraph office on November 6. But his private secretary John Nicolay watched "the appalling shadow of his mighty task and responsibility" pass over him as he donned his overcoat around 1:30 A.M. and headed home in a melancholy mood. "It seemed as if he suddenly bore the whole world upon his shoulders, and could not shake it off."

Lincoln faced the unnerving prospect that by the time he took his oath of office on March 4—four months after the election—the Union would be in ruins. Southern radicals were already clamoring for secession. Meanwhile, even though Lincoln lacked the constitutional authority to act as president, people in both the North and the South looked to him for leadership as the nation plunged into a period of dangerous uncertainty.

Years later, Lincoln's first vice president, Hannibal Hamlin, chided eulogists for "constructing a Lincoln who was as great the day he left Springfield as when he made his earthly exit four years later." As president-elect, Lincoln was uncertain about whether the secession movement represented the bluster of a minority or a groundswell of popular Southern sentiment. Nor could he confidently predict whether Northerners would insist on holding the Union together or bid good riddance to the slave states. Moreover, he struggled at first with his own natural tendency to let pressing questions simmer until solutions bubbled to the surface. Should he try to reach some accommodation with Southern moderates in hopes of averting war? Or would that merely encourage the radical secessionists, who

would interpret any accommodation as weakness and grow more convinced the North would never fight?

Only at his inauguration did he muster the will to attack the secessionists head on. By then it was too late to save the Union peacefully.

During the long winter interlude before he took office, Lincoln initially did nothing, hoping the crisis would pass. But when his inaction proved counterproductive and the secessionist momentum intensified, he felt obliged to alter course. Still, he moved quietly and indirectly, fearing that his words and deeds might provoke Southern moderates into joining the secessionists. Only at his inauguration did he muster the will to speak boldly and attack the secessionists head on.

By then it was too late to save the Union peacefully.

Lincoln had sought the presidency by means that invited confusion. He won the Republican nomination largely on the strength of his House Divided speech of 1858, in which he declared that America could not continue half slave and half free. But in the general election the Republicans promised to leave slavery alone in the states where it existed, and Lincoln embraced that promise without ever overtly disavowing the uncompromising message of the House Divided address.

In the mid-19th century presidential candidates didn't campaign for themselves, nor was it thought seemly for presidents-elect to speak on the record. But given the turmoil surrounding his election, many people thought Lincoln must explain his position on the unfolding crisis. A pointed appeal came from George Prentice, the editor of the *Louisville Journal*. Prentice was a discouraged Southern Unionist who urged Lincoln to make a public statement that would "take from the disunionists every excuse or pretext for treason."

Rebel Administration. Jefferson Davis (left) and Alexander Stephens were sworn in as president and vice president of the new Confederacy a month before Lincoln's inauguration. Stephens was on friendly terms with Lincoln and initially argued against secession.

"If what I have already said has failed to convince you, no repetition of it would convince you," Lincoln replied. His answer was a dodge; he wouldn't speak because he didn't want to commit himself before he had to.

The rumblings of secession increased, however, and Lincoln realized he had to give some sign of his thinking. Lyman Trumbull was a senator from Illinois who had been elected as a Democrat but subsequently converted to Republicanism. He and Lincoln were known to be close, and his words were often taken as coming from Lincoln. Two weeks after the election Lincoln wrote a brief passage for Trumbull to insert in a speech at Chicago. "I have labored in and for the Republican organization," Trumbull said, for himself and Lincoln, "with entire confidence that whenever it shall be in power, each and all of the states will be left in complete control of their own affairs respectively, and at as perfect liberty to choose, and employ, their own means of protecting property, and preserving peace and order within their respective limits, as they have ever been under any administration."

Lincoln's proxy statement failed dismally. It lacked the authority that words spoken by Lincoln himself would have carried, and its second-hand character suggested a timidity that augured ill for Lincoln's administration or his cause. Southern secessionists concluded that a man without the courage to speak

in his own voice would be a president without the nerve to challenge their separatist designs. Northern radicals complained that the Trumbull statement was a retreat from the moral clarity of the House Divided speech.

The criticism reinforced Lincoln's caution. "This is just what I expected, and just what would happen with any declaration I could make," he told a friend. "These political fiends are not half sick enough yet. 'Party malice' and not 'public good' possesses them entirely. 'They seek a sign, and no sign shall be given them.'"

Lincoln's diffidence encouraged others to take the stage. The secessionists called conventions and drafted resolutions to implement their separatist aims. Northern Unionists and Southern moderates weighed a constitutional amendment guaranteeing the future of slavery in the states where it already existed. Lame duck president James Buchanan sent an envoy, Duff Green, to test Lincoln's thinking on such an amendment.

"I do not desire any amendment," Lincoln told Green. An amendment, he reasoned, would be difficult to pass and nearly impossible to repeal. He blanched at the idea of grafting slavery so egregiously onto America's fundamental law. But he wouldn't rule it out entirely, if only because amending the Constitution was the prerogative of Congress and the states, not the president.

More promising, to Lincoln's view, was the approach of Alexander Stephens, a Georgia moderate Lincoln had known since the 1840s, when they served in the House of Representatives together. As Georgians debated their response to Lincoln's election, Stephens gave a widely noted speech opposing rash action. "I do not anticipate that Mr. Lincoln will do anything to jeopardize our safety or security," he said. "He can do nothing unless he is backed by power in Congress. The House of Representatives is largely in the majority against him. In the Senate he will also be powerless."

Lincoln read newspaper summaries of Stephens' remarks, and he wrote Stephens asking if he had prepared them for publication. Stephens replied that he had not, but that the news reports fairly characterized what he had said. He went on to offer Lincoln encouragement in his efforts to hold the nation together. "The Country is certainly in great peril and no man ever had heavier or greater responsibilities resting upon him than you have in this present momentous crisis," he said.

Lincoln appreciated the gesture, and he tried, through Stephens, to allay the concerns of Southern moderates. "Do the people in the South really entertain fears that a Republican administration would, directly or indirectly, interfere with their slaves?" he asked Stephens. "If they do, I wish to assure you, as once a friend and still, I hope, not an enemy, that there is no cause for such fears. The South would be in no more danger in this respect than it was in the days of Washington."

You think slavery is right and ought to be extended, while we think it is wrong and ought to be restricted. That I suppose is the rub.

Yet Lincoln conceded to Stephens that the issue ran deeper than political assurances. Southerners and Northerners had irreconcilable views on the morality of slavery. "You think slavery is right and ought to be extended, while we think it is wrong and ought to be restricted. That I suppose is the rub."

That was the rub, and it chafed the more as Lincoln's inauguration neared. A desperate Congress convened committees to find an arrangement to hold the Union together. Proposals included one to resurrect a popular sovereignty scheme advanced by Lincoln's old nemesis Stephen Douglas, by which residents of frontier territories would vote to permit or ban slavery. Lincoln still declined to issue a public statement, but he wrote Republican members of Congress to stiffen their resolve against any retreat on slavery in the territories. "Entertain no proposition for a compromise in regard to extension of slavery," he urged William Kellogg, a Republican representative from Illinois. "The instant you do, they have us

under again; all our labor is lost. . . . The tug has to come and better now than later." Lincoln told Elihu Washburne, another Illinois Republican: "Hold firm, as with a chain of steel."

Lincoln perceived Southerners' aggressiveness on the slave issue as inevitable. Their current demands were but the start. "If we surrender, it is the end of us, and of the government," he asserted privately. "They will repeat the experiment upon us ad libitum." The sole way out of the present impasse, Lincoln said, was by a route neither Northerners nor Southerners would accept: "a prohibition against acquiring any more territory." It was a great irony of American history that this very solution—which Lincoln and nearly every contemporary rejected as unworkable—had already been effected, in political practice if not in political theory. The continental expansion that was causing all the trouble had ended in 1848. The only substantial piece of North America to be added to the United States after 1860 was Alaska, which was unsuited to a large population of any sort, slave or otherwise.

As the winter dragged on, Lincoln realized he had underestimated the South. Those who spoke of secession were not bluffing. He decided he must state his position—albeit still not quite for public consumption. Thurlow Weed, the New York Republican boss whose support had been central to Lincoln's election, had convened Northern governors to prepare a riposte to the South. "I am unwilling to see a united South and a divided North," Weed wrote Lincoln. "Thus united, your administration will have its foundation upon a rock." What could Lincoln tell the governors, even in private, about his intentions?

Lincoln's response echoed what he had told other Republicans: He was "inflexible on the territorial question"—no slavery outside the Southern states. He added: "My opinion is that no state can, in any way lawfully, get out of the Union, without the consent of the others; and that it is the duty of the President, and other government functionaries, to run the machine as it is."

But the machine was already breaking up. South Carolina, amid great fanfare, had passed an ordinance of secession on December 20, and in the succeeding weeks several other states prepared to follow suit and leave the Union.

On February 11, Lincoln left Springfield for Washington. The psychological strain of the long, hard winter showed in his face and bearing; an acquaintance remarked that his body "heaved with emotion and he could scarcely command his feelings." Lincoln's voice broke as he told his Springfield neighbors, "I now leave, not knowing when, or whether ever, I may return."

The strain intensified as he headed east. The newspapers en route reported on the provisional Congress of the Confederate States of America, meeting in Montgomery, Ala. Seven states—South Carolina, Mississippi, Florida, Alabama, Georgia, Louisiana and Texas—sent delegates, although the Texans had to await the ratification of secession by the people of the Lone Star State. Lincoln read of the election of Jefferson Davis to be president of the Confederacy, and days later of Davis' inauguration with Alexander Stephens as his vice president. He also read that the Southern states were seizing the federal forts on their soil.

The progress of a president-elect en route to his inauguration was a once-in-a-lifetime event for many of the towns through which Lincoln's train passed, and at every stop people gathered and insisted that he speak. He was too good a politician not to oblige. "If the United States should merely hold and retake its own forts and other property, and collect the duties on foreign importations, or even withhold the mails from places where they were habitually violated, would any or all these things be 'invasion' or 'coercion'?" he asked an audience at Indianapolis. Then he waffled: "I am not asserting anything. I am merely asking questions."

At Philadelphia he learned that Allan Pinkerton, a detective hired by the railroad company to preempt sabotage, had heard rumors of an assassination plot in Baltimore, where secessionist sympathies ran strong. Lincoln at first resisted altering his schedule, but when additional evidence suggested real danger, he was persuaded. He disguised himself as an invalid and slipped through Baltimore in the dead of night.

He soon regretted that decision. Southern newspapers ridiculed his lack of courage; even Republican papers feared he had diminished himself on the verge of his inauguration.

All of Washington was on edge as Lincoln prepared to take his oath of office on March 4. General Winfield Scott, the army commander, stationed infantry, cavalry and artillery troops conspicuously about the capital, and special squadrons of policemen lined Pennsylvania Avenue. The great majority of the visitors who crowded the streets were from the Northern states—"judging from the lack of long-haired men in the crowd," an eyewitness observed. When the members of the House of Representatives were summoned to join the inaugural procession to the east side of the Capitol, their jostling for position escalated to curses, threats and near-fisticuffs. Chief Justice Roger B. Taney, whose decision in the *Dred Scott* case had elicited Lincoln's House Divided prophecy, visibly trembled as he stood near Lincoln on the rostrum.

Lincoln felt the tension as he looked out on the crowd. And he couldn't help reflecting that his caution had done nothing to ease the nation's crisis, which grew more acute by the day. Inaction had simply encouraged others to seize the initiative.

But now it was his turn—finally. He commenced by reiterating what he had been conveying in private: that slavery in the South was secure. "I have no purpose, directly or indirectly, to interfere with the institution of slavery in the States where it exists. I believe I have no lawful right to do so, and I have no inclination to do so."

Sadly, he continued, Southern radicals were not so tolerant. "A disruption of the Federal Union, heretofore only menaced, is now formidably attempted."

No disruption would be allowed. An unexpected steel entered Lincoln's voice—a tone few had anticipated and none in public heard. "The Union of these States is perpetual," he said. Secessionists would search in vain for constitutional authorization for their plan. "No government proper ever had a provision in its organic law for its own termination." If, as the secessionists

Inauguration Day. With the unfinished Capitol as a backdrop, Lincoln finally addressed the nation's uncertain future.

contended, the Union was a union of states rather than of peoples, this afforded no easier exit, for, having been created by all the states, the Union required the consent of all the states to be destroyed. "No State, upon its own mere motion, can lawfully get out of the Union. . . . The Union is unbroken."

The Union of these States is perpetual. No State, upon its own mere motion, can lawfully get out of the Union. . . . The Union is unbroken.

And Lincoln vowed it would remain unbroken. "To the extent of my ability I shall take care, as the Constitution itself expressly enjoins upon me, that the laws of the Union be faithfully executed in all of the States."

The secessionists blamed Lincoln personally for endangering the peace of the Union; they had it just backward, he said. "In your hands, my dissatisfied fellow-countrymen, and not in mine, is the momentous issue of civil war. The Government will not assail you. You can have no conflict without being yourselves the aggressors. You have no oath registered in Heaven to destroy the Government, while I shall have the most solemn one to 'preserve, protect, and defend it.'"

These were fighting words. The secessionists had doubted Lincoln's resolve; his long silence had corroborated their doubts, to the point of encouraging their secession. But they could doubt him no longer. To speak of civil war was to make it possible.

Lincoln had never fought a civil war; none of his contemporaries had. He had only the vaguest notion of what it would mean or how it would be done. Yet if the secessionists persisted in their destructive ways, they would provoke a civil war.

He let his words hang in the March air above the Capitol grounds. Applause had interrupted him earlier; now the thousands were silent as they pondered his promise, and his threat. He gave both a moment to sink in.

Then he concluded more hopefully: "We are not enemies, but friends. We must not be enemies. Though passion may have strained, it must not break our bonds of affection. The mystic chords of memory, stretching from every battlefield and patriot grave to every living heart and hearthstone all over this broad land, will yet swell the chorus of the Union, when again touched, as surely they will be, by the better angels of our nature."

H. W. BRANDS is a history professor at the University of Texas and the author of 16 books. His latest is *Traitor to His Class,* a biography of Franklin Roosevelt.

Lincoln and the Constitutional Dilemma of Emancipation

EDNA GREENE MEDFORD

> The President shall be Commander in Chief of the Army and Navy of the United States, and of the Militia of the several States, when called into the actual Service of the United States.
>
> —U. S. Constitution, Article II, Section 2

On the afternoon of January 1, 1863, following nearly two years of bloody civil war, Abraham Lincoln set in motion events that would reconnect the detached cord of Union and that would begin to reconcile the nation's practices to its avowed democratic principles. Interpreting Article II, Section 2 of the Constitution broadly, the president used his war powers to proclaim freedom for those enslaved laborers caught in the dehumanizing grip of one of the Confederacy's most sacrosanct institutions. His bold move challenged prevailing notions of presidential prerogative and triggered criticism from his supporters as well as his opponents. While many abolitionists bemoaned the limited scope of the president's actions, alleging that he freed those persons over whom he had no control, while exempting from his edict those under Union authority, his more conservative critics charged that he had exceeded the powers the Constitution invested in the executive.

Lincoln anticipated the criticism. He knew that most abolitionists would be satisfied with nothing less than universal emancipation and that, contrarily, pro-South forces would find in his actions reason to brand him a betrayer of American liberties. Given that slavery evoked such polarization in the North, he realized that whatever action he took on the institution posed considerable danger to the goal of the war—preservation of the Union.

Although influenced by the practical considerations of containing the rebellion—that is, not losing any more slaveholding states to the Confederacy—Lincoln's greatest challenge regarding emancipation was to achieve it without violating constitutional guarantees. He understood slavery to be the cause of the war but he believed that the Constitution denied the president any easy solution for its eradication. Whatever his personal views on slavery (and there is incontrovertible evidence that he hated the institution on moral grounds as well as practical reasons), law and custom had deemed enslaved people property.[1] Because the Constitution protected property rights, Lincoln felt compelled to operate within those constraints. As war propelled him inexorably toward emancipation, he sought authority to do so within the framework that the Constitution provided.

The Civil War began as a struggle over national union, one half of the American people believed it indissoluble and fought to preserve it, while the other half wished to withdraw from it and secure their own identity. Northern attempts at appeasement and diplomacy having failed, war became the only recourse for a president convinced that secession was unconstitutional. Hence, in his first official act after hostilities commenced, Lincoln called up the state militias "to maintain the honor, the integrity, and the existence" of the nation.[2] The decision had not been an easy one. When he spoke before Congress in special session on July 4, 1861, he explained that.

"It was with the deepest regret that the Executive found the duty of employing the war-power, in defense of the government, forced upon him. He could but perform this duty, or surrender the existence of the government."[3]

Defense of the government ultimately led Lincoln to strike at the heart of the South's reason for challenging national union. It would prove even harder than prosecuting the war itself, because the Constitution—compromise document that it was—reflected the ambivalence of the framers over the issue of slavery. Lincoln had acknowledged "not grudgingly, but fully, and fairly," the constitutional rights of the slaveholder, but the treatment of slavery in the Constitution suggested to him that the framers had deliberately paved the way for the institution's eventual extinction.[4] The founding fathers and the earliest Congress were hostile to slavery; they tolerated it "only by necessity," he argued. The framers even excluded the words "slave" and "slavery" from the Constitution and chose instead to refer to those held in bondage as "persons" from whom "service or labor may be due." This was a deliberate attempt, thought Lincoln, to keep the idea of "property in man" out of this democratic document.[5] The founding fathers hid it away "just as an afflicted man hides away . . . a cancer, which he does not cut out at once, lest he bleed to death."[6] Hence, the Supreme Court's ruling in *Scott v. Sandford*, which declared that slaveholders could not be prohibited from taking their chattel wherever they wished, was "based upon a mistaken statement of fact . . . that the right of property in a slave is distinctly and expressly affirmed in the Constitution." That document was "literally silent" about any right of slaveholders to take their human property into the territories.[7]

Lincoln had always believed that Congress could prevent slavery from spreading into the territories, over which it had jurisdiction. But the government, he believed, did not have the constitutional authority to touch the institution where it had already been established. Indeed, the 1860 Republican platform on which he was elected to the presidency declared:

That the maintenance inviolate of the rights of the States, and especially the light of each State to order and control its own domestic institutions according to its own judgment exclusively, is essential to that balance of power on which the perfection and endurance of our political fabric depend.[8]

Lincoln did not stand down from this position when in the weeks following his election several southern states seceded and formed the Confederate States of America. Far from seizing upon this as an opportunity to move against slavery, the newly elected president attempted to reassure the secessionists and their non-seceding slaveholding brothers that he had "no purpose, directly or indirectly, to interfere with the institution of slavery in the States where it exists. I believe I have no lawful right to do so, and I have no inclination to do so." Lincoln promised that "all the protection which, consistently with the Constitution and the laws, can be given, will be cheerfully given to all the States when lawfully demanded as cheerfully to one section, as to another."[9] It was a position he held throughout the war.

In promising to uphold the laws, Lincoln was speaking primarily about enforcement of the Fugitive Slave Act, passed in 1850 as one of the compromises after the war with Mexico resulted in the ceding of millions of acres to the United States. The Missouri Compromise had maintained a balance of free and slave states since 1820, but this new acquisition threatened to give advantage to one section over the other. In an effort to stay the rising crisis, Congress had proposed a series of measures that would appease each region. The Fugitive Slave Act aimed to assure southerners that the northern people would be equally obligated to protect the rights of the slaveholder. The law imposed fines on anyone who refused to assist in the apprehending of a fugitive or who facilitated any effort to prevent recovery. This attempt by Congress to resolve the conflict may have pleased the South, but it evoked anger and frustration among northerners who had no desire to become slave catchers.[10]

After the secessionist attack on Fort Sumter ignited armed conflict, Lincoln's declaration of noninterference met with increased criticism within the Union and initiated direct challenge to the administrations position. Undeterred by the president's pledge, enslaved African Americans had themselves seized the opportunity to obtain their freedom by flight. As Union troops advanced on the Confederacy, fugitives from slavery met them and offered loyalty, labor, and information in exchange for asylum. Even in the ostensibly loyal border states, black men and women sought to secure freedom as the chaos of war blurred distinctions between rebel and Unionist slaveholders.[11]

Without specific guidelines for dealing with fugitives, Union Commanders in the field implemented their own solutions. Some of them saw the advantage to sheltering runaways and chose to employ them in erecting defense against southern forces or utilized them in a variety of noncombatant occupations. General Benjamin Butler's declaration that these fugitives were contraband of war encouraged other commanders to embrace the designation.[12] But for every General Butler there was a Henry Halleck who barred fugitive slaves from the camps under his command. In the first months of the war, the Lincoln administration chose not to make any additional public pronouncements on the issue of fugitives, but the president, eager to keep the conflict contained and of short duration, privately queried the general-in-chief, Winfield Scott, if it "would be well to allow owners to bring back [slaves] which have crossed the Potomac" with Union troops.[13] As a consequence, runaways were banned from the Union camps of the Department of Washington and were prohibited from following soldiers on the move.[14]

Congress's attempt to turn the South's "peculiar institution" to the North's advantage and the emancipating actions of commanders in the field left Lincoln less than enthusiastic and, in some instances, downright perturbed. In August 1861, Congress had passed the First Confiscation Act, which provided for seizure of any property (including enslaved persons) that had been used to wage war against the government. The act did not address the status of the confiscated slaves once the war was over. Yet, concerned that such action would strengthen the resolve of the rebels and would likely be overturned by constitutional challenge, Lincoln reluctantly signed the measure and made little effort to enforce it.[15]

General John C. Frémont's proclamation of August 30 gave Lincoln even greater concern. As commander of the Department of the West, Frémont declared martial law in Missouri and issued a proclamation stipulating that "the property, real and personal, of all persons in the state of Missouri who shall take up arms against the United States . . . is declared to be confiscated and their slaves are hereby declared freemen."[16] Frémont's proclamation differed from the First Confiscation Act in that property could be seized without having been employed against the Union. Moreover, the human property thus confiscated was declared free. Citing concern that the decree might "alarm our southern Union friends, and turn them against us—perhaps ruin our rather fair prospect for Kentucky," Lincoln asked, and later commanded, the unyielding Frémont to place his proclamation in conformity with Congress' confiscation measure.[17]

In a letter written in late September to friend Orville H. Browning, fellow Republican and U.S. senator from Illinois, Lincoln reiterated these political concerns, especially the importance of securing the loyalty of Kentucky. But it was the constitutional question that was paramount. Lincoln argued that the general's proclamation, specifically the part which stipulated the liberation of the slaves, was "purely political, and not within the range of military law, or necessity." He challenged the notion that:

"If a commanding General finds a necessity to seize the farm of a private owner, for a pasture, an encampment, or a fortification, he has the right to do so . . . as long as the necessity lasts. . . . But to say the farm no longer belong to the owner, or his heirs forever, and this as well when the farm is not needed for military purposes as when it is, is purely political, without the savor of military law about it."[18]

Lincoln believed that this applied to slaves as well. Human property could be confiscated, "But when the need is past, it is not for [the confiscator] to fix their permanent future condition. That must be settled according to laws made by law-makers, and not by military proclamations. . . . Can it be pretended that it is any longer the government of the U.S. . . . wherein a General, or a President, may make permanent rules of property by proclamation?."[19]

When eight months later, General David Hunter, commander of the Department of the South, declared martial law and freed the slaves within the three states under his jurisdiction, an exasperated Lincoln rescinded the order, declaring that as president he would "reserve to myself" the question of whether or not as commander in chief he had authority to emancipate the slaves.[20]

Contrary to his response to the emancipating actions of commanders in the field, Lincoln did not challenge Congress's authority to free enslaved people in the District of Columbia when on April 11, 1862, that body approved a measure to emancipate "persons held to service or labor" in the city. As a federal enclave, Washington was under the jurisdiction of Congress, and hence, it had the constitutional authority to end slavery there. The city had been steadily moving toward eradication of the institution for some time, and so fewer than 3,200 African Americans out of a total black population of 11,000 were affected directly.[21] Nevertheless, many white Washingtonians challenged Congress's actions because they thought the maximum amount of three hundred dollars per slave was inadequate compensation and because they imagined that a free city would quickly become overrun with fugitives from slavery in Maryland and Virginia.[22]

But acknowledgement of constitutional authority did not suggest that the District Emancipation Bill was to Lincoln's liking. Weeks before, he had proposed a plan for gradual, compensated emancipation, implemented by the border states. In this way, constitutional constraints would be recognized while emancipation would sever the bond between the slaveholding Union states and their sisters in rebellion.[23] But none of those states had exhibited much interest. Hence, when Congress stepped in to implement emancipation for the District of Columbia, Lincoln was somewhat ambivalent. While the measure was making its way through Congress, he expressed his uneasiness "as to the time and manner of doing it." He preferred the initiative to come from one of the border states, but if this could not be achieved quickly, he hoped that the bill would stipulate an emancipation that was gradual, provided compensation to the owners, and was voted on by the people of the District.[24]

When Lincoln signed the District Emancipation Bill after delaying for five days, he sent a message to Congress that officially voiced his concerns. The president reminded them that he had "ever desired to see the national capital freed from the institution in some satisfactory way."[25] But he proposed an "amendatory or supplemental act" that would guarantee sufficient time for which to file claims for compensation. Moreover, he hinted at "matters within and about this act, which might have taken a course or shape, more satisfactory to my jud[g]ment."[26] Presumably, he was disturbed that emancipation had been carried out absent any opportunity for District residents to shape it as they did not have a vote.

One last action on the part of Congress would address the issue of emancipation of enslaved people before Lincoln issued his preliminary proclamation in September 1862. In July, Congress had passed the Second Confiscation Act. The measure, intended "to suppress Insurrection, to punish Treason and Rebellion, to seize and confiscate the Property of Rebels," provided for the freeing of all slaves of persons who were "adjudged guilty" of committing treason against the United States.[27] Again, certain features of the bill disturbed Lincoln, and again he responded by submitting written objections to Congress. While expressing his pleasure that loyal Unionist slaveholders were not touched by the measure and that persons charged with treason would enjoy "regular trials, in duly constituted courts," the president found it 'startling' that Congress could free a slave who resided in a state unless "it were said the ownership of the slave had first been transferred to the nation, and that congress had then liberated him." But what troubled Lincoln most about the Second Confiscation Act was the idea that forfeiture of title to the slave extended beyond the life of the rebel owner. The act, Lincoln believed, violated Article III, Section 3 of the Constitution that stipulated: "The Congress shall have Power to declare the Punishment of Treason, but no Attainder of Treason shall work Corruption of Blood, or Forfeiture except during the Life of the Person attainted."[28] The enforcement of the Second Confiscation Act would do just that by denying the property rights of the heirs of the person committing treason. Lincoln's objections led Congress to pass a joint resolution that disallowed any "punishment or proceedings under the act that would lead to forfeiture beyond the offender's natural life."[29]

The president's concerns regarding the Second Confiscation Act were no trivial matter. He was only two months away from issuing his Preliminary Emancipation Proclamation, which would announce his intention to make "forever free" those slaves in states and parts thereof still in rebellion by January 1, 1863. While the Constitution did not expressly give the president the authority to free slaves, Lincoln claimed such authority through the war powers. "The Constitution invests its Commander-in-Chief with the law of war, in time of war," he declared. "By the law of war, property, both of enemies and friends, may be taken" or destroyed if doing so hurts the enemy and helps the cause.[30] Hence, Lincoln claimed the right to issue the proclamation as a "fit and necessary war measurer."[31] By claiming military necessity, he sidestepped the constitutional concerns that had attended Congress's effort to legislate freedom under the clause regulating punishment for treason.

Despite objections to the proclamation, Lincoln declined to rescind the decree. "The promise [of freedom] being made, must be kept," he declared.[32] But his resoluteness masked the fear that his decree would face legal challenge. Moreover, he recognized that while freeing enslaved people in the Confederacy, slavery as an institution had not been abolished. Hence, during the summer of 1864, he joined Congress in pressing for the passage of a constitutional amendment banning slavery. When in February 1865, Congress passed the Thirteenth Amendment and submitted it to the states for ratification, Lincoln declared it "a King's cure for all the evils."[33] Interestingly, shortly thereafter, he drafted a recommendation to Congress that proposed that compensation payments be made to all the slaveholding states—including those currently in the Confederacy—provided the states were not in rebellion by April. The recommendation was never delivered to Congress because the president's cabinet unanimously rejected it.[34]

As he moved toward emancipation, Lincoln looked to the Constitution for guidance, ever careful to conform to what he believed were the guarantees of that document. Since enslaved people were deemed property, he felt it imperative to address the legality of efforts to liberate them from the perspective of the constitutional rights of the slaveholder. Although he acknowledged the humanity (albeit inferior to whites, in his estimation) of black men and women, issues of emancipation within the context of constitutional constraints precluded any humanitarian sentiment as a part of "official duty." "What I do about slavery, and the colored race, I do because I believe it helps to save the Union," he had declared. "[A]nd what I forbear, I forbear because I do not believe it would help to save the Union."[35] Despite the limitations it placed on presidential emancipation, the Constitution had given him the authority to save the Union and begin the destruction of slavery throughout the nation.

Notes

1. In his speech on the Kansas-Nebraska Act at Peoria, Illinois, on October 16, 1854. Lincoln had declared: "I hate [slavery] because of the monstrous injustice . . . I hate it because it deprives our republican example of its just influence in the world—enables the enemies of free institutions . . . to taunt us as hypocrites." See "Speech at Peoria," in *The Collected Works of Abraham Lincoln* (hereinafter cited as *Collected Works*). 8 vols., ed. Roy P. Basler (New Brunswick, NJ: Rutgers University Press. 1953), 2:255.

2. "By the President of the United States a Proclamation, April 15, 1861," *Collected Works,* 4:331–32.

3. "Message to Congress in Special Session, July 4, 1861," in *Collected Works,* 4:421.

4. Speech at Peoria, October 16, 1854, *Collected Works,* 2:256.

5. Address at Cooper Institute, February 27, 1860, *Collected Works,* 3:545.

6. Speech at Peoria, October 16, 1854, *Collected Works,* 2:274.

7. Address at Cooper Institute, February 27, 1860, *Collected Works,* 3:543–44.

8. Quoted in First Inaugural Address, 1861, *Collected Works,* 4:263.

9. Ibid.

10. For discussion of the Fugitive Slave Act and the Compromise of 1850, see Stanley W. Campbell, *The Slave Catchers: The Enforcement of the Fugitive Slave Law, 1850–1860* (Chapel Hill, NC: University of North Carolina Press. 1968).

11. See Harold Holzer, Edna Greene Medford, and Frank Williams, *The Emancipation Proclamation: Three Views* (Baton Rouge: Louisiana State University Press. 2006), 6–9.

12. Three fugitives from a rebel master sought asylum at Fortress Monroe (Virginia) in late May 1861, claiming that they were about to be taken out of Virginia and employed against the Union. As commander of the fort, Butler declared the men "contraband of war" and set them to labor for the Union. "Benj. F. Butler to Lieut. Gen. Winfield Scott. May 24, 1861." *The War of the Rebellion: A Compilation of the Official Records of the Union and Confederate Armies* (hereinafter *O.R.*), 128 vols. (Washington: Government Printing Office, 1880–1901), ser. 2, 1:752.

13. Lieutenant Colonel Schuyler Hamilton to Brigadier General Irwin McDowell, Washington, July 16, 1861, *O.R.,* ser. 2, 1:760.

14. General Orders, No. 33, July 17, 1861, Headquarters Department of Washington, in *O.R.,* ser. 2, 1:760.

15. See Allen C. Guelzo, *Lincoln's Emancipation Proclamation: The End of Slavery in America* (New York: Simon and Schuster, 2004), 45.

16. Proclamation of John C. Frémont, August 30, 1861, *O.R.,* ser 1, 3:467.

17. To John C. Frémont, September 2, 1861, *Collected Works,* 4:506.

18. To Orville H. Browning, September 22, 1861, *Collected Works,* 4:531.

19. Ibid.

20. "Revocation of the Hunter Proclamation," *Collected Works,* 5:222.

21. Constance McLaughlin Green, *The Secret City: A History of Race Relations in the Nation's Capital* (Princeton: Princeton University Press, 1967), 33. At 1860, the total population of the District (including Washington and Georgetown) was just over 75,000.

22. Ibid., 59–60.

23. Message to Congress, March 6, 1862, *Collected Works,* 5:145.

24. Letter to Horace Greeley, March 24, 1862, *Collected Works,* 5:169.

25. Message to Congress, April 16, 1862, *Collected Works,* 5:192.

26. Ibid.

27. See Holzer, Medford and Williams, *The Emancipation Proclamation: Three Views,* 137–40.

28. To the Senate and House of Representatives, July 17, 1862, *Collected Works,* 5:329.

29. Ibid.

30. To Hon. James C. Conkling, August 26, 1863, *Collected Works,* 6:408.

31. The Final Emancipation Proclamation, *Collected Works,* 6:29. See also Daniel Farber, *Lincoln's Constitution* (Chicago: University of Chicago Press. 2003), 152–57.

32. To Hon. James C. Conkling, August 26, 1863, *Collected Works,* 6:409.

33. "Response to a Serenade," February 1, 1865, *Collected Works,* 8:255.

34. "Message to the Senate and House of Representatives," February 5, 1865, *Collected Works,* 8:261.

35. Letter to Horace Greeley, August 22, 1862, *Collected Works,* 5:388–89.

EDNA GREENE MEDFORD is associate Professor and director of Graduate Studies in the Department of History at Howard University. Specializing in nineteenth-century African American history, she also teaches both graduate and undergraduate courses in Civil War and Reconstruction, Colonial America, the Jacksonia's Era, and Comparative Slavery. She has published more than a dozen articles and book chapters on African Americans, especially during the one of the Civil War. Her publications include the coauthored work, *The Emancipation Proclamation: Three Views,* Baton Rouge: Louisiana State University Press, 2006.

From *OAH Magazine of History,* January 2007, pp. 19–21. Copyright © 2007 by Organization of American Historians. Reprinted by permission via the Copyright Clearance Center.

Steven Hahn Sings the Slaves Triumphant

The Pulitzer Prize–winning historian recasts the Civil War as a black revolt that forged African American activism.

GENE SANTORO

Steven Hahn contends that blacks played a more active role in bringing an end to slavery than historians generally recognize. Indeed, in his latest book, *The Political Worlds of Slavery and Freedom,* he characterizes the Civil War as "the greatest slave rebellion in modern history." He argues that some Northern black communities may have functioned like Haitian or Brazilian "maroons"—independent sites peopled and governed by runaway slaves that were vital to sustaining black political and military struggles for emancipation.

Why Do You Call the Civil War a Slave Rebellion?

It's true that there was no big bloody uprising, like in Haiti. But the Confederates had no confusion about what the slaves were doing—fleeing north, refusing to work, demanding wages and so on. It was rebellious behavior, and they wanted government intervention to put it down. In *Black Reconstruction,* W.E.B. Du Bois writes about the "general strike" among slaves. You don't have to be a Marxist like him to see that he was really saying slaves were important political actors in the Civil War.

What about the Abolitionist Movement?

The public still has this idea that, with the exception of Harriet Tubman, white people are rescuing black people. But historians have learned that the abolitionist movement was made chiefly of people of African descent. In the 1830s and 1840s in the Northern states, blacks had access to a public sphere of politics, and held conventions to press against discrimination and for political rights, which carried through the Civil War. They're the ones who subscribed to abolitionist newspapers. They set up

and staffed the Underground Railroad. They knew where to go in order to be hidden and protected, or get employment.

The abolitionist movement was chiefly people of African descent

What Made You Think Runaway Slaves Had a Key Role in All This?

In other slave societies, maroons, or runaway slave communities, establish independence, support revolts and become important politically. In the United States, it appeared that outside of Spanish Florida, the lower Mississippi and a few swamps, not much was going on that way. But then I started thinking about slavery and emancipation as a long national experience, not a sectional one, and I started to speculate.

How?

There were still slaves in the North at the time of the Civil War, even though they lived in states where theoretically slavery wasn't legal. Free blacks' status in the North could be contested; they could be kidnapped. Most people in the North, including Lincoln, supported the Fugitive Slave Law. So slavery was effectively legal everywhere. Then how do you think about the communities of African Americans in the Northern states? Historians write as if Northern and Southern blacks had little to do with each other, yet we know by the end of the antebellum period a lot of African Americans in the North were born in the

South. What if some of these communities were like maroons? The people in them were fugitives from slavery who had to arm and defend themselves against paramilitary invasions, just as maroon communities elsewhere did.

For Example?

In Lancaster County, Pa., in 1851, there was a shootout between around 100 blacks and a Maryland slaveowner who was looking for four runaway slaves with his son and friends and a U.S. marshal. This is the kind of situation where the maroon analogy makes sense. Here are black people across the Mason-Dixon line in Pennsylvania, collected among themselves out in a rural area. Many of them are fugitives from slavery. They are armed. They have networks of communication designed to alert them to trouble. The slaveowners get deputized by the federal government.

How Did Slaves Push Emancipation?

When the war starts, the federal government doesn't really have a policy about slavery. Lincoln goes out of his way to assure Southern slaveholders that he will not tamper with, as he puts it, a "domestic institution." He tells Southerners that as the Union Army is marching through, if they need help putting down slave rebellions, the army will do that. Now, part of the reason is that he knows Northern sentiment is divided and he doesn't want to be distracted from saving the Union. But slaves have their own ideas about what's going on, and they act by running away to Union camps. They have local intelligence: Where's the Union Army? What's going on? Initially, the Union side doesn't want them and sends them back, so it's a risky undertaking.

What Changes the Situation?

Fairly early on, the Union side learns that the Confederacy is using slave labor to build fortifications. So the logic becomes, if we send them back, they'll be used against us. All of a sudden they're declared contraband of war, which still acknowledges they're property. But little by little, as the Union Army moves into the deeper South, slaves come in the hundreds and thousands. As the war drags on, they realize that black labor and, eventually, 200,000 black Union soldiers, will be important in saving the Union. So slavery becomes destabilized by what the slaves did.

How Does This Shape the Emancipation Proclamation?

Most people think it just establishes the idea of freedom and frees slaves in areas where the Union Army isn't. But they forget about the provision allowing blacks to enlist. This is a huge and amazing move, very different from the preliminary proclamation Lincoln issued in September 1862. Because of African-American participation in the war, they were in a position to make claims afterward about citizenship and equality.

How Did All This Change America?

The Civil War completed the Revolutionary period's nation-building process. Look at the world of the 1850s. The sovereignty of the federal government was in dispute and local sovereignties were emphasized. There was a nativist movement looking to deprive growing numbers of immigrants of any political rights. Then look at the country in the late 1860s and 1870s, where you have the Reconstruction amendments, when the idea of national citizenship for the first time comes into being, when you begin a massive process of enfranchisement after a decade and a half of disfranchisement, including women's suffrage. Obviously this process was painfully slow, and met with serious pushbacks all along the way. But if the war had ended in an armistice instead of unconditional surrender, none of this would have happened for much longer. Slavery might have continued deep into the 20th century.

How Does Barack Obama Fit into This Picture?

Obama is clearly part of a new segment of African descent in the United States. As immigration laws changed in the 1960s and 1970s, more people from Africa and the Caribbean came here, some with a good deal of education and resources. He's also the product of the civil rights movement and affirmative action, which really contributed to the growth of a black middle class. That segment of the black population is much more integrated with other groups. So his election is a tribute to what the struggle for civil rights accomplished, but it could also reemphasize class distinctions. He is going to run into problems with African Americans who expect a lot of things from him, which as president of the entire country, he won't be able to deliver.

A Slave's Audacious Bid for Freedom

DAVID W. BLIGHT

Mobile, Alabama, August 1864

One hot summer day in wartime Mobile, a city garrisoned by 10,000 Confederate troops, 17-year-old Wallace Turnage was driving his owner's carriage along Dauphin Street in the crowded business district when a worn harness broke, flipping the vehicle on its side. Thrown to the ground, Turnage narrowly avoided the crushing wheels of a passing streetcar. The stunned teenager shook himself off, then set off for the house of his owner, the rich merchant Collier Minge. Turnage was no stranger to hardship: he had already been sold three times, losing contact with his family. Ugly scars on his torso bore witness to many severe beatings and even torture. Yet his life was about to get even worse before it got better.

Born in Green County near Snow Hill, North Carolina, Turnage, the son of a 15-year-old slave woman named Courtney and an 18-year-old white man, Sylvester Brown Turnage, was thus one of the nearly quarter million slave children of mixed race in the 1850s, many the products of forced sexual unions. In the spring of 1860, Turnage's indebted owner had sold the 13-year-old for $950 to Hector Davis, a slave trader in Richmond, Virginia, leaving the boy to survive as best he could, orphaned in a dangerous and tyrannical world. One of Richmond's richest dealers in human property, Davis owned a three-story slave jail and auction house. By one estimate, slave traders in Richmond during the late 1850s netted $4 million per year (approximately $70 million in 2008 dollars). Davis often sold nearly $15,000 worth of slaves per week.

For the next several months, Turnage prepared his fellows in the "dressing room" for the auction floor. One day he himself was told to climb up on the block and sold to an Alabama planter, James Chalmers, for $1,000. Three days later he found himself on a large cotton plantation near Pickensville, Alabama, close to the Mississippi line.

It was mid-1860, a pivotal election year during which the American union was dissolving under slavery's westward expansion. Now a field slave, the young man had to adapt to another alien environment, falling prey to fear, violence, and loneliness. After several whippings, he ran away for the first of five times.

In the aftermath of the Civil War, Turnage wrote an extraordinary narrative, only recently discovered, of his path to freedom. In beautiful, if untutored and unedited prose, Turnage described a runaway's horrific struggle for survival. His fight with the slave system was one desperate collision after another, amidst the double savagery of slavery and war. Each of the first four times that he broke for liberty, he crossed the Mississippi line and headed north along the Mobile and Ohio Railroad, yearning, as he wrote, "to get home," which for him must have vaguely meant North Carolina. Each escape had been prompted by a violent encounter with an overseer. On one occasion, when the overseer approached him with a cowhide whip ready, Turnage stood his ground, "spoke very saucy," and fought long and hard, his foe nearly biting off his ear. For this resistance he was pushed facedown on the ground, his hands tied to a tree, and given 95 lashes.

During one bid for freedom, he traveled some 80 miles across the war-ravaged country, hiding among fencerows and gullies. Taken in by other slaves, betrayed by one couple, chased and mauled by bloodhounds, he struggled to outlast winter cold, starvation, and Confederate patrols. One sadistic slave-catcher, who held him in a cabin until his owner arrived, pistol-whipped and stabbed him, then pitched him into a burning fireplace in a drunken rage. Locked in neck chains and, at times, wrist chains attached to other fugitives, Turnage learned the logic of terror but also somehow summoned the strength never to surrender to his own dehumanization.

For all the miseries and dislocation of war, Turnage remained far too valuable for Chalmers to let escape. But after the fourth runaway in early 1863, the cotton planter sold him at the slave jail in Mobile, where he fetched the robust price of $2,000. Turnage labored in Mobile as a jack-of-all-trades house slave for the Minge family over the next 15 months until that August day in 1864 when the carriage flipped.

When Turnage arrived at the Minge house with news of the ruined carriage, his mistress excoriated him. He "got angry and spoke very short with her," and then fled "down into the city of Mobile," where for a week he "wandered from one house to another where I had friends." Hiding in haylofts and sheds, Turnage was discovered one day in a stable by a "rebel policeman" who pressed a cocked pistol to his breast. Dragged by the neck to the "whipping house," Turnage was soon confronted by his master, who ordered him stripped, strung up by his wrists on the wall, subjected to 30 savage lashes with a device "three leathers thick," and then told to walk home. On the way back, he took a different turn and simply walked out of Mobile, striding at dusk through a huge Confederate encampment, undoubtedly mistaken for a black camp hand.

For the next three weeks, Turnage traversed the snake- and alligator-infested swamps of the Foul River estuary, moving 25 laborious miles along the western shore of Mobile Bay, where on August 5, Adm. David Farragut's fleet won the largest naval battle of the Civil War. Turnage remembered seeing warships in the distance and hearing guns. In fear and desperate hunger, he crossed the Dog and Deer rivers, then somehow swam the fearsome Foul River, where he was "troubled all day with snakes." Today this extensive, beautiful wetland offers a gentle yet forbidding waterscape; alligators crawl in their wallows, laughing gulls squawk everywhere as delta grass—"broom sage" to Turnage—sways waist-high in the summer breeze.

After reaching Cedar Point, the southern tip of the mainland, he could make out the stars and stripes flying above a Union-occupied island fort. He made a "hiding place in the ditch" to protect himself from the swamp water and ducked Confederate patrols, growing "so impatient seeing the free country in view and I still in the slave country." The sun may have been blinding and his body all but spent, but Turnage's choices were clear: "It was death to go back and it was death to stay there and freedom was before me; it could only be death to go forward if I was caught and freedom if I escaped." This timeless expression of the human will to choose freedom at whatever risk manifests itself in most slave narratives.

Turnage was a desperate hero. After praying especially hard one night, he discovered that the tide had swept in an old rowboat, as if "held by an invisible hand." Grabbing a "piece of board," he began to row the rickety craft into the waves of Mobile Bay. A "squall" bore down on him, "the water like a hill coming with a white cap on it." Just as the heavy seas struck his boat, he heard "the crash of oars and behold there was eight Yankees in a boat." Turnage jumped into the Union craft just as his own vessel capsized. For a few long moments the oarsmen "were struck with silence" as they contemplated the gaunt young man crouched in front of them. Looking back to the shore, he could see two Confederate soldiers glaring after him. As the liberators' boat bounced on the waves, he inhaled his first breaths of freedom.

The Yankees took him to the sand island fort, wrapped him in a blanket, fed him, and gave him a tent to sleep in for the night—likely the first acts of kindness he had ever experienced from white people. The next day they took him in a skiff to Fort Gaines on Dauphine Island, the long sandbar at the mouth of Mobile Bay. In that fortress, whose cannon-crowned brick walls stand intact to this day, Turnage was interviewed by Gen. Gordon Granger, commander of all Union forces in the Mobile region, who was eager for intelligence about the city, which he hoped soon to capture. Granger offered Turnage the choice of enlisting in a newly raised black regiment as a soldier or becoming a servant to a white officer. Turnage opted for the job of mess cook for one Capt. Junius Turner of a Maryland regiment, whom he accompanied to the end of the war, marching into Mobile with the Union army in April 1865.

Sometime shortly after the war he traveled to North Carolina and retrieved his mother and four half-siblings. He moved to New York City, struggled to make a living as a common laborer, and managed to keep his family together until he died in 1916. He was married three times, losing his first two wives at a young age, and fathered seven children, only three of whom survived infancy under the grueling hardships of the black urban poor.

His memoir's final paragraph is a stunning, prayerful statement about the meaning of freedom.

Sometime in the 1880s, gripped by the dogged desire to be remembered, Turnage put down his narrative, which comes to an abrupt end after his dramatic escape at sea and liberation. But the final paragraph is a stunning, prayerful articulation of natural rights and the meaning of freedom: "I had made my escape with safety after such a long struggle and had obtained that freedom which I desired so long. I now dreaded the gun and handcuffs and pistols no more. Nor the blowing of horns and the running of hounds; nor the threats of death from the rebels' authority. I could now speak my opinion to men of all grades and colors, and no one to question my right to speak." As one of the "many thousands gone" prophesied in the old slave spiritual, Wallace Turnage crafted his own emancipation hymn.

How the West Was Lost

CHRIS SMALLBONE

At the beginning of the nineteenth century the United States neither owned, valued nor even knew much about the Great Plains. This vast tract of grassland which runs across the centre of the continent was described as the 'Great American Desert', but by the end of the century the United States had taken it over completely. As the 'new Americans' (many of them black) pushed the frontier to the west, they established their culture at the expense of that of the indigenous peoples, then known to the incomers as 'Indians'.

The great natural resource of the Plains was the buffalo, which migrated in vast herds. The peoples of the Great Plains hunted and ate the buffalo, made tepees from their hides and utilized most other parts to make tools, utensils and weaponry. Some of them, for example the Mandan and Pawnee, lived in semi-permanent villages; others, like the Lakota and Cheyenne, lived a nomadic life. When necessary, as in life or death situations of war or in securing food in the hunt or moving camp they could be very organized and disciplined, but normally life was very loosely structured. Different peoples or nations were distinguished by language or dialect and in variations of customs and beliefs. But all depended upon nature for survival and had a spiritual approach to it.

Before the arrival of the new Americans the native groups were often in conflict with neighbouring peoples for resources such as horses and land. The latter resulted in some movement in their patterns of settlement. Thus, the Cheyenne and Arapaho had divided into northern and southern groups in the 1820s. Some Cheyenne and Arapaho moved south, following reports of large numbers of wild horses and vast buffalo herds in the land south of the Platte River, while others remained north of the Platte near the Black Hills where they effectively became a separate group, closely allied with the Lakota. Other peoples, such as the Pawnee, Crow and Arikara (or Rees), had become enemies of the Lakota when supplanted by them earlier in the century. The northern Cheyenne and Arapaho were an exception, most other peoples in the northern Plains were enemies of the Lakota. Indeed the name for them adopted by the new Americans, Sioux, was the Ojibwe word for enemy. In the mid-eighteenth century the Lakota had moved gradually westwards from what was to be Minnesota, defeating other peoples as they went and pushing them into new hunting grounds.

In 1840, when the Oregon Trail from Independence, Missouri to the Pacific was first used, the frontier of the United States was roughly at the line of the Mississippi-Missouri, only about one third of the way across the continent. Just two generations later, by 1890, the indigenous peoples had been supplanted and the western frontier no longer existed. Apart from one or two later additions, today's map of the United States was firmly in place.

To understand how this took place one needs to step outside the strict chronology of the events. The new Americans split the Plains environment and those who depended upon it into two. This began in the 1840s with the overland trails to Oregon and California, initiating the age of the Wagon Train, and was cemented by the completion of the transcontinental and Kansas Pacific Railroads in the late 1860s. A series of treaties were signed, confining the native Americans to ever-smaller areas, and every opportunity was taken for incursion into these areas by prospectors, hunters, and settlers, supported by soldiers.

Even before the trails were opened, trading posts were established at key communications points, such as at the confluence of the North Platte and Laramie rivers in Wyoming, where fur traders Robert Campbell and William Sublette built Fort William in 1834. In 1849 it was bought by the US military to protect and supply emigrants travelling the Oregon Trail and renamed Fort Laramie. In the early 1840s relationships between the travellers and the native Americans on the trail had been good, but as the decade wore on relations became more tense, especially as numbers of the emigrants escalated with the California Gold Rush in 1849. Numbers of those seeking a quick fortune far exceeded those steadier individuals who wished to raise crops in the western coastlands of Oregon and California. As these numbers increased so did incidents between the two cultures. The settlement of the Plains did not become a problem for the native Americans until later, especially in the post-Civil War expansionist mood, when the 'sodbusters' were spurred on by the offer of free land through the Homestead Act of 1862. In the late 1840s the concern for the native Americans was that traffic down the Oregon Trail was keeping the buffalo from their traditional habitat in this area. As the numbers of incidents increased the government sought to alleviate the problem by attempting to keep the native Americans away from the trail. In doing so they used a method already used to legitimize riding roughshod over the eastern native Americans: the Treaty.

The various treaties between the US and the indigenous peoples of the west were of as little value as they had been in the east. In 1851 the US Indian agent Thomas Fitzpatrick invited all of the peoples of the Plains to a meeting in the vicinity of Fort Laramie. It was attended by members of the Lakota (Sioux), Cheyenne, Arapaho, Shoshone, Assiniboine, Crow, Mandan, Hidatsa, and Arikara nations. All these peoples still ranged widely across the central Plains, whereas the Comanche and the Kiowa, who did not attend the Fort Laramie meeting, were far in the south, in the vicinity of the Santa Fe Trail, and a separate treaty was signed at Fort Atkinson with them two years later.

By the 1851 Treaty of Fort Laramie, the government bound 'themselves to protect the aforesaid Indian nations against the commission of all depredations by the people of the said United States' and promised annuity goods for fifty years (later amended by the Senate to fifteen years). The native American chiefs guaranteed safe passage for settlers along the Platte River, and accepted responsibility for the behaviour of their followers in specified territories and recognized 'the right of the United States government to establish roads, military and other posts'. However, military posts already existed on the Oregon Trail: Fort Kearny had already been established in Nebraska as a stopping-off point and garrison in 1848, Fort Bridger in Wyoming as a fur-trading post in 1843, as well as Fort Laramie itself. Nor was the United States army a disciplined force: as emigrant William Kelley commented on the troops at Fort Kearny:

A most unsoldierly looking lot they were: unshaven, unshorn, with patched uniforms and a lounging gait. The privates being more particular in their inquiries after whiskey, for which they offered one dollar the half-pint; but we had none to sell them even at that tempting price.

It is not surprising that conflicts arose with native Americans.

Also, noble words meant little when the arbiters of 'justice' attempted to mete it out in a summary manner. Only three years after the treaty, Lieutenant Grattan attempted to bully Conquering Bear's Lakota into giving up a visitor who was accused of helping himself to a lame cow. His troops were annihilated, which led to retaliatory action by the Army, when any available native Americans were punished, regardless of whether they had been involved in the original action. This approach reflected the Army's attitude generally, as indeed had Grattan's action in the first place.

However little value could be placed on the promises in the treaties, their terms stand as clear indicators of the new Americans perceptions of how to deal with what they called the 'Indian Problem', at any one point. The Treaty of 1851 was an attempt to protect travellers on the Oregon Trail, which had become of high importance as a result of the discovery of gold in California in 1848. However, the commitment to protecting 'Indian nations' from 'depredations' by US citizens was of far lower priority to the new Americans and was never properly enforced.

Similarly in a treaty signed in 1861 at Fort Lyon in the southern Plains, the Cheyenne promised to remain in the vicinity of the Arkansas River and not to interfere with the gold-miners along the Smoky Hill Trail from Kansas City to Denver attracted to the area from 1858 onwards. Yet only three years later, in November 1864, an estimated 200 peaceful men, women and children of the Southern Cheyenne and Arapaho were massacred by the Third Colorado Regiment of volunteers and regular troops at Sand Creek. The leader of the outrage, John Chivington, fed the bloodlust of his troops, and was fond of the chilling phrase which rationalized the killing of infants: 'Nits make Lice'.

The idea of limiting to set areas peoples accustomed to a free-ranging existence following their source of life—the buffalo herds—was as unrealistic as it was racist. The concept of the native Americans' land being restricted to a reservation dated from the earliest treaties, and was consolidated in the 'removal' of eastern peoples into Indian Territory (later Oklahoma) in the 1830s under the direction of President Andrew Jackson. The National Park concept is generally credited to artist George Catlin, known for his paintings of native Americans. In 1832 he advocated that the wilderness might be preserved, 'by some great protecting policy of government . . . in a magnificent park . . . A nation's Park, containing man and beast, in all the wild and freshness of their nature's beauty!' In 1864, Congress donated Yosemite Valley to California for preservation as a state park. The second great Park, Yellowstone, was founded in 1872, during the presidency of Ulysses S. Grant, who developed an 'Indian Peace Policy' at this time which aimed to 'civilize' them. By 1876 this policy had increased the number of houses seven-fold, the acres under cultivation sixfold, the ownership of livestock by fifteen times, and tripled the number of teachers and schools. The concept of the reservation was surely similar to that of National Parks and as such was recognition that the new Americans saw the native Americans as no more or less significant than the flora and fauna.

The native Americans unleashed a robust raiding campaign in response to the massacre at Sand Creek which interfered with the US government's wish to expand and consolidate economically after of the Civil War (1862-65). The Union-Pacific and Kansas-Pacific railroads were built across the Plains in the 1860s. To confine the Southern Cheyenne and Arapaho and to protect the settlers, travellers, railroad workers and miners, the US government perceived the need for another treaty later in the decade and despatched a 'Peace Commission'. This resulted in the treaty of Medicine Lodge Creek, signed in 1867 between the US Army and 5,000 Southern Cheyenne, Arapaho, Comanche, Kiowa and Kiowa-Apache. Under its terms the indigenous peoples gave up their claims to 90 million acres in return for reservations in central Indian Territory (Oklahoma). Yet just four years later, after a method of tanning the buffalo hides to produce a good-quality leather was developed, the buffalo-hunters moved in. They annihilated the buffalo, in a wasteful and devastating manner, in a few short years. In 1872-73 three million buffalo perished and by 1874 the hunters had moved so far south that the Treaty of Medicine Lodge Creek was a dead letter. All the land given to the Cheyenne and Arapaho had been stripped of the buffalo on which they depended. This was recognized by General Philip Sheridan when he said of the buffalo hunters:

These men have done (more) in the last two years, and will do more in the next year to settle the vexed Indian question, than the entire regular army has done in the last thirty years.

The sorry remnants of the Southern Cheyenne and Arapaho united with the Comanche and Kiowa, and fought back in a last-ditch attempt at resistance: the Red River War (1874-75). Now without the animal that had long been their prime source of existence, they were harried and starved into submission. They were encircled in the Texas Panhandle by five columns of troops, who came at the native Americans from all directions, keeping them on the move, giving them no rest. The troops burned and destroyed whatever possessions they left behind, including tepees and winter food stores, as they hastily withdrew their families to safety. A small group of a few dozen warriors still roaming free despite constant harassment came into Forts Sill and Reno in Oklahoma in 1875, where they were humiliated, and seventy-one men and one woman, many indiscriminately chosen, were transported to prison in Miami, Fort Marion.

As the land available to the native Americans shrank, some chiefs refused to accept this and fought back against the Army. This allowed the new Americans to claim that the native American leaders could not control their followers and any agreements were therefore broken. This development supported the new American claim to Manifest Destiny whereby they justified their behaviour as the act of 'taming' a savage wilderness. Later commentators refined this argument to suggest that the native Americans had no cultural tradition of commitment to a permanent system of leadership and government.

It was undoubtedly true that the indigenous peoples functioned with loose social structures based on respect being given to an individual based on their qualities rather than on the office they hold, with no lasting obligation to follow their leaders' directives. However, the new Americans did not show themselves to be any more committed to acting upon agreements or attempting to enforce the rule of law. For as long as the land was seen as a useless desert, the new Americans were content to leave it to the native Americans. However, as soon as something of value was discovered—usually precious metals but, also the buffalo once the market had been established for their hides—the new Americans themselves violated the treaties with impunity. Thus when buffalo-hunters went to Fort Dodge in 1872 to ask if they could hunt south of the Cimarron, thereby violating the Treaty of Medicine Lodge Creek, Colonel Irving Dodge had replied,

Boys, if I were a buffalo hunter, I would hunt where the buffalo are.

While in the southern Plains the native Americans were driven south, confined to ever-smaller areas and ultimately defeated, those in the north were more successful at repelling the invaders in the short term. The Lakota were themselves usurpers, for they had moved into the northern Plains in the late eighteenth century from the north and displaced peoples such as the Crow, Pawnee and Arikara, who remained so hostile to them that they proved willing to ally with the Army against the Lakota. As in the south, miners moved into the area, despite the Treaty of 1851 and this resulted in armed conflict. When gold was discovered in Virginia City, Montana, in 1862, Forts Phil Kearney and C.F. Smith were built to protect miners using the Bozeman Trail taking them north from the Oregon Trail. Helped by Crazy Horse, the Lakota chief Red Cloud led his Lakota

and Northern Cheyenne warriors in a war in the Powder Valley of Wyoming in 1866-68 which culminated in these forts being evacuated and burned. A second Treaty of Fort Laramie (1868) followed, very much on terms dictated by the native Americans which reaffirmed the principles set out in the earlier treaty of 1851. It granted the Lakota a large area in Dakota including the Black Hills, important for hunting, a source of lodge poles and an area sacred to them: the US army withdrew from the forts they had built and they were burned by the exuberant Lakota and northern Cheyenne.

Yet the advantage was to be short-lived; once again the discovery of gold by an expedition led by George Armstrong Custer in 1874, was to result in the rules being rewritten. Attempts to hoodwink the native Americans into selling the Black Hills in 1875 met with a rebuff: commissioners were told by Red Cloud that the asking price was $600,000,000, a figure so far in excess of the Commissioners' valuation that it rendered negotiation futile. Tactics rehearsed in the southern Plains were now re-enacted in the north. Lakota and Northern Cheyenne were given notice to 'come in' to Fort Robinson in Nebraska: those not doing so would be deemed 'hostile'. Three encircling columns under Generals Gibbon, Crook and Terry were assembled to harry and destroy. However, the Lakota chose to fight. This surprised the arrogant Custer who commanded Terry's troops but who underestimated his foe and chose to ride the glory trail in defiance of all logic. In the south the tactics of relentless pursuit had worked, not because of fatalities experienced by the native Americans, but because when their homes were attacked the priority of the warriors was to get their families to safety. Their abandoned possessions could then be commandeered or destroyed. The choice of Custer fitted with the expectation that the Lakota and northern Cheyenne would try to escape as had happened in the south. In September 1867 he had been court-martialled for deserting his command, ordering deserters to be shot, damaging army horses, failing to pursue Indians attacking his escort and not recovering bodies of soldiers killed by Indians; but it was his reckless direct approach appealed to his superiors.

However the Lakota and their allies proved more than a match for their enemies. At the battle against General Crook at the Rosebud River in June 1876, it was only a rearguard action fought by a Crow contingent supporting the Army which enabled General Crook to withdraw, and ten days later Custer's force was wiped out at the Little Big Horn by Lakota and Northern Cheyenne warriors.

When the news of Custer's defeat hit the newsstands in the east, the country was in the midst of centenary celebrations. A shocked nation recoiled; public opinion hardened and resources were found to put more troops in the field. The victors of the Little Big Horn were driven north into Canada.

While in most cases incursions onto land 'granted' to the native Americans in both areas was linked in both northern and southern Plains to the discovery of gold, the eventual supplanting of groups in the south was not. Here it was as a result of the native Americans fighting back after their source of life, the buffalo, had been decimated on the very land that had been promised to them less than a decade previously. The defeat in the south came at the end of a long line of losses that followed each discovery by the new Americans that the land of the Great Plains was not as useless as they had first thought. The native Americans were driven south by the slaughter of the buffalo. The buffalo had been wiped out by 1878 in the south, and two years later the hunters moved in on the northern herd, protected by the post-Little Big Horn US military campaign against the victors. By 1884 few buffalo remained, and in 1885 they were virtually extinct. On the northern Plains, although the Lakota and their allies achieved some military successes, they were ultimately to suffer the same fate: the loss of land promised to them. They were driven further away from the heart of the Great Plains. The Oregon Trail and the railroad which carried travellers, information and goods to link east and west of the nation, was also the dividing line between north and south for the vast buffalo herd and the native Americans who relied on them.

The result for all native Americans of Plains was the same: confinement on reservations. A law was passed in 1871 which formally ended the practice of treaties which had considered the native Americans to be separate nations from the United States. Native American culture was undermined by the practice of removing young children from their families to be 'educated' in residential schools where they were beaten if they spoke their native tongue. Finally in 1887 a law was passed under which the president of the United States was given the power to divide up the reservations, which resulted in another boom-time for the land speculators. Gold, the bison and protecting travellers provided short term reasons for conflict, but ultimately in the clash of cultures, as Red Cloud, Oglala Lakota, observed:

> The white man made us many promises, more than I can ever remember, but they never kept but one; they promised to take our land and they took it.

This article first appeared in *History Today,* April 2006, pp. 42–49. Copyright © 2006 by History Today, Ltd. Reprinted by permission.

Creating a Military Image: Lincoln as Commander in Chief

WILLIAM C. DAVIS

O f the many eternal questions that surround Abraham Lincoln, surely one of the most pertinent must be the matter of how this civilian, unschooled and inexperienced in war, managed to build and then successfully lead the largest military establishment yet seen on the planet. How did he create an army from virtually nothing, and having done that, how did he keep men volunteering in their hundreds of thousands year after weary year, and sustain their will to see the war through to the end? Like so many questions surrounding the sixteenth president, the answers seem to lie more in the basic makeup of the man rather than in preparation or experience. They reveal once again, as in innumerable instances throughout history that great leadership is not learned, but comes from inner and often instinctive gifts honed unconsciously by life's daily successes and failures. No president had more or better preparation for the White House than Lincoln's predecessor James Buchanan, and yet he holds an unassailable claim to being among the worst chief executives in our history. Buchanan's successor, by contrast, had less preparation than all but a few of his fellow presidents, and yet he is consistently judged to be the greatest of them all.

When Lincoln took office, he inherited not only a crisis, but also a military that was woefully unprepared to deal with that crisis. America had no real professional military tradition. The Revolution had been fought entirely by volunteers. The second war with Britain in 1812–1815 saw the United States Army number barely 6,000, and again the young nation relied on volunteers, half a million of them, and even then the American forces were disintegrating when peace came. The war with Mexico in 1846–1848 was also fought overwhelmingly by volunteers who augmented a well-trained but small professional military. The volunteer ethic was firmly ingrained in the American character, north and south alike, when the new crisis came, yet there was no national militia system in place so that Washington could summon volunteers from the states directly. If the nation needed men quickly, it must depend on the sufferance and good will of the governors to raise state volunteers to loan to the nation. It was a process born out of the jealously guarded privileges of the states and the basically frugal "small government" ethos of young America, but it was hardly a process capable of dealing expeditiously with a major crisis, especially when a third of those governors would be hostile to that government.

Lincoln meets with General George B. McClellan in a carefully decorated tent near Antietam, Maryland, October 4, 1862. (Image courtesy of Library of Congress, LC-B8171-7948.)

Lincoln's actual schooling for confronting this conundrum was nothing more than that of any other rural American youth of his time. Like most schoolboys, he was interested in soldiers and soldiering. Even rural Kentucky and southern Indiana had enough Revolutionary veterans to sustain circulation of an oral history of the war for independence, and his father Thomas could remind his son that grandfather Abraham Lincoln had fought with the Continentals. Lincoln himself was almost 5 years old when the second war with Britain ended, and surely the child Lincoln was at least conscious that his country was at war, especially since forty regiments of Kentuckians went off to that war, and Kentuckians made up almost two-thirds of all American volunteers killed in that conflict.

More to the point, among young Lincoln's first readings was Mason Locke Weems's *The Life of Washington,* published in the year of Lincoln's birth. Half a century later, even as he was on his way to face his greatest test, Lincoln thought back to Weems. "I remember all the accounts there given of the battle fields and struggles for the liberties of the country," he told the New Jersey Senate on February 21, 1861. "There must have been something more than common that those men struggled for".[1] That feeling never left him, nor did the lessons of Weems's book of patriotic homilies. They venerated not just Washington, but also the American volunteer, weaving the leader and the led inextricably into a fabric patterned by duty and self-sacrifice. Washington stirred the patriotism and won the respect of the volunteers, and they in turn gave their time, their suffering, and their lives. As he made his way to Washington in 1861, Lincoln understood that he would have to do the same.

It helped, perhaps, that Lincoln had some fleeting personal experience of the volunteer soldier. He enlisted twice in militia units during the Black Hawk War of 1832. He never saw action, but he did help find the bodies of five men slain by the Indians, seeing first-hand the price a volunteer could pay. As a captain of his small company, he also saw the nature of the volunteer soldier—unruly, undisciplined, sometimes insubordinate, at best a civilian on loan to the military. When some of his men got drunk, Lincoln was himself punished for failing to maintain discipline, and soon afterward he was punished again for failing to follow orders.[2] He learned precious little about planning a war, but gained invaluable insights into the mind of the kind of men he would have to call upon in 1861.

Lincoln's practical military experience, miniscule as it was, ceased in 1832, and for almost 30 years afterward he had almost no opportunity to practice or develop the managerial skills necessary to equip him for the challenge of 1861. His fleeting efforts to run rural mercantile establishments failed miserably. Thereafter as a circuit riding attorney he had no one to manage except himself until, by the 1850s, he became a leading member of the Illinois bar and could employ a law clerk. But still, there were few demands that required him, as an executive, to bring men and resources together. Not until his run up to the senatorial contest in 1858 against Stephen Douglas did he have to coordinate the work of others, make decisions about advisors, weigh issues and audiences, and set priorities that affected anything more than his own day-to-day family and professional life. But through all those years, with an active and growing practice, and as he became more and more immersed in state and then national politics, he found himself required to make judgments about men—whom to trust, who had valuable skills in spite of character or personality shortcomings, and perhaps most valuable of all, how to subordinate his own pride and ego to the greater good of securing his aims. None of this told him a thing about how to raise an army or move soldiers around the landscape, but it did gain him invaluable experience in how to "read" the experienced soldiers he would one day need to do those things for him.

Thus, as he took his oath of office in 1861, Abraham Lincoln had the experience to understand some important truths. He found a Regular Army numbering barely over 13,000, spread among 200 army posts from Maine to California. If he had to raise an army and fight to hold the Union together, he would have to depend overwhelmingly on volunteers; there simply not being time to raise and train a professional army. He knew Americans would volunteer at their leaders' call, but he also knew from observation that they could not be taken for granted. They would suffer the boredom of camp and field, and they would fight and even die, but only so long as they believed they were accomplishing something worthwhile. They would follow officers they respected or feared, but rank itself did not awe them. Discipline and blind obedience were foreign to them. In donning uniforms they would not surrender their right to voice their views. Above all, they had to believe in their leaders and their cause, or they would just go home.

Lincoln was always a quick study, and throughout the war he included works on military strategy among the journals and newspapers that were his primary reading, though his suggestions and active involvement in strategic matters always showed the simplicity and directness that characterized him even before the war came. More than that, however, he grasped that—like Weems's Washington—he had to be a leader to every segment of the population. Thus while he would spend a great deal of time closeted with war ministers and generals, he showed that he had learned well the lesson of his early reading in Weems that a leader must first have the personal loyalty of his army. Lincoln's instinct told him that a starting point toward that objective was visibility. After the firing on Fort Sumter and Lincoln's first call for 75,000 volunteers to put down the rebellion, he personally met thousands of the arriving volunteers in the streets of Washington, at the railroad depot, and at boat landings. Often he had his wife Mary with him, and sometimes his young sons, too, displaying the First Family to young volunteers whom he would soon be calling his "boys" as well. Lincoln understood intuitively that merely seeing a president was a memorable experience, especially for these farm boys. It gave the volunteers a face to put to the cause, and Lincoln accurately gauged the effect. "He looks like a good honest man," a Rhode Island volunteer wrote on June 24, 1861, after marching past the president, "and I trust that with God's help he can bring our country safely out of its peril".[3] Every soldier who saw the president, or spoke with him, or heard him speak, was likely to go off to war an ambassador for the president. As for Lincoln, every face he saw enhanced his understanding of the men he was to lead, and gave him the confidence he needed that he could succeed if they all did their job.

For the rest of the war Lincoln kept himself before his soldiers whenever he felt it would be to good effect. Significantly, he did not appear much in public before civilian audiences. He made only a few public addresses, and rarely left Washington. He relied on his published public letters and his supporters in Congress and the state houses to sustain civilian morale. And he relied on his armies achieving successes that, in their turn, would be the most potent civilian morale builders of all. Thus it was that Lincoln would never during the course of the war visit his major armies west of the Appalachians. Under leaders like U.S. Grant, William T. Sherman and George Thomas, they made their own morale by an almost unbroken chain of victories stretching from Fort Donelson in February 1862 right to the end in 1865. Thus, too, in managing his commanders, when a general was active and engaged, Lincoln left him alone, intruding only occasionally to offer aid or an idea, but deferring always to the general's own judgment. Only the troubled commanders were to see and hear from Lincoln often, and again more to offer aid and encouragement than criticism.

Unfortunately, there was one army and series of commanders who needed a great deal of attention, and it was symbolically the most important of all. Lincoln's first army, the one he raised in April and May of 1861 in Virginia, went off to defeat in the Battle of First Bull Run on July 21. The fault lay not in the men or their commanders, but in the newness of it all, the rush that did not allow proper training and equipping, the unrealistic expectations born of inexperience, and simple bad luck. Lincoln himself was out in the streets of Washington as the defeated men streamed back into the capital. Repeatedly he told them that this had not been their fault. The blame lay with him and his administration, and he promised he would not let them down again. Defeat was humiliating enough. Lincoln understood that if he could shift the blame to his own shoulders, it would make the burden of defeat for his soldiers a little lighter. And he gave them hope. "We certainly needed some encouragement," wrote a private of the 2d Wisconsin after Lincoln's visit to his regiment. "There was stamped on his face a fresh, vigorous, healthy and courageous outlook that inspired confidence".[4]

For the next two years it would be the misfortune of the army, soon to be dubbed the Army of the Potomac, to endure a succession of commanders unequal to the task before them, a task made the more difficult by the fact that they faced the finest army and commander the Confederacy had, in Robert E. Lee and the Army of Northern Virginia. When George B. McClellan proved unable to handle the responsibility of army command, Lincoln relieved him of that command in the fall of 1862, even though "Little Mac" was inordinately popular with the soldiers. But Lincoln gauged his timing well, and waited until he felt that his own popularity with the men, coupled with their frustration at McClellan's inactivity, would be enough for him to weather any protest, as indeed it was. McClellan's successors, first Ambrose Burnside, and then Joseph Hooker, were each allowed one defeat before Lincoln replaced them, too, and with no outcry from the soldiers, for by this time generals could come and go, but they were Lincoln's soldiers, and now in words borrowed from a song they called him "Father Abraham."

Then George G. Meade took command in the summer of 1863 and turned back Lee's invasion of the north at Gettysburg. Lincoln at last had a general who could give him victories and use his army as a tool to sustain morale in the field as well as at home. When Lincoln brought Grant east to assume overall command of Union armies, he had many motives. One of them was to bring Grant's luster as the north's most successful general to the eastern theater. The western armies did not miss a pace with Grant gone, and while Meade, a winning general, still directly commanded the Potomac army, Grant brought enormous prestige and moral force to bear against Lee. Grant's promotion lent

renewed confidence to the soldiers in the field and to the civilians at home whose support Lincoln still needed to finish a job still far from done.

Through it all, Lincoln allowed an unprecedented accessibility. There was virtually an open door at the White House. Some days lines of people simply formed and Lincoln met them one by one, and many of them were soldiers. Some came with a petition, others simply wanted to shake the hand of the president, and Lincoln fully understood the value of those brief minutes with his "boys." "I feel—though the tax on my time is heavy—that no hours of my day are better employed than those which thus bring me again within direct contact and atmosphere of the average of our whole people," he told his staff. "The do not want much, and they get very little".[5]

In eloquent illustration of the egalitarian spirit of the volunteers, they felt perfectly at liberty to ask Lincoln in person or by letter for whatever favors they thought he might grant. He often told the soldiers to bring their problems to him, and they took him at his word. He wrote letters for them, contacted relatives, got furloughs for sick men, and responded to parents' pleas to give fatherly advice to their sons in uniform. In a military establishment that all told enlisted about two million men during the war, the president's direct intervention in soldier concerns was miniscule in terms of numbers. He had interviews with about 2,000 soldiers in the White House, and perhaps intervened personally by letter in several hundred other instances. Yet here again, as with the 100,000 or more who saw him personally in Washington or when he reviewed the Army of the Potomac, every one of these instances created another ambassador. Every happy applicant for a furlough, every soldier who shook the president's hand in the White House, would help bind his messmates and his family ever closer to this man and his cause.

And the president showed that he had learned the lessons offered him when he was a volunteer. He was invariably sympathetic to entreaties from soldiers for fairness and compassion. He knew that the military life was foreign to Americans, and that in the clash between military discipline and the independent spirit of young volunteers, many otherwise good men would run afoul of army regulations. As a result, more than any president before or after him, Lincoln showed patience and understanding when it came to military justice. "Fair play is a jewell [sic]," he told his secretary of war when one boy's case came up. "Give him a chance if you can".[6] More than 100,000 Union soldiers would come before courts martial, and in every instance that found its way to his desk, Lincoln gave them a chance if he could. He was patient with insubordination, sleeping on guard duty, drunkenness, even cowardice and desertion, never losing sight of the fact that these men were not professional soldiers, and they lived by a different ethic. Whenever possible he commuted sentences of jail time or pay forfeiture or dismissal from the service, instead simply imposing an appropriate extension of the soldier's enlistment term. Thus he won the loyalty of the man saved from harsh punishment, as well as the gratitude of any family at home depending on that soldier's pay, and at the same time got several extra months of active service from the man. And as the war approached its close, he also helped to insure that men could go home proud of their service rather than in shame and humiliation.[7]

The president took advantage, if in a passive way, of one other avenue of morale-building. Understanding the value of being seen, of giving his soldiers and his people an image to put with the name, he would be the first—and for some years the only—chief executive to recognize the power of the photograph. The era of mass-produced prints from a single negative began in 1850 with the appearance of the albumen process that made a negative of a glass plate. Innumerable positive prints could be made on sensitized paper. Even before the war Lincoln displayed some instinctive appreciation of photography, despite his humorous (and self-conscious) protestations of his own ugliness. He often said that a widely reproduced photograph made of him in February 1860 at the time of his Cooper Union speech was responsible for making him president. Whether he was serious or only joking, either way the comment reveals his awareness of the potential power of the camera.

As a result, while he rarely initiated sittings for a photographer, Lincoln as president seems never to have refused a request to sit for the lens. At least seventy times he faced the camera, sure in the knowledge that the photographers would capitalize on their images by reproducing them, or else selling the images to the New York firms that mass-produced album-sized photographs for a hungry northern public. Soon soldiers were carrying his small carte de visite portrait in their knapsacks, while their families at home added a Lincoln photo to their albums of sons, brothers, friends and fathers in uniform. Thus, the president, who rarely went beyond the environs of Washington or the army in Virginia, was still seen regularly by millions across the Union. Whether or not Lincoln actively encouraged this is open to debate. What is not debatable is that he understood the power of the image, and did nothing to discourage it.[8]

That power of imagery was just a part of the peculiar legacy that Lincoln left as the first president to conduct a major war. His successors who governed in peacetime, fortunately, did not have to meet the challenges he met. Yet all of the later "war presidents" echoed at least some of his actions. Most notably, they all heeded—or gave the appearance of heeding—Lincoln's words in his first inaugural that there could be no war unless the South was the aggressor. William McKinley, Woodrow Wilson, Franklin D. Roosevelt, Harry Truman, Lyndon Johnson, George H. W. Bush, and George W. Bush, all had personal or administration agenda calling for going to war. Yet each held off unilateral action until the opposing side either committed an overt act or, in the case of Johnson and the latter Bush, actions or circumstances arose that could be manipulated into a pretext. Just as Lincoln waited until the attack on Fort Sumter to call for volunteers, all of these presidents capitalized upon opportunities handed them by events, such as the Zimmerman telegram, the attack on Pearl Harbor, or the September 11, 2001 terrorist attacks. Whether the manner of their use of those events to expand executive power to take America to war was judicious is another question, but all of them to some degree followed Lincoln's example.

That said, none of Lincoln's successors except perhaps FDR exercised the degree of hands-on management of military affairs that he employed. By Wilson's time and thereafter, the military establishment had grown so large that it was no longer practical. Wilson and his successors dealt with chiefs of staff, but rarely ever directly with commanders in the field. Lincoln was the first wartime president to visit American troops in the field, and while such visits were good for soldier morale, that was mainly a side effect of Lincoln's need to confer with his commanders. Only FDR, Johnson, and the Bushes visited troops in the field during their wars, but by that time the intended morale effect was more at home than with the soldiers themselves. Truman, like Lincoln, would relieve an army commander in asserting the primacy of the civil authority over the military. Today a president can still take the nation to war, but after that the role is largely one of maintaining and manipulating popular opinion while leaving the conduct of military affairs to the Pentagon. Lincoln, in his time, paid far less attention to sustaining public will because for his public the question was far more pressing, the issues more stark, and the war itself on their hearths.

Something else that defies debate is the conclusion that the instincts that led Lincoln to pursue these means to build the morale of northern soldiers and civilians, and to bind them all to the cause of the Union, did not derive alone from his very limited experience in elective office. One lackluster term in Congress and four terms in the Illinois House of Representatives cannot account entirely for his understanding of the motivations and personality of the common people. That intuition came chiefly from his being one of them, though in most respects he was the least common of men. He understood human fear and insecurity because he had been afraid and insecure. He understood the exuberance of young America because he had felt it himself. He knew that the common folk would respond to respect, an appreciation for their comfort in adversity, and above all "fair play," because his own life had been a constant quest for the same.

Of course these things alone did not win his war, save his Union, and make him the greatest of all American presidents. Wedded to these instinctive attributes was what happily proved to be a superior executive skill born of limited experience, enormous common sense, a keen and curious mind, and an abiding personal humility. No one in 1861 would have been able to point to the ungainly Illinoisan and predict, on the basis of his past, that he was destined for greatness. There is perhaps the most lasting lesson. Few presidents had less training or experience as an executive than Lincoln, and yet he stands as our best. The raw material necessary for him to become what he became was there within him all the time.

Notes

1. Address to New Jersey Senate, February 21, 1861, Roy P. Basler, ed., *The Collected Works of Abraham Lincoln,* vol. 4 (New Brunswick: Rutgers University Press, 1953–1955), 235, 236. Hereafter cited as Basler, *Collected Works.*

2. William H. Herndon and Jesse Welk, *Herndon's Life of Lincoln: The History and Personal Recollections of Abraham Lincoln* (New York: Albert and Charles Boni, 1930), 77–78, 83.

3. Robert H. Rhodes, ed., *All for the Union: The Civil War Diary and Letters of Elisha Hunt Rhodes* (New York: Crown, 1991), 20–21.

4. Michael E. Stevens, ed., *As if It Were Glory: Robert Beechan's Civil War from the Iron Brigade to the Black Regiments* (Madison: Madison House, 1997), 12.

5. Harold Holzer, ed., *Dear Mr. Lincoln: Letters to the President* (New York: Perseus, 1993), 3.

6. Lincoln to Simon Cameron, August 10, 1861, Basler, *Collected Works* vol. 4, 480.

7. An extended discussion of Lincoln's policy toward courts martial and military discipline will be found in William C. Davis, *Lincoln's Men: How President Lincoln Became Father to an Army and a Nation* (New York: Free Press, 1999), 166 *passim*.

8. The authoritative work on Lincoln in photographs is Charles Hamilton and Lloyd Ostendorf, *Lincoln in Photographs: An Album of Every Known Pose* (Dayton, OH: Morningside, 1985).

WILLIAM C. DAVIS is professor of history at Virginia Polytechnic Institute and State University. He is the author or editor of more than 50 books and numerous documentary screenplays on the Civil War and southern history. Davis also worked as the on-camera senior consultant for 52 episodes of the Arts & Entertainment Network/History Channel series "Civil War Journal" as well as a historical consultant for several television and film productions, including "The Blue and the Gray," "George Washington," and "The Perfect Tribute." Davis is the only three-time winner of the Jefferson Davis Award given for book-length works on Confederate history. His most recent book is *The Pirates Laffite: The Treacherous World of the Corsairs of the Gulf* (Orlando: Harcourt, 2005).

The American Civil War, Emancipation, and Reconstruction on the World Stage

EDWARD L. AYERS

Americans demanded the world's attention during their Civil War and Reconstruction. Newspapers around the globe reported the latest news from the United States as one vast battle followed another, as the largest system of slavery in the world crashed into pieces, as American democracy expanded to include people who had been enslaved only a few years before.[1]

Both the North and the South appealed to the global audience. Abraham Lincoln argued that his nation's Civil War "embraces more than the fate of these United States. It presents to the whole family of man, the question, whether a constitutional republic, or a democracy . . . can, or cannot, maintain its territorial integrity." The struggle. Lincoln said, was for "a vast future," a struggle to give all men "a fair chance in the race of life."[2] Confederates claimed that they were also fighting for a cause of world-wide significance: self-determination. Playing down the centrality of slavery to their new nation, white Southerners built their case for independence on the right of free citizens to determine their political future.[3]

People in other nations could see that the massive struggle in the United States embodied conflicts that had been appearing in different forms throughout the world. Defining nationhood, deciding the future of slavery, reinventing warfare for an industrial age, reconstructing a former slave society—all these played out in the American Civil War.

By no means a major power, the United States was nevertheless woven into the life of the world. The young nation touched, directly and indirectly, India and Egypt, Hawaii and Japan, Russia and Canada, Mexico and Cuba, the Caribbean and Brazil, Britain and France. The country was still very much an experiment in 1860, a representative government stretched over an enormous space, held together by law rather than by memory, religion, or monarch. The American Civil War, played out on the brightly lit stage of a new country, would be a drama of world history. How that experiment fared in its great crisis—regardless of what happened—would eventually matter to people everywhere.

More obviously than most nations, the United States was the product of global history. Created from European ideas, involvement in Atlantic trade, African slavery, conquest of land from American Indians and European powers, and massive migration from Europe, the United States took shape as the world watched. Long before the Civil War, the United States embodied the possibilities and contradictions of modern western history.

Slavery was the first, most powerful, and most widespread kind of globalization in the first three centuries after Columbus. While colonies came and went, while economies boomed and crashed, slavery relentlessly grew—and nowhere more than in the United States. By the middle of the nineteenth century, the slave South had assumed a central role on the world stage. Cotton emerged as the great global commodity, driving factories in the most advanced economies of the world. The slaves of the South were worth more than all the railroads and factories of the North and South combined; slavery was good business and shrewd investment.

While most other slave societies in the hemisphere gradually moved toward freedom, the American South moved toward the permanence of slavery. Southerners and their Northern allies, eager to expand, led the United States in a war to seize large parts of Mexico and looked hungrily upon the Caribbean and Central America. Of all the slave powers—including the giants of Brazil and Cuba, which continued to import slaves legally long after the United States—only the South and its Confederacy fought a war to maintain bondage.[4]

Ideas of justice circulated in global intercourse just as commodities did and those ideas made the American South increasingly anomalous as a modern society built on slavery. Demands for universal freedom came into conflict with ancient traditions of subordination. European nations, frightened by revolt in Haiti and elsewhere and confident of their empires' ability to prosper without slavery, dismantled slavery in their colonies in the western hemisphere while Russia dismantled serfdom.

Black and white abolitionists in the American North, though a tiny despised minority, worked with British allies to fight the acceptance of slavery in the United States. A vision of the South as backward, cruel, and power-hungry gained credence in many places in the North and took political force in the Republican party. The global economy of commodities and ideology, demanding cotton while attacking slavery, put enormous and contradictory strains on the young American nation.[5]

Meanwhile, a new urge to define national identity flowed through the western world in the first half of the nineteenth century. That determination took quite different forms. While some people still spoke of the universal dreams of the French and American Revolutions, of inalienable attributes of humankind, others spoke of historical grievance, ethnic unity, and economic self-interest. Many longed for new nations built around bonds of heritage, imagined and real.[6]

White Southerners, while building their case for secession with the language of constitutions and rights, presented themselves as a people profoundly different from white Northerners. They sought sanction for secession in the recent histories of Italy, Poland, Mexico, and Greece, where rebels rose up against central powers to declare their suppressed nationhood, where native elites led a "natural, necessary protest and revolt" against a "crushing, killing union with another nationality and form of society".[7]

As the South threatened to secede, the Republicans, a regional party themselves, emphasized the importance of Union for its own sake, the necessity of maintaining the integrity of a nation created by legal compact. It fell to the United States, the Republicans said, to show that large democracies could survive internal struggles and play a role in world affairs alongside monarchies and aristocracies.[8]

Once it became clear that war would come, the North and the South seized upon the latest war-making strategies and technologies. From the outset, both sides innovated at a rapid pace and imported ideas from abroad. Railroads and telegraphs extended supply lines, sped troop reinforcements, and permitted the mobilization of vast armies. Observers from Europe and other nations watched carefully to see how the Americans would use these new possibilities. The results were mixed. Ironclad ships, hurriedly constructed, made a difference in some Southern ports and rivers, but were not seaworthy enough to play the role some had envisioned for them. Submarines and balloons proved disappointments, unable to deliver significant advantages. Military leaders, rather than being subordinated by anonymous machinery, as some expected, actually became more important than before, their decisions amplified by the size of their armies and the speed of communication and transport.[9]

The scale and drama of the Civil War that ravaged America for four years, across an area larger than the European continent, fascinated and appalled a jaded world. A proportion of the population equal to five million people today died and the South suffered casualties at a rate equal to those who would be decimated in Europe's mechanized wars of the twentieth century.

The size, innovation, and destructiveness of the American Civil War have led some, looking back, to describe it as the first total war, the first truly modern war. Despite new technologies and strategies, however, much of the Civil War remained old-fashioned. The armies in the American Civil War still moved vast distances on foot or with animals. The food soldiers ate and the medical care they received showed little advance over previous generations of armies. The military history of the Civil War grew incrementally from world history and offered incremental changes to what would follow. Although, late in the war, continuous campaigning and extensive earthen entrenchments foreshadowed World War I, Europeans did not grasp the deadly lesson of the American Civil War: combining the tactics of Napoleon with rapid-fire weapons and trenches would culminate in horrors unanticipated at Shiloh and Antietam.[10]

Diplomacy proved challenging for all sides in the American crisis. The fragile balance of power on the Continent and in the empires centered there limited the range of movement of even the most powerful nations. The Confederacy's diplomatic strategy depended on gaining recognition from Great Britain and France, using cotton as a sort of blackmail, but European manufacturers had stockpiled large supplies of cotton in anticipation of the American war. British cartoonists, sympathetic to the Confederacy, ridiculed Abraham Lincoln at every opportunity, portraying him as an inept bumpkin—until his assassination, when Lincoln suddenly became sainted. Overall, the North benefited from the inaction of the British and the French, who could have changed the outcome and consequences of the war by their involvement.[11]

Inside the United States, the change unleashed by the war was as profound as it was unexpected. Even those who hated slavery had not believed in 1861 that generations of captivity could be ended overnight and former slaves and former slaveholders left to live together. The role of slavery in sustaining the Confederacy through humbling victories over the Union created the conditions in which Abraham Lincoln felt driven and empowered to issue the Emancipation Proclamation. The Union, briefly and precariously balanced between despair and hope, between defeat and victory, was willing in 1862 to accept that bold decision as a strategy of war and to enlist volunteers from among black Americans.[12]

The nearly 200,000 African Americans who came into the war as soldiers and sailors for the Union transformed the struggle. The addition of those men, greater in number than all the forces at Gettysburg, allowed the Union to build its advantage in manpower without pushing reluctant Northern whites into the draft. The enlistment of African Americans in the struggle for their own freedom ennobled the Union cause and promised to set a new global standard for the empowerment of formerly enslaved people. The world paid admiring attention to the brave and disciplined black troops in blue uniforms.[13]

The destruction of American slavery, a growing system of bondage of nearly four million people in one of the world's most powerful economies and most dynamic nation-states, was a consequence of world importance. Nowhere else besides Haiti did slavery end so suddenly, so completely, and with so little compensation for former slaveholders.[14] Had the United States failed to end slavery in the 1860s the world would have felt the difference. An independent Confederate States of America would certainly have put its enslaved population to effective use in coal mines, steel mills, and railroad building, since industrial slavery had been employed before secession and became more common during wartime. Though such a Confederacy might have found itself stigmatized, its survival would have meant the evolution of slavery into a new world of industrialization. The triumph of a major autonomous state built around slavery would have set a devastating example for the rest of the world, an encouragement to forces of reaction. It would have marked the repudiation of much that was liberating in Western thought and practice over the preceding two hundred years.[15]

Driven by the exigencies of war, Northern ideals of color-blind freedom and justice, so often latent and suppressed, suddenly if briefly bloomed in the mid-1860s. The Radical Republicans sought to create a black male American freedom based on the same basis as white male American freedom: property, citizenship, dignity, and equality before the law. They launched a bold Reconstruction to make those ideals a reality, their effort far surpassing those of emancipation anywhere else in the world. The white South resisted with vicious vehemence, however, and the Republicans, always ambivalent about black autonomy and eager to maintain their partisan power, lost heart after a decade of bitter, violent, and costly struggle in Reconstruction. Northern Democrats, opposing Reconstruction from the outset, hastened and celebrated its passing.[16]

If former slaves had been permitted to sustain the enduring political power they tried to build, if they had gone before juries and judges with a chance of fair treatment, if they had been granted homesteads to serve as a first step toward economic freedom, then Reconstruction could be hailed as a turning point in world history equal to any revolution. Those things did not happen, however. The white South claimed the mantle of victim, of a people forced to endure an unjust and unnatural subordination. They won international sympathy for generations to follow in films such as *Birth of a Nation* (1915) and *Gone With the Wind* (1939), which viewed events through the eyes of sympathetic white Southerners. Reconstruction came to be seen around the world not as the culmination of freedom but as a mistake, a story of the dangers of unrealistic expectations and failed social engineering. Though former slaves in the American South quietly made more progress in landholding and general prosperity than former slaves elsewhere, the public failures of Reconstruction obscured the progress black Southerners wrenched from the postwar decades.[17]

When the South lost its global monopoly of cotton production during the Civil War, governments, agents, and merchants around the world responded quickly to take the South's place and to build an efficient global machinery to supply an ever-growing demand in the world market. As a result, generations of black and white sharecroppers would compete with Indian, Brazilian, and Egyptian counterparts in a glutted market in which hard work often brought impoverishment. The South adapted its economy after the war as well. By the 1880s, the South's rates of urban growth, manufacturing, and population movement kept pace with the North—a remarkable shift for only twenty years after losing slavery and the Civil War—but black Southerners were excluded from much of the new prosperity.[18]

As the Civil War generation aged, younger men looked with longing on possible territorial acquisitions in their own hemisphere and farther afield. They talked openly of proving themselves, as their fathers and grandfathers had, on the battlefield. Some welcomed the fight against the Spanish and the Filipinos in 1898 as a test of American manhood and nationalism. The generation that came of age in 1900 built monuments to the heroes of the Civil War but seldom paused to listen to their stories of war's horror and costs.

The destruction of slavery, a major moral accomplishment of the United States Army, of Abraham Lincoln, and of the enslaved people themselves, would be overshadowed by the injustice and poverty that followed in the rapidly changing South, a mockery of American claims of moral leadership in the world. Black Southerners would struggle, largely on their own, for the next one hundred years. Their status, bound in an ever-tightening segregation, would stand as a rebuke to the United States in world opinion. The postwar South and its new system of segregation, in fact, became an explicit model for South Africa. That country created apartheid as it, like the American South, developed a more urban and industrial economy based on racial subordination.

Americans read about foreign affairs on the same pages that carried news of Reconstruction in the South. Even as the Southern states struggled to write new constitutions, Secretary of State William Henry Seward purchased Alaska in 1867 as a step toward the possible purchase of British Columbia. President Grant considered annexation of Santo Domingo, partly as a base for black Southern emigration; he won the support of black abolitionist Frederick Douglass, who wanted to help the Santo Domingans, but was opposed by Radical Republican Senator Charles Sumner.

Americans paid close attention to Hawaii in these same years. Mark Twain visited the islands in 1866, and Samuel Armstrong—the white founder of Hampton Institute, where Booker T. Washington was educated—argued that Hawaiians and former slaves in the South needed similar discipline to become industrious. At the same time, Seward signed a treaty with China to help supply laborers to the American West, a treaty that laid the foundation for a large migration in the next few decades. In 1871, American forces intervened militarily in Korea, killing 250 Korean soldiers. The leaders of the Americans admitted they knew little about their opponents, but brought the same assumptions about race to the conflict that they brought to their dealings with all non-Europeans everywhere, Koreans—like Hawaiians, Chinese, American Indians, and African Americans—needed to be disciplined, taught, and controlled.

No master plan guided Americans in their dealings with other peoples. In all of these places, the interests of American businessmen, the distortions of racial ideology, and hopes for partisan political advantage at home jostled with one another. As a result, the consequences of these involvements were often unclear and sometimes took generations to play out. Nevertheless, they remind us that Americans paid close attention to what was happening elsewhere, whether in the Franco-Prussian War (1870–1871), where the evolution of warfare continued to become more mechanized and lethal, or the Paris Commune (1871), where some thought they saw the result of unbridled democracy in chaos and violence—and wondered if Reconstruction did not represent a similar path.

Some people around the world were surprised that the United States did not use its enormous armies after the Civil War to seize Mexico from the French, Canada from the English, or Cuba from the Spanish. Conflict among the great powers on the European Continent certainly opened an opportunity and the United States had expanded relentlessly and opportunistically throughout its history. Few Americans, though, had the stomach for new adventures in the wake of the Civil War. The fighting against the American Indians on the Plains proved warfare enough for most white Americans in the 1870s and 1880s.[19]

The United States focused its postwar energies instead on commerce. Consolidated under Northern control, the nation's economy proved more formidable than ever before. The United States, its economic might growing with each passing year, its railroad network and financial systems consolidated, its cities and towns booming, its population surging westward, its mines turning out massive amounts of coal and precious minerals, its farms remarkably productive, and its corporations adopting new means of expansion and administration, became a force throughout the world. American engineers oversaw projects in Asia, Africa, and Latin America. American investors bought stock in railroads, factories, and mines around the globe. American companies came to dominate the economies of nations in Latin America.[20]

Americans became famous as rich, energetic, and somewhat reckless players amid the complexity of the world. As the Civil War generation aged, younger men looked with longing on possible territorial acquisitions in their own hemisphere and farther afield. They talked openly of proving themselves, as their fathers and grandfathers had, on the battlefield. Some welcomed the fight against the Spanish and the Filipinos in 1898 as a test of American manhood and nationalism. The generation that came of age in 1900 built monuments to the heroes of the Civil War but seldom paused to listen to their stories of war's horror and costs.

The American Civil War has carried a different meaning for every generation of Americans. In the 1920s and 1930s leading historians in a largely isolationist United States considered the Civil War a terrible mistake, the product of a "blundering generation." After the triumph of World War II

and in the glow of the Cold War's end, leading historians interpreted the Civil War as a chapter in the relentless destruction of slavery and the spread of democracy by the forces of modernization over the forces of reaction. Recently, living through more confusing times, some historians have begun to question straightforward stories of the war, emphasizing its contradictory meanings, unfulfilled promises, and unintended outcomes.[21]

The story of the American Civil War changes as world history lurches in unanticipated directions and as people ask different questions of the past. Things that once seemed settled now seem less so. The massive ranks, fortified trenches, heavy machinery, and broadened targets of the American Civil War once seemed to mark a step toward the culmination of "total" war. But the wars of the twenty-first century, often fought without formal battles, are proving relentless and boundless, "total" in ways the disciplined armies of the Union and Confederacy never imagined.[22] Nations continue to come apart over ancient grievances and modern geopolitics, the example of the United States notwithstanding. Coerced labor did not end in the nineteenth century, but instead has mutated and adapted to changes in the global economy. "A fair chance in the race of life" has yet to arrive for much of the world.

The great American trial of war, emancipation, and reconstruction mattered to the world. It embodied struggles that would confront people on every continent and it accelerated the emergence of a new global power. The American crisis, it was true, might have altered the course of world history more dramatically, in ways both worse and better, than what actually transpired. The war could have brought forth a powerful and independent Confederacy based on slavery or it could have established with its Reconstruction a new global standard of justice for people who had been enslaved. As it was, the events of the 1860s and 1870s in the United States proved both powerful and contradictory in their meaning for world history.

Notes

1. For other portrayals of the Civil War in international context, see David M. Potter, "Civil War," in C. Vann Woodward, ed., *The Comparative Approach to American History* (New York: Basic Books, 1968), pp. 135–451 Carl N. Degler, *One Among Many: The Civil War in Comparative Perspective,* 29th Annual Robert Fortenbaugh Memorial Lecture (Gettysburg, PA: Gettysburg College, 1990); Robert E. May, ed., *The Union, the Confederacy, and the Atlantic Rim* (West Lafayette, IN; Purdue University Press, 1995); Peter Kolchin, *A Sphinx on the American Land: The Nineteenth-Century South in Comparative Perspective* (Baton Rouge: Louisiana State University Press, 2003). My view of the workings of world history has been influenced by C. A. Bayly, *The Birth of the Modern World, 1780–1914: Global Connections and Comparisons* (Malden, MA: Blackwell, 2004). Bayly emphasizes that "in the nineteenth century, nation-states and contending territorial empires took on sharper lineaments and became more antagonistic to each other at the very same time as the similarities, connections, and linkages between them proliferated." (p. 2). By showing the "complex

interaction between political organization, political ideas, and economic activity," Bayly avoids the teleologital models of modernization, nationalism, and liberalism that have dominated our understanding of the American Civil War.

2. Lincoln quoted in James M. McPherson, *Abraham Lincoln and the Second American Revolution,* reprint (New York: Oxford University Press: 1992, 1991), p. 28.

3. The seminal work is Drew Gilpin Faust, *The Creation of Confederate Nationalism: Ideology and Identity in the Civil War South* (Baton Rouge: Louisiana State University Press, 1988). For an excellent synthesis of the large literature on this topic, see Anne S. Rubin, *A Shattered Nation: The Rise and Fall of the Confederacy, 1861–1868* (Chapel Hill: University of North Carolina Press, 2005).

4. For a useful overview, see Robert W. Fogel, *Without Consent or Contract: The Rise and Fall of American Slavery* (New York: W. W. Norton, 1989).

5. David Brion Davis, *Slavery and Human Progress* (New York: Oxford University Press, 1984); Davis, *The Problem of Slavery in the Age of Revolution, 1770–1823* (Ithaca, NY: Cornell University Press, 1975), and Davis, *Inhuman Bondage: The Rise and Fall of Slavery in the New World* (Oxford University Press, 2006).

6. For helpful overviews of the global situation, see Steven Hahn, "Class and State in Postemancipation Societies: Southern Planters in Comparative Perspective," *American Historical Review* 95 (February 1990): 75–98, and Hahn, *A Nation Under Our Feet: Black Political Struggles in the Rural South From Slavery to the Great Migration* (Cambridge, MA: Belknap Press of Harvard University Press, 2003).

7. Quoted in Faust, *Creation of Confederate Nationalism,* p. 13.

8. There is a large literature on this subject, not surprisingly. A useful recent treatment is Susan-Mary Grant, *North Over South: Northern Nationalism and American Identity in the Antebellum Era* (Lawrence: University of Kansas Press, 2000). Peter Kolchin also offers penetrating comments on nationalism in *A Sphinx on the American Land,* 89–92.

9. Brian Holden Reid, *The American Civil War and the Wars of the Industrial Revolution* (London: Cassell, 1999), 211–13; John E. Clark Jr., *Railroads in the Civil War: The Impact of Management on Victory and Defeat* (Baton Rouge: Louisiana State University Press, 2001); Robert G. Angevine, *The Railroad and the State: War, Politics, and Technology in Nineteenth-Century America* (Stanford, CA: Stanford University Press, 2004).

10. For a range of interesting essays on this subject, see Stig Forster and Jorg Nagler, eds., *On the Road to Total War: The American Civil War and the German Wars of Unification, 1861–1871* (Washington, DC: The German Historical Institute, 1997).

11. See D. P. Crook, *The North, the South, and the Powers, 1861–1865* (New York: Wiley, 1974), R. J. M. Blackett, *Divided Hearts: Britain and the American Civil War* (Baton Rouge: Louisiana State University Press, 2001), James M. McPherson, *Crossroads of Freedom: Antietam* (Oxford: Oxford University Press, 2002), May, ed., *The Union, the Confederacy, and the Atlantic Rim,* and Charles M. Hubbard, *The Burden of Confederate Diplomacy* (Knoxville: University of Tennessee Press, 1998).

12. See Allen C. Guelzo, *Lincoln's Emancipation Proclamation: The End of Slavery in America* (New York: Simon and Schuster. 2004).

13. See Joseph T. Glatthaar, *Forged in Battle: The Civil War Alliance of Black Soldiers and White Officers* (New York: Free Press, 1990).

14. See Leon Litwack, *Been in the Storm So Long: The Aftermath of Slavery,* 1st Vintage ed. (New York: Vintage, 1980, 1979) and the major documentary collection edited by Ira Berlin, Leslie S. Rowland, and their colleagues, sampled in *Free At Last: A Documentary History of Slavery, Freedom, and the Civil War* (New York: The New Press, 1992).

15. See Davis, *Slavery and Human Progress,* for a sweeping perspective on this issue.

16. The classic history is Eric Foner, *Reconstruction: America's Unfinished Revolution, 1863–1877* (New York: Harper and Row, 1988), I have offered some thoughts on Reconstruction's legacy in "Exporting Reconstruction" in *What Caused the Civil War? Reflections on the South and Southern History* (New York: W. W. Norton, 2005).

17. On the legacy of Reconstruction, see David W. Blight, *Race and Reunion The Civil War in American Memory* (Cambridge, MA: Belknap Press of Harvard University Press, 2001).

18. For a fascinating essay on the South's loss of the cotton monopoly, see Sven Beckert, "Emancipation and Empire: Reconstructing the Worldwide Web of Cotton Production in the Age of the American Civil War," *American Historical Review* 109 (December 2004): 1405–38. On South Africa: John W. Cell, *The Highest Stage of White Supremacy: The Origins of Segregation in South Africa and the American South* (Cambridge: Cambridge University Press, 1982) and George M. Fredrickson, *White Supremacy: A Comparative Study in American and South African History* (New York: Oxford University Press, 1981).

19. See the discussion in the essays by Robert E. May and James M. McPherson in May, ed., *The Union, the Confederacy, and the Atlantic Rim.*

20. For the larger context, see Eric J. Hobsbawm, *The Age of Empire, 1875–1914* (New York: Pantheon, 1987) and Bayly, *Birth of the Modern World.*

21. I have described this literature and offered some thoughts on it in the essay "Worrying About the Civil War" in my *What Caused the Civil War?*

22. Reid, *American Civil War,* p. 213.

Bibliography

Surprisingly, no one book covers the themes of this essay. To understand this era of American history in global context, we need to piece together accounts from a variety of books and articles. For recent overviews of different components of these years, see Jay Sexton, "Towards a Synthesis of Foreign Relations in the Civil War Era. 1848–1877," *American Nineteenth-Century History* 5 (Fall 2004): 50–75, and Amy Kaplan, *The Anarchy of Empire in the Making of U. S. Culture* (Cambridge, MA; Harvard University Press, 2002).

Robert F. May, in the introduction to the book he edited, *The Union, the Confederacy, and the Atlantic Rim* (West Lafayette, IN: Purdue University Press, 1995), provides a useful summary of the larger context of the war. Though it is older, the perspective of D. P. Crook, *The North, the South, and the Powers, 1861–1865* (New York: Wiley, 1974) brings a welcome worldliness to the discussion. On the crucial debate in Britain, see Howard Jones, *Union in Peril: The Crisis Over British Intervention in the Civil War* (Chapel Hill: University of North Carolina Press, 1992) and R. J. M. Blackett, *Divided Hearts: Britain and the American Civil War* (Baton Rouge: Louisiana State University Press, 2001).

James M. McPherson offers characteristically insightful, and hopeful, analysis in several places. Perhaps the single best focused portrayal of the interplay between events in the United States and in the Atlantic World is in his *Crossroads of Freedom: Antietam* (Oxford: Oxford University Press, 2002). McPherson's essay, " 'The Whole Family of Man': Lincoln and the Last Best Hope Abroad," in May, ed., *The Union, the Confederacy, and the Atlantic Rim,* makes the fullest case for the larger significance of the war in encouraging liberal movements and belief around the world.

Peter Kolchin's, *A Sphinx on the American Land: The Nineteenth-Century South in Comparative Perspective* (Baton Rouge: Louisiana State University Press, 2003), offers an elegant and up-to-date survey that puts the conflict in the larger context of emancipation movements. A useful overview appears in Steven Hahn, "Class and State in Postemancipation Societies: Southern Planters in Comparative Perspective," *American Historical Review* 95 (February 1990): 75–98.

Another pioneering work is Drew Gilpin Faust, *The Creation of Confederate Nationalism: Ideology and Identity in the Civil War South* (Baton Rouge: Louisiana State University Press, 1988). Faust changed historians' perspective on nationalism in the South, which had been considered largely fraudulent before her account. Building on Faust are two recent books that offer fresh interpretations: Anne S. Rubin, *A Shattered Nation: The Rise and Fall of the Confederacy, 1861–1868* (Chapel Hill: University of North Carolina Press, 2005) and Susan-Mary Crant, *North Over South: Northern Nationalism and American Identity in the Antebellum Era* (Lawrence: University of Kansas Press, 2000).

On the much-debated issue of the relative modernity and totality of the Civil War, see Stig Förster and Jörg Nagler, eds., *On the Road to Total War: The American Civil War and the German Wars of Unification,* 1861–1871 (Washington, DC: The German Historical Institute, 1997); the essays by Stanley L. Engerman and J. Matthew Gallman, Farl J. Hess, Michael Fellman, and Richard Current are especially helpful. Brian Holden Reid, in *The American Civil War and the Wars of the Industrial Revolution* (London: Cassell, 1999), offers a concise but insightful portrayal of the war in larger military context.

For a powerful representation of the role of slavery in this history, David Brion Davis's works are all helpful. His most recent account synthesizes a vast literature in an accessible way: *Inhuman Bondage: The Rise and Fall of Slavery in the New World* (Oxford University Press, 2006).

Excellent examples of what might be thought of as the new global history appear in Sven Beckert, "Emancipation and Empire: Reconstructing the Worldwide Web of Cotton Production in the Age of the American Civil War," *American Historical Review* 109 (December 2004): 1405–38; and Gordon H. Chang, "Whose 'Barbarism'? whose 'Treachery'? Race and Civilization in the Unknown United States-Korea War of 1871," *Journal of American History* 89 (March 2003): 1331–65.

EDWARD L. AYERS is Dean of the College of Art and Sciences at the University of Virginia, where he is also the Hugh P. Kelly Professor of History. He has published extensively on nineteenth-century Southern history, his most recent publication being *In the Presence of Mine Enemies: War in the Heart of America, 1859–1863 (2003),* which received the Bancroft Prize. An earlier book, *The Promise of the New South (1992),* was a finalist for both the Pulitzer Prize and the National Book Award. In addition, Ayers has created and directs a prize-winning Internet archive, "Valley of the Shadow: Two Communities in the American Civil War," containing original sources related to two towns at either end of the Shenandoah Valley, one in Virginia and the other in Pennsylvania.

Test-Your-Knowledge Form

We encourage you to photocopy and use this page as a tool to assess how the articles in *Annual Editions* expand on the information in your textbook. By reflecting on the articles you will gain enhanced text information. You can also access this useful form on a product's book support website at *http://www.mhhe.com/cls*.

NAME: DATE:

_____

TITLE AND NUMBER OF ARTICLE:

_____

BRIEFLY STATE THE MAIN IDEA OF THIS ARTICLE:

_____

LIST THREE IMPORTANT FACTS THAT THE AUTHOR USES TO SUPPORT THE MAIN IDEA:

_____

WHAT INFORMATION OR IDEAS DISCUSSED IN THIS ARTICLE ARE ALSO DISCUSSED IN YOUR TEXTBOOK OR OTHER READINGS THAT YOU HAVE DONE? LIST THE TEXTBOOK CHAPTERS AND PAGE NUMBERS:

_____

LIST ANY EXAMPLES OF BIAS OR FAULTY REASONING THAT YOU FOUND IN THE ARTICLE:

_____

LIST ANY NEW TERMS/CONCEPTS THAT WERE DISCUSSED IN THE ARTICLE, AND WRITE A SHORT DEFINITION:

We Want Your Advice

ANNUAL EDITIONS revisions depend on two major opinion sources: one is our Advisory Board, listed in the front of this volume, which works with us in scanning the thousands of articles published in the public press each year; the other is you—the person actually using the book. Please help us and the users of the next edition by completing the prepaid article rating form on this page and returning it to us. Thank you for your help!

ANNUAL EDITIONS: United States History, Volume 1, 21/e

ARTICLE RATING FORM

Here is an opportunity for you to have direct input into the next revision of this volume.
We would like you to rate each of the articles listed below, using the following scale:

1. **Excellent: should definitely be retained**
2. **Above average: should probably be retained**
3. **Below average: should probably be deleted**
4. **Poor: should definitely be deleted**

Your ratings will play a vital part in the next revision.
Please mail this prepaid form to us as soon as possible.
Thanks for your help!

RATING	ARTICLE	RATING	ARTICLE
	1. America's First Immigrants		20. Fallen Timbers Broken Alliance
	2. 1491		21. The Best of Enemies
	3. A Desperate Trek across America		22. Cliffhanger
	4. Brave New World: The Watercolors That John White Produced in 1585 Gave England Its First Startling Glimpse of America		23. The Revolution of 1803
			24. Women in the Early Republic
	5. Champlain among the Mohawks, 1609: A Soldier-Humanist Fights a War for Peace in North America		25. The Everyday Life of Enslaved People in the Antebellum South
	6. The Birth of America: Struggling from One Peril to the Next, the Jamestown Settlers Planted the Seeds of the Nation's Spirit		26. Liberty Is Exploitation: The Force of Tradition in Early Manufacturing
			27. Play Ball!
	7. Strangers in a New Land: Henry Hudson's First American Adventure		28. The Change Agent
			29. The Inebriated Election of 1840
	8. Blessed and Bedeviled		30. The Awful March of the Saints
	9. The Real Pirates of the Caribbean		31. The Emancipation Question
	10. Wilderness Ordeal		32. Abolitionist John Doy
	11. The Gain from Thomas Paine		33. There Goes the South
	12. Benjamin Franklin: Revolutionary Spymaster		34. Lincoln and the Constitutional Dilemma of Emancipation
	13. Dirty Little Secret		
	14. God and the Founders		35. Steven Hahn Sings the Slaves Triumphant
	15. The Rocky Road to Revolution		36. A Slave's Audacious Bid for Freedom
	16. March on Quebec		37. How the West Was Lost
	17. A Day to Remember: July 4, 1776		38. Creating a Military Image: Lincoln as Commander in Chief
	18. The Baron DeKalb: Plotter or Patriot?		
	19. Getting Out: The First Rule of Holes		39. The American Civil War, Emancipation, and Reconstruction on the World Stage

BUSINESS REPLY MAIL
FIRST CLASS MAIL PERMIT NO. 551 DUBUQUE IA

POSTAGE WILL BE PAID BY ADDRESSEE

McGraw-Hill Contemporary Learning Series
501 BELL STREET
DUBUQUE, IA 52001

ABOUT YOU

Name _____   Date _____

Are you a teacher? ❏ A student? ❏
Your school's name _____

Department _____

Address _____   City _____   State _____   Zip _____

School telephone # _____

YOUR COMMENTS ARE IMPORTANT TO US!

Please fill in the following information:
For which course did you use this book?

_____

Did you use a text with this ANNUAL EDITION? ❏ yes ❏ no
What was the title of the text?

_____

What are your general reactions to the Annual Editions concept?

_____

Have you read any pertinent articles recently that you think should be included in the next edition? Explain.

_____

Are there any articles that you feel should be replaced in the next edition? Why?

_____

Are there any World Wide Websites that you feel should be included in the next edition? Please annotate.

_____

May we contact you for editorial input? ❏ yes ❏ no
May we quote your comments? ❏ yes ❏ no

NOTES

NOTES

NOTES

NOTES

NOTES

NOTES

NOTES

NOTES